BITCH IN A BONNET

RECLAIMING JANE AUSTEN FROM THE STIFFS, THE SNOBS, THE SIMPS AND THE SAPS

VOL. 1
SENSE AND SENSIBILITY · PRIDE AND PREJUDICE
MANSFIELD PARK

ROBERT RODI

2nd edition, October 2013

ISBN: 1469922657
ISBN-13: 978-1469922652

The chapters in this book were originally published as blog entries. They have been minimally edited for this collection in order to maintain the feeling of reading through Jane Austen's major novels in something akin to real time—in essence, of live-blogging the Jane Austen canon.

CONTENTS

INTRODUCTION
A PROPOSITION, AND A PLAN

Like many people, I feel I have a claim on Jane Austen. Though mine seems to me more binding than most: both she and I are authors of satiric novels. I'm not proposing myself as her equal, merely observing that we work the same mine. She habitually strikes gold and I some baser metal, but it's still the same job. I use her tools, I know her trade. We're colleagues.

And yet whenever I'm asked for my chief inspirations, hers is the name I consistently avoid mentioning. I'm a man, after all, and more than that a man of the world; while Austen is widely regarded as a woman's writer; scratch that, a particular kind of woman's writer, quaint and darling, doe-eyed and demure, parochial if not pastoral, and dizzily, swooningly romantic—the inventor and mother goddess of "chick lit." The wildly popular movies and TV serials based on her books are filled with meaningful glances across well-appointed rooms, desperate dashes over rain-pelted pastures, and wedding bells ecstatically clanging over oceans of top hats and shimmering pelisses.

Well, all that's a load of crap. It's not Jane Austen, it's "Jane Austen"—a great writer reduced to a marketing brand, literature retooled as product, genius reconfigured as kitsch.

It's high time I came to my colleague's rescue.

Jane Austen was—*is*—a sly subversive, a clear-eyed social Darwinist, and the most unsparing satirist of her century. She's wicked, arch, and utterly merciless. She skewers the pompous, the pious, and the libidinous with the animal glee of a natural-born sadist. She takes sharp, swift swipes at the social structure and leaves it, not lethally wounded, but shorn of it prettifying garb, its flabby flesh exposed in all its naked grossness. And then she laughs.

Despite her admittedly limited palette, her psychological acuity easily matches Shakespeare's, and her wit as well; like him, she's also violently allergic to sentimentality of any stripe. If she were alive today, she'd be either a snarky old Doris Lessing type, in tweeds and sensible shoes, abusing journalists who dared approach her, or a flamboyantly fang-toothed fag hag. Either way, you wouldn't want to cross her. Her tongue could kill at twenty paces.

How did someone whose vision is so darkly, even bleakly, comic—whose work brims with vicious, gabbling grotesques, most of whom are never adequately (or even minimally) punished for their sins (as Dickens, not so many years later, felt compelled to punish his)—become the patron saint of the turgid, chest-heaving, emotionally pornographic genre called "Regency Romance"?

I don't know, and I don't care. I only care to stop it—to fire the opening salvo that will, I hope, ignite the barrage of indignation that brings this travesty to a halt and restores, once and for all, the spit and vinegar to Jane Austen's public profile, raising her to the pantheon of gadflies that she might take her place beside Voltaire and Swift, Twain and Mencken. My goal is to make the world acknowledge, at long last, the bitch in the bonnet.

To that end, I'll be rereading the entire Austen corpus, one novel at a time, in the order of their original publication, and sharing with you my bellicose pronouncements along the way. Should be a kick.

But it won't be for the faint of heart. Those of you who fear taking offense...consider yourself forewarned. Offense will be generously on offer. So spare yourself, and go mewl in the corner with your goddamn Georgette Heyer.

PART ONE
SENSE AND SENSIBILITY

CHAPTERS 1-5

The opening pages of Jane Austen's first published novel give no indication that her reputation, in this post-literate age, hinges on something rather hazily labeled "romance." In fact an impartial reader might find *Sense and Sensibility*, at the outset, to read more like a ledger sheet. Austen explains in exhaustive (and exhausting) detail the means by which the female members of the Dashwood family (mother and three daughters) are reduced from easy living in stately Norwood House to a hardscrabble existence in a mere cottage, with just "two maids and a man" to look after them. (No romantic notions about them, either; once they've been mentioned, they might as well be a microwave oven, a sewing machine, and an Oreck XL Upright for all thc humanity they're allowed. Shakespeare at least gave his plebians all the best jokes, and Dickens couldn't get his to shut up.) I expect that people who might have skimmed over these initial pages previously will pay more attention to them now; I know I did. As someone whose 401k has been pretty much decimated and who's seen the value of his house tumble down beneath his mortgage, I've suddenly developed a keen interest in the mechanics of financial collapse. Misery loves company, even if it's fictional.

The principal agent of the Dashwoods' ruin is the wife of their stepbrother, Mrs. John Dashwood, the first of many monsters in Austen's fiction. What makes her monstrous—as opposed to merely wicked, or venal—is her thorough and transcendent shamelessness. She is, as Quentin Crisp once described Joan Crawford, radioactive with belief in herself. She's proud, insensitive, and has a sense of entitlement that threatens to devour the entire space-time continuum. For that reason, she's a startlingly timely figure, as we're just now reaping the rewards of years of "self-esteem" programs in junior and middle schools, which have produced a generation of Gap-clad Mrs. John Dashwoods who carry cell phones and drive SUVs and who will feel thoroughly justified in running you down with the latter because dammit *who said you could get in their way.* (And I bet more than one of them has a totebag slung on her passenger seat bearing the slogan AN ELIZABETH IN A DARCY-LESS WORLD.)

Mrs. John Dashwood (on whom Austen bestows the name Fanny—one of her old reliables; she'll recycle it repeatedly throughout her novels) pretty much steals the show in the early chapters of *Sense and Sensibility*, the way Shelob the giant spider steals the show in the third *Lord of the Rings* film. Fanny's attack is no less lethal; when she hears that her father-in-law has extracted a promise from his son to look after the "interest" of his stepmother and stepsisters—and that her husband intends to fulfill the vow by settling a few thousand pounds on them—she begins methodically demolishing every single inference that has led to this generous impulse, from asking what "interest" really means, to questioning the extent to which her husband even owes his father a deathbed promise at all. When John Dashwood contemplates paying his sisters an annuity, then, instead of a large lump sum, Fanny has one of the best lines in the book. Speaking of her mother having been saddled with similar obligations to three old servants, she says:

> *"Twice a year these annuities were to be paid; and then there was the trouble of getting it to them; and then one of them was said to have died, and afterward it turned out to be no such thing."*

The utter cad! Turning up *alive* like that. People are just no damn good.

She then goes on to say, of her sister Dashwoods:

> *"They will live so cheap! Their housekeeping will be nothing at all. They will have no carriage, no horses, and hardly any servants; they will keep no company, and have no expenses of any kind! Only conceive how comfortable they will be! Five hundred a year! I am sure I cannot imagine*

> *how they will spend half of it; and as to your giving them more, it is quite absurd to think of it. They will be much more able to give* you *something."*

Soon she has so far undermined her husband's finer impulses, that he begins to think himself spectacularly beneficent if he sends his step-sisters a fresh fish every now and then. It's a wonderfully comic scene, first revealing, then reveling in, human nature at its appalling worst.

Then there's this scene, as Fanny watches the family's belongings being moved from Norwood:

> *Mrs. John Dashwood saw the packages depart with a sigh: she could not help feeling it hard that as Mrs. Dashwood's income would be so trifling in comparison with their own, she should have any handsome article of furniture.*

This is bravura stuff; world-class ghastliness. Fanny Dashwood has booted her mother-and-sisters-in-law from the only home they've ever known, and wheedled them out of obtaining a single penny of their inheritance; now she has the sheer cojones to resent them taking their own possessions with them, because what do *poor* people need nice things for.

But with this Fanny is moved offstage, and a lot of the energy of the novel goes with her. We're left with the displaced Dashwood sisters as principals, which is not, at this point, entirely cause for rejoicing. All we know of them so far is that Elinor governs her feelings, and Marianne indulges hers. Maybe that's all we need to "get" them; after all, these are well-known character types, not only in literature but in life. (Marianne is the girl outside the bar, alternately shrieking "Wooo!" and throwing up on the sidewalk, and Elinor is the one pulling up to the curb to rescue her, saying, "This is absolutely the *last* time I do this," which even she doesn't believe.)

But alas, Austen is not yet at the height of her powers. This is the only time in the canon where she presents us with two heroines instead of one, and we can see, for the first and only time, some of the thematic scaffolding holding up the narrative. Elinor represents the legacy of the Age of Reason; Marianne, the new Romantic movement that urges instead the primacy of feeling. This was the great matter of the early 19th century, driven by thinkers like Rousseau and Baudelaire, and debated hotly in coffee houses all across England (in those days, coffee houses being breeding grounds of intellectual ferment, not hipster ennui).

It's fairly easy to tell which side of the argument Austen favors. True, she's a little bit in love with Marianne, who sweeps through the novel in a whirl of muslin. She's more filly than human; you almost expect her to neigh and paw the floor with her foot. But Elinor is steadfast; Elinor is measured in all things; she's a goddamn bionic woman. She self-calibrates so much you can practically hear her go *whirr, click*. There's nothing remotely attractive about her except her reliability and her faultless good manners, and when a writer puts a character like this at the center of a novel—like a bottle of milk in the middle of a sumptuous feast—you just know you're seeing a self-projection. "Here's me, all scrubbed of imperfections," she's saying. It's a feat she'd try time and again in future novels, with both greater and lesser success (Elinor is a dish of tepid tea next to Lizzy Bennet; but she's a feral, howling she-wolf next to Fanny Price).

What we still don't have, five chapters into the Austen corpus, is a hint of romance. And by that, I mean the passionate, worlds-colliding, pull-the-sky-down-from-the-heavens-because-your-hand-touched-mine-in-the-barouche business people have come to expect from Austen because of the way Austen "fans" go on about her.

Oh, sure, we have—in Elinor and Fanny Dashwood's brother, Edward Ferrars—a He and a She, and the stirrings of interest between them, and a Great Impediment, in the form of an iron-fisted mother (on Edward's side) and a lack of fortune (on Elinor's; Austen never forgets that ledger sheet, and never lets us forget it either). But the manner in which this epic, thwarted love is put forth is scarcely the stuff of Hollywood films:

> *He was not handsome, and his manners required intimacy to make them pleasing. He was too diffident to do justice to himself; but when his natural shyness was overcome, his behaviour gave every indication of an open affectionate heart.*

Jesus. Put *that* in a personal ad and see how many Elizabeths-Seeking-Darcys flood your freakin' In Box.

So Austen has, a little perversely, given her melba-toast heroine a rye-crisp hero. It doesn't bode well for the narrative, from the reader's point of view; but to her credit, she allows Marianne to stop twirling around like Stevie Nicks in a pashmina long enough to rebuke her sister for her mealy-mouthed praise of her fella:

> *"Esteem him! Like him! Cold-hearted Elinor! Oh! worse than cold-hearted! Ashamed of being otherwise. Use those words again and I will leave the room this moment."*

Elinor of course remains stolid and temperate; Marianne remains voluble and reactive. And as Reason and Romanticism bang away at each other like copper pots, we're left longing for Mrs. John Dashwood to come back into the story, having figured out a way to extort Marianne's piano from the parlor where the movers have just set it, and as long as the men are still here could they please move the island of Britain a few inches to the left, thank you and good afternoon.

But never mind; other grotesques are just around the corner.

CHAPTERS 6-10

These are, in the main, restaging chapters. The Dashwood family has left the splendor of Norland and now arrives at, and settles into, Barton Cottage—comfortable enough, but "as a cottage it was defective, for the building was regular, the roof was tiled, the window shutters were not painted green, nor were the walks covered with honeysuckles." (A swipe at Merchant and Ivory, 200 years early.) There's a lot of bustling about and discussion of plans for certain rooms, and a lot of rhapsodizing over the splendid prospect, which Marianne can't wait to go galloping over like My Friend Flicka. For the modern reader, the narrative will flag a bit here.

The entrance of the Dashwoods' cousin and new landlord, Sir John Middleton, provides a little zing of energy; he's got the kind of brash manners that, though "carried to a point of perseverance beyond civility...could not give offense." At least, not to anyone but Marianne, who allows herself to be provoked by Sir John's frank language and, being unable to keep even the most fleeting of her feelings to herself, tells him so in no uncertain terms:

> *"That is an expression, Sir John...which I particularly dislike. I abhor every commonplace phrase by which wit is intended...Their tendency is gross and illiberal; and if their construction could ever be deemed clever, time has long ago destroyed all its ingenuity."*

Sir John, for his part, "did not much understand this reproof; but he laughed as heartily as if he did." He's too likable to be awful. In fact we get the idea that his brand of boozy blathering is just the kind the author herself might like to encounter at a party. (I always think of her as that kinda gal: "If you can't say anything nice, come and sit by me.")

Sir John's wife, by contrast, is a cold fish, though she too stops short of actual monstrosity; she's just too inert. Her mother, Mrs. Jennings, is nearer the mark; a "good-humored, merry, fat, elderly woman, who talked a great deal," she relentlessly teases the Dashwood girls "on the subject of lovers and husbands" and "pretended to see them blush whether they did or not." In 21st century terms, she's the equivalent of the overly tanned, henna-haired grandmothers who mortify adolescents by making wild remarks about their developing breasts and asking earnest questions about their periods. But even she isn't a grotesque; she's too sociable, too generous of spirit.

Still, when Austen gathers these three borderline horrors in a single room, the combination of their deficiencies ignites some wonderful comic fireworks, as in this scene, in which Marianne is called upon to play the piano for them:

> *Sir John was loud in his admiration at the end of every song and as loud in his conversation with others while the song lasted. Lady Middleton frequently called him to order, wondered how anyone's attention could be diverted from the music for a moment, and asked Marianne to sing a particular song which Marianne had just finished.*

But the chief business of these chapters is to introduce a pair of rivals for Marianne's attention. There's Colonel Brandon, a taciturn, deeply feeling man who at thirty-five might as well be wrapped up in a sarcophagus for all that Marianne can see in him. Mrs. Jennings's persistent jokes about his affection for her openly disgust her: "When is a man to be safe from such a wit if age and infirmity will not protect him?" she says, in the same way she'd decry someone sticking a decrepit old dog with a poker.

And then there's Willoughy, the first of Austen's cads. (There's one in every book, serving almost exactly the same function: to distract the heroine from the more discreet charms of the hero.) Willoughy makes his debut by rescuing Marianne from a windswept hillside where she's taken a tumble while exulting in the rough weather. Poor Marianne; she's a would-be Bacchante, but lacks the motor skills for cavorting in a tempest. Still, Willoughy is on first sight a pretty tasty consolation prize: he's handsome, gallant, passionate, and quick-witted; he loves all the same books and music as Marianne, which as any sixteen-year-old can tell you means they're fated to be lovers till the crack of doom. (Marianne is exactly the kind of girl to have an Ideal Boyfriend's Reading List; she probably updates it monthly.)

In fact, Willoughby is so perfect he's ghastly; every time he opens his mouth, you cringe—you know something coy and clever and adorably wicked is coming that will make you want to push him down a flight of stairs. Elinor is scandalized by the way he makes fun of Colonel Brandon; but then Elinor would be scandalized by bent collar-stays. More to the point, *we're* scandalized by the way Willoughy and Marianne flit around together, like seagulls on a beach, shrieking and flapping and pecking at shiny things in the sand. We know instinctively: Nothing good can come of this.

Is it wrong that we can't wait to see it happen...?

CHAPTERS 11-15

Mrs. Jennings starts talking two pages into Chapter 11 and only gains steam as the narrative progresses. Austen describes her as an "everlasting talker" who "had already repeated her own history to Elinor three or four times; and had Elinor's memory been equal to her means of improvement, she might have known very early in their acquaintance all the particulars of Mr. Jennings's last illness and what he said to his wife a few minutes before he died." She talks so much that she basically has to be shoved off-page for Austen to get anything done, and even then you can practically hear her still chirping away in the margins, like someone on the phone in the next room. I have a friend who once told me, when describing an evening of particular volubility, that he'd only stopped talking half an hour after he fell asleep. Mrs. Jennings will stop talking about three weeks after she's laid in earth.

In one chapter she finally gets a whiff of Elinor's secret romantic life, through the agency of the youngest Dashwood sister, Margaret, who innocently lets it slip that there is a young man whom Elinor admires, and that his name begins with F. Mrs. Jennings is on it like a bloodhound; you half expect her to go down on all fours and start sniffing Elinor's hem for further clues. Fortunately, the ever considerate Colonel Brandon comes to her rescue and steers the conversation in a less mortifying direction.

But no good deed goes unpunished, and soon it's the colonel's turn to feel the heat of unwanted curiosity. We learn of a mystery surrounding him, something that can't but make him more attractive to the reader. (Not that he's been unattractive to us before; but all we've seen him do, really, is keep his dignity while Marianne and Willoughby pelt him with spitballs.) He receives news that compels his immediate departure for London, and so off he goes, even though his leaving completely torpedoes a pleasure outing scheduled for that very morning. That's how we know it's something capital-S serious; Colonel Brandon is the kind of man who'd rather endure root canal surgery than disappoint anyone. But though filled with regret, he's steadfast in his resolve to go; and equally firm in his polite refusal to tell Mrs. Jennings the cause of his departure, despite her asking him point-blank about six thousand times. She does everything but climb into his lap to persuade him. He leaves just in time; another minute and she'd have grabbed his hat and run off with it, saying, "You can have it back when you've told us your business in town."

Even when he's safely away, Mrs. Jennings keeps pursuing him. She spends almost an entire page wildly conjecturing on what might or might not be the cause of his sudden flight. Give her credit for self-esteem; it never occurs to her that it might be due to her own habit of mauling her guests like a great white shark. Finally, she reaches what is for her a definitive conclusion: it must be about Miss Williams. When Marianne asks who that might be, Mrs. Jennings is thrilled to be able to show off some secret knowledge:

> *"What? Do you not know who Miss Williams is? I am sure you must have heard of her before. She is a relation of the Colonel's, my dear; a very near relation. We will not say how near, for fear of shocking the young ladies." Then lowering her voice a little, she said to Elinor, "She is his natural daughter."*

Austen doesn't actually indicate any nudge-nudge, wink-wink interpolations in this passage, but I'm pretty sure they were there. In fact I'd bet on Elinor discovering a big bruise on her ribcage when she undresses that night. I also like the bit about Mrs. Jennings "lowering her voice a little;" you should always do that when you're preparing to announce something you've just said you can't possibly announce. (And need I add, Mrs. Jennings's lowered voice is probably still more than sufficient to carry to the cheap seats.)

Meanwhile, Marianne and Willoughby's whirlwind romance takes a huge leap—and suffers the inevitable nasty landing. Elinor hears from Margaret (who, after being a ghostly presence for the first ten chapters, suddenly becomes a regular Greek chorus in these) that Marianne has granted Willoughby a rather extraordinary favor:

> *"[T]hey were whispering and talking together as fast as could be, and he seemed to be begging something of her, and presently he took up her scissors and cut off a long lock of her hair, for it was all tumbled down her back; and he kissed it, and folded it up in a piece of white paper, and put it into his pocket book."*

This is about as close as we come to eros in the entire Austen canon, and I gotta give our gal props: it's hot stuff. Marianne's naked neck; her tumbling hair; those cold, hard scissors; the furtive kiss Willoughby gives the lock before hiding it away (in white paper, yet)... and all of it secretly observed by a child. Austen dispatches this news and then moves on to the next bit of business, and we're like, "Whoa, whoa, whoa! Back up there, sister, and open a window! I feel me a *swoon* comin' on." The irony, of course, is that scenes like this are exactly what people have been taught to expect from Austen; but she very rarely goes this route, and when she does, she never lingers, and never embroiders. She gives you the goods like a legal secretary, and then gets on with the story; and it's this very fleetness and directness that carries the erotic impact. (Imagine the scene as written by Dickens: suffocated by cushiony prose and sewn up tight with violin glissandos.)

It's this incident—Marianne's metaphorical surrendering of her body to Willoughby—that causes a modern reader's eyebrow to raise when we find out, later, that Willoughby has taken her to the house of his wealthy patron, Mrs. Smith, and shown her over all its rooms, without Mrs. Smith knowing she was there. The tour was supposed to have been secret, but Mrs. Jennings found out about it. (Of course she did; she's a Regency Columbo.) Elinor is shocked; she must suspect, as we do, that Marianne's criticism of the house's unfashionable furniture is partly due to the lack of comfort to be found there when you're flat on your back with your ankles in the air.

But Marianne isn't likely to be trapped into anything so common as remorse. When Elinor dismisses her exultations over the house with

"[T]he pleasantness of an employment does not always evince its propriety," Marianne just flat-out ain't havin' it:

> *"On the contrary, nothing can be stronger proof of it, Elinor; for if there had been any real impropriety in what I did, I should have been sensible of it at the time, for we always know when we are acting wrong, and with such a conviction I would have had no pleasure."*

Prediction: Marianne will soon discover chocolate, and weigh 270 pounds by Michaelmas.

Then we have an appalling scene in which Willoughby hears of Mrs. Dashwood's plans to improve the cottage, and he grandstands for three unendurable pages, absolutely forbidding her to alter as much as an atom of a place he considers the zenith of earthly perfection, and where he has found such unsurpassable happiness, and which he will reproduce brick for brick when he is master of his own property, and someone get a tub of water and help me hold his head under it for however goddamn long it takes, thanks, appreciate it.

But never mind, because a few heartbeats later Willoughby's gone. Mrs. Smith is sending him away indefinitely, and he makes sheepish goodbyes to Elinor and Mrs. Dashwood, having already provoked Marianne to flee the room *in extremis.* Which would have much more impact were Marianne not the type to flee every room *in extremis.* When we next see her, she's making a puny effort to compose herself at the dinner table, but is "without any power because she was without any desire of command over herself." Marianne is basically a three-act play, and everyone else in the household is her audience; and when she bolts offstage for the interval they all sit around and talk excitedly about what might happen next.

As for Willoughy, loathsome as he is, we sort of hate to see him go because there's no one to take his place—no oily grotesque to keep to narrative percolating. But have faith, Austen won't leave us abandoned for long.

CHAPTERS 16-20

With Willoughby gone, Marianne settles into the serious business of being a Tragic Heroine. She shuns her family's company and takes to solitary pursuits like wandering off to isolated scenic points where she can feel the full weight of her solitude, or tormenting herself by plonking down on the piano bench and going over all the music written in Willoughby's hand.

But here's where Austen's psychological savvy begins bleeding through: because rather than continue to portray Marianne as the personification of Romanticism, she presents her as an actual human being, one who's *chosen* Romanticism and is striving to live according to what she sees as its precepts. In other words, while Marianne is absolutely indulging her feelings, she's doing it self-consciously; she is, at least in part, striving for an effect. For example, immediately after Willoughby's departure, we learn that she would be "ashamed to look her family in the face the next morning had she not risen from her bed in more need of repose than when she lay down on it." Suddenly we can conjure an image of Marianne swooping downstairs and dropping limply across the length of a couch, then loudly clearing her throat until someone notices her.

Ultimately, of course, "such violence of affliction" can't be supported, and within a few days Marianne has segued into a "calmer melancholy," one in which she actually has to *work* herself into a fit of tears. Youth, with all its energy and optimism, is slowly reclaiming her, but she's putting up one helluva fight.

Now that Austen has sufficiently lashed Marianne, she turns her whip on Elinor; and where Marianne was tortured by the sudden departure of her great love, Elinor is wracked by the sudden appearance of hers. Edward Ferrars literally rides into the narrative, and the shock is so great Marianne even forgives him for not being Willoughby. Though she can't forgive him for the lack of poetry in his soul, which grates on her increasingly over the ensuing days. When she ecstatically points out the various grandeurs of the surrounding landscape, he can't see past the practicalities:

> *"It is such a beautiful country," he replied; "but these bottoms must be dirty in winter."*
>
> *"How can you think of dirt, with such objects before you?"*
>
> *"Because," replied he, smiling, "among the rest of the objects before me, I see a very dirty lane."*

Of course Elinor isn't bothered by Edward's leaden outlook, because she's not any more given to "transporting sensations" than he is. They're both wound up so tight, they might actually repel bullets. But even Elinor is abashed by Edward's demeanor on his arrival: he's cool, distant, and uneasy in the Dashwoods' company, and insists on staying no more than a week. (Things have obviously changed since the 19th century; these days, a houseguest who stays longer than a week can drive his hosts to distraction, divorce, and possibly manslaughter.) Elinor, like many women before and since, is completely flummoxed by the way her man is acting; her spirits soar at some flickering gesture that seems to indicate his high regard for her, then a few minutes later he'll be all standoffish again, and she'll be reduced to wondering why the chump bothered to come at all.

Edward does, however, seem to come alive in his exchanges with Marianne over the differences in their respective characters, a subject which seems to be of consuming interest to the both of them. (These days, they'd share a blog on the subject.) Many pages are spent in comparison and contrast, and Edward actually gets off some good lines at Marianne's expense:

> *"I like a fine prospect, but not on picturesque principles. I do not like crooked, blasted trees. I admire them much more if they are tall, straight*

> *and flourishing. I do not like ruined, tattered cottages. I am not fond of nettles, or thistles, or heath blossoms. I have more pleasure in a snug farmhouse than a watchtower, and a troop of tidy, happy villagers please me better than the finest banditi in the world."*
>
> *Marianne looked with amazement at Edward, with compassion at her sister. Elinor only laughed.*

Then Marianne notices that Edward wears a ring with a lock of hair in it, and she comments on it; Edward blushes and stammers. Elinor concludes the lock of hair must be hers, and that Edward's embarrassment must be over his having got it from her by some clandestine means. This is an interesting variation on the earlier chapter in which Willoughby ardently begged a lock of Marianne's hair, and Elinor was shocked to learn that Marianne allowed him to take one. Elinor, however, is quite pleased to believe that Edward has stolen a lock from her—presumably because she has the satisfaction of knowing her worth to him, without having had to surrender herself metaphorically to him. But I'd love to know exactly *how* she thought Edward got the lock of hair without her knowledge: did he perhaps sneak up on her while she was sleeping, and have his way with her scalp? Because that's inching uncomfortably close to a rape fantasy. I like my Austen nasty, but this is going a tad too far.

Despite such unsettling undercurrents and some very lively dialogue, we begin to weary a little of Marianne pining for Willoughby in his absence, and Elinor pining for Edward in his presence. Austen, perhaps sensing this, sends Edward packing. We're then treated to a few paragraphs detailing how Elinor handles his loss: it's the exact inversion of Marianne's behavior. Instead of languishing, she hurls herself into activities and employments. Instead of forbidding the mention of her beloved's name, she brings him up constantly. But this, too, has an element of self-consciousness in it: Elinor, like Marianne before her, is trying to persuade herself that she's the woman she pretends to be, by persuading others of it first.

By now we've had our fill of introspection and are beginning to pine, ourselves—for Sir John and Mrs. Jennings, whom we long to have burst back into the narrative. And what do you know, here they come—and hey! They've got company! Unexpected company, as we find out when Mrs. Jennings comes "hallooing" at the window:

> *"I have brought my other son and daughter to see you. Only think of their coming so suddenly! I thought I heard a carriage last night while we were drinking our tea, but it never entered my head it could be them. I thought of nothing but whether it might not be Colonel Brandon come back again; so I said to Sir John, 'I do think I hear a carriage; perhaps it is Colonel Brandon come back again—'"*

It's okay if you skim over this anecdote, because you get plenty of chances to hear it again; Mrs. Jennings retells it about ninety times over the course of the next three pages. She also introduces her daughter Charlotte, who talks as much as she does, but from an entirely different motive. Mrs. Jennings is driven to speak by a heightened sense of occasion; her great aspiration is to narrate the history of the world and every single person in it. Her daughter Charlotte, however, is a mindless natterer, one of those "Talking, talking, talking to keep Mr. Death away" types. When she catches sight of the drawings hung in the cottage, she launches into fulsome praise:

> *"Oh! Dear, how beautiful these are! Well! How delightful! Do but look, mama, how sweet! I declare they are quite charming; I could look at them forever." And then sitting down again, she very soon forgot that there were any such things in the room.*

Like Jack Spratt and his wife, Charlotte and her husband represent opposing principles, for Mr. Palmer barely speaks at all, and when he does, it's invariably a snarl. (He's no sooner been introduced to the Dashwoods than he takes up a newspaper and spends the rest of the chapter reading it. When at length Lady Middleton asks him if there's any news in the paper, he replies, "No, none at all," and goes on reading.) But to his wife he's especially brutal: he virtually refuses to dignify her with any conversation whatsoever, even when she asks him a direct question. She, of course, accepts this with nearly idiotic delight:

> *"Mr. Palmer does not hear me," said she, laughing; "he never does sometimes. It is so ridiculous!"*

I love that "he never does sometimes." A little soupçon of genius, right there.

Elinor thinks she has Mr. Palmer's number: she attributes his contemptuous treatment of others to a conscious desire to appear their superior—a motive "too common to be wondered at," but "not likely to attach anyone to him except his wife." Who, it seems to me, is the person he'd most like to *de*tach. Though his disdain for her can't be total, since she shows up pregnant; but I can imagine the sexual attraction she still holds for him might be one of the things he most resents about her. Whatever his psychology, he's good to have around, because every time he opens his mouth you gasp with admiration at his bravura hostility:

> *"You and I, Sir John," said Mrs. Jennings, "should not stand upon such ceremony."*
>
> *"Then you would be very ill-bred," cried Mr. Palmer.*
>
> *"My love, you contradict everybody," said his wife with her usual laugh. "Do you know you are quite rude?"*
>
> *"I did not know I contradicted anybody in calling your mother ill-bred."*

It's a hit-and-run performance, because as quickly as the Palmers arrive, they're off again. This is Austen's first published novel, and she's still learning her craft; she keeps coming up with extraordinary comic creations, like Fanny Dashwood and Mr. Palmer, who weave into and out of the narrative in a way that only tantalizes the reader. Even Mrs. Jennings, who's more of a fixture, is largely incidental to the story. In her next novel, she'll have learned her lesson, and epic grotesques like Mrs. Bennet, Mr. Collins and Lady Catherine will be essential to the mechanism of the plot. And in the very next chapters of *Sense and Sensibility* we'll see her finding her way there, as she introduces her first full-scale comic horror, who is also a pivot on which the plot turns: Miss Lucy Steele.

CHAPTERS 21-25

Austen must have had a roaring good breakfast the day she started writing chapter 21, because it crackles with comic energy. The Palmers are booted offstage only to make way for a new pair of arrivals, sisters who are essentially picked up by Sir John in Exeter after being discovered to be relations of Mrs. Jennings, and whom he promptly invites to come stay at Barton Park. His wife is alarmed at the thought that "she was very soon to receive a visit from two girls whom she had never seen in her life," and she takes no comfort in the assurances of her husband that they're capital sorts of girls because his opinion on such matters "went for nothing at all." But since she can't wriggle out of the responsibility he's thrust on her, she resigns herself to it "with all the philosophy of a well-bred woman" and contents herself with merely berating her husband about it "five or six times a day."

The two young ladies arrive, and from the moment they step out of the coach they are determined to make themselves adored by everyone. The way the two Miss Steeles go about this is by continually exclaiming the perfection of everything they see, as if they'd just fallen through a time vortex from the 9th century and are stunned into astonishment by things like glass windows and area rugs. Lady Middleton is only too happy to take this flattery at face value, declaring them "to be very agreeable girls indeed, which for her ladyship was extravagant admiration."

Sir John, for whom it's painful "even to keep a third cousin to himself," begins nagging the Dashwood sisters to come and meet his new pets, repeatedly declaring them "the sweetest girls in the world;" a testimonial wasted on Elinor, who knows "that the sweetest girls in the world are to be met with in every part of England, under every possible variation of form, face, temper, and understanding." But Sir John ain't having any of her danged reluctance:

> *"How can you be so cross as not to come? Why they are your cousins, you know, after a fashion. You are my cousins, and they are my wife's; so you must be related."*

Elinor and Marianne eventually relent, if only to stop Sir John bleating in their faces like an air-horn. And what they find underwhelms them: the oldest Miss Steele, Anne, is "nearly thirty, with a very plain and not a sensible face, nothing to admire;" the younger, Lucy, is prettier, with "a sharp quick eye and a smartness of air, which though it did not give actual elegance or grace, gave distinction to her person." Oooh! Flamed by faint praise! Watch your step, Austen's on lethal form here.

And in fact worse is to come. Elinor and Marianne look on in horror as the two Miss Steeles try to cement their favor with Lady Middleton by allowing her horde of devil children to torment them with "impertinent incroachments and mischievous tricks".

> *[Lady Middleton] saw their sashes untied, their hair pulled about their ears, their workbags searched, and their knives and scissors stolen away, and felt no doubt of its being a reciprocal enjoyment..."John is in such spirits today!" said she, on his taking Miss Steele's pocket handkerchief and throwing it out of the window. "He is full of monkey tricks."*

Nodding your head yet?...Oh, yeah, we all know that family. They invariably get the table next to ours at our favorite restaurants, or the seats right behind ours on any given airplane. They're the reason alcohol was invented. Also possibly murder.

Finally the children are dragged away, though not before having extorted every iota of attention from those only too willing to reward bad behavior. When they're gone, the Dashwood and Steele sisters are left alone, and the latter just can't stop gushing with pleasure—as, presumably, they pull their skirts down from over their heads and pop any dislocated joins back into place:

> *"I never saw such fine children in my life. I declare I quite dote upon them already, and indeed I am always distractedly fond of children."*
>
> *"I should guess so," said Elinor with a smile, "from what I have witnessed this morning."*

Then Anne Steele, the elder, who seems "very much disposed for conversation," leaps right over the kind of preliminary cocktail-type chatter we engage in when meeting someone new, to plunge into "feelings"—in particular, what the Dashwoods think of Devonshire and how sorry they must be to have left Sussex. She also goes on and on about "beaux" in a way that easily marks her as what we used to call "boy crazy," and she has an annoying fondness for the phrase "prodigious handsome," and would really like to know exactly how prodigiously so the beaux of Elinor and Marianne might be, and she doesn't care if they're Devonshire beaux or Sussex beaux as long as they're beaux.

In a Jane Austen novel, this is about as bad as it gets. She might as well ask them what feminine hygiene products they use; the effect couldn't be any worse. Even the younger sister, Lucy, seems to realize that Anne is going too far, and offers occasional muted apologies, in the way of someone who follows a squatting dog around the room, picking up its droppings but unable to get it to stop.

By the time the visit is over, the damage has been done:

> *This specimen of the Miss Steeles was enough. The vulgar freedom and folly of the eldest left her no recommendation, and as Elinor was not blinded by the beauty or the shrewd look of the youngest to her want of real elegance and artlessness, she left the house without any wish of knowing them better.*

At this point, we may think we know where this is headed: Anne Steele is going to be our new favorite freak, forever bursting into rooms without knocking, then crinkling her nose and asking What's that funny smell—with Lucy lagging behind as a kind of footnote to her foolishness.

But oh, no. Austen pulls a fast one on us. Anne Steele's clumsy awfulness is just a screen for the hair-wilting horror of Lucy, who is lying in wait like a crocodile while the narrative gently laps up against her scaly sides. She's biding her time for the perfect moment to snap... and it comes shortly after Sir John lets it slip that the prodigiously handsome beau Elinor favors over any other has a name that begins with an F. And lest anyone doubt him, he goes on to prove it: "His name is Ferrars," he says in an audible whisper, "but pray do not tell it, for it's a great secret."

Those of us who have read the novel before can pinpoint this as the exact moment when the wheels start turning behind Lucy's eyes; and in the very next chapter she delivers a masterful performance, asking Elinor, in all apparent innocence, whether she's ever met her sister-in-law's mother, Mrs. Ferrars, and apologizing if the question seems an odd one.

It absolutely seems an odd one to Elinor, but she answers it anyway: no, she has never seen Mrs. Ferrars in her life.

> *"I am sure you think me very strange for inquiring about her in such a way," said Lucy, eyeing Elinor attentively as she spoke, "but perhaps there may be reasons—I wish I might venture; but, however, I hope you will do me the justice of believing that I do not mean to be impertinent."*

Not impertinent, no; Lucy—whom Elinor has already marked out as woefully deficient in manners, breeding, and even speech (she has particular trouble with pronouns)—can't be called in any way impertinent. In fact, she's just the opposite. She has a bombshell for Elinor, but rather than fling it in her face, she's going to hint at it, allude to it, tease it like a hank of raw wool, so that when she finally does reveal it, it'll seem almost like it was Elinor who drew it out of her. And so she smirks and scowls, boasts and blushes—parries and feints, really, is what it amounts to, and she's the only one armed with a sword. But Elinor, who wasn't born yesterday, is perfectly aware she's being prompted, and refuses to play along, so that the performance is cut short and Lucy must reveal her shocking secret: She is engaged to Edward. Not that she can simply come out and *say* so: she has to shroud it like the prize tucked away in a whole Happy Meal of unwieldy verbiage:

> *"[I]f I dared tell you all, you would not be so much surprised. Mrs. Ferrars is certainly nothing to me at present, but the time may come—how soon it will come must depend upon herself—when we may be very intimately connected."*

She could be the goddamn Riddler on *Batman.*

Elinor, of course, is completely knocked flat. At first she can't believe that they're talking about the same Edward Ferrars, and Lucy takes an almost feline glee in reassuring her that yes they are, in every particular—"Mr. Edward Ferrars, the eldest son of Mrs. Ferrars of Park Street, and brother of your sister-in-law, Mrs. John Dashwood, is the person I mean; you must allow that *I* am not likely to be deceived as to the name of the man on who all my happiness depends."

Then Elinor considers she may be lying; but she produces a miniature of Edward, and a letter in his hand. There's no doubt left to cling to. But she's Elinor; she governs her emotions. She doesn't dissolve into pudding, she looks the problem square in the face—she looks *past* it—and so she sees things clear. She doesn't doubt Edward's love for her; nor does she doubt that his attachment to Lucy is a folly of his youth that he's now outgrown but can't honorably acquit himself of. She feels tremendous pity for him.

Meantime, Lucy strolls along beside her, almost purring; you can picture her licking flecks of gore off her lips. She's had a good meal and could probably now use a nap.

But then she makes the mistake of overplaying her hand; having slashed Elinor down to size, she now tries, pathetically, to solicit her pity. She tremulously confesses that she and Edward seldom see each other—"we can hardly meet above twice a year. I am sure I wonder my heart is not quite broke." After which she grandly produces a handkerchief, but Elinor, Austen tells us, "did not feel very compassionate." Seeing that this gambit hasn't worked, Lucy switches tacks and tries to make Elinor an ally, admitting her confusion in this swirl of affairs and pleading for Elinor's advice on what to do. Which, of course, is exactly the kind of appeal that brings out Elinor's inner Margaret Thatcher:

> *"Pardon me," replied Elinor, startled by the question, "but I can give you no advice under such circumstances. Your own judgment must direct you."*

The two women part ways after that, Elinor grievously wounded but still standing tall. Lucy, for her part, ambles off to play her role of secret fiancée to the hilt. It's at about this point we realize her elder sister Anne is her chief audience and fan club, and that the lurid aspects of the whole affair have had an adverse reaction on Anne's already-existing tendency to romantic hysteria. In this condition, no prodigiously handsome young gentleman within a dozen miles is safe from her; but we don't care about that. We care about Edward; and from what we've just seen of Lucy Steele, we know the boy's in some deeeep shite.

Elinor, unlike Marianne, doesn't run to the nearest cliffside to pose tragically against the setting sun; she goes someplace close and quiet and works out a program that incorporates all the hard data she's collected in the past few hours. And one thing becomes crystal clear to her: all of Lucy's blushing shyness and sisterly entreaties are actually poses, calculated to convey one message only: *Hands off my man.* Well, fine; Elinor would never pursue someone who's promised elsewhere; she has her pride, if nothing else. But she takes solace in her certainty that Edward's engagement to Lucy can no longer be a welcome one to him; and she weeps for him. This is where Austen gets us: we've seen Marianne weeping, how many times?...A dozen? Nine hundred? Three thousand?...and we've remained sympathetic but largely unmoved. When Elinor weeps, we feel it in our gut.

Suddenly Mrs. Jennings decides it's time to return to her house in London, and says she can't possibly endure life in town without the Dashwood girls joining her there. And it must be both of them, not just one: "It would be more comfortable for them to be together because if they got tired of me, they might talk to one another and laugh at my odd ways behind my back." She begs, she pleads, she cajoles, but Elinor is adamant. Personally, I don't know why Mrs. Jennings even bothers asking. The force of her personality is such that, when she leaves Barton Park, all of Norton College will probably uproot itself and be pulled after her, as in a tractor beam.

But in the end it's Marianne who pushes for the scheme. Elinor, who has spent the entire novel being shocked on every third page, is now shocked again. When it occurs to her that, aha!—Willoughby is in town!—which explains Marianne's motives, it doesn't make her any less uneasy.

> *That Marianne, fastidious as she was, thoroughly acquainted with Mrs. Jennings's manners, and invariably disgusted by them, should overlook every inconvenience of that kind, should disregard whatever must be most wounding to her irritable feelings, in her pursuit of one object, was such a proof, so strong, so full of the importance of that object to her, as Elinor, in spite of all that had passed, was not prepared to witness.*

But Elinor is overruled by Mrs. Dashwood, who's only too delighted to send her youngest daughter careering after a man who's rejected her. To complete Elinor's dismay, the Steele sisters are to follow shortly thereafter, as guests of the Middletons.

The day of departure finds Marianne in—what else?—a flood of tears.

> *Her unwillingness to quit her mother was her only restorative to calmness; and at the moment of parting, her grief on that score was excessive. Her mother's affliction was hardly less, and Elinor was the only one of the three who seemed to consider the separation as anything short of eternal.*

Sometimes, you just gotta give Austen the last word.

CHAPTERS 26-30

We're now twenty-five chapters into this fifty-chapter novel; so how much actual romance has the supposed über-romantic novelist given us? Halfway through her freshman effort, you'd expect to be suffocated by endless scenes of heaving bosoms, passionate embraces, and manly hands gripping Empire waists. Where is it all, then...? Where are the smoldering stares, the writhing limbs, the pull of erotic longing across spectacularly manicured lawns (with at least one gamboling lamb for color)?

Fact is, there's been nothing of the sort. All we've had are a few noisy chapters of Marianne and Willoughby's circus-tumbler carousing; some basset-hound moping from Colonel Brandon; and occasional scenes of Elinor and Edward looking mutely at each other from opposite sides of a revolving door. Scarcely the stuff "chick lit" is made of.

What we've had instead is a constant, contentious, and consistently sidesplitting parade of dopes, dupes, cranks, curmudgeons, gorgons, graspers, and rhymes-with-witches. Clearly Austen better get it in gear pretty goddamn fast, if she's going to produce something worthy of a Hollywood blockbuster—the kind whose budget for lip gloss exceeds her entire lifetime earnings.

And whaddaya know, she does. Against our expectations, in these next chapters Austen turns the narrative on its head and gives us one of the most deeply felt, tenderly delineated, and beautifully realized love stories in all of 19th century literature.

But not the one you're thinking of. (Unless you're almost unendurably brilliant, as I hope at least some of you are.)

The Dashwood sisters are now in London at Mrs. Jennings's invitation, and Marianne is filled with "the rapture of delightful expectation" of seeing Willoughby again. Elinor, noticing this, can't help feeling "how blank was her own prospect, how cheerless her own state of mind in comparison." It's not jealousy, exactly; it can't be—Elinor's still not as certain of Willoughby as Marianne is. But she resolves that if in fact he shows real pleasure and affection at Marianne being essentially dropped into his lap as from an overhead plane, she "must then learn to avoid every selfish comparison and banish every regret which might lessen her satisfaction in the happiness of Marianne."

Her selflessness is set in stark relief against her sister's navel-gazing. Marianne doesn't say a word to Mrs. Jennings during the coach ride to London, so Elinor has to bear the entire weight of the conversation, which frankly doesn't seem like it would be *that* big a burden. For someone like Mrs. Jennings, the response to an inquiry as simple as "What's new?" could conceivably take up most of a transatlantic crossing, if not a mission to Mars.

Yet Marianne remains in withdrawal when she gets to Mrs. Jennings's house. She writes Willoughby immediately to let him know she's arrived, which Elinor only discovers through chance observation; Marianne explains herself to no one, in fact barely speaks to anyone, seems only half-aware of there being anyone else in the house. Instead she spends her time banging gently against the front window, like a moth. Finally, after many glacial hours, there's a rap on the front door, and Marianne whips herself up like a dervish:

> *[S]he could not help exclaiming, 'Oh Elinor, it is Willoughby, indeed it is!' and seemed almost ready to throw herself into his arms, when Colonel Brandon appeared.*
>
> *It was too great a shock to be borne with calmness, and she immediately left the room.*

You almost have to laugh; Colonel Brandon has the worst timing of anyone this side of Ron Goldman. But of course it's a little heartbreaking as well, because he's too shrewd not to see the Kabuki-like look of horror he's brought to the face of the woman he loves.

Marianne's flight from the room once again leaves Elinor in sole charge of an awkward conversation, which neither she nor Brandon really has the heart for but in which they doggedly persist anyway, because that's the kind of people they are, goddammit. Fortunately, Mrs. Jennings ends their torment by sailing in and immediately grabbing the oars from both of them:

> *"Well, Colonel, I have brought two young ladies with me, you see—that is, you see but one of them now, but there is another somewhere. Your friend Miss Marianne, too—which you will not be sorry to hear. I do not know what you and Mr. Willoughby will do between you about her. Aye, it is a fine thing to be young and handsome. Well! I was young once, but I never was very handsome—worse luck for me. However I got a very good husband, and I don't know what the greatest beauty can do more. Ah! Poor man! He has been dead these eight years and better. But Colonel, where have you been to since we parted? And how does your business go on? Come, come, let's have no secrets among friends."*

If *Sense and Sensibility* were a play instead of a novel, Mrs. Jennings would steal the show at every performance. She's absolutely the equal of Lady Bracknell or Madame Arcati.

The next morning her daughter Charlotte arrives and greets the Dashwood sisters in her own inimitable manner:

> *"Mr. Palmer will be so happy to see you," said she; "what do you think he said when he heard of your coming with mama? I forget what it was now, but it was something so droll!"*

In fact, it seems like everybody in the world keeps arriving *except* Willoughby, which drives Marianne to increasing extremes, not just of anxiety but of outright gracelessness. Elinor has to hop on one foot and juggle oranges to keep Mrs. Jennings from noticing Marianne's rudeness, which Mrs. Jennings thankfully seems too busy talking to do—even though Marianne's agitation is so great that by this point, she could rattle the wheels off a landau just by sitting in it.

There's a temporary respite when Mrs. Jennings comments, over breakfast, on how unusually fine the weather has remained, and how lucky the huntsmen are to be able to extend their sport. Marianne lunges at this like a golden retriever at a Frisbee: "I had not thought of *that.* This weather will keep many sportsmen in the country." And so she gets reset to zero. She dashes off a letter to Willoughby's country address and then goes pathetically through the motions of daily life, less attuned to where she is and why than to any meteorological phenomenon that might bring him to town the sooner. "Don't you find it colder than it was in the morning, Elinor? There seems to me a very decided difference. I can hardly keep my hands warm even in my muff."

Then disaster: they return from an outing one afternoon and find that Willoughby's left his card. "Good God," Marianne cries, "he has been here while we were out!" A pretty dicey epithet for an Austen heroine; no doubt Elinor is shocked.

Disaster, yes; and yet also a sign that he's alive and well and in town, and was standing right at Mrs. Jennings's door! Marianne doesn't exactly drop to all fours and kiss the stoop, but she does run off to be alone with his card, which is a pretty close second on the Completely Lost It scale.

Best of all, if he came once, he's bound to come again. Except he doesn't, and Austen is absolutely merciless in the way she ratchets up Marianne's agony—masterfully playing it against Mrs. Jennings's obliviousness and Elinor's helplessness so that we can barely sit still while reading it. We're tempted to avert our eyes, as though we're watching a school bus careening towards the edge of a cliff. Take the scene in which a note is brought in and laid on the table:

> *"For me?" cried Marianne, stepping hastily forward.*
> *"No, ma'am, for my mistress."*
> *But Marianne, not convinced, took it instantly up.*
> *"It is indeed for Mrs. Jennings; how provoking!"*

This kind of behavior, in Austen-land...do I really even need to tell you? Marianne might as well be staggering around the parlor in her underwear, slugging gin right from the bottle.

Ironically, while Willoughby keeps Marianne twisting in the wind, the whole town is talking about them as though they're engaged—the result of Marianne writing to him so openly and injudiciously. Colonel Brandon comes to call (we can imagine him peering around the door jamb this time, to make sure the coast is clear) and asks Elinor if it's true, if there's really no hope for him. Elinor, confused herself, thinks it kinder to "say more than she really knew or believed," just to spare him further torment. He takes it manfully; of course he does. He's a man. One of Austen's better exemplars of the species. (You can sort of tell I'm a Brandon booster, huh?)

Then the inevitable occurs, on a night when Marianne attends a ball "wholly dispirited, careless of her appearance." You can almost see her with her hair out of curl, and a big gravy stain on one sleeve. Of *course* that's when she runs into Willoughby. She really should've thought of it earlier; if you're anxious to see the one you adore, just go out in a sweat-stained T-shirt and with spinach stuck in your teeth; you're guaranteed to run into him.

The interview doesn't go well; Willoughby pretends to be no more than a casual acquaintance of the Dashwoods, though he doesn't do a very good job of it—his face colors and his jaw contorts as Marianne basically dissolves into a puddle of plasma and petticoats before him. Elinor observes all this, and is comforted that Willoughby apparently *does* feel how badly he's behaving; that he hasn't just been callously toying with Marianne all along. And then, strangely, she finds herself not only no longer in danger of jealousy of Marianne, but at the opposite extreme: she at least can always be certain of Edward's love, even if she can't have him, whereas Marianne will now always know she was dispensable to Willoughby. (He's dispensed with her in favor of an heiress worth a walloping fifty thousand pounds, but still.)

Marianne goes to pieces after this, and takes to her room like the madwoman in the attic, and Elinor practically has to turn somersaults while whistling the overture from *Die Zauberflöte* to keep Mrs. Jennings from noticing. In fact she does the job too well, because Mrs. Jennings, she learns, is still happily promoting the idea of a Marianne-Willoughby match. Elinor asks her please to desist, says there's no substance to it, it was only ever a kind of fancy, but Mrs. Jennings scoffs; it must be true, because it's being broadcast all over town. Distressed, Elinor asks who's broadcasting it, and Mrs. Jennings replies, *she* is. No doubt with a rebuking look at Elinor for being so stupid.

Elinor goes up to see Marianne, and finds her prostrate in her distress.

> *Elinor drew near, but without saying a word; and seating herself on the bed, took her hand, kissed her affectionately several times, and then gave way to a burst of tears, which at first was scarcely less violent than Marianne's.*

And thus the opening salvo in the love story I mentioned earlier: these sisters, who were intended to represent opposing philosophical principles—Reason vs. Romanticism—have become fully rounded individuals; the genius of their creator has by degrees pulled her away from her original design and toward something much more profound. We know, of course, that the one enduring love of Austen's own life was her sister, Cassandra; but for the purposes of this treatise I choose to ignore biography and take the works on their own terms, since for any writer, that's all we can ever be certain of. (I sometimes think we're lucky to have virtually nothing on the particulars of Shakespeare's character and affairs; imagine the groaning shelves of dissertations on how, say, his abscessed teeth were the driving force behind the problem plays.) Certainly the most affecting, truest, and most palpable love story in *Sense and Sensibility* is that of Elinor and Marianne. From this moment, they come together—Reason unmanned, Romanticism ravaged—and bolster each other; restore each other; balance each other's deficits and draw ballast from each other's strengths, even as the teeming world of freaks and ogres continues to press in on them.

Speaking of which, the Middletons and the Palmers arrive on the scene. Go on, admit it, you're happy to see them, even though you know their endless gabble on the subject of Willoughby's perfidy will drive Marianne to the brink of opening her wrist with an oyster fork.

Mrs. Jennings is the first to see the silver lining:

> *"Well, my dear, 'tis a true saying about an ill wind, for it will be all the better for Colonel Brandon. He will have her at last: aye, that he will. Mind me now if they an't married by Midsummer. Lord! How he'll chuckle over this news! I hope he will come tonight. It will be all to one a better match for your sister. Two thousand a year without debt or drawback—except the little love child, indeed; aye, I had forgot her, but she may be 'prenticed out at small cost, and then what does it signify?"*

Colonel Brandon does come that night; he hears the news from Elinor; and Mrs. Jennings, observing them, is absolutely astonished that he remains downcast and ashen, that he doesn't leap up and do the Macarena on hearing that the woman he loves has been cast aside and is in anguish. For the first time since the novel began, she's speechless.

CHAPTERS 31-35

Austen etches a finely drawn portrait of the rejected and dejected Marianne, going over and over the particulars of her history with Willoughby and reaching a different conclusion each time—sometimes condoning him (he's broke, he has no choice but to marry a rich girl), sometimes condemning him (he led her on, the chump). Elinor bravely endures all this while trying to provide some ballast for Marianne's wind-whipped emotions; it's a job only she can do because Marianne refuses to see anyone else, and has a particular aversion to the seemingly solicitous Mrs. Jennings. "All that she wants is gossip," Marianne sneers, "and she only likes me now because I supply it." Which is a little ingenuous of her. She's spent the past several months careering around England like a cross between Isadora Duncan and Yoko Ono, but God forbid anyone should *comment.*

Mrs. Jennings fans the flames against herself when she hands Marianne a letter with the words, "Now, my dear, I bring you something that I am sure will do you good." Of *course* Marianne thinks it's from Willoughby, and is crestfallen when it turns out to be from her mother. Mrs. Jennings might as well have said, "My dear, who do you think is at the door with a dozen roses? Mr. Willoughby!...KIDDING."

Eventually Mrs. Jennings tires of trying to glean good material from the eight seconds per day that Marianne skitters across her line of sight, so she decides to bundle up what she's got and take it on the road. She "could not be easy till the Middletons and Palmers were able to grieve as much as herself." When she's finally gone, Marianne creeps out of her room on the assumption that it's safe, only to have Colonel Brandon appear and send her scurrying back like Punxsatawney Phil at the sight of his shadow.

But it's really Elinor that Brandon has come to see. He's ready to divulge his Great Secret, which actually is, even by our standards, pretty great indeed. Turns out he had a childhood sweetheart whom he lost to his brother; he joined the army to put distance between them, only to return and find that his brother had mistreated her and she had left him. By the time Brandon found her again she was a fallen woman who was also (rather conveniently for the narrative) mortally ill; what's more, she had a child whom she entrusted to Brandon's care. This daughter—the Miss Williams mentioned earlier in the novel by (who else) Mrs. Jennings—has only recently repeated her mother's sad history, by falling prey to a heartless seducer. Guess who. No, go on, really. Take a wild stab.

Elinor is profoundly shocked (as opposed to her everyday level of shocked) by this revelation of Willoughby's villainy, and earnestly thanks Brandon, who explains that he's kept silent all this time because he thought Marianne's influence might "reclaim" Willoughby. Which is taking Christian charity about a mile and half too far, in my opinion. But just when you begin to wonder whether Brandon might be a seriously world-class wuss, you get this:

> *"Eliza had confessed to me, though most reluctantly, the name of her lover; and when he returned to town, which was within a fortnight after myself, we met by appointment, he to defend, I to punish his conduct. We returned unwounded, and the meeting, therefore, never got abroad."*

They had a *duel*, baby! Most people gloss right over this significant detail. Me, I'm only sorry that at this stage of her career, Austen wasn't yet experimenting with multiple points of view (once past the exposition of the initial chapters, *Sense and Sensibility* is told entirely from Elinor's perspective). She'd do so in later novels, but man, I'd love to have "been" there for this event, and to have seen how Austen handled things like exploding gunpowder and bullets ripping through the air adjacent to Brandon's and Willoughby's well-manicured cheeks.

Elinor of course relates all this to Marianne, with the effect that her feelings for Colonel Brandon significantly alter. She no longer reflexively flees from him as if he were all four horsemen of the Apocalypse put together, and in fact goes that one better by actually speaking to him ("even voluntarily," Austen adds).

So now we're thinking Marianne will be all, "Phew! Narrow escape. On with my life!" But no, despite what she's learned she remains as wretched as before. "She felt the loss of Willoughby's character yet more heavily than she had felt the loss of his heart." Which just makes us want to take her by her slim little shoulders and shake her like a Regency martini.

Meanwhile, Mrs. Jennings has whipped all her relations into such an affronted frenzy that none of them can say enough bad about the infamous Willoughby. For Mrs. Jennings's own part, "she hated him so much that she resolved never to mention his name again, and she should tell everybody she knew how good-for-nothing he was." (This is the first incidence of a joke Austen will use repeatedly over the years, and I will laugh like a fool every goddamn time.) Only Lady Middleton, spiritually torpid as ever, takes no part in the general outrage; to Elinor's relief, the best she can manage is indifference. She offers a few token words in support of her husband's ire, then...

> *...having thus supported the dignity of her own sex and spoken her decided censure of what was wrong in the other, she thought herself at liberty to attend to the interest of her own assemblies and therefore determined (though rather against the opinion of Sir John) that as Mrs. Willoughby would at once be a woman of elegance and fortune, to leave her card with her as soon as she married.*

Then we hear that Willoughby has indeed wed the heiress for whose sake (or rather for whose shekels) he dumped Marianne. And a kind of bleak, Scandinavian stillness comes over the novel. It lasts almost three whole paragraphs. Then, thank sweet merciful Jesus, the Miss Steeles come barreling back, entering London society with all the effortless grace of a locomotive run amok.

Elinor is sorry to see them, but no sorrier than Lucy is to see her; after all, Elinor's chances of running into their mutual heartthrob Edward are far greater in town than they were in the country. Lucy makes her feelings abundantly clear in a sisterly greeting that wields italics like a sabre:

> *"I should have been quite disappointed if I had not found you here* still... *But I always thought I* should. *I was almost sure you would not leave London yet awhile; though you* told *me, you know, at Barton, that you should not stay above a* month...*I am amazingly glad you did not keep to your* word."
>
> *Elinor perfectly understood her and was forced to use all her self-command to make it appear that she did not.*

But the Miss Steeles aren't the only previous cast members Austen's gathering up, like ingredients for a meal she's been keeping in the larder for just this moment. John Dashwood and his wife Fanny are coming to London too, and since Fanny is Edward's sister, Lucy is convinced that Elinor plans to use this to get the upper hand over her: "I suppose you will go and stay with your brother and sister, Miss Dashwood, when they come to town," she snarls sweetly. When Elinor assures her she will do no such thing, Lucy says, "Oh yes, I dare say you shall." Lucy is the Joe Wilson of *Sense and Sensibility.*

We're longing to see Fanny Dashwood again, of course, and it's a kind of torture knowing she's in town wreaking her particular brand of havoc—frightening horses, driving porters to suicide—without us being in on it. But hearing Lucy mention her raises the tantalizing idea of those two women in the same room, which is so exciting we have to put the book down and just *think* about it for a while, the way, as children, we'd devote half an afternoon to wondering who'd win a fight between Godzilla and Mothra.

But Austen has some other business to take care of before anything so felicitous can happen. First is a chapter in which Elinor, by some great effort—possibly involving winches and a crane—gets Marianne out of the house for some shopping. Or rather, for some bartering: Elinor seeks to exchange "a few old-fashioned jewels of her mother." Austen slips in these little nods to the sisters' pennilessness every so often, lest you're tempted to forget the Ledger Sheet.

Unfortunately the jeweler's shop is crowded, and Elinor and Marianne are forced to sit and wait, during which time they have plenty of opportunity to observe one customer in particular, a young man whose manner imprints on Elinor "the remembrance of a person and face of strong, natural, sterling insignificance, though adorned in the first style of fashion." What follows is brilliant little burlesque as this self-important oaf transacts the selection and purchase of a toothpick case (how Austen must have howled when she settled on *that* detail) with only slightly less scrupulousness than Julius Caesar conducted his conquest of Gaul. And soon we realize that while we're impatiently awaiting more of Lucy and Fanny, Austen has snuck a whole new monster under our noses; she's almost taunting us with her virtuosity.

The fatuous gentleman goes off, "having named the last day on which his existence could be continued without the possession of the toothpick case," presumably never to be seen again. Ah, but Austen isn't finished surprising us yet. We learn that John Dashwood intends to honor his fraternal obligations by calling on his sisters, and we shift in our seats awaiting some good toxic doses of Fanny...only to have John show up alone, his wife being "too much engaged with her mother that really she had no leisure for going anywhere."

But our disappointment is swiftly ameliorated by John's superb comic performance. Removed from Fanny's outsize shadow, he reveals himself to be a perfectly splendid cretin. He spends most of the chapter complaining woefully of his poverty, the way only someone both obscenely rich and invincibly self-involved can:

> *"I have made a little purchase within this half year: East Kingham Farm; you must remember the place where old Gibson used to live. The land was so very desirable for me in every respect, so immediately adjoining my own property, that I felt it my duty to buy it. I could not have answered to my conscience to let it fall into any other hands. A man must pay for his convenience, and it has cost me a vast deal of money."*

When not bemoaning how skint he is, he delivers to Elinor the interesting news that a wife has been selected for Edward, a certain Miss Morton who comes with an "Honorable" before her name and thirty thousand pounds a year, so she could pretty well be as big as a manatee and four times as ugly and still be thought a brilliant match. To encourage Edward to accept her, his mother has agreed to settle an income of a thousand pounds on him when the marriage takes place: "A thousand a year is a great deal for a mother to give away; but Mrs. Ferrars has a noble spirit." Later John meets Colonel Brandon, whose income he learns is two thousand, and Austen amplifies his almost heroic obliviousness by having him decide that Brandon and Elinor are meant for each other, despite Elinor's very firm insistence on the contrary. The way he speaks to her would, if she were anyone but Elinor, pretty much provoke bodily harm, possibly with drawn blood:

> *"[Marianne] was as handsome a girl last September as any I ever saw —and as likely to attract the men...I remember Fanny used to say that she would marry sooner and better than you did; not but what she is exceedingly fond of you, but so it happened to strike her. She will be mistaken, however; I question whether Marianne now will marry a man worth more than five or six hundred a year, at the utmost, and I am very much deceived if you do not do better."*

He also nags Elinor on the subject of whether Mrs. Jennings's generosity in hosting her in town might indicate that the lady will leave her a bequest in her will. "He had just compunction enough for having done nothing for his sisters himself to be exceedingly anxious that everybody else should do a great deal."

Now that John has met (and approved) the Middletons and Mrs. Jennings, of course he invites them to dinner, and since the Miss Steeles are the Middletons' guests they're invited as well ("though Lucy was certainly not elegant and her sister not even genteel"). This is the first opportunity for us to see so many of the novel's principals under one roof together; it's also our chance to meet Edward and Fanny's mother, Mrs. Ferrars, the first of Austen's magnificent gorgons; she's the run-up to Lady Catherine de Bourgh. Austen is careful to point out that Mrs. Ferrars is thin, and that she's "not a woman of many words; for unlike people in general, she proportioned them to the number of her ideas". This makes her the anti-Mrs. Jennings; and while Austen is often hard on the latter, it's clear, by the viciousness with which she depicts the former, that she vastly prefers overweight blabbermouths to emaciated mutes.

The entire party is one of Austen's best set pieces; the characters all get the chance to make idiots of themselves in their own idiosyncratic ways. But pride of place goes to Lucy Steele who, as Edward's secret fiancée, is in a high flutter at the prospect of finally meeting his mother —but not so much so that she doesn't seize the chance to rub Elinor's nose in it: "There is nobody here but you that can feel for me. I declare I can hardly stand. Good gracious! In a moment I shall see the person that all my happiness depends on—that is to be my mother!" Elinor of course knows Mrs. Ferrars intends to marry Edward to Miss Morton, so she responds to Lucy's taunting with genuine sympathy—"to the utter amazement of Lucy, who, though really uncomfortable herself, hoped at least to be an object of irrepressible envy to Elinor."

Neither Mrs. Ferrars nor Fanny have forgotten Edward and Elinor's mutual attraction, so they've made up their minds to be as rude to Elinor as possible, to put her off any idea of taking up pursuit of him again. Unfortunately, the chief means they choose to accomplish this is to make a big deal of Lucy—essentially saying, "See, bitch, we like even *this* piece of trash better than you"—which has a very different effect on Elinor than the one intended: "She could not but smile to see the graciousness of both mother and daughter towards the very person—for Lucy was particularly distinguished—whom of all others, had they known as much as she did, they would have been most anxious to mortify."

But Marianne—who, of course, can't hold back an emotion any more than she could a team of mustangs—finally emerges from her gloom long enough to notice how badly Elinor's being treated. She opens a whole can of whoop-ass on Fanny and Mrs. Ferrars, then flounces off to a corner and bursts into tears. Colonel Brandon just about faints in admiration, but is interrupted by John Dashwood who, with his wonderful ability to say not only the wrong thing but the most spectacularly wrong of all wrong possibilities, points out to the Colonel that Marianne *"was* remarkably handsome a few months ago; quite as handsome as Elinor. Now you see it is all gone."

Lucy sails out of the experience with the wind at her back, in such a confusion of joy that her pronouns occasionally come out correctly by sheer accident. She can't stop talking about how Mrs. Ferrars singled her out for such extravagant attention, and since Elinor is the only one alive who knows what that attention means to her, she's the only one Lucy can badger on the subject. Elinor for her part is amazed that Lucy's "vanity should so very much blind her as to make the attention which seemed only paid to her because she was *not Elinor* appear a compliment to herself." But Lucy, while possessing the sheer animal cunning of a feral cat, can't be said to be the sharpest tack in the corkboard.

It's during one of these occasions—when Lucy has Elinor cornered in Mrs. Jennings's drawing room and is repeatedly lashing her with new observations on Mrs. Ferrars's wonderfulness—that the door opens, and Edward walks in. Edward, who had prudently avoided John Dashwood's party so as not to be trapped in a social setting with both Lucy and Elinor, has now plunged blindly in to a situation inconceivably more awkward.

> *He seemed to have as great an inclination to walk out the room again as to advance farther into it. The very circumstance, in its unpleasantest form, which they would each have been most anxious to avoid, had fallen on them. They were not only all three together but were together without the relief of any other person.*

Edward, never the most silver of tongues, is struck dumb; and Lucy, with the pretense of secrecy to uphold, doesn't dare put herself forward—though she does a lot of really excruciating glancing and eyelash-batting, as though trying to communicate in Morse code. So the burden of conversation again falls to Elinor; really, how many times in the narrative has she had to do this?...Make polite chatter when no one else can or will? A hundred and fifty years later she could've had quite a career in international relations. Imagine her moderating peace talks at Camp David.

As if that weren't enough to prove her mettle, she actually gets up and leaves the room—she leaves *Edward and Lucy alone*—with the excuse of fetching Marianne. "[S]he really did it, and *that* in the handsomest manner, for she loitered away several minutes on the landing place with the most high-minded fortitude before she went to her sister." Talk about making a deposit in the karma bank! In her next life, Elinor's definitely coming back a butterfly. Or a majority shareholder in Microsoft, take your pick.

Marianne descends on Edward in complete exultation. She clutches him, she squeezes him; she all but devours him like a praying mantis. For her, he represents romantic fidelity; Elinor has yet to tell her of his youthful commitment to Lucy. Unfortunately, in her ignorance Marianne keeps saying things that make everyone else in the room wish the earth would open up and swallow them whole. "Oh! don't think of me!" she tells Edward with tears a-brimming. "Don't think of *my* health. Elinor is well, you see. That must be enough for both of us." You can practically hear the static electricity crackle around Lucy. I picture her hair lifting an inch off her shoulders.

From here it becomes a kind of ridiculous contest: Marianne determined to keep Edward in conversation till Lucy finally leaves; and Lucy determined to stay put till the sun goes nova, if that's what it takes. If they were teenage boys in Chevys it would be a game a chicken, and the resultant collision would mash both to pulp. In the present circumstances it ends with Marianne's defeat; preordained, I think. After all, she's merely human, while Lucy is a Terminator in periwinkle.

And so the four characters part ways, in various stages of ignorance over Lucy and Edward's secret engagement. Lucy of course knows, but has told only Elinor. Elinor can tell neither Edward nor Marianne of her knowledge because Lucy swore her to secrecy. Edward doesn't know that Lucy has told Elinor. And Marianne knows jack about it, period. It's a gorgeous mess, a cat's-cradle of human gut strings, some still warm and dripping. And Austen will be twanging them like a fiddle over the course of the next few chapters.

CHAPTERS 36-40

Like a master torturer, Austen keeps coming up with new ways to throw her characters together in mutual mortification. The latest gambit involves Charlotte Palmer giving birth, so that her mother, Mrs. Jennings, rushes off to be at her side—handing her houseguests, the Dashwood sisters, into the care of her other daughter, Lady Middleton, who is also hosting the Miss Steeles. Mrs. Jennings can't help congratulating herself on having come up with this arrangement; she's blissfully oblivious to the fact that Elinor and Marianne loathe both their new hostess and their fellow guests, and that the loathing is warmly reciprocated. The antagonism between the two pairs of sisters is well recorded, but now we learn that Lady Middleton dislikes the Dashwoods too, for any number of reasons—among them their love of reading, for which "she fancied them satirical, perhaps without exactly knowing what it was to be satirical, but *that* did not signify. It was censure in common use, and easily given." When even Lady Middleton—whose performance in prior chapters might be called, at best, somnambulant—starts showing some comic flair, you know Austen's really hit her stride. Then there's this:

> *Their presence was a restraint both on [Lady Middleton] and on Lucy. It checked the idleness of one and the business of the other. Lady Middleton was ashamed of doing nothing before them, and the flattery which Lucy was proud to think of and administer at other times she feared they would despise her for offering.*

Only Anne Steel seems immune to the general tension. She's no fonder of the Dashwoods, but is ready to forgive them in a heartbeat if they'll just give her a "full and minute account" of *l'affaire* Willoughby. Or if not that, if they'll at least tease her about a certain Doctor for whom she has long insisted she has no feelings at all; to her dismay, it appears everyone in the house now actually believes her.

Then Fanny Dashwood is dragged reluctantly back into the narrative, leaving a long trail of heel marks on the floor. A fashionable caller, hearing Fanny's sisters-in-law spoken of, misconstrues that they're staying with her, and so later extends an invitation to "a small musical party" to not only John and Fanny, but Elinor and Marianne as well. Fanny is obliged to send a carriage for them, and even worse "must be subject to all the unpleasantness of appearing to treat them with attention; and who could tell that they might not expect to go out with her a second time?" Not that Fanny has to *meet* that expectation; but "that was not enough, for when people are determined on a mode of conduct which they know to be wrong, they feel injured by the expectation of anything better from them." This is the very worst of Elinor and Marianne's crimes against her: by their very existence, they make her *self-aware.*

The party that follows is a bit of a bust. Austen dismisses the whole event with a few well-sharpened barbs:

> *The party, like other musical parties, comprehended a great many people who had real taste for the performance, and a great many more who had none at all; and the performers themselves were, as usual, in their own estimation and that of their immediate friends the first private performers in England.*

Austen then reveals that Elinor is "neither musical nor affecting to be so," which is a pretty good indication that Austen herself isn't. And in fact most of her heroines have only the most perfunctory relationship with music (an exception might be Anne Elliot), and seem only glancingly apologetic about it. Even Marianne, who as Romanticism's avatar must be deeply musical, is never given any specific enthusiasms—pieces, composers, or the like. Similarly, Austen never talks much about food—we're treated to many meals, but scarcely ever a description of what's eaten there—and while a number of her characters are clergymen, few religious thoughts or sentiments ever issue from her pen. She seems to lack both sensuality and spirituality...to have been an entirely practical woman. That may not have been the case, but given the world she created on the page—all we can ever really know of her inner life—it's a fair assumption.

The chief business of the musical party is to reintroduce the "coxcomb" we met in an earlier chapter, bombastically transacting the purchase of a toothpick case. He is revealed to be Mr. Robert Ferrars, the brother of Edward and Fanny, and when Elinor is introduced to him he goes spiraling off into another hilarious monologue, the principal subject of which is himself. Any topic can be turned in this direction; when Elinor's residence in a cottage comes up, for instance, he plunges into a dissertation on his own love of cottages, how he would build one if had any money to spare, and how he advises absolutely everybody to build them too.

> *"My friend Lord Courtland came to me the other day on purpose to ask my advice, and laid before me three different plans of Bonomi's. I was to decide on the best of them. 'My dear Courtland,' said I, immediately throwing them all into the fire, 'do not adopt either of them, but by all means build a cottage.' And that, I fancy, will be the end of it."*

You find yourself wishing Elinor would bring up scarlet fever, or tin mines, or the Cherokee nation, just to see how Robert Ferrars manages to bring it all around to himself again.

Meanwhile, the mistaken notion that Elinor and Marianne are residing with their brother during Mrs. Jennings's absence, has suggested to John Dashwood the propriety of their actually doing so: "The expense would be nothing, the inconvenience not more," he adds, somewhat muting the philanthropy of the original notion. Fanny nearly gives birth herself when she hears about it: the last thing she'll ever do is put Elinor in Edward's path. But she can't really admit this to her husband, so instead she tells him that it's certainly a fine idea, and gosh she'd just *love* to have the girls 'round, but she's only just decided to invite the Miss Steeles, and she can't have them *all.* John sees the sense in this and leaves off inviting his sisters for another year—"at the same time, however, slyly suspecting that another year would make the invitation needless by bringing Elinor to town as Colonel Brandon's wife and Marianne as *their* visitor."

Lucy is over the moon at being invited to stay with Edward's sister; she practically carries her bag downstairs, hurls it on the coach, and takes the whip hand herself in her zeal to get there. If the horse were to go lame en route, she'd put the bit between her own teeth and haul that sucker right up to Fanny's front door. She feels actually within reach of her goal: the blessing of the Ferrars clan on the announcement of her engagement to Edward.

And so it seems to Elinor, too, as news of the mutual admiration—almost adoration—between Fanny and Lucy trickles back to her. But then Mrs. Jennings is brought back into the novel, and it's as though she's heard about Robert Ferrars's full-page monologue on cottages and has returned to defend her title as *Sense and Sensibility*'s champion power-talker. (You can picture her rolling up her sleeves and saying, "Right, then...it's *on*.") And what a throw-down: it takes her *three* full pages—filled with preambles, asides, disquisitions, and interjections—to deliver the news that Anne Steele (who she for some reason calls Nancy) was so far gone in her confidence of Lucy's eventual success that she went and told Fanny about the engagement to Edward.

Fanny's reaction is both immediate and extreme, and if the Richter scale had existed back then, it would register about the same magnitude as the Great Chilean Quake of 1960. The Miss Steeles are summarily thrown out of the house, so suddenly that John Dashwood has to beg his wife to allow them at least time to pack. We don't hear whether Fanny agreed, and I personally like to think she just hurled their things out the window one by one, while Anne and Lucy scampered around the front walk trying to catch them as they flapped to the ground.

Elinor is, naturally, riveted by this news, and her first thought is of compassion for Edward. Her second is that her vow of secrecy is now moot, and that she'd better tell Marianne about what's happened before she hears it from someone else. Marianne always requires careful handling, like a soufflé, or nitroglycerin.

What follows is the emotional core of the novel, as Marianne learns to her astonishment that all the while Elinor was comforting her over Willoughby, she was suffering a heartache just as piercing. The scene runs for several pages, and there's not a missed beat anywhere in it; I wouldn't be surprised if it were the first scene Austen wrote (since it provides the thematic crux of the novel: Romanticism comprehending the strength of Reason) and thus were also the one she most reworked (since we know that she, unlike Shakespeare, was a tireless reviser). It's two sisters seated on a bed talking, and yet you can scarcely breathe while you're reading it; it's wave after wave of tension and release, tension and release, all in Austen's most plangent cadences:

> *"I have many things to support me. I am not conscious of having provoked the disappointment by any imprudence of my own, and I have borne it as much as possible without spreading it farther. I acquit Edward of all essential misconduct. I wish him very happy; and I am so sure of his always doing his duty that though now he may harbour some regret, in the end he must become so. Lucy does not want sense, and that is the foundation on which everything good may be built."*

This dramatic encounter, however, ends on a comic note; Austen is above all a social satirist. Marianne feels such a burden of guilt for having exulted in her grief while Elinor was forced to hide hers, that Elinor has to comfort her *again*. At which point you begin to wonder why Elinor doesn't just comfort her with a sharp blow to the base of her skull, and be done with it.

She does extract from her a promise not to show her disappointment to others, which Marianne tries to honor the next morning while listening to Mrs. Jennings yammer on about how happy she is for Lucy. But she's really put to the test when John Dashwood comes to call, expressly to reassure everyone that his wife, after a bout of hysterics, is now recovering from the shock of Edward's betrayal. "She has borne it all with the fortitude of an angel! She says she never shall think well of anybody again; and one cannot wonder at it after being so deceived!"

He then delivers the news that Edward has refused to renege on his engagement to Lucy in favor of one with Miss Morton, with the result that he's been disinherited by his mother and barred from her house forever. Marianne's vow of silence takes some heavy taxing here, as both she and Mrs. Jennings writhe and groan in agony over Edward's disgrace, which John Dashwood misinterprets as moans of dismay at Fanny and Mrs. Ferrars having to endure so much effrontery. Marianne, in fact, has to get up and walk about the room to keep from erupting into outrage; I can easily see her grabbing a letter opener and stabbing a few pillows on her way around the perimeter.

After their brother has gone, Elinor and Marianne go all melty over Edward's sterling character. "Elinor gloried in his integrity and Marianne forgave all his offences in compassion for his punishment." And Marianne in addition gets to admire the way Elinor is handling all this —even to the point of rejoicing that the man she loves refuses on principle to end his engagement to her rival. It's quite a comparison to the way she herself has behaved, and she doesn't miss that:

> *She felt all the force of that comparison; but not as her sister had hoped, to urge her to exertion now; she felt it with all the pain of continual self-reproach, regretted most bitterly that she had never exerted herself before; but it brought only the torture of penitence without the hope of amendment.*

In other words, from Marianne's point of view, this is still all about *her.*

Later, while walking in the park with Mrs. Jennings, Elinor runs into Anne Steele, who informs her that after he was disinherited, Edward came to see Lucy and offered to let her out of the engagement, since his material prospects are now so vastly inferior to what they were when she first accepted him. Lucy steadfastly refused, and the end result was an agreement that they wait to marry until Edward gets "a living"—i.e. is offered the curacy of a parish somewhere. Since he hasn't even taken orders yet, that's probably a long way off.

But Anne can't report any more because at this point, she says, a caller arrived, and she was "forced to go into the room and interrupt them."

> *"I do not understand what you mean by interrupting them," said Elinor; "you were all in the same room together, were not you?"*
>
> *"No, indeed, not us. La! Miss Dashwood, do you think people make love when anybody else is by? Oh for shame!...No, no, they were shut up in the drawing room together, and all I heard was only by listening at the door."*

Elinor nearly expires when she realizes she's been gobbling up intelligence that has been obtained illicitly, and she refuses to hear any more, even after Anne tells her it's all right, Lucy would do exactly the same if the situation were reversed. Which is about as reassuring to Elinor as "But everybody else cheats on *their* taxes" would be to an IRS auditor.

Back at the house, Elinor is trying desperately to induce Repressed Memory Syndrome when Colonel Brandon comes to call, and we see their conversation through Mrs. Jennings's eyes. Elinor blushes a lot; the Colonel is insistent to the point of being ardent; and at one point he can be overheard apologizing for how bad his house is. To Mrs. Jennings, it's obvious that the Colonel is proposing marriage. Of course she thinks that. Brandon could strangle Elinor with his bare hands and then bash her head in with a poker and Mrs. Jennings would think, "Such passion! Lawd, but he's smitten."

We then get the conversation replayed from Elinor's perspective, and learn that Colonel Brandon, appalled by Edward's family's treatment of him, has come to offer him a small living that he has in his gift; a *very* small one, as it happens, which explains his apology over the state of the house. Elinor's blushes are all on Edward's behalf. The Colonel, a bashful benefactor, is adamant that Elinor to be the one to give him the news.

When he leaves, Austen gives us a kind of 19th century Abbott & Costello routine, in which Elinor and Mrs. Jennings discuss at length what's just happened, without realizing that they're in fact talking about two entirely different things.

> *"...And as to the house being a bad one, I do not know what the Colonel would be at, for it is as good a one as ever I saw."*
>
> *"He spoke of its being out of repair."*
>
> *"Well, and whose fault is that? Why don't he repair it?"*

Mrs. Jennings is called away, and Elinor sits down to write Edward; but Edward thwarts her by showing up in person. "She had not seen him before since his engagement became public and therefore not since his knowing her to be acquainted with it; which with the consciousness of...what she had to tell him, made her feel particularly uncomfortable for some minutes." In fact there's an awful lot of awkwardness and throat-clearing and dragging-the-toe-across-the-carpet, in that special way Edward and Elinor have. If Edward were any more abashed, he might just ball his fist and slug her, like a lovestruck six-year-old. But cooler heads prevail, and when they're feeling up to articulacy again, they sit down and Elinor gives him the news.

He is, of course, gobsmacked, and there's a heart-in-the-mouth feeling to the whole scene:

> *"Colonel Brandon giving me a living! Can it be possible?"*
>
> *"The unkindness of your own relations has made you astonished to find friendship anywhere."*
>
> *"No," replied he with sudden consciousness, "not to find it in you; for I cannot be ignorant that to you, to your goodness, I owe it all. I feel it. I would express it if I could; but as you well know, I am no orator."*

They're two lost souls, conducting themselves with grace and honor against their own deepest longings. What do you even call that?...The only word that comes to mind is, civilization.

CHAPTERS 41-45

Thanks to Colonel Brandon, the way is clear for Edward and Lucy to marry. Lucy is, appropriately, abashed with gratitude, and stands ready to "worship him as a saint"—though "secretly resolved to avail herself at Delaford, as far as she possibly could, of his servants, his carriage, his cows, and his poultry."

Elinor, meawhile, realizes it's been a week since her brother John came to call with the news that Edward's perfidy had made his wife ill; she figures she'd better bite the bullet and pay a return visit to see how Fanny's doing. Neither Marianne nor Mrs. Jennings will go with her, since so far from even feigning solicitude over Fanny's health, they'd be only too happy to slip the ebola virus into her Earl Grey. So it's up to Elinor alone "to run the risk of a tête-à-tête with a woman whom neither of the others had so much reason to dislike."

She's greeted by John, who's completely stunned at the news of Colonel Brandon having given a living to Edward—*given* it as a gift, when he might have sold it for a tidy profit. It just doesn't make sense to him.

> *"Well, I am convinced that there is a vast deal of inconsistency in almost every human character. I suppose, on recollection, that the case may probably be this. Edward is only to hold the living till the person to whom the Colonel has really sold the presentation is old enough to take it. Aye, aye, that is the fact, depend upon it."*

It's as though, having been an exemplar of stinginess his entire adult life, the idea of Christian charity actually panics him. He has to abolish it even as a credible concept.

Having done so, he asks Elinor not to bring up the matter with Fanny, as it can only cause her pain. They haven't even dared tell Mrs. Ferrars the news, and hope to keep it from her as long as they can, though "When the marriage takes place, I fear she must hear of it all." Elinor is perplexed:

> *"But why should such precaution be used?...She has done with her son; she has cast him off forever and has made all those over whom she had any influence cast him off likewise. Surely, after doing so, she cannot be imagined liable to any impression of sorrow or of joy on his account. She cannot be interested in anything that befalls him. She would not be so weak as to throw away the comfort of a child and yet retain the anxiety of a parent!"*

This is Elinor at her most rational; and it's up to John, of all people, to remind her that she's made no accounting for the contradictions of human nature. It's one of the rare instances of someone actually scoring a point off her; we're reminded that, while Marianne may still be a quivering mass of gelatinous emotion, Elinor remains pretty tightly sewn up with her own limitations.

But in the present instance she recovers quickly, grabbing the ball and running with it when John informs her that Edward's much-desired engagement to Miss Morton will now be Robert's.

> *Elinor, smiling at the grave and decisive importance of her brother's tone, calmly replied:*
>
> *"The lady, I suppose, has no choice in the affair."*

Aaaand they're 1-1 at the end of the first quarter.

Then John, in a kind of ecstasy of obliviousness and odiousness, takes Elinor's hand and delivers a very long and very roundabout speech in which he takes great care to imply rather than state outright, that Mrs. Ferrars has expressed the opinion that however objectionable Elinor may have been as a choice for Edward, she'd have been vastly preferable to Lucy. "'It would have been beyond comparison,' she said, 'the least evil of the two, and she would be glad to compound *now* for nothing worse'...But I thought I would just tell you of this because I knew how much it must please you."

Having delivered this *coup de grâce,* John goes off to fetch Fanny, leaving Elinor in the care of the just-arrived-on-the-scene Robert Ferrars, who can barely contain his mirth over the whole situation:

> *He laughed most immoderately. The idea of Edward's being a clergyman and living in a small parsonage house diverted him beyond measure; and when to that was added the fanciful imagery of Edward reading prayers in a white surplice and publishing the banns of marriage between John Smith and Mary Brown, he could conceive nothing more ridiculous.*

Elinor fixes on him "a look that spoke all the contempt it excited," but which "gave no intelligence to him." I'd have preferred to have her deliver an actual response—a defense of the office of clergyman—but as I noted earlier, seldom in Austen's canon is holy orders depicted as an actual calling (Edmund Bertram being a notable exception). It's just a profession, no different from the law or government; merely one of the few avenues of endeavor open to a gentleman. Robert Ferrars's laughter springs from a view of the church devoid of any spiritual component; and I'm guessing Elinor's silence does as well.

When Robert mentions Lucy Steele, Elinor asks whether he's ever met her, and he replies that he has. "The merest awkward country girl," he says in a withering dismissal, "without style or elegance, and almost without beauty."

Remember this, please, for later.

Fanny finally shows her face; but after the bravura boorishness of John and Robert, she's a disappointment. Elinor sees in her "something like confusion of countenance" which is compounded by her actually treating Elinor in a manner resembling cordiality. It's our first indication that she really *has* been made ill by the tumult in her family, and it comes as a shock. We've been accustomed to think of her as more than a little inhuman. But hey, even Frankenstein's monster got all weepy when he threw that little girl in the river by mistake.

And with that, it's time to pull up our tent pegs and leave town; the London sojourn has come to an end, and though Marianne has been longing to get away, when it comes to the point of it she goes to pieces.

She can barely bring herself to say goodbye to "the house in which she had for the last time enjoyed those hopes and that confidence in Willoughby which were now extinguished forever." Me, I think a nice, firm shove down the stairs might snap her out of it.

A few paragraphs later, the entire party arrives at the Palmers' country house, Cleveland, which Austen describes for us in meticulous, almost loving detail. "[I]t had its open shrubbery and closer wood walk; a road of smooth gravel winding round a plantation led to the front; the lawn was dotted over with timber..." On and on it goes, like a listing sheet written by a Remax agent. Austen may exhibit no great interest in food or music, but she's clearly a connoisseur of real estate. (Just wait till the next novel; she goes right off the rails over Pemberley.)

The first thing Marianne does after entering the house is turn on her heels and go back out again, to spend an afternoon darting about the grounds like an overly caffeinated wood sprite. She winds up at a Grecian-style temple where, given the way she's behaving, we almost expect her to strip naked and ritually disembowel a squirrel. But all she does is stare moonily over the horizon and imagine she can see Willoughby's estate, Combe Magna. Which, since it's thirty miles distant, she can't. Never mind, "she resolved to spend almost every hour of every day while she remained with the Palmers in the indulgence of such solitary rambles." Those squirrels may not be so safe, after all.

Elinor, a more indoors kind of gal, takes the time to renew her acquaintance with Mr. Palmer and finds her opinion of him improving. Despite his sarcasm and air of superiority, she finds she actually likes him, and the only way he really suffers is in comparison with Edward. I'm sorry Austen reforms him this way; I was looking forward to several chapters of his acid tongue. First she de-fangs Fanny, now Mr. Palmer...you almost get the sense she's grown bored with them. (She won't make this mistake in the next novel; there, the grotesques will remain actively hideous all the way to the end.) Palmer's wife, Charlotte, however, doesn't disappoint; on surveying the house on her return, she doesn't know which is funnier, the sorry state of her greenhouse or the ailments and deaths of her livestock. I suppose if a fire had consumed the servants' quarters and the servants with it, she might have split a seam.

As a consequence of all her frolicking *al fresco,* Marianne catches a cold. At first it doesn't seem serious, but the physician lets slip the word "infection," which puts Charlotte in a fright for her baby—whose illness would apparently not be *nearly* as funny as that of her hens. She grabs up the child and bolts, and Mr. Palmer is obliged to follow, albeit reluctantly; but Mrs. Jennings, "with a kindness of heart which made Elinor really love her, declared her resolution of not stirring from Cleveland as long as Marianne remained ill," and she turns out to be a darned good nurse into the bargain, with quite a bit more experience than Elinor. She also urges Colonel Brandon to stay, "as she should want him to play at piquet of an evening while Miss Dashwood was above with her sister," but really because she's contriving to keep him close to his one true love...whichever sister she imagines that to be, at this point; it's hard to keep track.

Unfortunately, Mrs. Jennings is also fond of predicting the worst possible outcome for any misfortune, so she's basically got Marianne nailed up in a pine box while the ailing girl's symptoms aren't much beyond a runny nose and a tendency to droop over pillows, which is pretty much what Marianne has always been like, except for the runny nose. Alas, just as certain quantum physicists tell us that saying something often enough can actually alter the fabric of reality to make it so, Marianne worsens, and is soon in so deep a crisis that Elinor sends Colonel Brandon to fetch her mother from Barton. The scenes that follow, in which Elinor hovers over the desperately ill Marianne, are harrowing enough if you know how to read between the lines. Austen, never keen to wallow in extremes of emotion, speaks of Elinor's "distress" and "alarm," which basically means she's lunging wildly around the sickroom spouting the Regency equivalent of "OMFG." Dickens would have lashed into this scene with two carving knives and a bib; much as I love him, I find Austen's astringency more emotionally affecting.

The crisis passes, and Elinor watches color and animation return incrementally to Marianne. She feels an ecstasy of relief that she won't have to greet her mother with worse news than that which summoned her. Hearing a coach in the yard, she thinks, Why, there's Mum now and rushes down to meet her—

—except it isn't Mum. It's Willoughby. Elinor tries to duck back out of the room, but he asks her to stay "in a voice rather of command than supplication." She refuses, supposing that the servants neglected to tell him that Mr. Palmer isn't home, to which he hurls back: "Had they told me...that Mr. Palmer and all his relations were at the devil, it would not have turned me from the door!"

Elinor figures the quickest way to be rid of him is to hear him out, so she agrees on the condition that he be brief. Oh, Elinor, as freakin' *if.* Once this blowhard starts yapping, you'll be here the rest of the 19th century.

He leads off by saying, "Your sister...is out of danger. I heard it from a servant. God be praised! But is it true? Is it really true?" When Elinor remains silent, he says, "For God's sake, tell me, is she out of danger or is she not?" He's been in the house five minutes and has already invoked the devil once and God twice, which is pretty dicey stuff for an Austen novel.

Elinor admits that Marianne is on the mend. Then she asks him what he means by trespassing this way, and he tells her he intends, "if I can, to make you hate me one degree less than you do *now*" and to offer an apology by opening "my whole heart to you, and by convincing you that though I have been always a blockhead, I have not been always a rascal." And then he plunges into a very lengthy, very urgent recounting of all his objectionable behaviors, offering, of course, a perfectly rational and understandable explanation for each one of them, and stressing that he really did—in fact still does—love Marianne, and is miserable in his present marriage.

The predominant themes here are "I'm so misunderstood" and "It's not my fault," twin refrains you can hear resounding yet today, when spoiled, sulking, sponging latter-day Willoughbys are excused by anointing them with the denomination "man-child," as though there's something innocent and natural about them that civilization hasn't yet corrupted with its touch. We're back to Reason vs. Romanticism, only here Elinor is seeing for the first time her real opposite. Marianne at least recognizes the deficiencies of pure feeling; she suffers guilt over her failure to rise above it. Willoughby, though, seeks pity; he asks for exoneration in a manner suggesting the things he's done were beyond his control. In his mind, *he's* the victim...because he's *unhappy.* "I owe such a grudge to myself for the stupid, rascally folly of my own heart that all my past sufferings under it are only triumph and exultation to me now." Sounds like a fine sentiment on first hearing, sure. But imagine Edward saying it. Imagine Brandon. They'd rather eat live weasels than let a single such self-dramatizing syllable pass their lips.

Elinor won't give him an inch. And when he begins to talk trash about his wife, she hands his sorry ass right back to him:

> *"You are very wrong, Mr. Willoughby, very blameable...you ought not to speak in this way either of Mrs. Willoughby or my sister. You have made your own choice. It was not forced on you. Your wife has a claim to your politeness, to your respect, at least. She must be attached to you or she would not have married you. To treat her with unkindness, to speak of her slightingly is no atonement to Marianne, nor can I suppose it a relief to your own conscience."*

But in the end, she gives him what he came for. "Yes, you have certainly removed something—a little," she tells him. "You have proved yourself, on the whole, less faulty than I had believed you." Less faulty because weak and spoiled, instead of vicious and unfeeling; not the kind of distinction to billow the sails of most men, but Willoughby's all over it. He makes ready to leave, but has one more cringe-inducing scene to play:

> *"...I shall now go away and live in dread of one event."*
>
> *"What do you mean?"*
>
> *"Your sister's marriage."*
>
> *"You are very wrong. She can never be more lost to you than she is now."*
>
> *"But she will be gained by someone else."*

I've heard—unbelievably—people refer breathlessly to this passage, as though there's something heroically romantic about it. Let's get it straight: Willoughby has just said he'd be happier to have Marianne remain a penniless spinster for the rest of her life; that would give him some peace of mind as he lay awake at night bewailing his awful fate in the lavish master bedroom of his wife's sprawling manor house. This, my friends, is a cretin; a venal, self-obsessed schmuck.

But...a *charming* cretin; a *handsome* self-obsessed schmuck. And now, for the first time, we see Elinor give way to emotion. Having discovered that Willoughby is less loathsome than she previously thought, she cracks open the door a bit and that's it: he slips right through. After he's gone, she finds herself thinking of him with "a tenderness, a regret, rather in proportion...to his wishes than his merits." But still, she's no fool; she realizes what's happening:

> *She felt that his influence over her mind was heightened by circumstances which ought not in reason to have weight: by that person of uncommon attraction, that open, affectionate, and lively manner which it was no merit to possess; and by that still ardent love for Marianne, which it was not even innocent to indulge.*

When Elinor's mother arrives and after joyfully reuniting with Marianne—goes off on a tirade against Willoughby, Elinor says nothing to defend him. She herself may harbor some kind of affectionate pity for him; but only because he's gone. It's safe now to feel for him against her better judgment; safe, in short, to yield to feeling... to be like Marianne. Reason dips a toe in Romanticism.

Romanticism, upstairs in bed looking all dewy after her fever, must now return the favor.

CHAPTERS 46-50

Home stretch now. Marianne mends, verrrry slowly—is it just me, or were Regency women total goddamn creampuffs? They're always having to sit down because they've exhausted themselves walking across a garden or something. And when they fall sick, they seem to recover one molecule at a time. Here, days go by before Marianne dares to take her first few tentative steps outside, leaning on Elinor's arm and basically giving the impression that one stiff wind would flay the skin right off her.

Anyway, her convalescence—and a return to Barton—have given her plenty of time for reflection, and the result is "a mind awakened to reasonable exertion." In fact, quite a bit more than reasonable: "I mean never to be later in rising than six, and from that time till dinner I shall divide every moment between music and reading. I have formed my plan and am determined to enter on a course of serious study." Mm-*hmmm.* This is the 19th century equivalent to, "I just joined a gym and I'm going to go every day before work. I'll be doing aerobics and free weights, and on alternating days spinning and Pilates. No, seriously. Look, I just bought these Air Jordans and everything."

Elinor keeps silent, but she gets it, "smiling to see the same eager fancy which had been leading [Marianne] to the extreme of languid indolence and selfish repining, now at work in introducing excess into a scheme of such rational employment and virtuous self-control."

Only one thing hinders Marianne's new resolve to become an intellectual titaness: Willoughby. If only she "could be allowed to think that he was not *always* acting a part, not *always* deceiving me," she would have peace of mind. Elinor asks her how, then, she'd explain his behavior. "Oh! How gladly would I suppose him only fickle, very, very fickle." Then, the key exchange:

> *"Do you compare your conduct with his?"*
>
> *"No. I compare it with what it ought to have been; I compare it with yours."*

Romanticism bows before Reason, and just in time, 'cause I'm getting pretty tired of talking about them. So long, guys, thanks for the nice theme and everything! Let's stay in touch, 'kay? You on Facebook?

Marianne then says, "My illness, I well knew, had been entirely brought on by myself, by such negligence of my own health as I had felt even at the time to be wrong. Had I died, it would have been self-destruction." This is pretty strong talk for an Austen character. The text doesn't say so, but I bet Marianne had to sit down and rest afterwards. Then she remarks on her desire "to have time for atonement to my God and to you all," which is one of the very few references to the deity in the Austen canon, and possibly the only one that is explicitly spiritual in nature. Religious feeling seems, on the evidence of these books, to have been incidental to Austen's character, if not entirely reflexive—a conditioned cultural response to which she gave little thought.

A few more paragraphs are devoted to Marianne wallowing in self-reproach, after which Elinor takes pity on her and tells her about her startling encounter with Willoughby during Marianne's illness. It's a risk, of course; even though it's exactly what Marianne has *said* she longs to hear, that doesn't mean she really *wants* to hear it. Elinor worries that, on learning that Willoughby, weak and vacillating though he may be, still loves her, she might go right back into Fainting Monkey mode.

But in fact Marianne takes it all with admirable stoicism, though some evident internal quaking is going on; and of course there are tears, but quiet ones, not her usual Sarah-Bernhardt-on-amphetamines histrionics. And her only words, as the conversation draws to a close and she heads for her room, are "'Tell mama."

Elinor complies; and what follows are several pages of some pretty serious Willoughby-bashing. No kidding, by the time the Dashwood women are through, there's not enough left of him to carry away in a pail. And it's not even a WWF-style smackdown; just a point-by-point dissection of his petty failings, which is somehow even more devastating. The key passage is this one:

> *"At present," continued Elinor, "he regrets what he has done. And why does he regret it? Because he finds it has not answered towards himself. It has not made him happy. His circumstances are now unembarrassed. He suffers from no evil of that kind; and he thinks only that he has married a woman of a less amiable temper than yourself. But does it thence follow that had he married you he would have been happy? The inconveniences would have been different. He would then have suffered under the pecuniary distresses which, because they are removed, he now reckons as nothing. He would have had a wife of whose temper he could make no complaint, but he would have been always necessitous, always poor, and probably would soon have learned to rank the innumerable comforts of a clear estate and good income as of far more importance, even to domestic happiness, than the mere temper of a wife."*

When I talk of Austen having the psychological acuity of Shakespeare...there it is right there, baby.

With Willoughby now processed, stamped, and filed under "Later For Your Sorry Ass," Elinor becomes impatient for news of Edward. She sends out some feelers, but doesn't get much in return; her brother John can only "conclude him to be still at Oxford," and then stops mentioning his name altogether. But then one morning the Dashwood manservant returns from Exeter, which was a lucky errand for him because it earns him possibly the biggest speaking role of any servant in the whole of Austen—she even, in a positive rush of democratic fervor, gives him a name. Thomas. It comes in midway through the scene, almost as an afterthought, but never mind; it happens.

Anyway, Thomas makes the most of his big break, and gabbles on almost as volubly as Mrs. Jennings about how he supposes everyone must know Mr. Ferrars is now married, and how he himself knows it because he spotted him in a coach in Exeter with Mrs. Ferrars, or Miss Steele that was, and how Mrs. Ferrars sends back very particular compliments to the Dashwood sisters and apologizes for not visiting them but promises to do so very, very, very soon, and some other things that are basically just code for *nyaahh-nyaah-nyaaah,* and indeed Elinor "recognized the whole of Lucy in the message and was very confident that Edward would never come near them."

After which we have the delightful line, "Mrs. Dashwood could think of no other question, and Thomas and the tablecloth, now alike needless, were soon afterwards dismissed." Thank you, Thomas. We have your head shot, we'll call you.

Elinor descends into a kind of stunned state of mourning. "She now found that in spite of herself, she had always admitted a hope while Edward remained single that something would occur to prevent his marrying Lucy"—and she torments herself by imagining Edward and Lucy's life at Delaford, with Lucy as a kind of tireless, bustling hausfrau, relentlessly working over Colonel Brandon, Mrs. Jennings, and anyone else with a more than unusually weighty purse for every advantage they might provide her, like a kind of rustic English version of a Chicago ward boss.

Then one day a gentleman rides up to the cottage and Elinor is convinced it's Colonel Brandon, come to give them some good, hard news so that she can finally abolish all frivolous conjecture (along with everything else frivolous, already taken care of long ago). Then she looks out the window and does a classic vaudeville double-take because it's not Colonel Brandon climbing down from his horse. It's Edward. "I *will* be calm," she tells herself; "I *will* be mistress of myself." And she has to; all the rest of the household, now realizing who's at the door, are waiting to take their cue from her. If she runs riot around the room, or gives the Tarzan yell, or smashes a vase over Edward's skull, they'll all do the same.

Edward comes tentatively in and bashfully takes a seat, and then a conversation ensues in which stammering and blushing and hemming-and-hawing play so principal a part, it's like watching a stage play where everyone's forgotten their lines and the prompter's just dropped dead. Finally, Elinor, "resolving to exert herself, though fearing the sound of her own voice," pipes up:

"Is Mrs. Ferrars at Longstaple?"

> *"At Longstaple!" he replied with an air of surprise. "No, my mother is in town."*
>
> *"I meant," said Elinor," to inquire after Mrs.* Edward *Ferrars."*
>
> *She dared not look up; but her mother and Marianne both turned their eyes on him. He coloured, seemed perplexed, looking doubtingly, and after some hesitation, said, "Perhaps you mean—my brother—you mean Mrs.—Mrs. Robert Ferrars."*

Now it's time for *everybody* to do a double-take—actually more like the rarely executed triple, with extra points for eye-bulging on the dismount. This quite naturally unnerves Edward, who gets up and crosses the room, and "apparently from not knowing what to do; took up a pair of scissors that lay there, and while spoiling both them and their sheath by cutting the latter to pieces"—lovely detail, that—he speaks:

> *"Perhaps you do not know—you may not have heard that my brother is lately married to—to the youngest—to Miss Lucy Steele."*

Oh, hell yeah. *Snap*, homies.

And how does Miss I-Will-Be-Mistress-Of-Myself handle the news? ...Go on, guess. She *bolts from the room in tears.* That's right, she does a *total Marianne.*

How much you want to bet when Austen finished that scene she was all smug and superior for a whole day?...Like, Hello, I just pulled off an *ironic transference.* And excuse me, a *major* one. Do you have any idea how hard that is? So yeah, why don't you just do your *own* goddamn needlework for a change.

But the upshot is this: Edward's free. He loves Elinor. Elinor loves him. So what happens now? Ladies and gentlemen, I give you Jane Austen:

> *How soon he had walked himself into the proper resolution...how soon an opportunity of exercising it occurred, in what manner he expressed himself, and how he was received, need not be particularly told.*

Whoa whoa WHOA. Back the frack up, Chuckles. Slap me some rewind. It's the Big Mo'—Edward getting down on one knee, declaring his love for Elinor, and asking if she'll do him the honor of being his wife—and Austen, the supposed progenitor of "Regency romance," the patron saint of "chick lit," the inspiration for who even knows how many craptacular costume dramas with dewy close-ups of heaving bazooms and quivering lips—Austen tell us the details "need not be particularly told"? WTF? Can it be that all those people who gave her that reputation are...dare I say it?...Hell yeah I do: knuckle-dragging subliterates?

Because she's right: the details *don't* need to be told. Everything we need to know about Elinor and Edward was clearly and movingly presented to us at their last meeting: the interview in which Elinor advised him of Colonel Brandon's gift of the Delaford living. There, without a word of apology, explanation, or reproach, they came together to build a world in which neither of them had a scintilla of a chance of happiness—because that was the only world in which they could live with honor. It's perhaps the most indelibly romantic scene in the book, if not in all of 19th century English literature. We don't, after that, need to see them fluttering and cooing and whirling giddily about the garden, the sun glinting off their pearly-whites. We don't, in short, need the crashing banality of a Final Rose Ceremony.

What we also don't need, is an explanation for Lucy Steele's sudden switcheroo. Unlike Elinor and Edward, who spend several pages puzzling over it, we've got Lucy's number: we've known for some time that she's a classic grifter, and when Edward's stock was devalued, of *course* she'd turn her battering ram of flattery on Robert, whose almost Olympian self-regard made him the easiest target she'd chosen to date. How long before her shameless fawning undermined his initial aversion to her?...You'd probably have needed a stopwatch.

Once they've got this doped out, Elinor and Edward can't but savor the lovely irony of it. Elinor tells him, "[Y]our mother has brought on herself a most appropriate punishment...she has actually been bribing one son with a thousand a year to do the very deed which she disinherited the other for intending to do."

Edward, wise in this respect at least, tells her, "She will be more hurt by it, for Robert always was her favorite. She will be more hurt by it, and on the same principle will forgive him much sooner." Which is of course what happens. Lucy Steele even manages to worm her way into Mrs. Ferrars's black, shrunken olive-pit of heart. Clearly she's a force to reckoned with; sycophancy has become, for her, a kind of super-power.

Mrs. Ferrars also grudgingly gives a nod to the marriage of Edward and Elinor, because at this point disapproving would just look stupid. She also agrees to some slight augmentation of their income, which is really the only thing they lacked to be completely content. Mrs. Jennings visits them at Michaelmas and finds them to be "one of the happiest couples in the world. They had, in fact, nothing to wish for but the marriage of Colonel Brandon and Marianne, and rather better pasturage for their cows."

Ah, yes, Brandon and Marianne; remember them? Austen saves the resolution of their story for the final two pages—then dispatches it with a wryness that pulls the rug out from under anyone who's waited all this time for grand passion and deathless declarations:

> *[Marianne] was born to overcome an affection formed so late in life as at seventeen, and with no sentiment superior to strong esteem and lively friendship, voluntarily to give her hand to another—and that other, a man who had suffered no less than herself under the event of a former attachment, whom, two years before, she considered too old to be married, and who still sought the constitutional safeguard of a flannel waistcoat!*

Here are a few things you won't find in *Sense and Sensibility*: a passionate kiss or a violent embrace...a kiss or embrace of any kind, for that matter...any portrayal of a marriage proposal...any depiction of a wedding ceremony...anyone speaking the words "I love you."

Here are a few things you *will* find in *Sense and Sensibility:* ruthlessness ...venality...arrogance...avarice...fecklessness...snobbishness...shamelessness...two or three of the most unbridled talkers in all of western literature...and an authorial voice that merrily mocks them all into immortality.

I rest my case. In Jane Austen, we have one of the great social satirists of all time. Because she was a woman, living at a time when marriage was the only means by which a woman could alter the condition of her life, that's what she wrote about. To call her, for that reason, a writer of romances is the kind of cloddish thinking she'd take relish in eviscerating. Two or three strokes of her scalding pen, and there'd be you all over the cobblestones.

Praise her, by all means; venerate and cherish her. But...be wary around her. Girl's *watching* you.

PART TWO
PRIDE AND PREJUDICE

CHAPTERS 1-5

Jane Austen's second published novel is one of the best known and best loved in the English language, so much so that it's almost impossible to see it clearly any longer; it's become a set of fixed images and responses in our collective mind. Perhaps only Dickens's "A Christmas Carol" has undergone so thorough a metamorphosis from literary work to cultural bulwark, bogged down by the accumulated accretions of generations who know it only second- or thirdhand...or who know it only by reputation, a kind of ripple effect across the surface of western civilization; familiarity by osmosis. Whenever it's mentioned we no longer even hear the dissonance in the title; it's just a series of syllables, a consumerist trigger—not *Pride and Prejudice,* but *Pridenprejudice.* It is, in these postliterate days, less a novel than a brand. And like all powerhouse brands, it's proved capable of spawning sub-brands, the most successful (and in my opinion the most insidious) being that which currently boasts legions of frenzied, maenad-like devotees who'd as soon rip Austen's moldering carcass to shreds than grant her even a posthumous claim on her own creation. I speak, of course, of the great, the dreaded, invoke-it-at-your-peril, *Darcy.*

What's been lost in all this, alas, is the original novel, which, when it's read these days at all, is undertaken by people who already "know" it, who are convinced they've always known it, that they knew it *in utero;* they don't just read it, they read it with intent. We all strive to find what we need in stories; we furnish what we can, in between the lines, to make the text more amenable to us—to *reflect* us better. But with the possible exception of the New Testament, no other seminal text has been so greedily trawled for evidence of the reader's own transcendent superiority. *Pride and Prejudice* is the kind of book certain people make a point of visibly carrying with them in public, exhibiting it like a designer label. Or a weapon.

Astonishing, then, to read it afresh. Make a conscious effort to clear away the layers of received opinion, the yellowing varnish of endlessly parroted consensus, and you find a lean, feisty, *spiky* little novel, limber and fleet-footed and occasionally even vicious. A bantamweight boxer of a novel. Readers don't fall for *Pride and Prejudice;* they're knocked down. And while they're on the mat they see twittering birds around their heads, like in cartoons. No wonder so many people are deranged about it. They've had their brainpans jostled. Their vision's still screwy, they talk too loud, and under stress they've been known to wet themselves.

This most famous of Austen's works begins with one of the most famous first lines in literary history: "It is a truth universally acknowledged that a single man in possession of a good fortune must be in want of a wife." What nobody ever seems to get anymore is that Austen is being ironic here—she's starting as she means to go on. The "truth" that is "universally acknowledged" is actually neither; it's the kind of ludicrous attempt to co-opt the conventional wisdom we hear all the time in the modern world ("Everybody knows trees cause air pollution"). Austen even exposes the irony in the next paragraph, when she allows that even the single man in question might not be aware of the "truth" about him.

From there she gets right down to business. We're thrown into the hearth and home of the Bennet clan, a gentleman and his wife and their five grown daughters. Anyone expecting a Dickensian scene of domestic felicity is in for a rude shock. The Bennet home is if anything a kind of capital-b Bedlam, with Mrs. Bennet as the chief lunatic and her husband the sadistic warden who keeps poking her with a stick through the grate.

Both the senior Bennets are, in fact, major comic creations. Mrs. Bennet is all impulse, pure id; the delay between her having a feeling, and speaking it, cannot be measured by any instrument known to man. It's like her synapses are actually in her tongue. She rages, she rants, she pouts, she preens, she exults—sometimes all in the space of a single sentence. Her husband, whose regard for her is clearly long gone, likes to amuse himself by orchestrating this cacophony of feeling, directing it first this way, then that, like a pinball player knocking about a little silver ball. His chief method of doing this is by affecting not to understand a word of what she says to him, even the plainest and most obvious statement of fact. This happens repeatedly in the first chapter, with such frequency that you'd think any idiot would sit up and say, "Hey, *wait* a minute—are you busting my chops, here?" But Mrs. Bennet is not just any idiot. She's world championship material; a Wonder Woman of imbecility.

And Mr. Bennet is an utterly ruthless tormenter. It's fairly clear that he's revenging himself on his wife for getting old and silly on him; but Austen skillfully implies an element of self-loathing as well. He can't forgive her for losing her youth and beauty; but he can't forgive himself for not having seen that's all she *ever* had going for her.

The chief prod to Mrs. Bennet's hysteria is that she has five unmarried daughters and a limited income. This is why she's in such a state of high excitement when the novel opens; she's just heard news of a gentleman—the aforementioned "single man in possession of a good fortune"—moving into the neighborhood. "What a fine thing for our girls!" she trills to her husband, who of course pretends not to understand her.

> *"How so? how can it affect them?"*
>
> *"My dear Mr. Bennet," replied his wife, "how can you be so tiresome! You must know that I am thinking of his marrying one of them!"*
>
> *"Is that his design in settling here?"*

This is exactly the kind of response that causes Mrs. Bennet to sputter bits of foam; but she manages all the same to make her point, which is that Mr. Bennet had better introduce himself to this newcomer, Mr. Bingley, immediately, so that he can then become acquainted with the rest of the family. But Mr. Bennet sees no point in that; if his marrying one of the girls is all that matters, why not just send over all five for him to choose from, like a pack of hunting dogs?

It's here that Mr. Bennet first expresses some degree of partiality for one of his brood, when he adds that he may have to put in a good word for "my little Lizzy." All his daughters, he declares, are silly and ignorant, but "Lizzy has something more of quickness than her sisters." Elizabeth Bennet's "quickness" is at the very heart of the novel, and of the character's extraordinary appeal to generations of readers, and I sometimes wonder whether a certain type of female devotee—lethally smart, socially inept, unappreciated by her family and disdained by her peers—might still latch on so needily to Lizzy Bennet as a personal avatar if the first words regarding her super-specialness didn't come from her father. My own observation of the "Lizzies" and their ilk is that, whoa baby, *major* Daddy issues.

As for the other Bennet sisters: Lydia, the youngest, is the most like her mother—all wild, unchecked feeling—and is for that reason her mother's favorite, which she both knows and uses to her advantage. Mary is bookish but very far from wise; she's always trying to come forth with some pithy maxim or aphorism, but it invariably ends up sounding like bad advertising copy. Kitty coughs, and...well, basically Kitty coughs. And then there's Jane, who possesses no flaw of any kind: she has beauty, grace, charm, humility, and sweetness of temper. By page 19 you're more than ready to push her in front of a train.

In the end Mr. Bennet does visit Mr. Bingley; Austen doesn't say why, but it's pretty clear he'd be only too happy to have one less mouth to feed. If he really can foist one of his daughters onto this new arrival, all the better. But of course he doesn't *tell* anyone he's paid the call; instead he waits for his wife to snarl about how tired she is of hearing Mr. Bingley's name since *they're* never to know him; then he produces the news of his acquaintance as though it were something he'd agreed to all along, leaving Mrs. Bennet to do one of those whiplash reversals that over time have basically shredded her grey matter to confetti. If someone treated his dog the way Mr. Bennet treats his wife, PETA would be after him with pitchforks.

And yet, we laugh. Of course we do. It's *funny*. It's also funny when Mrs. Bennet says, "If I can but see one of my daughters happily settled at [Mr. Bingley's] Netherfield...and all the others equally well married, I shall have nothing to wish for." We hoot because this is exactly the kind of mindless babble you get from women like her. She doesn't even hear herself. She might as well add, "And if I can but fly like a bird and live forever" into the mix.

Next thing you know there's a ball, and in Austen that always spells trouble. She likes lining up all her characters so that they sweep around the room in perfect harmony, while in the ether above them all bloody hell's breaking loose. In this case the hell is principally provoked by one of Mr. Bingley's guests, a regal young man who enters the hall like Admiral Perry stepping foot on the island of Japan. This is Mr. Darcy.

> *The gentlemen pronounced him to be a fine figure of a man, the ladies declared he was much handsomer than Mr. Bingley, and he was looked at with great admiration for about half the evening, till his manners gave a disgust which turned the tide of his popularity; for he was discovered to be proud, to be above his company, and above being pleased; and not all his large estate in Derbyshire could then save him from having a most forbidding, disagreeable countenance, and being unworthy to be compared with his friend.*

Even worse, by Austen's yardstick, is that he refuses to dance—unless it's with one of Bingley's two sisters, whose noses are as determinedly tilted skyward as his; they're like three sea lions balancing invisible hoops. And when Bingley—who of course is having just a swell time, never better, love these peeps and hey how about that Jane Bennet number, *woof*—corners his friend and pleads with him to dance, Darcy flatly refuses: "At such an assembly as this, it would be insupportable. Your sisters are engaged, and there is not another woman in the room whom it would not be a punishment to me to stand up with." Bingley bravely urges him on, pointing out that Elizabeth Bennet is both very pretty and at present without a partner. Darcy looks over to where Lizzy is seated, and either not knowing or not caring that she can easily overhear him, declares: "She is tolerable; but not handsome enough to tempt *me*; and I am in no humour at present to give consequence to young ladies who are slighted by other men."

So here's my message of good will to all those aggrieved single women, smoldering with affronted self-esteem, who go angrily about their lives carrying tote bags that read AN ELIZABETH IN A DARCY-LESS WORLD: Ladies, I can help you! I know for a fact that there are very, very many men who would be only too happy to step reluctantly into your life, offend all your friends *en masse,* and then insult you in particular. You just say the word, I'll have a whole rugby team of Darcys on your doorstep.

But then, I'm willing to bet these women meet such men all the time. And I'm guessing that they, like Lizzy, don't recognize a potential Great Romantic Hero in any of them; or maybe they do, and that's the point. They don't want a *potential* romantic hero; they want one who's already fully fitted out and ready to drive off the showroom floor. God forbid they should have to do any of the body work themselves. Or that, like Lizzy, they'd have to recognize some of their *own* failings into the bargain. What, are you fuggin' *kidding* me...?

Good luck with that, chiquitas. 'S'all I'm sayin'. Cheers, stay in touch.

Anyway, Lizzy is sufficiently self-confident to laugh off the incident, in fact to report it merrily to her friends and family, which only increases the general loathing of Darcy. Lizzy doesn't mind being the figure of fun; it doesn't leave a scratch on her. She's invincibly well-adjusted. She knows it, too; when Jane, the next day, is all bewilderment at Mr. Bingley having paid her the compliment of asking her to dance a *second* time, Lizzy rolls her eyes and says, "Compliments always take *you* by surprise, and *me* never."

We're then introduced to another family in the neighborhood, the Lucases. Austen's brief introductory sketch of its paterfamilias is a small comic gem all on its own, and a wonderfully coherent psychological profile as well; by the time you finish it, you'd be easily able to pick him out of a *Where's Waldo*-style crowd. It's worth quoting in full, because it shows how Austen's comic genius can manifest itself even in the swiftest, most fleeting strokes:

> *Sir William Lucas had been formerly in trade in Meryton, where he had made a tolerable fortune and risen to the honour of knighthood by an address to the King, during his mayoralty. The distinction had perhaps been felt too strongly. It had given him a disgust to his business and to his residence in a small market town; and quitting them both, he had removed with his family to a house about a mile from Meryton, denominated from that period Lucas Lodge, where he could think with pleasure of his own importance, and unshackled by business, occupy himself solely in being civil to all the world. For though elated by his rank, it did not render him supercilious; on the contrary, he was all attention to everybody. By nature inoffensive, friendly and obliging, his presentation at St. James's had made him courteous.*

Sir William has a daughter, Charlotte, who's Lizzy's best friend. She is, we are told, "a sensible, intelligent young woman, about twenty-seven." We already know she's no looker, because a few pages earlier, during a scene in which Mrs. Bennet recounts for her husband the goings-on at the ball so exhaustively that the poor man is nearly driven to taking refuge under his desk, she says of Mr. Bingley's dance partners: "First of all, he asked Miss Lucas. I was so vexed to see him stand up with her; but, however, he did not admire her at all; nobody can, you know."

Charlotte thus has all the necessary criteria for seeing the world as it is: she's smart, she's old, and she's unloved. And true to her nature, she speaks truth to Lizzy throughout the novel, though Lizzy—her supposed best friend—hears her without listening. She says something now, as the novel's principal womenfolk gather to talk over the ball—making this one of the chapters male readers may have some trouble with (except, say, the kind of male who giddily agrees to be part of the studio audience for *The View*). As the ladies rise to new heights of indignation over Mr. Darcy's insufferable pride, Charlotte interrupts them:

> *"His pride," said Miss Lucas, "does not offend* me *so much as pride often does, because there is an excuse for it. One cannot wonder that so very fine a young man, with family, fortune, everything in his favour, should think highly of himself. If I may so express it, he has a right to be proud."*

Such wise words alarm Mary, who's supposed to be the sage in the room. Accordingly she leaps into an extemporaneous discourse on pride that proves to be another comic high point. It's a small masterpiece of flat-footed, tone-deaf banality:

> *"Pride...is a very common failing, I believe. By all that I have ever read, I am convinced that it is very common indeed, that human nature is particularly prone to it, and that there are very few of us who do not cherish a feeling of self-complacency on the score of some quality or other, real or imaginary. Vanity and pride are different things, though the words are often used synonymously. A person may be proud without being vain.*

> *Pride relates more to our opinion of ourselves, vanity to what we would have others think of us."*

At this point, she's in serious danger of Lydia beaning her with a candlestick. Fortunately for her safety, a young Lucas lad chooses this moment to burst in and declare that if he were as rich as Mr. Darcy he'd drink a bottle of wine every day, prompting Mrs. Bennet to say that if she were to see him she'd take the bottle away from him, unleashing a repeated chorus of "No you shouldn't"/"Yes I should" which, Austen tells us, "ended only with the visit."

For the record?...If I were to meet Mrs. Bennet, a bottle of wine a day is about the first thing I'd recommend to her.

CHAPTERS 6-10

Finally, by Chapter 6, we have the first inkling of something that might be termed "romance" in this novel by the supposed queen of the genre. And what is it?...Mr. Bingley, who's basically a man-sized plush toy, has fallen for Jane, the vanilla ice-cream cone of the Bennet sisters. There's not enough erotic spark here to charge an AA battery. Sure, Jane returns the sentiment, but this is so far from evidence of a grand passion that even Lizzy reflects…

> *...that it was not likely to be discovered by the world in general, since Jane united with great strength of feeling a composure of temper and a uniform cheerfulness of manner, which would guard her from the suspicions of the impertinent.*

In other words, she smiles. A lot. In fact, I get the distinct impression Jane smiles more or less 24/7. Like she's been lobotomized, or injected with Joker venom.

Charlotte Lucas recognizes the peril in a woman presenting as chaste a face to a wooer as propriety demands she present to the public:

> *"If a woman conceals her affection with the same skill from the object of it, she may lose the opportunity of fixing him...In nine cases out of ten, a woman had better show* more *affection than she feels. Bingley likes your*

> *sister undoubtedly; but he may never do more than like her, if she does not help him on."*

Lizzy, of course, disagrees. One of the aspects of the novel no one ever seems to comment on, is the invariably crappy way Lizzy treats Charlotte pretty much throughout. She airily dismisses her advice, not even pausing to consider that advice is pretty much all Charlotte's got to offer. When their discussion broadens to encompass romantic accord in general, Charlotte says, pretty brilliantly, I think:

> *"Happiness in marriage is entirely a matter of chance. If the dispositions of the parties are ever so well known to each other, or ever so similar beforehand, it does not advance their felicity in the least. They always continue to grow sufficiently unlike afterwards to have their share of vexation, and it is better to know as little as possible of the defects of the person with whom you are to pass your life."*

Lizzy just laughs at this and says, "You know it is not sound, and that you would never act in this way yourself." This is one of the little moments of ironic foreshadowing that Austen sows through the narrative (as in the previous chapter, when Lizzy tells her mother she can safely promise her never to dance with Mr. Darcy).

In the meantime, Darcy, having now been forced several times into the company of the Bennets by the smallness of local society, finds his resistance to Lizzy's charms gradually eroding. He had "no sooner... made it clear to himself and his friends that she had hardly a good feature in her face, than he began to find it was rendered uncommonly intelligent by the beautiful expression of her dark eyes. To this discovery succeeded some others equally mortifying." Invariably, whenever *Pride and Prejudice* is adapted to film, the role of Lizzy is given to some sparklingly pretty actress; but it's clear from this passage, and others, that Lizzy isn't pretty in the conventional sense at all. There's a French term, *jolie laide*—literally, "pretty-ugly"—that is applied to women whose unusual or ungainly features combine, by some feminine alchemy, to create an allure more distinctive and oftentimes more powerful than conventional beauties can manage. It's ridiculous, for instance, to imagine Mr. Darcy disdaining at first sight a Lizzy who looks like Keira Knightley; but a Lizzy who looks like Sarah Jessica

Parker...? Then it makes sense that her brightness, quickness, and incandescence would only become apparent on a second or third meeting—and would accordingly have a more profound impact, by being both delayed and unexpected.

Lizzy is of course unaware of this transformation in Darcy's opinion of her, but she can't help noticing that he's always looking at her now, and even eavesdropping on her conversations. So she chooses the opportunity of a large party at Sir William Lucas's to confront him playfully on the subject, telling Charlotte, "He has a very satirical eye, and if I do not begin by being impertinent myself, I shall soon grow afraid of him." This is the opening salvo in their battle of wits, a battle in which—though they don't yet know it—their hearts are at stake. Darcy and Elizabeth are thus firmly in the tradition of the sparring lovers, an enduringly popular genre that goes back at least to Shakespeare (Katherine and Petruchio, Beatrice and Benedick) and right on up to modern times (the most iconic example being Tracy and Hepburn). But it's a *comic* tradition, a *comedic* genre; the lovers always end up in perfect accord, and because we're never in the slightest doubt about it, we don't feel the scalding heat of sexual attraction, or the torments of thwarted desire. Jane Austen is one-hundred percent Apollonian; the Dionysian genre of the romance novel is as alien to her as, say, science-fiction, or pornography. Despite recent attempts to turn *Pride and Prejudice* into *Wuthering Heights,* it remains what it is: not the story of a grand passion overriding all obstacles before it, but a comedy of manners—or rather, bad manners. Prejudice and pride, to name them. They're an affront to Apollonian order. When Darcy and Elizabeth finally do come together, their petty venalities wrung out of them, the effect isn't one of epic consummation, but of smiling serenity.

In the meantime, they seem, in the time-honored tradition of the genre, to be the only two people who are unaware of how perfectly matched they are. Mr. Bingley's unmarried sister, Caroline, who's clearly set her cap at Darcy (and not just her cap: her gloves, her shoes, her skirt, her petticoat, and pretty much anything else she can fling his way, like a fan at a Tom Jones concert circa 1969) is the first to pick up on the revealing spikes in tension anytime Darcy and Lizzy get within ten yards of each other. Sensing the danger to her own interest, she confronts it head on, attacking Darcy's attraction in a highly unusual manner: by forcing him to visualize it clear to its inconceivable end—

meaning marriage to Lizzy, and association of the Darcy name with the Bennet family. "You will have a charming mother-in-law, indeed," Caroline teases him, "and of course she will always be at Pemberley with you."

The rest of the Bennet clan aren't idle while all this is going on. We hear now that a militia regiment has arrived in Meryton for the winter, which effectively deranges Lydia and Kitty; from this point on they're like bulls in the ring, charging madly at anything that flaps red. And Jane receives an invitation to come to Netherfield and dine with Mr. Bingley's sisters while Bingley himself, along with Darcy, is out dining with the officers.

Mrs. Bennet is delighted by this invitation, because it gets Jane under Mr. Bingley's roof; the only problem is, Bingley himself won't be there. Never mind, that's a mere technicality to Mrs. Bennet, who might rouse herself to invent cold fusion if it meant marrying off one of her daughters. She notices that the sky looks ominous, and therefore insists that Jane go to Netherfield on horseback instead of by carriage; with any luck, there'll be a rainstorm and she'll be forced to spend the night.

The stratagem works a bit more thoroughly than she'd planned, because the storm breaks while Jane is en route, so that she arrives completely soaked, takes a chill, and is soon sufficiently unwell to warrant bed rest till she feels better. Mr. Bennet acidly consoles his wife that should Jane worsen and die, at least it will have been in pursuit of Mr. Bingley.

Hearing of Jane's illness, Lizzy decides to go and see her. "How can you be so silly," cries Mrs. Bennet, "as to think of such a thing in all this dirt! You will not be fit to be seen when you get there." Lizzy retorts that she'll be fit to be seen by Jane, which is all that counts. She then spurns her father's grudging offer of a carriage, remarking that the walk is only three miles.

Mary interjects, "I admire the activity of your benevolence...but every impulse of feeling should be guided by reason; and, in my opinion, exertion should always be in proportion to what is required." The only thing funnier than this gaseous declamation is the response of the Bennet clan: they completely ignore her.

Lizzy sets off—accompanied for the first part of the journey by Lydia and Kitty, on their way into Meryton to molest some more officers—and we see her "jumping over stiles and springing over puddles...and finding herself at last within view of the house, with weary ankles, dirty stockings, and a face glowing with the warmth of the exercise."

Her effect on the Netherfield party, assembled for breakfast, is sensational. To Bingley's sisters she might as well be the Swamp Thing, shambling into the parlor dripping with moss and algae. The idea that she actually walked all the way from Longbourn is utterly incredible to them. They greet her with the kind of note-perfect politeness that conveys contempt more effectively than a mouthful of vitriol. But Darcy, we're told, is "divided between admiration of the brilliancy which the exercise had given to her complexion, and doubt as to the occasion's justifying her coming so far alone."

We're aware now of what's going on. Austen doesn't usually show her hand so blatantly, but here you can almost sense her daring you to disapprove. Jane's illness is really just an excuse to get Lizzy inside Netherfield—enemy territory, as it were. She, the free-spirited country girl, shows up ankle-deep in mud, her features glowing (which is just 19th century for sweating like a horse), and somehow has to survive in a lion's den of cruel wit, vicious competition, and unforgiving fashion. The only way to manage it is the way she settles on naturally: by not caring. Let Bingley's sisters spit poison about her behind her back; let Darcy turn his withering, scornful looks on her; let Bingley's brother-in-law, Mr. Hurst, despise her for preferring a plain dish to a ragout. None of them matters a damn to her.

In fact Darcy's looks *aren't* scornful; they may be reluctant, and they're very likely defensive, but that's only because he finds himself fascinated without being able to account for it. He's helplessly in the grip of...something. And he's not soon evading it, either. When Jane proves unwilling to part with Lizzy at the end of the afternoon, Lizzy is prevailed upon to stay for dinner; and then to stay the night. And the next day she's urged to send for clothes so that she can stay indefinitely.

This turns Pemberley into a kind of arena, in which Darcy and Lizzy play out their drama of attraction-repulsion, using the only weapons available to them: mockery, ridicule, and humiliation. Caroline Bingley does her best to fan the flames ("Miss Eliza Bennet despises cards," she sneers when Lizzy declines to join them at the card table. "She is a great reader and has no pleasure in anything else").

At one point Caroline turns the topic of conversation to Darcy's sister, Georgiana—not the first time she's tried to use this paragon of female virtuosity to make Lizzy look bad by comparison. "It is amazing to me," says Mr. Bingley, on once again hearing Miss Darcy's praises sung, "how young ladies can all have the patience to be so very accomplished as they all are...I am sure I never heard a young lady spoken of for the first time without being informed that she was very accomplished."

This brings both Caroline and Darcy down on him like a flyswatter, declaring that for a lady to be *truly* accomplished she must possess a whole menu of virtues, talents, and achievements which they then proceed, over the course of nearly two-thirds of a page, to enumerate, stopping just shy of insisting that any woman worthy of praise must be able to translate Virgil into semaphore. "I am no longer surprised at your knowing *only* six accomplished women," Lizzy says. "I rather wonder now at your knowing *any.*" Caroline Bingley almost hops up and down in her seat, so happy is she to have been given this cudgel to use against her; and as soon as Lizzy leaves the room, she sneers:

> *"Eliza Bennet...is one of those young ladies who seek to recommend themselves to the other sex by undervaluing their own; and with many men, I dare say, it succeeds. But in my opinion, it is a paltry device, a very mean art."*
>
> *"Undoubtedly," replied Darcy, to whom this remark was chiefly addressed, "there is meanness in all the arts which ladies sometimes condescend to employ for captivation. Whatever bears affinity to cunning is despicable."*
>
> *Miss Bingley was not so entirely satisfied with this reply as to continue the subject.*

Given the active scorn of the Bingley sisters and the persistent friction between herself and Darcy, it's difficult to imagine how Lizzy's enforced stay at Nethefield could become any more uncomfortable—barring, say, her accidentally setting the house on fire or shooting Darcy's dog, both of which she's presumably got the presence of mind to avoid. But uh-oh, we've forgotten the worst potential mortification of all: a visit from Mama.

Sure enough Mrs. Bennet sails in—already talking—to see how Jane is doing, and if that isn't bad enough she's brought along Lydia and Kitty, which from Lizzy's point of view is just one Horseman of the Apocalypse short of a foursome. Mrs. Bennet satisfies herself that Jane is in no real danger, then goes back to Mr. Bingley and the others and launches into the kind of stream of semi-consciousness that even an Islamic jihad couldn't interrupt:

> *"I am sure...if it was not for such good friends I do not know what would become of [Jane], for she is very ill indeed, and suffers a vast deal, though with the greatest patience in the world, which is always the way with her, for she has without exception the sweetest temper I ever met with. I often tell my other girls they are nothing to her. You have a sweet room here, Mr. Bingley, and a charming prospect over that gravel walk. I do not know a place in the country that is equal to Netherfield. You will not think of quitting it in a hurry, I hope, though you have but a short lease."*

When Darcy dares to offer a comment, Mrs. Bennet rises to dizzying heights of indignation, and spends the next several pages firing off direct insults at him, despite both Lizzy and Bingley's efforts to deflect her onto other, less alarming topics. She's like one of those tennis-ball launchers, with the frequency turned up to full. When Lizzy desperately asks whether Charlotte Lucas has called while she's been at Netherfield, Mrs. Bennet says:

> *"Yes, she called yesterday, with her father. What an agreeable man Sir William is, Mr. Bingley—is not he? So much the man of fashion! So genteel and so easy! He has always something to say to everybody.* That *is my idea of good breeding; and those persons who fancy themselves very important and never open their mouths quite mistake the matter."*

Darcy bears all this by becoming increasingly rigid and aloof; it's like Mrs. Bennet is a literal gorgon, and is turning him slowly to stone.

Kitty and Lydia now make maters worse by virtually extorting a promise from Mr. Bingley that he'll host a ball at Netherfield; and then, thankfully for Lizzy, the visit ends before any further damage can be done. Though a tongue like Mrs. Bennet's is sure to retain a lethal capacity at a hundred yards at least, so she's probably not entirely safe till their carriage is well down the drive.

Caroline, seeing how deeply affronted Darcy is by Mrs. Bennet's behavior toward him, spends the next day pressing her advantage. Unfortunately, she's about as subtle as a golden retriever. She fawns shamelessly over Darcy while he attempts to write a letter, so much so you have to wonder how he resists plunging his pen right through her neck. She can't see that for a man like Darcy—who, as Charlotte Lucas astutely observed, has a right to be proud—flattery is nothing; it's surrounded him all his life; it's white noise. But Elizabeth Bennet's indifference to him—Elizabeth Bennet's muddy hem, Elizabeth Bennet's unapologetic freedom, Elizabeth Bennet's *jolie-laide* allure—these are things highly exotic to him, and rapidly becoming irresistible. When Caroline, taking a turn at the piano, plays a lively Scotch air, Darcy can't resist asking, "Do you not feel a great inclination, Miss Bennet, to seize such an opportunity of dancing a reel?" She doesn't reply, so he repeats the question.

> *"Oh!" said she, "I heard you before; but I could not immediately determine what to say in reply. You wanted me, I know, to say 'Yes' that you might have the pleasure of despising my taste; but I always delight in overthrowing those kind of schemes, and cheating a person of their premeditated contempt. I have therefore made up my mind to tell you that I do not want to dance a reel at all—and now despise me if you dare."*
>
> *"Indeed I do not dare."*
>
> *Elizabeth, having rather expected to affront him, was amazed at his gallantry; but there was a mixture of sweetness and archness in her manner which made it difficult for her to affront anybody; and Darcy had never been so bewitched by any woman as he was by her. He really believed that were it not for the inferiority of her connections he should be in some danger.*

Of course, the inferiority of her connections won't save him, poor sod. If they could, he'd be in for a real windfall; for we're about to be introduced to a Bennet cousin who's about as inferior as they come, and who will prove to be one of the towering buffoons in all of

English literature. Ladies and gentlemen, get your spit shields in place; here comes the Rev. Mr. Collins.

CHAPTERS 11-15

By Lizzy's third day at Netherfield, things have gotten very tense. Jane's condition is improving—she's even able to come downstairs for a while, to be fluttered over by Mr. Bingley, whose attentions she no doubt returns with more idiot smiling—but the atmosphere between Darcy and Lizzy is now virtually flammable. In a regular old dopey romance novel this would be just the thing to linger over; but this is a comedy of manners, and we're here to laugh, not get all starry-eyed. Thus we have the high comic relief of Caroline Bingley, who, dizzy for Darcy, continues to interpose herself between the two romantic adversaries, hop-skipping about to divert their attention from each other, completely clueless that should they by chance both turn their eyes toward each other while she's in the way, she'd go up like a matchstick, *whoompf.*

Even in the quiet moments, when each member of the Netherfield party is occupied by solitary pursuits, Caroline doesn't disappoint; she positions herself close to Darcy and basically does everything but shoot rubber bands at him to get him to notice her.

> *Miss Bingley's attention was quite as much engaged in watching Darcy's progress through* his *book, as in reading her own; and she was perpetually either making some inquiry, or looking at his page. She could not win him, however, to any conversation; he merely answered her question, and read on. At length, quite exhausted by the attempt to be amused with her own book, which she had only chosen because it was the second*

> *volume of his, she gave a great yawn and said, "How pleasant it is to spend an evening in this way! I declare after all there is no enjoyment like reading! How much sooner one tires of anything than a book! When I have a house of my own, I shall be miserable if I have not an excellent library."*
>
> *No one made any reply.*

Finally, in sheer desperation, Caroline strong-arms Lizzy into helping her draw Darcy's attention; a gambit that sadly backfires, because it sets off a bout of teasing that rapidly degenerates into their most heated exchange yet, during which Caroline wisely melts into the background, perhaps suddenly fearing the loss of one or more limbs. These two pages of increasingly acid accusations conclude with Lizzy telling Darcy that his defect is "a propensity to hate everyone."

> *"And yours," he replied with a smile, "is willfully to misunderstand them."*

I'm not sure how many thousands of schoolchildren have scrawled out these lines in a book report, with the words "statement of theme" somewhere attached, but I wish I had a nickel.

After this bout of fire-breathing, Darcy, we're told, "began to feel the danger of paying Elizabeth too much attention." Um, ya *think?* Accordingly he summons all his resolve and manages to ignore her completely for the remainder of her stay...which it turns out isn't long, because Lizzy's own take-away from the confrontation is a determination to get the high holy hell outta Dodge, even if it means she has to carry Jane home on her back through another monsoon, or twenty.

But that won't be necessary if Mr. Bingley will just lend them his carriage for the trip. And so he is applied to the next morning; but before he can respond Caroline, oozing insincerity from every pore—hell, there's insincerity visibly pooling beneath her feet—says what a shame they have to go so soon and couldn't they stay just *one* more night?...Which suggestion her brother leaps on with all the ardor of a hungry puppy, so that Lizzy has to give in, leaving Caroline "sorry that she had proposed the delay, for her jealousy and dislike of one sister much exceeded her affection for the other." This is the ironic genius of Caroline Bingley. She's a shallow, haughty, vengeful woman, and might have served perfectly well as a foil for Lizzy just so; but Austen has given her an additional, unexpected comic twist: she's unfailingly, unwittingly self-destructive. Time and again she sets out to harm Lizzy, and time and again hurts only herself in the process—as though she were continually hurling a boomerang at her, incapable of learning it's just going to whirl around and smack her in the face instead. She's Wile E. Coyote to Lizzy's Road Runner.

At this point, it's difficult to decide who my favorite character in the novel might be; Austen has heaped on us so many outstanding freaks and monsters. There's Caroline; Mr. and Mrs. Bennet, independently or in tandem; even the lethally prolix Mary, who's had only a few spotlight moments in the narrative so far—surely because if she spoke much oftener, she'd suck all the energy right out of the sun and bring about a premature end to life on Earth.

But now, what joy, Austen introduces a new character who makes all the others look like amateurs.

It begins with the Bennet family reassembled at Longbourn. Mr. Bennet interrupts breakfast to announce that he hopes his wife has "ordered a good dinner to-day, because I have reason to expect an addition to our family party." Mrs. Bennet immediately assumes this must mean Charlotte Lucas, and is sure her everyday meal service is good enough for *her* (Charlotte gets respect from no one in this novel; *no one*). Mr. Bennet tells her that in fact, "The person of whom I speak is a gentleman and a stranger." Mrs. Bennet now decides, with great delight (and with no clear grasp of the word "stranger") that it must be Mr. Bingley. So that her husband is forced to correct her a second time, interrupting her transports to say, "It is *not* Mr. Bingley...it is a person whom I never saw in the whole course of my life." Which is enough to stump his wife, who, given her complete ignorance of her husband's affairs, can have no idea what sort of person might be entirely new to him. Before she can think to blurt "The tsar of Russia!" her daughters have enticed the news from him: "It is…my cousin, Mr. Collins, who, when I am dead, may turn you all out of this house as soon as he pleases."

From the heights of rapture Mrs. Bennet now descends into the depths of indignation. Of course she does; think of the way Mr. Bennet has just presented this news it to her. He plucks her like a violin to get exactly the tone he desires, and it's always the most shrill and discordant one.

Jane and Elizabeth try to placate their mother by explaining the nature of an entail. "They had often attempted it before, but it was a subject on which Mrs. Bennet was beyond the reach of reason"—making it different from every other subject exactly how?—and so "she continued to rail bitterly against the cruelty of settling an estate away from a family of five daughters, in favour of a man whom nobody cared anything about."

Mr. Bennet assures his wife that her feelings for Mr. Collins will soften once she's heard the contents of a letter he's written, which Mr. Bennet received a month earlier. This might have an astute reader wondering why, if he's known of Mr. Collins's impending visit for so long, he's chosen to refrain from telling his wife about it till the morning of their guest's arrival, when she'll have to scramble to put on a better dinner than her usual. In fact it's just another example of Mr. Bennet's unashamed sadism. He actually enjoys distressing his wife. If it were remotely possible, he'd have preferred Mr. Collins to burst out of Mrs. Bennet's wardrobe at night, just as she's undressing for bed.

Mr. Collins's letter is summarily read aloud. He has, we learn, taken holy orders, and been fortunate enough to obtain a living from one Lady Catherine de Bourgh. Being thus settled, he'd now like to mend the breach that existed between his late father and Mr. Bennet.

> *"As a clergyman...I feel it my duty to promote and establish the blessing of peace in all families within the reach of my influence; and on these grounds I flatter myself that my present overtures of goodwill are highly commendable...I cannot be otherwise than concerned at being the means of injuring your amiable daughters, and...assure you of my readiness to make them every possible amends—but of this hereafter."*

"I cannot make him out," says Lizzy. "There is something very pompous in his style.—And what can he mean by apologizing for being next in the entail?—We cannot suppose he would help it, if he could.—Can he be a sensible man, sir?" To which Mr. Bennet replies, "No, my dear; I think not. I have great hopes of finding him quite the reverse. There is a mixture of servility and self-importance in his letter, which promises well. I am impatient to see him."

He appears—punctually, we're told—and is "a tall, heavy-looking young man of five and twenty. His air was grave and stately, and his manners were very formal." The strange mixture of obsequiousness and self-congratulation he displayed in his letter is, we now discover, pretty much the way he expresses himself in person as well; and in fact he's mastered the very difficult art of making one serve the other. His fawning compliments to Mrs. Bennet on the impeccable taste of her household are, he assures her, compliments indeed, because of his intimate knowledge of the taste of Lady Catherine, who is a virtual titaness of style.

It is in fact on the subject of Lady Catherine that Mr. Collins proves himself—to Mr. Bennet's great satisfaction, and ours—an inexhaustible blowhard, an oleaginous brute. The hilariously trivial anecdotes of Lady Catherine's attentions to him are meant to do double duty: to demonstrate his own humility before so exalted a personage, and to overawe the Bennets with his connection to her. Lady Catherine has, we are told, "asked him twice to dine at Rosings, and had sent for him only the Saturday before to make up her pool of quadrille in the evening." We can imagine the wide-eyed self-satisfaction with which such thrilling news is conveyed. Mr. Collins is, in short, a courtier by nature, and a thoroughly cretinous example of that odious breed. Here he is on the subject of Lady Catherine's daughter, Anne:

> *"She is a most charming young lady indeed. Lady Catherine herself says that in point of true beauty, Miss De Bourgh is far superior to the handsomest of her sex, because there is that in her features which marks the woman of distinguished birth. She is unfortunately of a sickly constitution, which has prevented her making that progress in many accomplishments, which she could not otherwise have failed of, as I am informed by the lady who superintended her education, and who still resides with them. But she is perfectly amiable, and often condescends to drive by my humble abode in her little phaeton and ponies."*

Mr. Collins isn't just a courtier, he's a proud one. He actually brags about it, telling the Bennets that he is "happy on every occasion to offer those little delicate compliments which are always acceptable to ladies...it is a sort of attention which I conceive myself peculiarly bound to pay." (His compliments are, by the way, neither little nor delicate;

they're fulsomely loaded whoppers. Here's one: "I have more than once observed to Lady Catherine that her charming daughter seemed born to be a duchess, and that most elevated rank, instead of giving her consequence, would be adorned by her." Sweet creeping Jesus.)

Unable to restrain himself, Mr. Bennet says, "May I ask whether these pleasing attentions proceed from the impulse of the moment, or are the result of previous study?" And Mr. Collins, blissfully unaware that he's being tweaked, replies:

> *"They arise chiefly from what is passing at the time, and though I sometimes amuse myself with suggesting and arranging such little elegant compliments as may be adapted to ordinary occasions, I always wish to give them as unstudied an air as possible."*

Mr. Bennet's expectations are "fully answered. His cousin was as absurd as he had hoped, and he listened to him with the keenest enjoyment". Mr. Bennet's daughters, however, are less taken with him; in particular the two youngest, for whom no male not in a red coat has any value at all, and certainly not some preening gasbag of a clergyman. Whenever he speaks, all they hear is a kind of multisyllabic drone; he might as well be addressing them in Swahili. Lydia, bored out of her mind, commits the grave error of making some remark to her mother while Mr. Collins is reading aloud to them from Fordyce's *Sermons to Young Women*, and he goes into a horrid sulk about it. It seems somehow right that, in addition to being an unregenerate sycophant, he's a great big baby.

He's also trouble. Because we now learn he's come to Longbourn with the intention of marrying one of its daughters. "This was his plan of amends—of atonement—for inheriting their father's estate; and he thought it an excellent one, full of eligibility and suitableness, and excessively generous and disinterested on his own part."

He settles first on Jane, as the eldest and loveliest; but Mrs. Bennet, apprised of his plan (and we can just imagine the Snoopy dance she does when she hears it), gently informs him that Jane is likely to be soon engaged. "Mr. Collins had only to change from Jane to Elizabeth," we're told, "and it was soon done—done while Mrs. Bennet was stirring the fire." Every once in a while a single detail—a grace note—

rings out with Austen's genius; that "done while Mrs. Bennet was stirring the fire" is one of them.

And so we have, in Mr. Collins, one of English literature's supremely realized buffoons; he's so finely and richly drawn, we might even call him Shakespearean. He's not quite Falstaff (who is?), but he's definitely the equal of Malvolio; I'd even say his superior. What especially comes through, in the sheer brio with which he's written, is Austen's enjoyment of this extraordinary creation of hers; I can imagine her putting down her pen and doubling over with laughter after she finishes each of his heroically fatuous soliloquys. She obviously knows she's struck gold in him, and she mines it with palpable pleasure.

Now comes an outing to Meryton, formulated by Lydia, who hasn't laid eyes on a red coat in probably half a day or longer and is beginning to look rather wan, like a vampire deprived of fresh blood. All the sisters—except, of course, Mary, whose intellect is too unwieldy to carry out of doors—agree to go along; and Mr. Bennet, who's had Mr. Collins following him around like a spaniel all day, puffing and crooning and repeating "Lady Catherine de Bourgh" like a mantra, pointedly invites his guest to accompany his daughters. (Though he's prepared, he tells Lizzy, "to meet with folly and conceit in every other room in the house, he was used to be free from them" in the sacred space of his library.) Fortunately Mr. Collins accepts the invitation; otherwise the genre of the Victorian murder novel might have been invented some thirty years early.

In Meryton, the party runs into Mr. Denny, a favorite officer of Lydia and Kitty, who remarkably doesn't turn tail and flee for his life at the sight of them. In Denny's company is an unfamiliar gentleman, one Mr. Wickham, who has just arrived with the intention of accepting a commission in the corps.

> *This was exactly as it should be; for the young man wanted only regimentals to make him completely charming. His appearance was greatly in his favour; he had all the best part of beauty, a fine countenance, a good figure, and very pleasing address.*

Kitty and Lydia are already circling this Mr. Wickham, all but tying bibs around their necks in anticipation of what a fine meal he'll make, when who should ride up the street but Mr. Bingley and Mr. Darcy. The former, seeing Jane, hurries on over to exchange a few civilities and, no doubt, several hundred thousand smiles; and the latter is bound to follow, but is resolute that he will not look at Lizzy. There is, for a few moments, a general milling about as the party accommodates the newcomers, during which, unseen by anyone but Lizzy, Darcy and Wickham catch sight of each other. "Both changed colour, one looked white, the other red," we're told, without being informed which hue was whose. This is followed by an extremely frosty mutual acknowledgment—a barely perceptible touching of the hats; just enough to avoid being a direct snub.

Lizzy is astonished by what she's seen; but there's scarcely time to reflect on it, for as soon as Bingley and Darcy have departed, Denny and Wickham do likewise, and the original party is summarily ushered into the apartment of their Aunt Philips for an emergency summit of urgent military gossip. Mrs. Philips is the sister of Mrs. Bennet, and is several degrees less batty than that lady, presumably because she's not laden with a full marching band of unmarried daughters; in fact, she appears to be childless. But she's still a pretty ditzy piece of work; for one thing, she goes all girlish over Mr. Collins, being so "awed by such an excess of good breeding" that she momentarily forgets about officers, to her nieces' great annoyance.

Mr. Collins, for his part, is reciprocally impressed, and on his return to Longbourn gratifies Mrs. Bennet by declaring that he has never in his life met a finer and more elegant woman than Mrs. Philips, with the obvious exception of...oh, you know.

CHAPTERS 16-18

From breathless bootlicker to breathtaking bounder: having introduced Mr. Collins, Austen now turns her attention to Mr. Wickham, who we met last time just long enough for him to flash a dazzling smile and twinkle his baby blues. Apparently everyone in Meryton got the same treatment, because when he shows up with his fellow officers for a dinner party at Aunt and Uncle Philips's, half the room is primed to swoon, the other half to scream, like bobby-socksers for the young Sinatra. Pushed to the periphery by such star power, Mr. Collins is left with Mrs. Philips as his sole admirer, and even that's at risk when he attempts to extol the furnishings of her apartment by declaring "he might almost have supposed himself in the small summer breakfast parlour at Rosings," which falls rather flat with his hostess till he hastily expounds on the magnificence of said parlour, in which "the chimney-piece alone had cost eight hundred pounds."

Mr. Wickham, meanwhile, chooses Lizzy to sit with, which is just fine by her, as she thinks he is *so* all that: "Mr. Wickham was as far beyond (the rest of the militia) as *they* were superior to broad-faced stuffy uncle Philips, breathing port wine, who followed them into the room." This is more than a tad uncharitable, considering broad-faced stuffy uncle Philips is paying to feed and entertain her tonight. But then I've often noticed a kind of chauvinism in Austen; handsome, trim, dashing young men might be dangerous or untrustworthy or in some other degree deficient...but men who aren't handsome, trim, dashing, or young, are worth pretty much flap all. I have a mental picture of

Austen, seated at some assembly next to a short, red-faced, flabby forty-year-old and doing her level best to pretend they're on separate planets. Absence of male beauty seems to strike her as almost a moral failing, worthy of the most ruthless derision (think of that famous passage from one of her letters to her sister Cassandra: "Mrs. Hall of Sherbourn was brought to bed yesterday of a dead child, some weeks before she expected oweing to a fright—I suppose she happened unawares to look at her husband"). She does eventually outgrow this girlish prejudice; so much so that in her last novel, *Persuasion,* she actively mocks Sir Walter Eliot's drag-queen-like preoccupation with his appearance, as well as his horror at the sun-weathered face of Admiral Croft, whose craggy maturity represents a new kind of male ideal for his creator.

But in the meantime she's beguiled by a pretty fella, as is Lizzy, who's so taken with Mr. Wickham's lounge-lizard charm that she feels even "the commonest, dullest, most threadbare topic might be rendered interesting by the skill of the speaker." Or by being able to watch the cleft in his chin while he speaks. Who we kidding here, Lizbot.

What Lizzy's dying to ask him, of course, is how he knows Mr. Darcy, and what's responsible for the perceptible Sharks vs. Jets vibe between them; but she doesn't dare inquire. Never mind, as it happens Wickham is only too happy to introduce the subject himself; a bit circuitously at first—he asks "in a hesitant manner how long Mr. Darcy had been staying there." But once he ascertains that Lizzy is no fan of the man, he's off to the races; he can't trash-talk fast enough. He could be Conan let loose on Leno. Or vice-versa.

We learn that Darcy and Wickham grew up together; Wickham's father was the steward of Darcy's father's estate, and Darcy senior was so fond of the young Wickham that he came close to preferring him to his own son, earning Wickham the younger Darcy's enmity. In fact Mr. Darcy promised to help advance the young man's career in the church by presenting him with a clerical living that was in his gift (which in those days meant income for life and jack-squat to do for it—every gentleman's dream). But by the time the living came free, Darcy senior had died and left the gift (along with everything else) to Darcy junior —who summarily awarded it elsewhere. Wickham has as a result been forced to endure the inhuman indignity of finding some kind of active profession, which is what's brought him to Meryton.

> *"Society, I own, is necessary to me. I have been a disappointed man, and my spirits will not bear solitude. I must have employment and society. A military life is not what I was intended for, but circumstances have now made it eligible."*

Yes, he really is this shameless. I mean, cue the goddamn violins already.

Yet Lizzy happily drinks the Kool-Aid. Swallows it down and asks for more, please. She's so scandalized she can barely sit still. She seems ready at any moment to lead a mob of villagers with torches on Netherfield, to drive Darcy from the house and run him off a cliff. She keeps remarking on her outrage, as if its intensity surprises even her; certainly it's in marked contrast to Wickham's own attitude, which is a kind of wounded resignation. This is really quite brilliant of him: whip someone else into furious indignation on his behalf, so he can sit quietly by and look adorably pitiable, like a puppy with its leg in a splint.

Lizzy hopes his plans to join the militia won't be scuttled by Darcy's presence here. "Oh! no," he assures her, "it is not for *me* to be driven away by Mr. Darcy. If *he* wishes to avoid seeing *me,* he must go."

At some point in this long confessional, Mr. Collins is heard to crow the name "Lady Catherine de Bourgh" (imagine) which surprises Wickham. "You know of course," he tells Lizzy, "that Lady Catherine ...and Lady Anne Darcy were sisters, consequently that she is aunt to the present Mr. Darcy." Lizzy replies that she did *not* know, but is keen to hear more, and Wickham is only too willing to oblige. "Her daughter, Miss De Bourgh, will have a very large fortune, and it is believed that she and her cousin will unite the two estates." Which information amuses Lizzy, as it means all Caroline Bingley's jumping through fiery hoops to snare Darcy, is predestined to failure.

The evening ends with Lizzy's head full of Wickham. She's like a twelve-year-old after a Justin Bieber concert. If she had a poster of him, she'd hang it above her bed. The next day she tells Jane his story of woe, and since Jane is equally incapable of believing either Darcy wicked or Wickham a liar, this has the same effect you see in old science-fiction movies when contradictory information is fed to a computer: she starts to rattle and shake, and smoke billows from her ears. Eventually she decides that nothing remains "but to think well of them both, and to defend the conduct of each, and throw into the account of accident or mistake, whatever could not be otherwise explained." She's like Lewis Carroll's White Queen, who strives to believe six impossible things before breakfast.

"They have both been deceived, I dare say," she tells Lizzy. "Interested people have perhaps misrepresented each to the other." Which prompts Lizzy to ask how, then, she would defend these hypothetical "interested people." "Do clear *them* too," she quips, "or we shall be obliged to think ill of somebody."

But Jane won't be mocked out of her conviction, even though Lizzy keeps laying on the pressure. At one point she sighs:

> *"It is difficult indeed—it is distressing. One does not know what to think."*
>
> *"I beg your pardon; one knows exactly what to think."*

This brief exchange is a wonderful distillation of the sisters' characters, and their chief failings. Jane is unable to believe the worst of anybody; Lizzy is only too ready to.

Their conversation is cut short by the arrival of Bingley, who issues a personal invitation to attend the promised ball at Netherfield—a prospect that is, Austen tells us, "extremely agreeable to every female of the family." Yes, even Mary. By her own standards she's fairly clawing the place apart in anticipation of the day: "I think it no sacrifice to join occasionally in evening engagements. Society has claims on us all; and I profess myself one of those who consider intervals of recreation and amusement as desirable for everybody."

Lizzy is so high-spirited at the idea of soon dancing the night away with Wickham that, even though she "did not often speak unnecessarily to Mr. Collins," she can't help asking him if he thinks it quite proper for a clergyman to accept an invitation to a ball. His reply:

> *"I am by no means of opinion," said he, "that a ball of this kind, given by a young man of character, to respectable people, can have any evil tendency; and I am so far from objecting to dancing myself that I shall hope to be honoured with the hands of all my fair cousins in the course of the evening..."*

In fact he requests Lizzy's favor for the first two dances, which she'd been saving for Mr. Wickham; so she now bitterly regrets the "liveliness" that prompted her to say anything more to Mr. Collins than "One side, chuckles" on the staircase. Even more mortifying, however, is that on reflection she begins to understand that his asking her for these opening dances is due to something more than gallantry. "It now struck her that she was selected from among her sisters as worthy of being the mistress of Hunsford Parsonage, and of assisting to form a quadrille table at Rosings, in the absence of more eligible visitors."

It isn't long before Mrs. Bennet is broadly hinting that she's all in favor of such a match. Lizzy pretends obliviousness, and for the moment contents herself with going along as usual, keeping her head low and hoping Mr. Collins doesn't make an offer...or that he falls into a manhole, or spontaneously combusts or something. Her focus remains on the ball, and on a full evening spent in the company of Wickham.

But on the night in question, she arrives at Netherfield to find Wickham isn't there. She initially assumes he wasn't invited, at Darcy's insistence (again: all too ready to believe the worst about someone), till she overhears Captain Denny saying that Wickham went to London on business the day before, and hasn't yet returned. Though he adds, with a "significant smile," that he doesn't imagine "his business would have called him away just now, if he had not wished to avoid a certain gentleman here."

So Darcy *is* behind Wickham's absence, if indirectly. Conveniently ignoring the fact that Wickham flatly told her Darcy would have to avoid *him,* not the other way around, Lizzy goes into a major snit on his behalf. It's all the excuse she needs to treat Darcy with the bare minimum of civility when he approaches her. "Attention, forbearance, patience with Darcy was injury to Wickham." Her coldness doesn't put Darcy off, however; possibly the fire in her eyes even turns him on a little. And so he slinks up behind her as she chats with Charlotte, and without warning asks her for a dance; she "took so much surprise in his application for her hand that, without knowing what she did she accepted him." She immediately regrets not having had the presence of mind to think of a way of turning him down—spitting at him, maybe, or moving her chair onto his foot—but Charlotte, ever the voice of reason, advises her "not to be a simpleton and allow her fancy for

Wickham to make her appear unpleasant in the eyes of a man of ten times his consequence." At this point, Charlotte's pretty well established herself as the story's Cassandra—and I don't mean Cassandra Austen; I mean the Trojan princess who was gifted with foresight but cursed always to have her warnings ignored.

Lizzy and Darcy have their dance, and at first it's an awkward one. Lizzy is determined to remain utterly silent, but soon realizes "it would be a greater punishment to her partner to oblige him to talk."

So they talk. And what talk! They thrust, they parry, they draw blood, they retreat; there's not a moment that doesn't scintillate. Beatrice and Benedick were never better, and in their rhythms you can hear the whole genre of 1930s screwball comedy being born.

> *"It is* your *turn to say something now, Mr. Darcy.* I *have talked about the dance, and you ought to make some kind of remark on the size of the room, or the number of couples."*
>
> *He smiled, and assured her that whatever she wished him to say should be said.*
>
> *"Very well.—That reply will do for the present.—Perhaps by and by I may observe that private balls are much pleasanter than public ones.—But now we may be silent."*
>
> *"Do you talk by rule, then, while you are dancing?"*
>
> *"Sometimes. One must speak a little, you know."*

It's like listening to Carole Lombard and William Powell. Or Barbara Stanwyck and Henry Fonda.

Lizzy, who's got more than a little debbil-chile in her, can't resist bringing up Wickham, just to see Darcy's reaction. "A deeper shade of *hauteur* overspread his features," Austen tells us, and I really hope she took the day off after that, because man, she earned it; what a freaking brilliant turn of phrase.

> *"Mr. Wickham is blessed with such happy manner as may insure his* making *friends—whether he may be equally capable of* retaining *them is less certain."*
>
> *"He has been so unlucky as to lose* your *friendship," replied Elizabeth with emphasis, "and in a manner which he is likely to suffer from all his life."*

Fortunately they're now interrupted by Sir William Lucas, or God knows what might have happened. One or both might have had their hair burst into flames. But Sir William, while preventing this, actually sets something worse in motion when, in the midst of his interminable account of how seeing Darcy and Lizzy dance has given him more untrammeled joy than anyone has ever known in the entire history of the human species, he makes an allusion to a "certain desirable event" and glances knowingly at Jane and Bingley, who are of course tucked away in a corner talking only to each other. (We're never privy to these intimate chats, which is just as well, as I suspect if we listened for thirty seconds we'd be compelled to plunge chopsticks into our ears. I'm willing to bet they go something like this: "I like soup. Do you like soup?" "I love soup! Do you like baby duckies?" "I love baby duckies!") Anyway, the result of Sir William's loose lips is that Darcy, now advised of a general expectation of an engagement, goes on red alert.

A short while later Caroline Bingley slithers up to warn Lizzy about becoming too enamored of Mr. Wickham, who is, she has it on the very best authority, a thoroughly punk piece of work.

> *"I pity you, Miss Eliza, for this discovery of your favorite's guilt; but really considering his descent, one could not expect much better."*
>
> *"His guilt and his descent appear by your account to be the same," said Elizabeth angrily; "for I have heard you accuse him of nothing worse than of being the son of Mr. Darcy's steward, and of that, I can assure you, he informed me himself."*

Thus far, the ball Lizzy so looked forward to has been nothing but a series of petty disappointments and grating annoyances. Little does she know that, compared to what comes next, it's been a goddamn Arcadian romp; because for the remainder of the party, her relations will put her through a virtual gauntlet of mortification. It's like the clock strikes ten and, poof!—the Bennet clan becomes the Addams Family.

Mr. Collins leads the charge. He's delighted to have discovered "that there is now in the room a near relation of my patroness," and he declares to Lizzy's horror that he will go and introduce himself to Mr. Darcy, and "entreat his pardon for not having done it earlier...It will be quite in my power to assure him that her ladyship was quite well yesterday sennight." Because, you know, Darcy might be losing sleep worrying about that.

Lizzy tries to persuade him that there's no cause for notice to be taken on either side, and if there were Mr. Darcy should initiate it, as "the superior in consequence." But Mr. Collins dismisses this with his patented brand of pompous cravenness (or craven pomposity, your pick): "I consider the clerical office as equal in point of dignity with the highest rank in the kingdom—provided that a proper humility of behaviour is at the same time maintained."

He then goes and makes such a show of self-abasement towards Darcy, while at the same time wielding his connection to Lady Catherine like a cudgel, that Darcy can only stare at him "with unrestrained wonder."

Mrs. Bennet is next; she sits at the dinner table trumpeting her pleasure at the coming nuptials of Jane and Mr. Bingley, which is "such a promising thing for her younger daughters, as Jane's marrying so greatly must throw them in the way of other rich men". When Lizzy tries to hush her, advising her that Mr. Darcy can hear every word, Mrs. Bennet retorts, even more shrilly, "What is Mr. Darcy to me, pray, that I should be afraid of him? I am sure we owe him no such particular civility as to be obliged to say nothing he may not like to hear."

Then it's Mary's turn. After "very little entreaty," she stakes her claim at the piano and begins to perform—croaking out a tune while banging away at the keys as though trying to drown out her own voice. After she finishes, she turns and scans the guests for "the merest hint of a hope that she might be prevailed on to favour them again," and obtaining this—possibly somebody sneezes, or breaks wind—she happily launches into another number; so that her father, seeing Lizzy's agonies, goes and all but slams the lid on her fingers, saying, "That will do extremely well, child. You have delighted us long enough."

By this time Mr. Collins has got his second wind, and now undertakes a loud dissertation on the duties and obligations of a clergyman that begins around the time of the dessert course and concludes the following Tuesday.

You know you've got a disaster on your hands when the best behaved Bennet is Lydia. To Lizzy, "it appeared that had her family made an agreement to expose themselves as much as they could during the evening, it would have been impossible for them to play their parts with more spirit or finer success." She's painfully aware of the effect it's had on Darcy and the two Bingley sisters, whose faces tell all; if they'd had cellular phones, they'd have been madly texting each other all night with OMGs and NFWs.

The final mortification comes when Mrs. Bennet somehow arranges it so that they have to wait for their carriage a quarter of an hour longer than everyone else. So they're not just the guests from hell, they're the guests from hell who *won't leave.* The Bingley sisters stand off to one side and yawn theatrically while ignoring everything Mrs. Bennet says (which can't be easy; it must be like trying to ignore a swarm of bees) and Darcy acts like he thinks if he just stands still enough, everyone will forget he's there.

And yet, with the notable exception of Lizzy, none of the family seems to realize the devastation they've just made of their reputations. In fact Mrs. Bennet thinks she's had a kind of triumph. She "quitted the house under the delightful persuasion that...she should undoubtedly see her daughter settled at Netherfield in the course of three or four months." And another daughter settled as well, though that providing less pleasure: "Elizabeth was the least dear to her of all her children; and though the man and the match were quite good enough for *her,* the worth of each was eclipsed by Mr. Bingley and Netherfield."

Mrs. Bennet is about to learn not to count her chickens before they hatch.

Actually, who am I kidding; Mrs. Bennet isn't ever going to learn anything.

CHAPTERS 19-23

Ladies and gentlemen, savor the moment: Jane Austen, the doe-eyed, dewy-cheeked, peaches-and-cream mother goddess of Regency romance, is about to dramatize her first marriage proposal. I advise you to set aside your hankies; you won't be needing them, unless it's to help prevent spraying saliva across the room. Because what follows is as brutally, cringe-makingly hilarious as any episode of *Curb Your Enthusiasm.*

Mr. Collins decides, the day after the disastrous ball at Netherfield, that the time has come to declare himself to Lizzy.

> *Having resolved to do it without loss of time, as his leave of absence extended only to the following Saturday, and having no feelings of diffidence to make it distressing to himself even at the moment, he set about it in a very orderly manner, with all the observances which he supposed a regular part of the business.*

Ah, the ardent lover!

He finds Lizzy at breakfast with her mother and Kitty, and asks to be granted the favor of addressing her alone. Lizzy, knowing what's coming, tries every possible gambit to escape the encounter short of actually climbing out the window, but her mother is adamant: "Lizzy, I *insist* upon your staying and hearing Mr. Collins." In Austen's world, the authority of a parent is unassailable, even a parent whose I.Q. is a few digits lower than her shoe size, so Lizzy is good and stuck. But she realizes it's probably "wisest to get it over as soon and as quietly as possible," and so sits down and steels herself. Possibly she sneaks in a good, stiff shot of rye; I know that'd be my action item.

Mr. Collins then launches into his epic, or at least epic-length, pronouncement of his violent affection, which taken out of context might be mistaken for a member of Parliament advocating corn subsidies. "Almost as soon as I entered the house I singled you out as the companion of my future life," he says. Love that "almost." After a bit more preamble, he gets down to brass tacks:

> *"My reasons for marrying are, first, that I think it the right thing for every clergyman in easy circumstances (like myself) to set the example of matrimony in his parish. Second, that I am convinced it will add very greatly to my happiness; and thirdly, which perhaps I ought to have mentioned earlier, that it is the particular advice and recommendation of the very noble lady whom I have the honour of calling patroness. Twice has she condescended to give me her opinion (unasked too!) on this subject; and it was but the very Saturday night before I left Hunsford—between our pools at quadrille, while Mrs. Jenkinson was arranging Miss De Bourgh's footstool, that she said, 'Mr. Collins, you must marry...Choose properly, choose a gentlewoman for my sake; and for your own, let her be an active, useful sort of person, not brought up high, but able to make a small income go a long way. This is my advice. Find such a woman as soon as you can, bring her to Hunsford, and I will visit her.'"*

And, what raptures, Mr. Collins thinks he's found just such a humble little workhorse in Lizzy. "[Y]our wit and vivacity," he tells her, "I think must be acceptable to [Lady Catherine], especially when tempered with the silence and respect which her rank will inevitably excite."

Lizzy has, by some great summoning of inner strength, not yet hurled anything across the room at him, so he's emboldened to continue in an even more condescending vein, touching the minuscule income she would bring to the marriage: "To fortune I am perfectly indifferent...On that head, therefore, I will be uniformly silent; and you may assure yourself that no ungenerous reproach shall ever pass my lips when we are married."

Lizzy, deciding it "absolutely necessary to interrupt him now" (possibly with a Howitzer) reminds him that she has yet to make an answer, and does so at once, gratefully but firmly refusing him in the most definitive manner possible. But Mr. Collins's self-regard is so stratospheric that Lizzy's flat rejection appears to him nothing more than coquetry; he knows very well "that it is usual with young ladies to reject the addresses of the man whom they secretly mean to accept," not only the first but sometimes the second and third time as well. Accordingly he's not discouraged; he knows he will eventually prevail.

So Lizzy is forced to restate her refusal in increasingly blunt language ("You could not make *me* happy, and I am convinced that I am the last woman in the world who would make *you* so"), which in turn forces Mr. Collins to do the same:

> *"[Y]ou should take it into farther consideration that in spite of your manifold attractions, it is by no means certain that another offer of marriage may ever be made you...As I must therefore conclude that you are not serious in your rejection of me, I shall choose to attribute it to your wish of increasing my love by suspense, according to the usual practice of elegant females."*

The more adamantly she digs in her heels, the more maddeningly Mr. Collins insists on seeing her as flirtatiously frolicking around him, teasing his nose with a plume. In the end, she throws up her hands (a better alternative might've been to throw up her breakfast—*that* would've cooled his ardor) and walks out on him.

Mrs. Bennet, seeing Lizzy leave the room, rushes back in to congratulate and thank Mr. Collins and possibly garland his head with flowers and exalt him in song. She's quite taken aback when he tells her the actual result of the interview; but after recovering from this thunderbolt, she reassures him he needn't worry, Lizzy will see reason. "She is a very headstrong foolish girl, and does not know her own interest; but I will *make* her know it." To which Mr. Collins replies, if she's really so headstrong and foolish, maybe Mrs. Bennet needn't bother.

Sensing a much-longed-for fish wriggling off the hook, Mrs. Bennet goes into panic mode, rushing about the house in a furor, raising the alarm; I picture her dashing into the kitchen and beating all the pots with a wooden spoon, like a Regency run-up to Alex Van Halen. Eventually she grabs Lizzy by the arm, hauls her into Mr. Bennet's library—where that gentleman had probably hoped to hunker down for the next geologic age or so—and dumps the whole matter unceremoniously into his lap. Thus forced into the patriarchal role he usually evades, he reluctantly rises to the occasion, calling Lizzy forward.

> *"I understand that Mr. Collins has made you an offer of marriage. Is it true?" Elizabeth replied that it was. "Very well—and this offer of marriage you have refused?"*
>
> *"I have, Sir."*
>
> *"Very well. We now come to the point. Your mother insists upon your accepting it. Is it not so, Mrs. Bennet?"*
>
> *"Yes, or I will never see her again."*
>
> *"An unhappy alternative is before you, Elizabeth. From this day you must be a stranger to one of your parents.—Your mother will never see you again if you do* not *marry Mr. Collins, and I will never see you again if you* do."

Possibly my favorite scene in all of Austen. Top five, for sure.

Despite this seemingly crippling setback, Mrs. Bennet doesn't give in, but keeps battering away at Elizabeth like a broken shutter in a thunderstorm. "I have done with you this very day," she howls. "I told you so in the library, you know, that I should never speak to you again, and you will find me as good as my word." Of course, when Mrs. Bennet says "I will never speak to you again," what she means is, "I will harangue you day and night without any respite except to take an occasional life-preserving breath," which is exactly what she does. "Nobody can tell what I suffer!" she laments at the conclusion of one such rant. "But it is always so. Those who do not complain are never pitied."

As for Mr. Collins, we're told that his pride is dinged, but since his regard for Lizzy is "quite imaginary" he suffers in no other way. In the end he's perfectly easy about withdrawing his suit, saying, with typical pomposity, that "resignation is never so perfect as when the blessing denied begins to lose somewhat of its value in our estimation." Snarky as that sounds, it's a notch or two nicer than the things he said when he was actually proposing to her.

You might think Mr. Collins would now be anxious to leave Longbourn—by either slinking away without ceremony, or departing with a great show of majestic contempt; but in fact he has no intention of leaving at all. "He was always to have gone on Saturday, and to Saturday he still meant to stay." It's part and parcel of his character that, as tone-deaf as he is to human relationships, it doesn't occur to him that his continued presence among his cousins is well beyond awkward. The Bennets thus learn the meaning of the phrase "the elephant in the room," though in their case with the aid of an actual elephant.

Meantime Lizzy takes solace in the return of Mr. Wickham, who explains his absence from the Netherfield ball thus:

> *"I found...as the time drew near that I had better not meet Mr. Darcy; that to be in the same room, the same party with him for so many hours together, might be more than I could bear, and that scenes might arise unpleasant to more than myself."*

So...he's a *philanthropist,* not a coward. Rrrright, got it. But alas Lizzy, dazzled again by those eyes and that chin, "highly approved his forbearance," not bothering to notice, much less question, the contradictions and evasions in his story. Or his use of the passive voice ("scenes might arise," indeed) always a favorite gambit among the cretins of our world. As when government officials say, "Mistakes were made," the implication being, Those darn mistakes, how'd *they* get in?

Lizzy has no such trouble analyzing a letter that arrives for Jane, in which Caroline Bingley announces the departure of the entire Netherfield party for London, with no plan of coming back again. "I do not pretend to regret anything I shall leave in Hertfordshire, except your society, my dearest friend," she writes, and it's pretty impressive that she sounds as clangingly insincere on the page as she does in person. You get the impression she's lost the ability to produce a simple declarative sentence; bitchy disingenuousness has locked on to her DNA like a retrovirus. If you came upon her wasting away in a desert wailing, "Please, please, I need water," your reaction would be, "Geez, sarcastic much? What did *I* do?"

Even worse for Jane, Caroline continues by saying how everyone is looking forward to seeing Mr. Darcy's sister, that paragon of perfectness, Georgiana, and how much cause they all have to hope for an attachment between that lady and her brother. Jane—perhaps the only human being on the face of the earth naïve enough to take Caroline Bingley at her word (in today's world she'd be busy emailing her bank account number to Nigerian diplomats)—is devastated by this news, but Lizzy isn't fooled for a moment:

> *"Miss Bingley sees that her brother is in love with you, and wants him to marry Miss Darcy. She follows him to town in the hope of keeping him there, and tries to persuade you that he does not care about you...No one who has ever seen you together can doubt his affection. Miss Bingley I am sure cannot...Could she have seen half as much love in Mr. Darcy for herself, she would have ordered her wedding clothes...[S]he is the more anxious to get Miss Darcy for her brother, from the notion that when there has been one intermarriage, she may have less trouble in achieving a second; in which there is certainly some ingenuity, and I dare say it would succeed, if Miss De Bourgh were out of the way."*

Jane feels marginally better on hearing this; then plummets back into dismay again.

> *"But, my dear sister, can I be happy, even supposing the best, in accepting a man whose sisters and friends are all wishing him to marry elsewhere?"*
>
> *"You must decide for yourself," said Elizabeth, "and if upon mature deliberation, you find that the misery of disobliging his two sisters is more than equivalent to the happiness of being his wife, I advise you by all means to refuse him."*

This is one of those moments—and there are many—when you're reminded that Austen was a child of the Enlightenment, and wrote from that serene, sunlit point of view. Lizzy doesn't tell Jane, as the chest-thumping, shadow-haunted Romantics would have her do, that capital-L love is its own highest value and must overrule all else, no matter the cost. No; Lizzy merely advises Jane to weigh the consequences to herself, and does so in such a way as to carry her point with a laugh.

While Lizzy consoles Jane in her unhappiness, Charlotte Lucas is performing the same function for Mr. Collins, which earns her Lizzy's fervent gratitude. But what Lizzy doesn't know is that Charlotte has an ulterior motive: she's out to snag Mr. Collins on the rebound. And she's been so solicitous of him that "she would have felt sure of her success if he had not been to leave Hertfordshire so very soon. But here she did injustice to the fire and independence of his character, for it led him to escape out of Longbourn House with admirable shyness, and hasten to Lucas Lodge to throw himself at her feet." I'd pay cash money to see Mr. Collins throw himself at anything; but as it happens he might have spared himself the effort. Charlotte very much does not require wooing; quite the opposite.

> *The stupidity with which he was favoured by nature must guard his courtship from any charm that could make a woman wish for its continuance; and Miss Lucas, who accepted him solely from the pure and disinterested desire of an establishment, cared not how soon that establishment were gained.*

In case we miss the point, we're reminded soon after that Mr. Collins "was neither sensible nor agreeable; his society was irksome, and his attachment to her must be imaginary. But still he would be her husband." And for women in early 19th century England, it was pretty much husband or nothing.

> *Without thinking highly of either men or of matrimony, marriage had always been [Charlotte's] object; it was the only honourable provision for well-educated young women of small fortune, and however uncertain of giving happiness, must be their pleasantest preservation from want.*

This is one of the bleaker storylines in the Austen canon, made all the more so by occurring in the author's most sparklingly bright novel. But it serves a purpose: Charlotte, with eyes wide open, has made the rational choice—the choice Lizzy disdained. If we're to feel the full measure of Lizzy's ultimate triumph, we have to understand the fate she escapes: that of choosing either dependent spinsterhood, or selling herself for security. Austen herself must have keenly felt the pull of these competing imperatives; my guess is that she hoped, through her writing, to achieve sufficient independence to avoid either. Unfortunately, her income was never up to the task.

Meanwhile, Charlotte asks Mr. Collins not to reveal their engagement to the Bennets, so that she can tell Lizzy of it first. Thus, on the eve of his departure, when Mrs. Bennet offers him the hospitality of their house on whatever occasion he chooses to return, he astonishes her by not only accepting, but by intending to do so "as soon as possible". She'd only offered out of politeness, the way you and I tell people "Drop by anytime," though both we and they know we'd pretty much have to kill them if they ever pulled a stunt like that. As for Mr. Bennet, he's so alarmed by the idea of Mr. Collins coming back that he tries to frighten him out of it by the only means possible: invoking Lady Catherine de Bourgh. "Risk anything rather than her displeasure; and if you find it likely to be raised by your coming to us again, which I should think exceedingly probable, stay quietly at home, and be satisfied that we shall take no offense."

Mary, meantime, is considering that she may be next in line for Mr. Collins's attentions, and she's totally up for it.

> *She rated his abilities much higher than any of the others; there was a solidity in his reflections which often struck her, and though by no means so clever as herself, she thought that if encouraged to read and improve himself by such an example as hers, he might become a very agreeable companion.*

Oh, if *only*. If ever two people deserved each other, we've got them right here. But possibly their similarities might have made it too much for us. I mean, there's a reason they never use Yosemite Sam *and* the Tasmanian Devil in the same cartoon.

Alas for Mary, Charlotte calls the next day to dash her hopes and to flabbergast Lizzy—who cries out, "Engaged to Mr. Collins! my dear Charlotte—impossible!" Which is Austenspeak for *Beeyotch, are you high?* Charlotte does her best to rise above "so direct a reproach" and calmly, dispassionately lays out her case. But Lizzy still struggles to accept the match; it seems to her completely out-of-balance—as if Charlotte had just announced sex-change therapy, or taken up spinning classes. She's humiliated for her friend, and finds that she has "sunk in her esteem".

But if her reaction is strong, Mrs. Bennet's is downright volcanic:

> *In the first place, she persisted in disbelieving the whole of the matter; secondly, she was very sure that Mr. Collins had been taken in; thirdly, she trusted that they would never be happy together, and fourthly that the match might be broken off. Two inferences, however, were plainly deduced from the whole: one, that Elizabeth was the real cause of all the mischief; and the other, that she herself had been barbarously used by them all; and on these two points she principally dwelt during the rest of the day.*

Mr. Bennet responds with more equanimity. He is gratified to discover "that Charlotte Lucas, whom he had been used to think tolerably sensible, was as foolish as his wife, and more foolish than his daughter!"

Now that Lizzy is "persuaded that no real confidence could ever subsist" between Charlotte and her anymore, she turns "with fonder regard to her sister, of whose rectitude and delicacy she was sure her opinion could never be shaken." Which is just as well, because Jane needs her support more than ever as time passes and, with it, any hope of Mr. Bingley's return. Lizzy herself begins to entertain doubts about Bingley; it occurs to her that his pliable, agreeable nature might have succumbed to the thuggish influence of his sisters and Mr. Darcy—aided and abetted by "the attractions of Miss Darcy and the amusements of London". And this is a possibility we ourselves entertain, knowing as we do that Bingley might be persuaded, in a weak moment, and with firm enough instruction, that left is right, and beef is chicken, and hands are feet.

Worse, the rumor of his coming no more to Netherfield has gained currency in Meryton, "which highly incensed Mrs. Bennet and which she never failed to contradict as a most scandalous falsehood." Pity Mrs. Bennet; she has a whole smorgasbord of devils to beset her now, chief of which is the fact that she will, because of the entail on Longbourn House, live to see Charlotte Lucas take her place there. For this anxiety, at least, her husband has the antidote: "My dear, do not give way to such gloomy thoughts. Let us hope for better things. Let us flatter ourselves that *I* may be the survivor."

But amidst all this torment, relief is on the way. Next time out, we meet some extended family members who are not only *not* demented, Felliniesque freaks, but who seem to be pretty decent, upright, straight-talking sorts. Amazingly, they won't bore us at all. Stay tuned for Aunt and Uncle Gardiner.

CHAPTERS 24-28

"Hope was over, entirely over"—an uncharacteristically melodramatic outburst from this most astringent of authors; but it's in relation to Jane Bennet, so she has to use stronger verbiage than usual to convince us that Jane's still waters really do run deep. Some of us remain not entirely persuaded that her desolation is as bad as all that. Anything might snap her out of it. A hobby—say, butterfly collecting. If she could bear to put the pins in.

Anyway, the prompt for this declaration of hopelessness is a letter from Caroline Bingley announcing that she and her brother are settled in town for the winter so hasta la vista, baby, have a nice spinsterhood. She also goes on about Georgiana Darcy in an almost girl-crush kind of way, and keeps hinting that there'll be a happy development very soon that will make them the fondest of sisters. Yeah, sure she's just saying it to quash any ideas Jane may have about marrying her brother, but I can't help wondering whether Caroline wouldn't really mind having the kind of sisterly relationship with Georgiana that involves late-night pillow fights in their underwear.

Seeing Jane in distress gets Lizzy righteously p.o.'ed, and for the first time her ire turns to Mr. Bingley himself. She "could not think without anger, hardly without contempt, on that easiness of temper, that want of proper resolution which now made him the slave of his designing friends, and led him to sacrifice his own happiness to the caprice of their inclinations." I have to agree with her. Bingley's one of nature's patsies; a natural-born schlemiel. Next to him, the average Woody Allen hero is a titan of self-confidence and drive.

Meanwhile she has to contend with Jane being all noble-of-spirit and saying things like: "I have this comfort immediately, that it has not been more than an error of fancy on my side, and that it has done no harm to any one but myself." Which makes you want to say, Not harm enough, sweetheart, and bean her with a hairbrush.

Lizzy herself has had quite enough of people behaving contrary to their established characters, and says so pretty bluntly, in one of the novel's more famous passages:

> *"There are few people whom I really love, and still fewer of whom I think well. The more I see of the world, the more I am dissatisfied with it; and every day confirms my belief of the inconsistency of all human characters, and of the little dependence that can be placed on the appearance of either merit or sense."*

She's talking about Bingley, of course, but also about Charlotte, which brings Jane to Charlotte's defense, arguing that there are up sides to her marriage to Mr. Collins that Lizzy is refusing to see: fortune, respectability, stability. She doesn't add, but could, that Mr. Collins might also choke on a chicken bone at any time, leaving his wife a respectable widow. Hey, it's probably crossed Charlotte's mind.

Lizzy ain't havin' it, though. "You shall not defend her, though it is Charlotte Lucas. You shall not, for the sake of one individual, change the meaning of principle and integrity, nor endeavour to persuade yourself or me that selfishness is prudence, and insensibility of danger, security for happiness."

She's laying it on a bit thick here; but we need to see that Lizzy's got some issues of her own. We need it because by this time we're pretty much crazy about her. She's good company…the best, in fact, Austen will ever give us (and don't start in on me, please; we're all entitled to have our favorites, and Lizzy's mine. You don't like it, write your own book).

The conversation turns back to Jane's own heartbreak, as Lizzy tries to convince her that Caroline and her sister are the snakes who have slithered between her and Mr. Bingley. Jane can't bring herself to believe it. "Why should they try to influence him? They can only wish for his happiness, and if he is attached to me, no other woman can secure it." Lizzy is ready with the answer for that: "They may wish many things besides his happiness; they may wish his increase of wealth and consequence; they may wish him to marry a girl who has all the importance of money, great connections, and pride."

But Jane is incapable of thinking ill of anyone, and pleads, "Let me take it in the best light, in the light in which it may be understood." I think Jane may spend too much time staring directly into the sun.

Mr. Bennet's take on the matter is predictably misanthropic.

> *"So, Lizzy," said he one day, "your sister is crossed in love, I find. I congratulate her. Next to being married, a girl likes to be crossed in love a little now and then. It is something to think of, and gives her a sort of distinction among her companions. When is your turn to come? You will hardly bear to be long outdone by Jane...Let Wickham be your man. He is a pleasant fellow, and would jilt you creditably."*

Lizzy, obviously accustomed to this kind of acerbic badinage with the old man, shoots back that not everyone can have Jane's good luck, and Mr. Bennet admits the truth of this; "...[B]ut it is a comfort to think that whatever of that kind may befall you, you have an affectionate mother who will always make the most of it." Probably they both howled and slapped their knees at this, though Austen doesn't say.

By now all Meryton has heard the news that Bingley and his circle will no longer return to Netherfield; and simultaneously the full scope of Mr. Darcy's culpability in *l'affaire* Wickham becomes current, which tanks his already foundering reputation among the locals. Wickham himself becomes the toast of the town. Which pretty much tells you all you need to know about the town.

Such is the state of affairs when Mr. and Mrs. Gardiner arrive to spend Christmas at Longbourn. This is Mrs. Bennet's brother ("a sensible, gentlemanlike man, greatly superior to his sister as well by nature as education") and his wife ("an amiable, intelligent, elegant woman and a great favourite with all her Longbourn nieces"). They're a couple of peaches, really; not a word to be said against them, and in fact "the Netherfield ladies would have had difficulty in believing that a man who lived by trade, and within view of his own warehouses, could have been so well bred and agreeable." No word about what he might think of *them*. But he's a gallant, courteous man, so maybe he'd just presume their corsets were too tight.

To Mrs. Bennet, the Gardiners' arrival offers two fresh sets of ears into which to pour her tale of woe: a pair of daughters on the brink of marriage, only to have it all go belly-up. Jane isn't to blame, of course, because she did her best to snare Bingley, but Lizzy just threw away her chance at Mr. Collins. Most blameworthy of all in the matter, in Mrs. Bennet's view, are Charlotte and her family: "The Lucases are very artful people indeed, sister. They are all for what they can get. I am sorry to say it of them, but so it is." I believe this is what is called, in psychological circles, projection.

The Gardiners are a kind of stroke of genius for the narrative; emotions have been running so high, and incident piling up even higher, that it comes as a relief suddenly to have these two still, beatific presences layered in like a balm. They give the narrative a much-needed pause, without which it might have escalated into a kind of opera buffa or even Grand Guignol. They also, by their solidity and shrewdness, remind us of how frantic and foolish everyone else has been acting.

Most useful of all, they're able to serve as course-correctors for Lizzy. She is, as we've seen, far too clever for her own good (which is a large part of her slightly jagged charm), and hardly anyone else in the novel is smart enough to call her on it—save possibly Mr. Bennet, but he lacks the inclination. (In fact he may actually prefer Lizzy at full tilt.) But when Lizzy trots out her usual routine for Aunt Gardiner, she's not allowed to take it very far; as, for instance, when she protests that Bingley's abandonment of Jane must be the work of saboteurs, because he'd been so violently in love with her just a few days before. Mrs. Gardiner shoots back: "But that expression of 'violently in love' is so hackneyed, so doubtful, so indefinite, that it gives me very little idea. It is as often applied to feelings which arise, from an half-hour's acquaintance as to a real, strong attachment. Pray, how *violent* was Mr. Bingley's love?"

It's a mild kind of shock to see someone subject Lizzy to the Socratic method and force her to define her terms. It's equally pleasurable to see Lizzy rise to the occasion; confronted with an actual grown-up speaking to her in grown-up fashion, she's able to summon sufficient maturity to meet her on level ground. Aunt Gardiner's conversation adds heft to Lizzy's.

Another example of this rapport occurs after Mrs. Gardiner's had a chance to observe Lizzy and Wickham together. "You are too sensible a girl, Lizzy, to fall in love merely because you are warned against it"—wonderful line!—"and, therefore, I am not afraid of speaking to you openly...Do not involve yourself, or endeavour to involve him in an affection which the want of fortune would make so very imprudent."

Lizzy can't help noting the seriousness of her tone. "Yes," says Mrs. Gardiner, "and I hope to engage you to be serious likewise." Lizzy breezily reassures her that Wickham "shall not be in love with me, if I can prevent it," and immediately Mrs. Gardiner nails her for flippancy. "I beg your pardon," she says, "I will try again." And she does, vowing in more sober terms to be on her guard against any va-va-voomage with Wickham.

> *"[B]ut since we see every day that where there is affection, young people are seldom withheld by immediate want of fortune from entering into engagements with each other, how can I promise to be wiser than so many of my fellow creatures if I am tempted, or how am I even to know that it would be wisdom to resist? All that I can promise you, therefore, is not to be in a hurry."*

Now that the Gardiners have splashed all our faces with a little cold water, we're ready for the burlesque to resume. And right on cue, Mr. Collins comes charging back to Hertfordshire to claim his blushing bride. Now that she's on the point of leaving, Charlotte finally experiences something like regret, and in a startling departure from her regular dispassionate manner, makes so emotional appeal for Lizzy to visit her in Hunsford that Lizzy is embarrassed into agreeing to it. "My father and Maria are to come to me in March," Charlotte tells her, "and I hope you will consent to be of the party. Indeed, Eliza, you will be as welcome to me as either of them."

Then, the wedding! Expecting one of those tour de force Austen set pieces?...Well, here it is, in its entirety:

> *The wedding took place; the bride and bridegroom set off for Kent from the church door, and everybody had as much to say or to hear on the subject as usual.*

Granted, it's just Mr. Collins's wedding; but in fact this is about as much detail as Austen ever expends on describing any such occasion, ever. Weddings bore her, and the unrelenting vulgarity of our modern wedding industry—which strives to turn each marriage ceremony into the kind of blockbuster apotheosis that makes grand opera look like a campfire singalong—would appall her into derisive laughter. For Austen, weddings are just the contract signing; the legitimization of the transaction. She has a highly pragmatic point of view, and she understands achingly well that what weddings are chiefly about, is property, not passion.

Meantime, Aunt and Uncle Gardiner have taken Jane back to London in an attempt to raise her spirits. Mr. Bingley is in London too, of course, but the Gardiners live in an unfashionable neighborhood (within view of Mr. Gardiner's warehouses, remember, so we can just imagine) and it's unlikely they'll run into each other. Still, convention dictates that Jane call on Caroline, which she does after having written her several times to no reply. Caroline is astonished to see her and scolds her for not having given her notice she was in town, which, to poor daft Jane, is just proof that her letters never reached her. (Caroline might have claimed all her mail was eaten by the invisible beast who lives under the stairs, and Jane would've bought that too.) She's also, damn the luck, arrived *just* as Caroline and her sister are going out *(liar, liar, petticoat on fire),* so a proper visit will have to wait till they return the call. Weeks pass, and Lizzy receives a letter from Jane:

> *"Caroline did not return my visit till yesterday; and not a note, not a line, did I receive in the meantime. When she did come, it was very evident that she had no pleasure in it; she made a slight, formal apology for not calling before, said not a word of wishing to see me again, and was in every respect so altered a creature that when she went away, I was perfectly resolved to continue the acquaintance no longer...But I pity her, because I am very sure that anxiety for her brother is the cause of it."*

Later in the letter, ruminating on Caroline's behavior since their acquaintance began, she says, "If I were not afraid of judging harshly, I should be almost tempted to say that there is a strong appearance of duplicity in all this." You begin to wonder what, exactly, Caroline would have to do to earn Jane's unconditional disapproval. Maybe blow a gaping hole in her midsection with a cannon. But then again Jane might just say, with her dying breath, "I cannot blame her, for I am sure I was in the way."

As Jane's friendship with Caroline skids to a halt, Lizzy's with Wickham wanes; he's found someone else to flirt with, and a more material prospect besides: a certain Miss King, who has a clear ten thousand a year. Lizzy is philosophical; she writes to Mrs. Gardiner:

> *"I should at present detest his very name, and wish him all manner of evil. But my feelings are not only cordial towards him; they are even impartial towards Miss King. I cannot find that I hate her at all, or that I am in the least unwilling to think her a very good sort of girl. There can be no love in all this."*

Shortly thereafter Lizzy begins her promised journey to Hunsford, in the company of Charlotte's father and sister. Maria is "a good-humoured girl, but as empty-headed as himself," and Sir William "could tell her nothing new of the wonders of his presentation and knighthood." As a result they "were listened to with about as much delight as the rattle of the chaise." Poor Lizzy, stuck in the 19th century when an iPod would've come in so handy.

In half a day they reach London, where they stop to visit the Gardiners and Jane. Lizzy is surprised to find that Mrs. Gardiner is far less sanguine about Wickham's abandonment of her, than she is herself. His turning his baby-blues on a rich heiress seems, Mrs. Gardiner says, too nakedly mercenary. Lizzy finds herself actually defending him:

> *"Pray, my dear aunt, what is the difference in matrimonial affairs between the mercenary and the prudent motive? Where does discretion end, and avarice begin? Last Christmas you were afraid of his marrying me, because it would be imprudent; and now, because he is trying to get a girl with only ten thousand pounds, you want to find out that he is mercenary."*

And besides, Lizzy argues, if Miss King doesn't object, why should they?...To which Mrs. Gardiner argues that this only shows some deficiency in the girl's character. Lizzy, worn down by a morning with the Lucases (so much so that Mrs. Gardiner might want to check her sherry decanter later), finally gives in and says, "Well...have it as you choose. He shall be mercenary, and she shall be foolish." She, for her part, is sick and tired of worrying herself over the Wickhams and Bingleys of the world, and declares:

> *"Thank Heaven! I am going to-morrow where I shall find a man who has not one agreeable quality, who has neither manner nor sense to recommend him. Stupid men are the only ones worth knowing, after all."*
>
> *"Take care, Lizzy; that speech savours strongly of disappointment."*

Very few others in the novel speak to Lizzy this way, daring to look beneath the effervescence of her manner and gauge her real meaning. Charlotte does; and, interestingly, so does Darcy. Lizzy hasn't quite connected those dots yet.

The visit concludes with the Gardiners inviting Lizzy to accompany them on a summer tour of the lake district, which Lizzy accepts rhapsodically. I mean, she all but cartwheels. You'd think she'd just been handed an airline ticket to Acapulco.

The next day brings Lizzy (and Lucas *pere et soeur)* to Hunsford Parsonage, where they're met at the door by Charlotte and Mr. Collins; in fact Mr. Collins all but knocks his wife over in his zeal to greet them. Lizzy discovers that "her cousin's manners were not altered by his marriage; his formal civility was just what it had been, and he detained her for some minutes" to inquire minutely after her family; then "as soon as they were in the parlour, he welcomed them a second time with ostentatious formality to his humble abode, and punctually repeated all his wife's offers of refreshment."

> *Elizabeth was prepared to see him in his glory; and she could not help fancying that in displaying the good proportion of the room, its aspect and its furniture, he addressed himself particularly to her, as if wishing to make her feel what she had lost in refusing him. But...she was not able to gratifiy him by any sigh of repentance.*

Lizzy watches Charlotte keenly for her reaction to her husband's manifold absurdities, perhaps expecting her to fling herself down a staircase in shame, or maybe just get right in his face and bark "Shut up!" But no, decorum is preserved: "Once or twice she could discern a faint blush; but in general Charlotte wisely did not hear." You can just bring yourself to believe this. Mr. Collins being one of Austen's ceaseless talkers—a character type in which she excels above any other; it makes me sorry she never wrote for the stage—it's entirely credible that after a while his voice becomes, for Charlotte, a kind of background hum; white noise. Then there's this subtle hint at how she endures him:

> *To work in his garden was one of his most respectable pleasures; and Elizabeth admired the command of countenance with which Charlotte talked of the healthfulness of the exercise, and owned she encouraged it as much as possible.*

Mr. Collins conducts a tour of the grounds, and "every view was pointed out with a minuteness which left beauty entirely behind...But of all the views which his garden, or which the country, or the kingdom could boast, none were to be compared with the prospect of Rosings, afforded by an opening in the trees that bordered the park nearly opposite the front of his house. It was a handsome modern building, well situated on rising ground."

We knows Austen's real estate fetish well enough by now, to recognize that last sentence as damning with faint praise. She's setting us up to be underwhelmed by Lady Catherine de Bourgh's much touted grandeur. Though, sadly, we don't get any advance dish from Charlotte; she dutifully takes the party line, as much as her integrity will allow, saying only that Lady Catherine is "a very respectable, sensible woman indeed." You get the feeling she rehearsed it in a mirror to get the proper neutral facial expression.

Despite this, the visit takes some of the chill off the relations between the two friends, and "Elizabeth in the solitude of her chamber had to meditate upon Charlotte's degree of contentment, to understand her address in guiding, and composure in bearing with her husband, and to acknowledge that it was all done very well." Charlotte has achieved a kind of independence which Lizzy herself yet lacks; and while Lizzy can't quite envy her, she acknowledges its value. In this I think she's pretty clearly speaking for her creator as well.

The next day there's a great tumult, with Maria shrieking so loudly that Lizzy, hurling herself downstairs, says, "I expected at least that the pigs were got into the garden, and here is nothing but Lady Catherine and her daughter." The nine-year-old in me wants to say, "And the difference is...?"

In fact it's not Lady Catherine but Mrs. Jenkinson, who looks after Miss De Bourgh, who requires looking after because of her poor health. Lizzy, noting the girl's sickly, cross appearance, cackles to herself, imagining her married to Darcy. "Yes, she will do for him very well. She will make him a very proper wife." It's unworthy of her, but we love her a little bit for it. We can't help it, we like us some bitchy Lizzy.

Miss De Bourgh's visit goes on for a while, though she doesn't descend from the phaeton, thus keeping Charlotte out in the cold; and meantime Sir William Lucas, "to Elizabeth's high diversion, was stationed in the doorway in earnest contemplation of the greatness before him, and constantly bowing whenever Miss De Bourgh looked that way."

Any time a novelist effects a change of scene, the way that Austen has just moved her narrative from Longbourn to Hunsford, it necessitates a certain amount of reshuffling; she has to get all her pieces in place before the action of the plot can recommence. Austen has made the best of it here, keeping us laughing just enough to hold us in abeyance for the next round of fireworks. Which begins next time out, as she at long last brings to the fore Lady Catherine de Bourgh, and we get to judge for ourselves what kind of dame she is. I'm not one for spoilers, but here's a hint: think the Antichrist in a silk pelisse.

CHAPTERS 29-33

The Hunsford party is invited to dine at Rosings the day after their arrival, the unexpected honor of which has Mr. Collins in such a state he doesn't know whether to faint, burst into song, or just run laps around the parsonage waving his hands above his head. "The power of displaying the grandeur of his patroness to his wondering visitors, was exactly what he wished for," and the fact of it coming so soon is almost deranging—or would be, if he weren't deranged already.

Sir William Lucas professes not to be surprised by the invitation, because of his intimate knowledge of "what the manners of the great really are...About the court, such instances of elegant breeding are not uncommon." You recall that he was presented at court, right? If not, never mind, he's sure to mention it again, once or twice or six hundred thousand times.

Mr. Collins spends the next day meticulously instructing everyone in "what they were to expect, that the sight of such rooms, so many servants, and so splendid a dinner might not wholly overpower them." On Lizzy, he confers even more unctuous advice: "Do not make yourself uneasy, my dear cousin, about your apparel. Lady Catherine is far from requiring that elegance of dress in us which becomes herself and her daughter...She likes to have the distinction of rank preserved."

Lizzy allows Mr. Collins the distinction of having his front teeth preserved, which is more than many of us would do under similar circumstances. Or perhaps she simply isn't quick enough to get her right hook in, because at this point Mr. Collins is a moving target, darting around the house like a gerbil in a Habitrail. "While they were dressing, he came two or three times to their different doors to recommend their being quick, as Lady Catherine very much objected to be kept waiting for her dinner." You get the impression that if Lizzy doesn't take him at his word, he might forcibly drag her away by her hair.

As they cross the park towards Rosings, with Mr. Collins pointing out everything of interest and where possible quantifying its cost, Sir William Lucas's knees begin visibly to wobble, and poor Maria pretty much dissolves into peat-like clumps and has to be shoveled up into a wheelbarrow and ferried to the front door. As for Lizzy, however, "Her courage did not fail her. She had heard nothing of Lady Catherine that spoke her awful from any extraordinary talents or miraculous virtue, and the mere stateliness of money and rank she thought she could witness without trepidation."

That's our gal! By this point in the novel, we're just about ready for TEAM LIZZY sweatshirts.

Finally they all find themselves before the August Personage herself. The Lucases stand with their backs arched, like frightened cats; a loud noise might set them tearing off in different directions. But once again, "Lizzy found herself equal to the scene," and has no trouble taking her hostess's measure. Lady Catherine, she finds, is "a tall, large woman, with strongly marked features, which might once have been handsome ...she was not conciliating, nor was her manner of receiving them, such as to make her visitors forget their inferior rank."

But Lady Catherine's Olympian self-importance and her air of almost imperial disdain, are completely lacking in her daughter. Miss De Bourgh is "pale and sickly; her features, though not plain, were insignificant; and she spoke very little, except in a low voice, to Mrs. Jenkinson," who is likewise a cipher. It's as though Lady Catherine were some kind of psychic vampire, her formidable vitality being fed by the life forces of the two feeble, shrunken appendages at her side. You wouldn't be surprised, really, to see her turn towards one or the other and suck away some of their aura through a straw.

The dinner scene is a comic tour de force. Mr. Collins is seated "at the bottom of the table, by her ladyship's desire, and looked as if he felt that life could furnish nothing greater." He proceeds to gush fulsomely over every dish, with Sir William doing his best to out-lickspittle him, "in a manner which Elizabeth wondered Lady Catherine could bear." But her hostess bears it just fine; in fact she gobbles up their flattery just as eagerly as they wolf down their pride. It's a weird kind of feeding frenzy, where the food is almost incidental.

For her part, Lizzy says nothing because there's no one to speak to; there's no conversation at the table except for Lady Catherine's epic pronouncements, and the two gentlemen's raptures over everything set before them. Miss De Bourgh, seated next to Lizzy, says not a word during the entire meal, and in fact we're beginning to wonder if she's capable of speech at all. Possibly if she attempted to say something, it might come out as a squeak or a howl or an oink. Or maybe Lizzy's just not paying attention, and Miss De Bourgh is trying to communicate with her in some other way, such as spelling out HELP ME with her peas.

After dinner Lady Catherine continues to hold forth on a wide range of subjects, and Lizzy notes that "nothing was beneath this great lady's attention which could furnish her with an occasion of dictating to others." And like a garden hose turned on full blast, jumping around the room and soaking everybody, Lady Catherine's attention occasionally lands on Lizzy. "She asked her at different times how many sisters she had, whether they were older or younger than herself, whether any of them were likely to be married, whether they were handsome, where they had been educated, what carriage her father kept, and what had been her mother's maiden name?"

Lizzy feels "all the impertinence of her questions, but answered them very composedly"—at least until Lady Catherine gets around to asking whether "any of her younger sisters are out"—meaning, out in society. Lizzy answers that all of them are, and then goes on to say that in her opinion, it would be "very hard upon younger sisters that they should not have their share of society and amusement because the elder may not have the means or inclination to marry early," which is a pretty democratic thing to say, so of course it alarms Lady Catherine, whose notions of social hierarchy are slightly to the right of the average Egyptian pharaoh. Their exchange degenerates from there, with Lady Catherine going relentlessly at Lizzy as though she were a door hanging slightly off its hinge that might be banged back into proper function.

The evening concludes with cards. Lizzy is stuck at a table with the unenviable company of Maria, Miss De Bourgh, and Mrs. Jenkinson, who between them have about half the wit required to play the game, and a third the physical strength required to shuffle the deck. The other table is more animated:

> *Lady Catherine was generally speaking—stating the mistakes of the three others, or relating some anecdote of herself. Mr. Collins was employed in agree-ing to everything her ladyship said, thanking her for every fish he won, and apologizing if he thought he won too many. Sir William did not say much. He was storing his memory with anecdotes and noble names.*

Afterwards the party "gathered round the fire to hear Lady Catherine determine what weather they were to have on the morrow," the implication being that the Almighty had better see to it or she'd be rapping at the pearly gates first thing demanding to know why not.

This is very much my Jane Austen. This entire sequence is everything I love about her: the brio with which she depicts the absurdities of human vanity, the ruthlessness with which she dissects fatuousness and venality, the delight she takes in skewering ambition and mocking the mighty. No one has ever done it better; no one has ever surpassed her in mirthful mercilessness.

After this rich comic feast, she gives us a chapter or two to catch our breath. Sir William departs after a week's stay at Hunsford, and Lizzy worries that Mr. Collins will now have more time to devote to her and Maria, but fortunately he passes most of his time "either at work in the garden, or in reading and writing, and looking out of the window in his own book room"—ah, the grueling life of a 19th century parson! His chief employment seems to be watching for Miss De Bourgh to drive by in her phaeton, at which time he invariably runs to inform Charlotte as though he's just seen a comet or a herd of wildebeest, or something equally miraculous, "though it happened almost every day."

Sometimes Lady Catherine descends on them to check out Charlotte's housekeeping and to tell her she's got it all wrong and draw up a new shopping list for her and rearrange the furniture and re-sod the lawn and while she's at it Charlotte herself could stand to be an inch taller. Lizzy soon learns that while Lady Catherine "was not in the commission of the peace for the county, she was a most active magistrate in her own parish...whenever any of the cottagers were disposed to be quarrelsome, discontented, or too poor, she sallied forth into the village to settle their differences, silence their complaints, and scold them into harmony and plenty."

After two relatively quiet weeks spent in this manner, Lizzy hears the news that Mr. Darcy is due at Rosings to visit his aunt. Lady Catherine "talked of his coming with the greatest satisfaction, spoke of him in terms of the highest admiration, and seemed almost angry to find that he had already been frequently seen by Miss Lucas and herself." Lizzy looks forward to observing Darcy and Miss De Bourgh together, and to be able to judge how hopeless Caroline Bingley's pursuit of him may be. You get the impression she'd be only too glad to write to Caroline saying, "We are all in the happy expectation of there being soon an attachment between them, which all their friends and family must greet with earnest felicity. P.S. Payback's a bitch, and so are you."

News of Darcy's arrival reaches the parsonage, followed almost immediately by Darcy himself. As they wait for him to enter the room, Charlotte says, "I may thank you, Eliza, for this piece of civility. Mr. Darcy would never have come so soon to wait upon me." Lizzy replies with the Regency equivalent of "Ssshhhyeah, right," but has no time to say more because Darcy's now among them...accompanied by his cousin, one Colonel Fitzwilliam, who is "about thirty, not handsome, but in person and address most truly the gentleman." He's another stock Austen type: the appealing, but not too dazzling, man of the world who will, by his attentions to the heroine, show the hero her real worth. And he jumps right in, chatting up Lizzy with genial ease while Darcy sits silently on the sidelines with his chest puffed up, like a waxwork of Napoleon Bonaparte. Lizzy, however, pierces Darcy's deflecting aura long enough to impishly ask, "My eldest sister has been in town these three months. Have you never happened to see her there?" Mr. Darcy admits that he hasn't been so fortunate, then starts looking very hard in the middle distance, as though using X-ray vision to detect an emergency somewhere that requires his swift intervention. And in fact he and Colonel Fitzwilliam depart soon after.

This is the last Lizzy sees of Darcy for some days. Colonel Fitzwilliam comes calling at the parsonage, where he's definitely flavor of the month among the ladies, but he comes alone. Nor is anyone invited back to Rosings for almost a week, and when they finally are, "Her ladyship received them civilly, but it was plain that their company was by no means so acceptable as when she could get nobody else", and she virtually ignores them, speaking entirely to her nephews.

Colonel Fitzwilliam, however, fixes his attentions on Lizzy; and they talk "so agreeably of Kent and Hertfordshire, of traveling and staying at home, of new books and music, that Elizabeth had never been half so well entertained in that room before"—which very much does *not* escape Mr. Darcy's notice. In fact, Lizzy and Fitzwilliam are having such a party together that it draws Lady Catherine's attention, their merriment being in marked contrast to the mood on her side of the room, where her tongue is poised to lash out and obliterate the merest suggestion of glee.

> *"What is that you are saying, Fitzwilliam? What is you are talking of? What are you telling Miss Bennet? Let me hear what it is."*
>
> *"We are speaking of music, madam," said he, when no longer able to avoid a reply.*
>
> *"Of music! Then pray speak aloud. It is of all subjects my delight. I must have my share in the conversation, if you are speaking of music. There are few people in England, I suppose, who have more true enjoyment of music than myself, or a better natural taste. If I had ever learned, I should have been a great proficient. And so would Anne, if her health had allowed her to apply. I am confident that she would have performed delightfully."*

This is the point at which, on my original reading of *Pride and Prejudice,* I nearly wet myself with joy. Lady Catherine, up to now a merely world-class ogre, here becomes a comic creation of indisputable genius. This is a woman so impossibly imperious that she will boldly trumpet achievements she's never achieved. And not just her own; she's equally ready to boast of her daughter's superiority based on what she might have accomplished but in fact hasn't. Even today it dizzies the mind to contemplate this kind of sociopathic arrogance—yet it's a particularly brilliant stratagem, because it's unarguable. Like, if I were to tell you, "Oh! The Internet would be so much more useful if only I had invented it." Well, you can't prove it wouldn't—any more than I can prove it would. But no one's going to ask Lady Catherine de Bourgh for substantiation. She could claim the ability to grow footmen from crystals under her bed, and everyone would just nod and try not to meet each other's eyes.

Lady Catherine then harangues Mr. Darcy about telling his sister Georgiana that she must practice if she's to excel at the piano. Mr. Darcy reassures her that Georgiana practices "very constantly," but Lady Catherine can't believe anyone is doing anything properly if she's not there to supervise it, and decides that "when I next write to her, I shall charge her not to neglect it on any account." Then, unable to contain this extremely urgent advice till she's next at her writing desk, she foists it instead on Lizzy, adding that since Charlotte doesn't have an instrument she can come to Rosings "and play on the pianoforte in Mrs. Jenkinson's room. She would be in nobody's way, you know, in that part of the house." Even Darcy cringes.

After coffee Lizzy does in fact find herself on the bench, urged by Colonel Fitzwilliam to play for him. Once again, they seem to be having a better time than anyone else, and Darcy, exhausted by his aunt —for whom "I must have my share in the conversation" is code for "I will now speak and you will shut your pie hole"—gradually moves away from her and stations himself by the piano. Within moments, he and Lizzy are at it again, tormenting each other in the most sparklingly brash dialogue ever written.

Lizzy accuses him of having come to stand over her in an effort to frighten her, but she refuses to succumb. "There is a stubbornness about me that never can bear to be frightened at the will of others. My courage always rises with every attempt to intimidate me."

He shoots back that she believes no such thing, she's just showing off. "I have had the pleasure of your acquaintance long enough to know that you find great enjoyment in occasionally professing opinions which in fact are not your own."

She hoots. "I am particularly unlucky in meeting with a person so well able to expose my real character, in a part of the world where I had hoped to pass myself off with some degree of credit." But then she retaliates by exposing *his* character to Colonel Fitzwilliam, revealing how the first time she met him, at the ball in Meryton, he danced only four dances, though "to my certain knowledge, more than one young lady was sitting down in want of a partner."

Darcy, beginning to sweat a little, insists that this was simply due to personal reserve; he didn't know anyone, and "I am ill qualified to recommend myself to strangers." Lizzy pounces on that, asking why someone of Mr. Darcy's lofty position and manifest advantages is unqualified to recommend himself to strangers, and Colonel Fitzwilliam, taking Lizzy's side (no fool, he) chimes in, "It is because he will not give himself the trouble." Possibly he and Lizzy high-five after that one; Austen doesn't say.

Darcy's now being both ganged up on *and* laughed at—his own particular double-barrel hell, sort of like what the rest of us might feel if we were stuck in an elevator with the cast of *Jersey Shore*. He tries to defend himself, insisting that unlike other people he doesn't possess the talent for chatting with strangers. "I cannot catch their tone of conversation, or appear interested in their concerns, as I often see done." To which Elizabeth delivers a scathing smackdown:

> *"My fingers," said Elizabeth, "do not move over this instrument in the masterly manner which I see so many women's do. They have not the same force or rapidity, and do not produce the same expression. But then I have always supposed it to be my own fault—because I would not take the trouble of practicing. It is not that I do not believe my fingers as capable as any other woman's of superior execution."*
>
> *Darcy smiled and said, "You are perfectly right. You have employed your time much better. No one admitted to the privilege of hearing you can think anything wanting. We neither of us perform to strangers."*

At just about this point Colonel Fitzwilliam must realize he is oh so *very* out of the running where Lizzy is concerned. No one hearing her and Darcy go at it hammer and tongs could reach any other conclusion but that these two were utterly made for each other. Except, of course, the two idiots themselves, who persist in torturing one another, and themselves, for their own ridiculous reasons. Those being, of course, pride on his part, prejudice on hers. Austen, who sort of clobbered us over the head with sense versus sensibility in her first novel, is here vastly more subtle about manipulating her theme.

I say that neither Lizzy nor Darcy is aware that they were made for each other; but Darcy at least realizes that there's something between them that renders him to some degree powerless. He's in the slow process of giving in to it, as we discover the next day when he comes calling at the parsonage and finds Lizzy alone. He apologizes for intruding; he'd thought to find all the ladies present. "They then sat down," Austen tells us, "and when her inquiries after Rosings were made, seemed in danger of sinking into total silence." This is a wonderful, and subtle, refutation of Darcy's earlier statement, "We neither of us perform to strangers"—because in fact he and Lizzy seem able to speak to each other *only* with an audience; with that buffer removed, without a single other soul present to serve as an alternate point of reference, they're marooned with the inescapable fact of each other, and it renders them both nearly mute. Lizzy is the better at small talk; she asks whether Mr. Bingley will return to Netherfield, and suggests that if he has no such plans "it would be better for the neighborhood that he should give up the place entirely, for then we might possibly get a settled family there." Darcy's replies are nearly monosyllabic.

But then he starts saying things that Lizzy can't figure out. Speaking of Charlotte, he says "It must be very agreeable to her to be settled within so easy a distance of her own family and friends," which astonishes Lizzy because Hunsford Parsonage is fifty miles from Lucas Lodge, which she'd scarcely call convenient. They debate the relative proximity of Charlotte's family, and then Darcy scoots his chair closer and says, "*You* cannot have a right to such very strong local attachment. *You* cannot have been always at Longbourn."

Lizzy has no idea how to respond. She couldn't be more surprised if he leapt up from his chair and started playing air guitar. Fortunately they're interrupted by Charlotte's return, upon which Darcy slinks away with a mumbled excuse, like he's been caught with his hand in the cookie jar; and Charlotte, who's no fool and knows exactly how many beans make five, says, "My dear Eliza, he must be in love with you or he would never have called on us in this familiar way," which makes Lizzy want to bend Charlotte's arm behind her and say, *"Take it back! Take it back!"*

And on reflection even Charlotte begins to doubt this initial impression, because Mr. Darcy's manner, when he does call, is so strained and silent; he might be in a gastroenterologist's waiting room for all the pleasure he seems to derive from it.

In the days that follow, Elizabeth repeatedly runs into Mr. Darcy on her "ramble" in the park. "She felt all the perverseness of the mischance that should bring him where no one else was brought; and to prevent its ever happening again, took care to inform him at first that it was a favorite haunt of hers. How it could occur a second time therefore was very odd! Yet it did, and even a third."

You read this and think, "Well, *duh,* Lizbot! Now you're just being stupid." Except Darcy's behavior during these meetings is scarcely the kind that would encourage her to think she's scored a conquest. He remains stiff, formal, and silent. Put a well-dressed mannequin on wheels for her to drag along like a pull-toy, and there'd be no difference.

And when Darcy does deign to speak, he sounds like his brains are addled. He makes a reference to Rosings that seems to imply that on Lizzy's next trip to Hertfordshire she'd be staying *there,* which Lizzy would probably not agree to even if Lady Catherine by some miracle offered it. Even if she offered it *at gunpoint.*

Eventually she concludes that Darcy must be presuming that when she returns to Kent, she'll be married to Colonel Fitzwilliam. This makes her a bit guarded when she next meets the colonel, on the day before his departure. She tries to keep the conversation light but they end up treading dangerous waters, as when she teases him for bemoaning his fate as an earl's youngest son; surely he's never experienced want or dependence! But he replies that while this may be true, he lacks self-determination; "Younger sons cannot marry where they like." They have to wed where there's money.

> *"Is this," thought Elizabeth, "meant for me?" and she colored at the idea; but recovering herself, said in a lively tone, "And pray, what is the usual price of an earl's younger son? Unless the elder brother is very sickly, I suppose you would not ask above fifty thousand pounds."*

But her ability to deflect perilous topics with a quip, fails her spectacularly a few minutes later, when they're speaking about Darcy—Lizzy of course being the one to introduce him into the conversation (she keeps bringing up how proud and pushy he is, sure, but the point is, she keeps *bringing him up*). Fitzwilliam says, in Darcy's defense, "From something that he told me in our journey hither, I have reason to think Bingley very much indebted to him." Lizzy's ears perk up and she presses for details. The colonel obliges: "…[H]e congratulated himself on having lately saved a friend from the inconveniences of a most imprudent marriage." Lizzy, now on full alert, boldly asks for Darcy's reasons; and if the colonel doesn't supply them, she may just kick his feet out from under him and pin him to the ground till he does. Fortunately, he immediately divulges: "I understood that there were some very strong objections against the lady."

Lizzy is thus propelled into such a turmoil of astonishment and anger that she all but loses cognizance of her companion. He could walk right off a cliff and it wouldn't register. She's consumed by righteous indignation, and by terrible shock; she'd presumed all along that Caroline Bingley had been the prime mover in her brother's abandonment of Jane, with Darcy just an accessory, but in fact it was the other way around. And she's been being *civil* to him all this while, when she might have been secretly spitting into his cup of Darjeeling!

Back in her room at the parsonage, she obsesses over that phrase, "very strong objections against the lady." She's not stupid; she knows Darcy can't but regard her family as a pack of ravenous hyenas. But she's convinced it's their humble station, not their apparent insanity, that really gets to him. He'd "receive a deeper wound from the want of importance in his friend's connections than from their want of sense," and she has a point. If Mrs. Bennet were a duchess, none of her shrill rudeness and incessant prattle would matter a damn to him; similarly, if Lady Catherine were merely a country widow, he wouldn't go anywhere near her, and would beat her off with his cane if she came anywhere near him.

Lizzy's so vexed by all this that she develops a headache, and accordingly bows out of accompanying the Collinses and Maria to tea at Rosings. This will have dramatic consequences in the next chapter, when Lizzy, who already has the distinction of enduring the most egregiously insulting marriage proposal in all of English literature, gets to beat her own record by suffering one exponentially worse. Good times!

CHAPTERS 34-37

The big moment arrives—the crux of the novel.

Lizzy, pleading a headache, has stayed behind at the parsonage while the Collinses and Maria have gone to tea at Rosings...where, we know by now, even the most benign headache might turn lethal. Then, "as if intending to exasperate herself as much as possible against Mr. Darcy," Lizzy dives back into all the letters she's received from Jane over the past few weeks, to trawl them for signs of heartache and distress. She can contrast these with "Mr. Darcy's shameful boast of what misery he had been able to inflict," and whip herself into a nice, cathartic fury. Possibly she'll even kick some of the furniture, or chase the dog with a broom.

This pleasant afternoon's diversion is interrupted, to Lizzy's "utter amazement," by the arrival of Mr. Darcy himself. He seems agitated, out of sorts; though it's easy to appear out of sorts when the only sorts you're ever in, is Cigar Store Indian. He inquires after Lizzy's health and she responds "with cold civility." They sit in silence for a while, staring at each other—it's a game of emotional chicken, and Darcy is the first to swerve. He leaps up, strides manfully around the room, then turns and delivers the lines that, for better or worse, are the foundation for what will, two centuries later, become the cult of Darcy, tended ferociously by legions of aggrieved vestal virgins decked out in Donna Karan:

> *"In vain have I struggled. It will not do. My feelings will not be repressed. You must allow me to tell you how ardently I admire and love you."*

The modern Darcyite thrills to the idea of bringing this proud man to his knees; for her, emasculation is the key to the scene's—if not the novel's—appeal. Perhaps, then, Austen erred in relating what follows as narrative instead of dialogue; for if we heard it from Darcy's own lips, it would somewhat take the bloom off the rose. In fact it would wilt it, wither it, and snap it at the stem.

> *He spoke well, but there were feelings besides those of the heart to be detailed, and he was not more eloquent on the subject of tenderness than of pride. His sense of her inferiority—of its being a degradation—of the family obstacles which judgment had always opposed to inclination were dwelt on with a warmth which seemed due to the consequence he was wounding, but was very unlikely to recommend his suit.*

Imagine the average Darcyite being told, "I know you're trash, I know my friends will drop-kick me to the curb the moment they see me with you, and who could blame them. But I can't help it. It's a mental illness. Marry me!" We're not talking Regency romance, we're talking Jerry Springer.

As for Lizzy, there's never a question in her mind that she's going to refuse him, but she feels an initial twinge of regret at causing him pain. By the time he's finished speaking that's no longer an issue. In fact she might now be ready to carve NO into his forehead with a letter opener. Especially since "she could easily see that he had no doubt of a favourable answer. He *spoke* of apprehension and anxiety, but his countenance expressed real security." Well, our gal can take care of that:

> *"...[I]f I could feel gratitude, I would now thank you. But I cannot—I have never desired your good opinion, and you have certainly bestowed it most unwillingly. I am sorry to have occasioned pain to anyone. It has been most unconsciously done, however, and I hope will be of short duration. The feelings which, you tell me, have long prevented the acknowledgment of your regard can have little difficulty in overcoming it after this explanation."*

Darcy "seemed to catch her words with no less resentment than surprise. His complexion became pale with anger, and the disturbance of his mind was visible in every feature." He draws himself up even more stiffly than usual—his hair might just brush the ceiling—and goes into a major snit. "I might, perhaps, wish to be informed why, with so little endeavour at civility, I am thus rejected. But it is of small importance."

Lizzy rolls up her sleeves and goes in for a three-point takedown.

> *"I might as well inquire," replied she, "why with so evident a design of offending and insulting me you chose to tell me that you liked me against your will, against your reason, and even against your character? Was not this some excuse for incivility, if I was uncivil? But I have other provocations. You know I have."*

And then she dares him to deny that he was the one who split up Jane and Bingley, "exposing one to the censure of the world for caprice and instability, the other to its derision for disappointed hopes, and involving both in misery of the acutest kind."

He doesn't deny it; why should he? "I did everything in my power to separate my friend from your sister...Towards *him* I have been kinder than towards myself." Ummm...not learning the lesson here, dude.

Lizzy then slaps him with his crimes against Mr. Wickham:

> *"You have reduced him to his present state of poverty, comparative poverty. You have withheld the advantages, which you must know to have been designed for him. You have deprived the best years of his life of that independence which was no less his due than his desert. You have done all this! And yet you can treat the mention of his misfortunes with contempt and ridicule."*

Darcy doesn't answer this; instead, adopting the gambit of cornered teenagers everywhere, he turns the whole interrogation back on Lizzy. "My faults, according to this calculation, are heavy indeed! But perhaps ...these offenses might have been overlooked, had not your pride been hurt by my honest confession of the scruples that had long prevented my forming any serious design."

And here's where we know the game is up. If Lizzy really felt about him as she claims to do—if she merely loathed him and wanted no part of him, ever—she'd now say, "Believe what you like, if it comforts you. Just believe it somewhere else, please. There's the door. Have a nice Hanoverian Era."

But she doesn't say that. Instead she mounts a full-bore assault, going after him so viciously that you can almost feel him flinch from the heat blasting into his face:

> *"From the very beginning, from the first moment, I may almost say, of my acquaintance with you, your manners impressing me with the fullest belief of your arrogance, your conceit, and your selfish disdain of the feelings of others, were such as to form that groundwork of disapprobation on which succeeding events have built so immovable a dislike; and I had not known you a month before I felt you were the last man in the world whom I could ever be prevailed on to marry."*

Whoa, whoa, *whoa*, Lizbot! Way to jump the shark there, kiddo!

Darcy, having somehow survived this volcanic spew, knows it's time to retreat, and he does so in high style.

> *"You have said quite enough, madam. I perfectly comprehend your feelings, and have now only to be ashamed of what my own have been. Forgive me for having taken up so much of your time, and accept my best wishes for your health and happiness."*

Now that right there is *my* Darcy—that's the first time I've really, genuinely liked him. I think he had me at "madam."

After he withdraws, Lizzy goes into a tizzy, and when the Collinses return she flees to her room lest Charlotte take one look at her and say, "Did Mr. Darcy just propose to you and you call him a conceited cretin from hell?" Because Charlotte is *that good.*

She wakes up the next morning in as miserable state as she went to bed. Still trying to evade Charlotte's piercing eye, she goes on a long walk to try to clear her head. Of course she runs into Darcy. He's been lying in wait for her, like a highwayman. He hands her an envelope, "with a look of haughty composure," and says merely, "Will you do me the honour of reading that letter?" What, no "madam"? C'mon, I like it when you call her madam!

Lizzy tears it open as soon as he's left her and plunges right in. (Again, if she really had no feelings for him, she'd wait till he was gone and then toss it aside with a little puff of disgust.) The text comprises a long and very stately defense of all his actions with regard to Jane and Bingley, and to Wickham. "You must, therefore, pardon the freedom with which I demand your attention; your feelings, I know, will bestow it unwillingly, but I demand it of your justice." This is Austen's move to rehabilitate him in our eyes, too, as up to now we haven't had a whole lot of reason to think good of him.

Regarding Jane and Bingley, he excuses himself in that he saw nothing in her behavior towards him that implied any more affection than she might show a kitten, or a plate of cookies. "Her looks and manners were open, cheerful and engaging as ever, but without any symptom of peculiar regard"—so score another one for Charlotte, who warned of exactly this: that if Jane didn't show her feelings, no one would believe they existed.

Darcy apologizes for having been mistaken in this regard. But in another area, he holds firm: "The situation of your mother's family, though objectionable, was nothing in comparison of that total want of propriety so frequently, so almost uniformly betrayed by herself, by your three younger sisters, and occasionally even by your father.—Pardon me.—It pains me to offend you."

He excuses both Jane and Lizzy herself from censure, and in fact compliments them on the way they comport themselves in the midst of such shrieking god-awfulness; he might as well ask, Are you by any chance adopted? Even so, he felt compelled to persuade his friend to give up the woman he'd fallen in love with—and Bingley, who's basically a big marshmallow man, soon yielded to his iron-fisted mentor. Darcy still can't blame himself for having done this; but there is "one part of my conduct in the whole affair on which I do not reflect with satisfaction; it is that I condescended to adopt to measures of art so far as to conceal from him your sister's being in town." By "the measures of art," he means "the measures of Caroline"—which really should've been his first clue it wasn't quite kosher.

As for his conduct towards Wickham, that's a more complex matter. Wickham, like most liars, knows how to season his falsehoods with just enough truth to make them credible; and in fact Mr. Darcy's father *did* promise to promote his career in the church, and to provide him with a clerical living when it fell due. But after the old man died, Wickham—who by this time Darcy knew to be not quite the golden boy his father had thought—decided against the church in favor of studying law, and asked Darcy, his new patron, to honor his father's intentions to the extent of providing "some more immediate pecuniary advantage in lieu of the preferment by which he could not be benefited." In other words, he wanted to cash out.

Darcy agreed; and with the settlement money Wickham ran wild, ran to seed, and ran to ground—then came crawling back to Darcy saying that hey, he'd changed his mind about that clerical living, so how about it? Darcy, not unreasonably, said something like, "Are you freakin' kidding me?" and booted his sorry ass out the door—with the predictable result that "His resentment was in proportion to the distress of his circumstances—and he was doubtless as violent in his abuse of me to others as in his reproaches to myself." Except of course Wickham was too smart for that; as we've seen, he's chosen a different tack, whimpering and batting his eyelashes and begging pitiably for scraps so that everyone *else* is driven to fury in *their* abuse of Darcy.

Darcy then cautions Lizzy: "I must now mention a circumstance which I would wish to forget myself, and which no obligation less than the present should induce me to unfold to any human being." So we immediately shift in our seats, expecting some juicy goods. And in fact it's pretty succulent stuff: To revenge himself on Darcy—and to get his hands on those funds after all—Wickham took a stab at seducing Darcy's sister Georgiana, "whose affectionate heart retained a strong impression of his kindness to her as a child, that she was persuaded to believe herself in love, and to consent to an elopement. She was then but fifteen, which must be her excuse." Fifteen-year-olds everywhere will love that. Fortunately the plot was discovered and foiled; and if the whole matter seems too incredible for Lizzy to believe, Darcy urges her to apply to Colonel Fitzwilliam for verification, since he shared Georgiana's guardianship and is thoroughly familiar with the whole sordid story.

Given Darcy's general gravitas, this letter chapter is the first in the novel that's completely devoid of laughs. Its appeal—which is considerable—comes from the plangent beauty of the language, which tolls like a particularly resonant bell, irresistibly gorgeous and undeniably masculine in character.

> *But I shall not scruple to assert that the serenity of your sister's countenance and air was such as might have given the most acute observer a conviction that, however amiable her temper, her heart was not likely to be easily touched. That I was desirous of believing her indifferent is certain—but I will venture to say that my investigations and decisions are not usually influenced by my hopes or fears. I did not believe her to be indifferent because I wished it; I believed it on impartial conviction, as truly as I wished it in reason.*

And these strong, insistent cadences wear away at Lizzy's resistance to the sentiments they convey. Her first reading of the letter is peppered by scoffs and dismissals and Regency synonyms for "As *if*," but her avidity to devour the whole betrays the thinness of her aversion to it. "She read, with an eagerness which hardly left her power of comprehension, and from impatience of knowing what the next sentence might bring, was incapable of attending to the sense of the one before her eyes."

After racing through the whole of the letter, she "put it hastily away, protesting that she would not regard it, that she would never look at it again." So of course, she resumes her walk for three-and-a-half steps, then stops and tears it back open and scours it line by line as though it's written in the Da Vinci Code. Her object, of course, is to find reasons to dismiss the whole thing, especially the account of Wickham's supposed villainy. "But every line proved more clearly that the affair, which she had believed it impossible that any contrivance could so represent as to render Mr. Darcy's conduct in it less than infamous, was capable of a turn which must make him entirely blameless throughout the whole." Welcome to Bizarro World, where everything am opposite!

She focuses her memory on Wickham, trying "to recollect some instance of goodness, some distinguished trait of integrity or benevolence, that might rescue him" from Darcy's slander, but of course there's nothing, because all Wickham ever did was preen and purr and flirt and flatter. Suddenly everything about him seems, in hindsight, very different, right from the way he behaved that first evening at her Aunt and Uncle Philips's party, when he'd told her all about his history with Darcy, and she'd come away so besotted with him.

> *She was now struck with the impropriety of such communications to a stranger, and wondered it had escaped her before. She saw the indelicacy of putting himself forward as he had done, and the inconsistency of his professions with his conduct. She remembered that he had boasted of having no fear of seeing Mr. Darcy—that Mr. Darcy might leave the country, but that* he *should stand his ground; yet he had avoided the Netherfield ball the very next week. She remembered also that till the Netherfield family had quitted the country, he had told his story to no one but herself; but that after their removal, it had been everywhere discussed; that he had no reserves, no scruples in sinking Mr. Darcy's character, though he had assured her that respect for the father would always prevent his exposing the son.*

She dissolves into self-rebuke; she's been an idiot, and she knows it. Darcy had started their acquaintance by insulting her, Wickham by flattering her; and so, like some silly bint she has "driven reason away, where either were concerned. Till this moment I never knew myself." Lizzy, meet Lizzy. Yes, she's something of a dork; give her time, you'll learn to love her for it.

As for Jane, she has to admit it; she'd been wrong there, too. Darcy had "declared himself to have been totally unsuspicious of her sister's attachment, and she could not help remembering what Charlotte's opinion had always been." Oh yeah, *snap*—Charlotte *finally* gets some cred! Too little, too late, though, huh? But even more mortifying is the section of the letter concerning her family. She'd thought their behavior to be less offensive to Darcy than their inferior rank, when just the opposite is true; she hasn't allowed herself to see how seriously, deep-dish ghastly her relations really are. And the knowledge that their Pirates of the Caribbean act is principally to blame for driving a decent man away from pursuing a life with Jane, is almost more than she can bear.

When she returns to the parsonage and learns she's missed both Darcy and Colonel Fitzwilliam, who had come to take their leave of her, she's actually glad. Facing either one of them would've been impossible.

The time's drawing near for her own departure, which, surprisingly, Lady Catherine views with some regret—though Lizzy rightly intuits that her feelings might be different if Lizzy were now known, as she could have been, as her nephew's finacee. In which case Lady Catherine would not only be eager to see the back of her, she might actually lash her ankle to the bridle of a horse and set it cantering off with Lizzy bump-bump-bumping along behind.

But as it's turned out, there's no cause for that, and Lady Catherine insists that Lizzy extend her visit. "I expected you to stay two months. I told Mrs. Collins so before you came." When Lizzy protests that her father has written to hurry her return, Lady Catherine waves a hand in dismissal. "Daughters are never of so much consequence to a father. And if you will stay another *month* complete, it will be in my power to take one of you as far as London, for I am going there early in June for a week." The only thing that could make this a greater *dis*incentive for Lizzy, is if she added, "We will be traveling in the barouche, with several hundred pounds of rotting sheep entrails."

Lizzy accordingly insists on the original plan, but since no plan can be satisfactory until Lady Catherine has lifted her leg on it, she says, "Mrs. Collins, you must send a servant with them. You know I always speak my mind, and I cannot bear the idea of two young women traveling post by themselves. It is highly improper," and so on and so forth, growing more heatedly indignant over the VERY IDEA of two young ladies hurling themselves across the country unescorted, till Lizzy manages to get a word in edgewise (probably by judicious use of a crowbar): "My uncle is to send a servant for us," she says.

"Oh!—Your uncle!" Lady Catherine sputters. "He keeps a man-servant, does he?—I am very glad you have somebody who thinks of those things. Where shall you change horses?—Oh! Bromley, of course.—If you mention my name at the Bell, you will be attended to."

Sorry, I just love Lady Catherine to smithereens. I could read an entire book of her just sitting in her drawing room re-ordering the whole of creation, saying things like How can it be August already, I gave no permission for it to be August, and Who allowed that Venus may be closer to the sun than we are, have it removed at once.

And so the Hunsford jaunt ends with Lizzy materially changed—her eyes opened with regard to Wickham, and more painfully with regard to her own family—but also deeply conflicted about Darcy. "His attachment excited gratitude, his general character respect; but she could not approve him; nor could she for a moment repent her refusal, or feel the slightest inclination ever to see him again."

She just doesn't know what to think about him. But she *keeps on* thinking about him. Gee, I wonder what *that* could mean.

CHAPTERS 38-41

Mr. Collins corners Lizzy on the morning of her departure, ostensibly to thank her for her kindness in visiting Charlotte, but really to twist the knife a little. Venturing to hope that she hasn't been bored by their simple, quiet life, he notes that of course there has been the compensating factor of their connection to Rosings, that Valhalla of all earthly glory.

> *"You see on what a footing we are. You see how continually we are engaged there. In truth I must acknowledge that, with all the disadvantages of this humble parsonage, I should not think any one abiding in it an object of compassion, while they are sharers in our intimacy at Rosings."*

In case that's not pointed enough, he adds, "Lady Catherine's great attention to Mrs. Collins you have been a daily witness of, and altogether I trust it does not appear that your friend has drawn an unfortunate—but on this point it will be as well to be silent." Rrrrrright. Mr. Collins could be hiding behind the sofa from an ax-wielding intruder combing the house in search of him, and still not find that a circumstance in which it's "as well to be silent." His will to talk is quite a bit stronger than his will to live. It's just that here, he's already made his point to Lizzy, and now he wants to watch her squirm as it sinks in. Take a look at Charlotte's love-monkey, cousin, and go on home a-cryin' "Should'a, would'a, could'a." What he's too stupid to realize is that Lizzy herself is thinking, Not if he were the last man— or rather, vaguely man-shaped organism—alive.

Mr. Collins now brags that "My dear Charlotte and I have but one mind and one way of thinking. There is in every thing a most remarkable resemblance of character and ideas between us. We seem to have been designed for each other." Where—on Planet Wrong? Or possibly he's really telling the truth, and this isn't our Mr. Collins at all, but an extra-dimensional counterpart who's momentarily blinked in from a parallel universe...maybe that one where Kirk is evil and Spock sports a van dyke.

Lizzy is briefly sorry to leave Charlotte alone in "such society." But then she gets over it, because Charlotte doesn't act pitiable: "Her home and her housekeeping, her parish and her poultry, and all their dependent concerns, had not yet lost their charms." Yeah, if I were saddled with Mr. Collins as a companion, a coop of idiot chickens would seem like a pretty sweet alternative.

Lizzy and Maria Lucas now ride off to London for another short stay at the Gardiners', where Jane is still a guest. Lizzy somehow resists telling her sister about Darcy's marriage proposal, despite the temptation to use her power to both flabbergast her and flatter her own vanity into the bargain. Girl's got strength of will, I'll give her that. Most of us would be blaring the news from the coach window before it even drew to a halt. By which time Jane would probably know all about it anyway, because we'd have texted her, emailed, blogged about it, and possibly appeared with Darcy on *Maury Povich.*

Lizzy, Jane, and Maria then set off for Longbourn. When they reach the inn at Hertfordshire where they're to meet Mr. Bennet's carriage, they're surprised by Lydia and Kitty, who give them a shout-out from the window of a second-story dining room; they might as well moon them while they're at it, it couldn't make any worse an impression on the locals. They are, however, thoughtful enough to have a lunch spread waiting for the returnees.

> *"And we mean to treat you all," added Lydia, "but you must lend us the money for we have just spent ours at the shop out there." Then, showing her purchases: "Look here, I have bought this bonnet. I do not think it is very pretty; but I thought I might as well buy it as not. I shall put it to pieces as soon as I get home, and see if I can make it up any better."*

In this single paragraph, Austen has restated Lydia's character in its entirety: impulsive, careless, a creature of whim and appetite—it's all right here. But she needn't have been so economical, because there are many, many paragraphs to follow. Lydia is another of Austen's epic talkers, and she blabs a blue streak for three solid pages, occasionally, by sheer law of averages, hitting on a topic of actual interest, such as the departure of the regiment from Meryton, and her idea that the Bennet family should follow them to their new camp at Brighton. "It would be such a delicious scheme, and I dare say would hardly cost anything at all. Mamma would like to go too of all things! Only think what a miserable summer else we shall have!" Lydia in full flow can make you regret exclamation points were ever invented. She assails you with them like pepper spray.

Lizzy, who's seen how Lydia and Kitty have run wild with *one* regiment at their disposal, blanches at the thought of how they'd behave with a whole division. And she's right; if this scheme goes down, Austen will end up writing *Fanny Hill* instead of *Pride and Prejudice.*

Then Lydia teases that she's got some news about Wickham. Jane and Lizzy exchange a glance, then dismiss the waiter. Lydia mocks them: "Ah, that is just like your formality and discretion. You thought the waiter must not hear, as if he cared." Lydia, of course, would say anything in front of anybody. She'd say it before the king and Parliament. Probably after hopping into his majesty's lap. As for the news about Wickham: he's not to marry Miss King after all. "There's for you! She is gone down to her uncle in Liverpool, gone to stay. Wickham is safe!" Lizzy privately observes that actually it's Miss King who's safe, while Jane, predictably, hopes no one's feelings have been bruised in the breakup. Lydia leaps in with, "I will answer for it, he never cared three straws for her. Who *could* about such a nasty little freckled thing?" Lizzy is "shocked to think that, however incapable of such coarseness of expression herself, the coarseness of the sentiment was little other than her own breast had harboured and fancied liberal!"

So yes, she's still suffering the shocks of incipient self-awareness. She's like Dorian Gray finally having a good, long look at that pesky portrait in the attic; only in her case, what she sees looking back at her from the canvas is Lydia. Talk about a wake-up call.

After lunch they all pile into the carriage, along with all of Lydia and Kitty's purchases—it must be like 1950s college students cramming into a phone booth—and ride home, with Lydia chattering away non-stop the whole journey, entertainingly but exhaustingly (she's perpetually on the verge of "dying of laughter"), and at a certain point you realize you haven't heard a peep from Maria Lucas for going on six pages. It's as if Lydia uses up so much life force that when she gets too close, borderline cases like Maria just blink out of existence. Either that, or the sisters absentmindedly ate Maria along with the cold meats and salad.

Back at Longbourn everything is noise and tumult, as we've come to expect; but at the first comparatively quiet moment (I think it occurs about 1878) Lizzy tells Jane about her second marriage proposal, and of Wickham's sordid history...though she pointedly doesn't tell her what she's discovered about Darcy's role in splitting up her and Bingley.

Jane is initially surprised by the proposal, though her "astonishment was soon lessened by the strong sisterly partiality which made any admiration of Elizabeth appear perfectly natural." But she remains slack-jawed over the news about Wickham; she "would willingly have gone through the world without believing that so much wickedness existed in the whole race of mankind as was here collected in one individual." Of course she wants to believe it's all some kind of misunderstanding, but can't do that without damaging Darcy's credentials. So she careens back and forth trying to clear one without indicting the other. Just when we think we might have the thrill of watching her head implode, Lizzy interrupts:

> *"This will not do...You will never be able to make both of them good for anything...There is but such a quantity of merit between them; just enough to make one good sort of man; and of late it has been shifting about pretty much. For my part, I am inclined to believe it all Mr. Darcy's, but you shall do as you choose."*

Having finally been able to unburden herself to Jane, Lizzy is obviously feeling lightheaded, if not downright giddy. Later, when Jane expresses sympathy for "poor Mr. Darcy" and his disappointed hopes and adds, "I am sure you must feel it so," Lizzy quips back: "Oh! No, my regret and compassion are all done away by seeing you so full of both. I know you will do him such ample justice that I am growing every moment more unconcerned and indifferent."

I mean, you can almost hear a rimshot.

Later, however, she's more reflective, and takes a jab at her own propensity to go for the killer crack:

> *"I meant to be uncommonly clever in taking so decided a dislike to Mr. Darcy...without any reason. It is such a spur to one's genius, such an opening for wit to have a dislike of that kind. One may be continually abusive without saying anything just, but one cannot be always laughing at a man without now and then stumbling on something witty."*

This is all very true and very fine, but we find ourselves hoping she doesn't mean it *too* much. We like our trash-talkin' Lizbot just the way she is.

The sisters then discuss whether the truth about Wickham ought to be revealed, but ultimately they decide against it; Mr. Darcy divulged the details in confidence, and besides, the regiment's leaving town in a few days, after which Wickham will be somebody else's problem. Jane adds that, "To have his errors made public might ruin him forever. He is now perhaps sorry for what he has done, and anxious to re-establish a character." Which makes you flip back to earlier chapters just to make sure you're not dreaming and yes, in fact Jane really *has* met him.

But maybe we should give Jane a pass here, 'cause the poor kid's pining. Now that they're home again, Lizzy has time to observe her more closely, and finds her outwardly her old self, but something vital has gone out of her—she seems to struggle through each day. Even Mrs. Bennet notices, which is saying something:

> *"Well, Lizzy...what is your opinion of this sad business of Jane's? For my part, I am determined never to speak of it again to anybody. I told my sister Philips so the other day."*

Yes, I know this is a joke Austen uses repeatedly, but I just keep finding it hilarious. So sue me. And when Lizzy tells her that she's pretty sure Bingley won't ever return to Netherfield, we get another trademark Mrs. Bennet response: "Well, my comfort is I am sure Jane will die of a broken heart, and then he will be sorry for what he has done." It's like she's been out of the narrative for a dozen chapters, so Austen is welcoming her back in with a medley of her greatest hits.

Finally, the dreaded week arrives in which the regiment is to pull up stakes. Austen tells us that "all the young ladies in the neighborhood were drooping apace," with the exception of Jane and Lizzy. But their lack of weepy dismay is more than made up for by Kitty and Lydia, who fling themselves about the house in transports of anguish, like actresses in an exceptionally morbid silent movie, all the while bemoaning their fate and invoking Brighton, Brighton, Brighton, Brighton, like an LP record with a skip in it.

Lizzy, witnessing these histrionics, "tried to be diverted by them; but all sense of pleasure was lost in shame. She felt anew the justice of Mr. Darcy's objections; and never had she before been so much disposed to pardon his interference in the views of his friend." Maybe now she's even asking *herself* if she might be adopted.

Suddenly Lydia's prayers are answered (or would be if she actually prayed, which I doubt; she seems to have less of an inner life than the average household cat). She's invited to Brighton as the guest of one Mrs. Forster, the new young wife of an officer in the regiment. "A resemblance in good humor and good spirits had recommended her and Lydia to each other, and out of their *three* months' acquaintance they had been intimate *two*."

Lydia is so enraptured by this sudden deliverance that she almost bursts like a piñata, and she and her mother gabble at each other with the velocity of dueling banjoes. Kitty, meanwhile, utterly forgotten, sulks in a corner and curses the unfairness of it all and does her best to cough up a lung.

Lizzy, no fool, sees Lydia's opportunity as "the death-warrant of all possible common sense" for her, and begs her father to forbid the expedition. But Mr. Bennet, as hands-off a dad as ever, can't be bothered to take the initiative. "Lydia will never be easy till she has exposed herself in some public place or other, and we can never expect her to do it with so little expense or inconvenience to her family as under the present circumstances."

Right here, the gods of foreshadowing make like the assembled cast of *Stomp*.

Lydia, meanwhile, marinates in lurid fantasies of conquering Brighton:

> *She saw with the creative eye of fancy, the streets of that gay bathing place covered with officers. She saw herself the object of attention to tens and scores of them at present unknown. She saw all the glories of the camp; its tents stretched forth in beauteous uniformity of lines, crowded with the young and the gay, and dazzling with scarlet; and to complete the view, she saw herself seated beneath a tent, tenderly flirting with at least six officers at once.*

It's like a mash-up of Merchant & Ivory and every Aaron Spelling TV show ever made.

It's about this time that Lizzy, who has been avoiding Meryton ever since her return so as not to run into Wickham, finally comes face to face with him at a party, and it's not pretty. Wickham, amazingly, gets all flirty with her again, as though she'll fall for his lounge-lizard act a second time; and why wouldn't she? She's just some dopey provinicial girl. Lizzy responds in the most feline way imaginable—giving him a little swipe here (telling him Darcy and Colonel Fitzwilliam spent three weeks at Rosings while she was at Hunsford), and a quick scratch there (yes, actually, she saw quite a lot of them), and watching his face sag a little with each revelation. It's the social-intercourse version of the death by a thousand cuts. Then she says she thinks Mr. Darcy "improves on acquaintance," which causes Wickham to flail desperately to get her back on his side.

> *"Is it in address that he improves? Has he deigned to add ought of civility to his ordinary style? For I dare not hope," he continued in a lower and more serious tone, "that he is improved in essentials."*
>
> *"Oh no!" said Elizabeth. "In essentials, I believe, he is very much what he ever was."*

Lizzy's almost purring with lethal contentment now, while Wickham veers between anxiety and confusion, like a mouse who still thinks he can get away from his tormentor but doesn't understand why his back legs don't work. Then Lizzy delivers the killing blow: "When I said that he improved on acquaintance, I did not mean that either his mind or manner were in a state of improvement, but that from knowing him better, his disposition was better understood."

Wickham, now reeling, makes some feeble speculation that Darcy was only making nice because of his aunt's presence, but clearly he's been shot down hard, and he knows it. When they part, Lizzy glides away in satisfaction, while he just slumps to the ground with a pair of X's where his eyes should be.

When the party ends Lydia returns with Mrs. Forster to Meryton to begin her big Brighton adventure, and Mrs. Bennet, who will be living vicariously through her (probably without knowing what "vicariously" means), bids her an enthusiastic farewell and advises her "not to miss the opportunity of enjoying herself as much as possible," as if this is something Lydia might neglect to do otherwise.

We'll soon find out exactly how much Lydia enjoys herself—as will all of Meryton. And all of Hertfordshire, and possibly all of England. Nice going with the advice, Mrs. B. I'm betting you and Polonious make a smashing pair out there in the literary afterlife. (And ain't *that* an idea for a play!)

CHAPTERS 42-45

The Education of Elizabeth Bennet continues apace, and boy, it is freakin' brutal. With the scales fallen from her eyes, Lizzy looks around and sees, as if for the first time, the desolation of her parents' marriage, and the culpability of her father in bringing it to this pass. She can no longer "banish from her thoughts that continual breach of conjugal obligation and decorum which, in exposing his wife to the contempt of her own children, was so highly reprehensible." In spite of his blatant cruelty, we've tended to like Mr. Bennet, so this comes as a bit of cold water in our faces. But there's more:

> *"[Lizzy] had never felt so strongly as now the disadvantages which must attend the children of so unsuitable a marriage, nor ever been so fully aware of the evils arising from so ill-judged a direction of his talents, talents which rightly used might at least have preserved the respectability of his daughters, even if incapable of enlarging the mind of his wife."*

She's gone beyond mere mortification at seeing her family through Darcy's eyes; she's now realizing that the way he views them is the way they are—that this is how they would appear to anyone lacking prejudice. Hell, it's how the average dog would see them.

It's not an epiphany she can easily escape; with the regiment gone and Lydia with them, there are fewer distractions to occupy her mind in place of this awful new reality she's been forced to accommodate. And this is the bleak, itchy, oppressive place in which we now find ourselves. We're 200-plus pages into *Pride and Prejudice,* and so far from anything resembling romance (Jane and Bingley's hummingbird flutterings excepted), what we've had is a constant stream of bitter conflict, class anxiety, disappointed hopes, hideous confrontations, and an entire degustation menu of shrill social barbarisms. It's all been wildly funny, sure, and handled with astonishing deftness, but that doesn't alter the fact that it's been pretty salty stuff. Rather than the dainty drawing-room woodcuts most publishers choose to illustrate their editions, the novel would be better served by something closer to the engravings of William Hogarth, with their anarchic groupings of wastrels and grotesques.

What Lizzy—and we—now need is an escape; a clean break, to put all this obloquy in perspective. Fortunately, the time of her expedition to the lakes with Aunt and Uncle Gardiner is fast approaching, and she's so worked up for this long-anticipated getaway that she can barely sit still. Come the day of the departure, if the Gardiners' coach doesn't carry her from Longbourn fast enough, she may just leap out and run on ahead.

Then bad news arrives: Mr. Gardiner's business will delay their setting out for another two weeks, which won't allow them sufficient time to travel all the way to the lakes. So instead they'll be taking a shorter tour, and go no farther northward than Derbyshire—which in Lizzy's mind is now synonymous with Pemberley. She momentarily balks; after the repercussions of her last snarling match with Darcy, she doesn't want to risk being found clomping around his home turf. "But surely," she thinks, "I may enter his county with impunity, and rob it of a few petrified spars without his perceiving me." Whereas in Kent, I'm pretty sure Lady Catherine has all the petrified spars numbered and catalogued.

The final few weeks at last run out and the party sets off on its journey. Austen, as little given to nature porn as she is to depictions of music, food, or finery, tosses off the travelers' initial experiences with a flick of her wrist:

> *It is not the object of this work to give a description of Derbyshire, nor of any of the remarkable places through which their route thither lay: Oxford, Blenheim, Warwick, Kenilworth, Birmingham, etc. are sufficiently known.*

And if you *don't* know them, she implies, that's *your* problem.

Lizzy's plan to give a wide berth to Pemberley, in the manner of a reconnaissance scout skirting an enemy camp, doesn't work, because the lure of the great house is like the pull of the moon on the tides, and the Gardiners see no reason to resist it. "My love, should you not like to see a place of which you have heard so much?" Mrs. Gardiner asks, quite reasonably.

Lizzy, who would rather be caught dead, naked, and with a gimp mask zipped over her face than be discovered gamboling about the grounds of Pemberley, tries to fast-talk her way out of this scheme, by saying how tired she is of great houses, and of staring at fine carpets and satin curtains, and anyway her feet hurt, and also she has nothing to wear, and look isn't it going to rain, and oh yes she thinks she has leprosy.

But the Gardiners overrule her since she's just being silly, and besides who's paying? So Lizzy's only recourse is to pray to the sweet lord baby Jesus that you-know-who isn't home at the moment. And when they check into an inn for the night, she in fact learns from a chambermaid that the family is *not* currently in residence. So fine, then, she's safe.

Except, of course, she's not safe at all. She doesn't know it yet, but we do. We can feel it coming...and it's too big to hold back. Ladies and gentlemen, prepare yourself, for at long last *Pride and Prejudice* is about to go capital-R romance, as the passions that have been simmering beneath the surface at last bubble up into bright, ecstatic, bodice-heaving love at first sight. And here's the moment it happens:

> *It was a large, handsome, stone building, standing well on rising ground, and backed by a ridge of high woody hills; and in front, a stream of some natural importance was swelled into greater, but without any artificial appearance. Its banks were neither formal nor falsely adorned. Elizabeth was delighted. She had never seen a place for which nature had done more, or where natural beauty had been so little counteracted by an awkward taste. They were all of them warm in their admiration; and at that moment she felt that to be mistress of Pemberley might be something!*

From this moment on, Lizzy's heart is utterly lost. This isn't to say she's not still our prickly, practical Lizbot; she'll try to resist this epic ravishment, even as she succumbs to the glories of Pemberley's interiors, which are "neither gaudy nor uselessly fine; with less of splendor, and more of real elegance, than the furniture of Rosings."

> *"And of this place," thought she, "I might have been mistress! With these rooms, I might now have been familiarly acquainted! Instead of viewing them as a stranger, I might have rejoiced in them as my own, and welcomed to them as visitors my uncle and aunt.—But no"—recollecting herself—"that could never be: my uncle and aunt would have been lost to me: I should not have been allowed to invite them."*
>
> *This was a lucky recollection—it saved her from something like regret.*

In other words, Pemberley's flawlessness is countered by the failings of its owner. She won't allow herself to regret the former if having it would've meant enduring the latter. And yet as the housekeeper, Mrs. Reynolds ("a respectable-looking, elderly woman, much less fine, and more civil, than [Lizzy] had any notion of finding her") leads her and the Gardiners through the house, Lizzy is astonished to hear her extol the virtues of her master: Mr. Darcy is so handsome, Mr. Darcy is so generous, Mr. Darcy is the most attentive brother, Mr. Darcy is the kindest landlord, Mr. Darcy can kill a lion with his bare hands, Mr. Darcy can dance the tarantella with a rose between his teeth.

And when Mrs. Reynolds learns that Lizzy is acquainted with him, her respect for her visibly increases, as though having been in Darcy's ennobling presence is enough to confer honor on any mere mortal. Possibly she believes his actual touch might cure scrofula, or banish male pattern baldness.

Lizzy reels from all this exaltation of Darcy; her own feelings for him have, of course, lately been softening, but this is too much, too soon. Like a passenger on a wave-tossed ship, she tries to keep her balance by grasping the railing of her skepticism; and she has one magnificently snarky moment, when Mr. Gardiner asks the housekeeper whether her master is much at home during the course of the year.

> *"Not so much as I could wish, sir; but I dare say he may spend half his time here; and Miss Darcy is always down for the summer months."*
>
> *"Except," thought Elizabeth, "when she goes to Ramsgate."*

All right, so she thinks it, rather than says it aloud; but then neither Aunt nor Uncle Gardiner knows the story of Georgiana's elopement, and possibly Mrs. Reynolds doesn't either. So she's the only one who can really appreciate her own vicious wit.

Then Mr. Gardiner speculates that if Mr. Darcy were to marry, Mrs. Reynolds might see more of him, and the housekeeper replies, "Yes, sir; but I do not know when *that* will be. I do not know who is good enough for him." It's like she's just read Lizzy's mind; she might as well shoot her a look that says, *Sure as hell not you, trash mouth.* A few minutes later, she adds, "I have never had a cross word from him in my life, and I have known him since he was four years old." And later, "I have always observed that they who are good-natured when children, are good-natured when they grow up; and he was always the sweetest-tempered, most generous-hearted boy in the world." It's like she's deliberately saying things to make Lizzy's head swivel around, Linda Blair-style.

> *"Some people call him proud; but I am sure I never saw anything of it. To my fancy, it is only because he does not rattle away like other young men."*

By this point Lizzy is feeling the need for some fresh air, and possibly a restorative bloodletting. Mrs. Reynolds hands them over to the gardener, who takes them out onto the grounds, where Lizzy, straying a little afield of the others, runs smack dab into Darcy. Well, of course she does. Mrs. Reynolds's lofty testimonial has served, in dramatic terms, as nothing more than an introduction—designed to whet the audience's appetite while he waits, just offstage, straightening his collar and checking his teeth, for the moment when he can stride out to our riotous acclaim.

Though in actuality his entrance proves to be a quiet moment. Austen masterfully subverts our expectations by relating the encounter in so breezy a manner that if we're skimming, we might just miss it:

> *As they walked across the lawn towards the river, Elizabeth turned back to look again; her uncle and aunt stopped also, and while the former was conjecturing as to the date of the building, the owner of it himself suddenly came forward from the road, which led behind it to the stables.*

As you can imagine, there's a lot of abashment over the next page and a half, with bouts of blushing and eyes darting hither and thither for avenues of escape, and stammered courtesies and fervent wishes for a face-saving brain aneurysm. Lizzy in particular is hugely embarrassed, being well aware of "the impropriety of being found there," and his continued civility makes it worse by the moment. Eventually, their ingenuity fails them and they just stand silently gawping at each other, till Darcy gives up the game and leaves.

The Gardiners, who have observed all this, rejoin Lizzy and ask if *that* was Mr. Darcy, though of course they know it was because they've just been paraded before five hundred separate portraits of him. And it's just as well the question is rhetorical, because Lizzy can't speak to answer it. She's writhing under the horror of having been found here, and is half mad with the idea that Darcy might think she's deliberately thrown herself in his path again. She wouldn't have blamed him if he'd erupted in indignation and kicked her sorry ass to the curb.

But...he didn't. In fact, he was more courteous than she's ever known him before.

It's definitely Confuse-A-Lizzy Day here in Derbyshire. If she saw a cat chasing a dog, or rain falling upwards, it couldn't disorient her any more than she already is. Her only wish is to hitch up her skirt and hightail it outta here, but the only realistic means of retreat is the Gardiners' carriage, and they aren't ready to go yet. Mr. Gardiner still has E tickets in his booklet and he's not budging till he's used them. Accordingly they set off on a long walk by the side of the lake, which leads them to all sorts of wonderful vistas that make the Gardiners ooh and aah and go lookee-lookee, but whatever these sights might be—a giant water slide, seals juggling hoops, hedges clipped to form scenes from the Kama Sutra—we'll never know, because Lizzy isn't paying attention. "Her thoughts were all fixed on that one spot of Pemberley House, whichever it might be, where Mr. Darcy then was. She longed to know what at that moment was passing in his mind, in what manner he thought of her, and whether, in defiance of everything, she was still dear to him."

Notice, please, how infinitely more attractive he suddenly is to her, now that she can imagine him *in that house.* I'm not blaming her. I mean, she's not entirely mercenary; he *has* been working his way under her skin lately, and just now, in really excruciating circumstances, his behavior was downright princely. But in terms of Lizzy giving way to his love for her, it's very much a matter of "You had me at six hundred acres." In this, she's echoing her creator's prejudices; as I've noted before, Austen is indifferent to fashion, music, religion, and food; but she's decidedly partial to male buffitude, and flat-out bonkers for real estate. Suddenly, Darcy is looking *so* all that.

And here he comes again, striding across the grounds, having had plenty of time to recover his wits, given that Mrs. Gardiner walks at a pace that makes the average glacier seem full of pep. (Fortunately Darcy diverts them from their present course, because by the time Mrs. Gardiner finished circumnavigating the lake, Victoria would be queen.) Darcy asks Lizzy to be introduced to her companions, which surprises her—and amuses her too, because he's now actually *asking* to become acquainted with the kind of people he's previously disdained. After making the introduction (something along the lines of, "This is my Uncle Gardiner, who has a house in Cheapside in full view of his warehouses") she watches to see how long it takes before he realizes his mistake and bolts. But whaddaya know:

> *That he was surprised by the connexion was evident; he sustained it however with fortitude, and so far from going away, turned back with them and entered into conversation with Mr. Gardiner. Elizabeth could not but be pleased, could not but triumph. It was consoling that he should know she had some relations for whom there was no need to blush.*

So there's progress made on both sides. Lizzy has now seen Darcy behave in a way that perfectly accords with his housekeeper's golden boasts about him; and Darcy has seen that Lizzy does not come from stock entirely tainted by the curse of the werewolf. In fact, the Gardiners charm him so effortlessly that he offers Mr. Gardiner, an avid fisherman, the use of his lake, and even throws in the loan of some first-rate fishing tackle.

Eventually Mrs. Gardiner, who's been leaning on Lizzy's arm, finds she needs greater support to continue—we're beginning to get the idea that Mrs. G is about the size of Pemberley itself—and so swaps Lizzy for her husband. This leaves Lizzy and Darcy to pair off, and gives them a chance to speak privately—very privately, as they presumably leave the older couple behind, with Mr. Gardiner trying to propel forward a wife who by this point might as well be slogging through quicksand.

Lizzy seizes the opportunity to tell Darcy they'd been assured of his absence or she'd never have trespassed on his home. Darcy explains he came back several hours earlier than anticipated, and that the rest of his party will follow the next day—and that Mr. Bingley and his sisters will be among them.

> *"There is also one other person in the party," he continued after a pause, "who more particularly wishes to be known to you—will you allow me, or do I ask too much, to introduce my sister to your acquaintance during your stay at Lambton?"*

I think here, right here, is where the Cult of Darcy comes screaming to life. Granted, it's a wonderful, heart-in-your-mouth moment, and it suckers you right in on a number of levels; on the other hand, it sets the bar for Perfect Boyfriend Material so spectacularly high that many women have never been able to be content with their own comparatively tepid lot—and in fact it has so completely deranged the present generation that they seem to exist in a state of perpetual and permanent aggrievement. It also, paradoxically, altered the mechanics of seduction. Prior to *Pride and Prejudice*, men who wished to woo women climbed walls or fought duels or tamed bulls or set sail for Troy; afterwards, they just asked if they could introduce their sisters. I do not say this without some regret. We have had to suffer many serious social and cultural repercussions because of this realignment, including the entire career of Jennifer Aniston.

Lizzy will of course be glad to meet Miss Darcy, and the visit concludes happily, with everyone won over by everyone else; though Mrs. Gardiner can't reconcile this nice Mr. Darcy with the villain who caused so much harm to poor Wickham. Lizzy is forced to hint, broadly, that not everything they've heard of Wickham's lamentable history can be completely trusted; and while Mrs. Gardiner is tempted to press her for the skinny on *that*, they find themselves suddenly in her old neck of the woods, and she's distracted by a cavalcade of memories, and by pointing out the sites of her girlhood, such as the shrubbery she used to make a circuit around for exercise when she had an hour or two to spare.

Lizzy naturally expects that Darcy will bring Georgiana to call the day after the girl returns to Pemberley; but in fact they show up the morning before that, which pretty much means Darcy must have allowed her about ninety seconds to drop her bags and splash some water on her face before hustling her off to Lambton. It's as though he fears Lizzy might change her mind and hop a freight train out of town before he can get the two women together.

His arrival, all but gasping for breath, and trailing Georgiana, who may well have lost a shoe along the way, makes a pretty strong impression on the Gardiners, who may be slow, but they ain't stupid. They look at Darcy, as he presents his sister to Lizzy like a Christmas present, and then at Lizzy, who is "amazed at her own discomposure" and totally showing it, and think, *Ohhhh.* Suddenly everything makes sense.

Georgiana Darcy is basically Anne De Bourgh; they're both timid, tentative, and insecure, and take refuge in silence because of it, leading people to presume them proud. The difference is, Georgiana has a brother who tries gently to prod her into putting herself forward, while Miss De Bourgh has a mother more than willing to do all her talking (and thinking) for her. Yet Lizzy takes to Georgiana instantly, in a way she never took to Anne at all, and you wonder about that till you read that "Elizabeth, who had expected to find in her as acute and unembarrassed an observer as Mr. Darcy had been, was much relieved by discerning such different feelings." Basically, she's just happy to be getting a free pass.

And then who should bound up the stairs but Mr. Bingley, apparently just now catching up with the Indy 500 Darcys. At the sight of him, all of Lizzy's anger dissolves, the way you can't stay mad at a big fluffy puppy even though he's wee'd all over your rug. Bingley is plainly dying for news of Jane, but can't bring himself to flout the laws of propriety by asking about her directly, and is thus reduced to peppering Lizzy with earnest questions about the welfare of all her relations, all her very *nearest* relations, all those with whom she might perhaps, oh, share a room, let's say, and whose initials might fall between I and K.

For her part, Lizzy is most interested in finally being able to observe Bingley and Georgiana in the same room together. Their complete indifference to each other convinces her that all of Caroline Bingley's endless prattle about the imminent "attachment" between them is, as is usually the case with Caroline, a big, fat, skankalicious lie. In fact Bingley seems more acutely aware of the absent Jane than of the present Georgiana; at one point he remarks to Lizzy that it's been a very long time since they've met, adding that, "It is above eight months. We have not met since the 26th of November, when we were all dancing together at Netherfield." This is veering dangerously towards the sentimental, but because it's Bingley—and because it's Austen—it comes off fine.

But the real revelation of the visit is Darcy, whose behavior continues to knock Lizzy flat on her tuckus.

> *Never, even in the company of his dear friends at Netherfield, or his dignified relations at Rosings, had she seen him so desirous to please, so free from self-consequence or unbending reserve as now, when no importance could result from the success of his endeavours, and when even the acquaintance of those to whom his attentions were addressed would draw down the ridicule and censure of the ladies both of Netherfield and Rosings.*

The visit ends with the Darcys inviting the Gardiners and Lizzy to dine at Pemberley. The Gardiners have now come full circle; they're total Darcy fans. If there were a gift shop at Pemberley, they'd go back and buy coffee mugs with his face on them. Lizzy, however, while very pleased with how well the visit went, is slightly more confused about her own feelings. She no longer hates him; but it takes her a while to pin down what she *does* feel for him.

> *She respected, she esteemed, she was grateful to him, she felt a real interest in his welfare; and she only wanted to know how far she wished that welfare to depend upon herself, and how far it would be for the happiness of both that she should employ the power, which her fancy told her she still possessed, to bring on the renewal of his addresses.*

But practical matters bring her back down to earth. Now that Georgiana has called on them, she and Mrs. Gardiner are obliged return the favor. And since Mr. Gardiner has been invited to fish at Pemberley the very next morning, that seems like the ideal opportunity.

And who should they find, lying in wait for them there like the Siamese cats from *Lady and the Tramp,* but Caroline and her sister Mrs.

Hurst. They greet Lizzy and Mrs. Gardiner coldly, with a single grudging curtsey. Georgiana tries to rouse herself to give them a proper welcome, and doesn't entirely succeed, which makes you start wondering whether, after her elopement with Mr. Wickham, Darcy kept her locked in a trunk beneath the stairs for a few years. Come on, girl, *snap to it.* It's not like you've got a Cruise missile constantly trained on your ass, like Anne de Bourgh.

The conversation gets off to an awkward start, because Caroline and Mrs. Hurst refuse to speak, and Georgiana can't bear to; so Georgiana's governess and Mrs. Gardiner take the burden upon themselves. Though I'm willing to bet Caroline interjects a couple of barely audible "tch" noises every so often, and when they turn to look at her she's all, What? I didn't say anything.

But alas, Caroline's campaign of icy inertia, which is doing a pretty fair job of making everyone within a quarter-mile feel the depths of her contempt, doesn't last. Darcy, who's heard of the ladies' arrival, has left the fishing party and returned to the house to give Georgiana some moral support. At the sight of him—and at the sudden static-electric charge that crackles across the room between him and Lizzy—Caroline can't help herself: she drops her strategy of victory-through-frostbite and switches to full-on Flame Queen; as if she might, with enough vitriol, be able to burn Lizzy down to slag right before Darcy's eyes.

She begins by loudly asking, "Pray, Miss Eliza, are not the ——shire militia removed from Meryton? They must be a great loss to *your* family." She's talking specifically about Wickham, and almost everyone in the room knows it; unfortunately, Caroline herself doesn't know that invoking Wickham is the surest way to distress Georgiana and infuriate Darcy. As ever, when Caroline throws a punch, it lands squarely on her own kisser.

Lizzy notices the profound effect Caroline's remark has had on Darcy and Georgiana—the latter of whom is now so upset she can't speak for the rest of the visit, and possibly the rest of the novel. But Caroline herself remains blithely ignorant of it, so much so that after Lizzy and Mrs. Gardiner have gone she dives right in again, crowing, "How very ill Eliza Bennet looks this morning, Mr. Darcy," and then commences a rundown of her many imperfections:

> *"Her face is too thin; her complexion has no brilliancy; and her features are not at all handsome. Her nose wants character; there is nothing marked in its lines. Her teeth are tolerable, but not out of the common way; and as for her eyes, which have sometimes been called so fine, I never could perceive anything extraordinary in them. They have a sharp, shrewish look, which I do not like at all; and in her air altogether, there is a self-sufficiency without fashion, which is intolerable."*

This machine-gun spray of bitchery provokes Darcy into protesting that "it is many months since I have considered her as one of the handsomest women of my acquaintance," after which he storms out; and, Austen tells us, "Miss Bingley was left to all the satisfaction of having forced him to say what gave no one any pain but herself."

Mrs. Gardiner and Lizzy ride back to Lambton avidly discussing everyone they've just seen *except* Mr. Darcy, all the while being acutely aware of exactly why they aren't discussing him. It's all very coy and cozy, and everything seems to be falling into place so neatly, that you venture to think, Okay, fine, I can see where this is headed. Is that, like, *it*, man?

No, that's not it. Because this is where Austen takes out a big ol' sledgehammer and smashes her little porcelain doll's house to smithereens.

CHAPTERS 46-49

"Lydia, oh Lydia, at risk of chlamydia / Lydia the SCAAAR-let lady / Any officer to offer / She'll let climb both on and off 'er"

Heh. I just now made that up. Apologies to the immortal Groucho.

And apologies to Lydia as well, because she's really not *that* free with her favors. Though she's not likely to be held up as a model of maidenly virtue anytime soon—as we, and her older sister, are about to find out.

Lizzy's still in Lambton with Aunt and Uncle Gardiner, and still looking forward to the promised dinner party at Pemberley, when two letters from Jane arrive for her simultaneously, "on one of which was marked that it had been missent elsewhere. Elizabeth was not surprised at it, as Jane had written the direction remarkably ill." Personally, I get the impression Jane writes as a rule with her tongue wrapped around her cheek. But we'll soon be marveling that under the circumstances, the girl could hold a pen at all.

Lizzy, left by the Gardiners to read the missives in private, begins by opening the earlier one first. It's from five days before, and seems initially to contain nothing remarkable—"an account of all their little parties and engagements, with such news as the country afforded"—whose horse kicked whose wife, how many times Kitty coughed, that kind of thing—but its latter portion, dated a day later, contains some startling news about You Know Who.

An express came at twelve last night, just as we were all gone to bed, from Colonel Forster to inform us that she was gone off to Scotland with one of his officers; to own the truth of it, with Wickham!—Imagine our surprise...So imprudent a match on both sides!...His choice is disinterested at least, for he must know my father can give her nothing.

Jane's inferring that the couple mean to marry (hence the reference to Scotland, whose village Gretna Green was a sort of no-questions-asked wedding capital—a Regency Las Vegas). But Lizzy, being of a more pragmatic bent, must have her suspicions, for as soon as she's finished with this first letter she "instantly seized the other," and for all we know rips it open with her teeth.

Its contents bear out her worst fears. "Imprudent as a marriage between Wickham and our poor Lydia would be," Jane writes, "we are now anxious to be assured it has taken place, for there is but too much reason to fear they are not gone to Scotland." Colonel Forster has tracked the pair's movements; the last sighting of them was on the road to London. Jane, ever the idiot—excuse me, optimist—continues:

My father and mother believe the worst, but I cannot think so ill of him. Many circumstances might make it more eligible for them to be married privately in town than to pursue their first plan; and even if he could form such a design against a young woman of Lydia's connections, which is not likely, can I suppose her so lost to everything?

Ahem. Have you met her...?

I shouldn't really be so hard on Jane; as a 21st century urban male, I have greater familiarity than a 19th century provincial virgin with the extreme lengths to which a hot-blooded young buck will go to satisfy his lust. Though I also know that even the most unregenerate lothario will have a sense of when it's really just not worth it anymore. And, I mean, we all know what a carriage ride with Lydia is like. Imagine one from Brighton to London. I'm willing to bet that somewhere around the halfway point, Wickham was wishing he'd just stayed in camp and banged a slattern for a shilling, already.

Jane concludes by wishing Lizzy back at Longbourn—and not only Lizzy:

> *My father is going to London with Colonel Forster instantly to try to discover her. What he means to do I am sure I know not; but his excessive distress will not allow him to pursue any measure in the best and safest way, and Colonel Forster is obliged to be at Brighton again to-morrow evening.*

In other words, Mr. Bennet might challenge Wickham to a duel, and when Colonel Forster is gone there won't be anyone to prevent him. So Uncle Gardiner is urgently needed.

The idea of Mr. Bennet and Wickham taking up arms against each other isn't an outlandish one; it's the way gentlemen resolved affronts to their honor back in those wild and wacky days—and in fact, in Austen's previous novel, you'll remember, it's revealed that Colonel Brandon and Mr. Willoughby, for very similar reasons, fought a duel; though in that instance neither was harmed. I guess they were both lousy shots.

By this time, Lizzy's worked herself into a frenzy of anxiety. She hurls herself towards the door with the intention of chasing down Mr. Gardiner, when her way is blocked by a servant admitting...Mr. Darcy. (Well, really—from a dramatic point of view, who else could it be? Lady Lucas? The Prince Regent? Lord Nelson and the crew of the HMS Elephant?) Seeing her in such obvious distress, he says, "Good God! what is the matter?" In Austen, it's always a sign that things are way, way busted when a gentleman invokes the Man Upstairs.

Fortunately, he then collects himself, and persuades Lizzy to send a servant after Mr. Gardiner—perhaps sensing that if allowed to continue the errand herself, she'd end up running headlong down the main street, tearing at her hair like Anna Magnani in some Italian neorealist film. With the servant thus directed (and may I once again note how, in Austen, the servant class are, with very, very rare exceptions, nameless, faceless, and voiceless? Modern though her sensibility may be in many respects, democratic or egalitarian it decidedly is not), Lizzy collapses into a chair. She confesses to Darcy that she isn't ill, just the recipient of some dreadful news from Longbourn, and then bursts into tears.

We don't often witness an Austen heroine losing control to such an extent; and what makes this particular instance even more cringeworthy, is the awareness of whom she's losing that control before. True, we've seen Darcy relax his stringent rectitude over the past few chapters, but that's been due to his growing admiration for Lizzy's steadiness of character and independence of mind. To see her reduced to blubbering helplessness...who's to say that this spectacle won't snap him right back to his former state of lofty douchebaggery? Already he's becoming more coolly formal, even as Lizzy reveals to him what's happened—and who's responsible.

> *"When I consider," she added, in a yet more agitated voice, "that I might have prevented it!—I who knew what he was. Had I but explained some part of it only—some part of what I learned to my own family! Had his character been known, this could not have happened. But it is all, all too late now."*

Darcy, of course, is the source of her knowledge of Wickham's true character, and it was his insistence upon confidentiality that prevented her from warning her family about him. So we can see his continued solicitude as stemming, in part, from a case of the guilts. But his manner is increasingly hands-off, and Lizzy soon notices. "He seemed scarcely to hear her, and was walking up and down the room in earnest meditation, his brow contracted, his air gloomy. Her power was sinking; everything must sink under such a proof of family weakness, such an assurance of the deepest disgrace."

And of course, it's at this worst of all possible junctures, that she finally sees her own wishes clearly; and "never had she so honestly felt that could have loved him as now, when all love must be in vain."

He soon takes his leave, and with such hilarious formality that his parting words are "This unfortunate affair will, I fear, prevent my sister's having the pleasure of seeing you at Pemberley to-day," as though the problem were a bad sprain or the sudden onset of trench foot. When he's gone, Lizzy allows herself the luxury of a few moments to throw "a retrospective glance over the whole of their acquaintance, so full of contradictions and varieties," and she "sighed at the perverseness of those feelings which would now have promoted its continuance, and would formerly have rejoiced in its termination." This is pretty nakedly valedictory; we're not left with any doubt that she expects never to see him again. She's no fool. She knows that in his mind she's now, by association, tainted goods.

The Gardiners burst back into the room, no doubt expecting to find Lizzy beset by wolves, or standing with a bloodied axe over the corpse of Caroline Bingley. When Lizzy tells them what's really gone down, they rise to the occasion, gearing up for an immediate departure—despite, we're told, Lydia having "never been a favourite with them".

On the journey back to Longbourn, the Gardiners have some second thoughts about the necessity of so much haste and anguish. Mr. Gardiner in particular succumbs to an almost Jane-level attack of Pollyannaitis.

> *"It appears to me so very unlikely that any young man should form such a design against a girl who is by no means unprotected and friendless, and who was actually staying in his colonel's family, that I am strongly inclined to hope the best. Could he expect that her friends would not step forward? Could he expect to be noticed again by the regiment, after such an affront to Colonel Forster? His temptation is not adequate to the risk."*

Lizzy openly scoffs. She asks why, if it's all so honest and above board, there's such furtiveness, such secrecy?...And then she reminds them that Wickham literally cannot afford to wed a woman who doesn't have at least *some* money. Lydia's charms, such as they are, are scarcely of the caliber to make him forget that. As for his reputation among the regiment...who knows how they would view these things? They're *soldiers*, after all, not the College of Cardinals. And as for fear of retribution from Lydia's "friends," Lizzy reminds them:

> *"Lydia has no brothers to step forward; and [Wickham] might imagine, from my father's behaviour, from his indolence and the little attention he has ever seemed to give what was going forward in his family, that* he *would do as little, and think as little about it, as any father could do in such a matter."*

Whoa. *Harsh*, chiquita.

Mr. Gardiner then asks, "But can you think that Lydia is so lost to everything but love of him as to consent to live with him on any other terms than marriage?" Which again makes you want to say, Hel-LO... Lydia Bennet?...Ya *think?*

Ceding this point, the Gardiners switch back to consideration of Wickham. Could *he* really be so awful? Lizzy, no longer in any mood to grant anyone the benefit of the doubt, lays it out flat: "We both know that he has been profligate in every sense of the word. That he has neither integrity nor honour. That he is as false and deceitful as he is insinuating." And he has bad posture and hairy ears and his penmanship is *vile*. The. Man. Is. A. Dog.

Not daring to contradict her, the Gardiners then wonder at Lizzy not having warned Lydia about him before she went to Brighton; and Lizzy excuses herself by swearing she can recall no hint of anything resembling affection, or even of interest, between the two; "and had anything of the kind been perceptible, you must be aware that ours is not a family on which it could be thrown away." Oh hell no. Mrs. Bennet alone would have made such a meal of it that the bones would still be worth gnawing on twenty years after the fact.

The carriage pulls up at Longbourn, and when the Gardiner children, who have gathered on the doorstep, see who it is, a joyful surprise "lighted up their faces, and displayed itself over their whole bodies in a variety of capers and frisks". I include this just because I love the image so much. Also, Capers and Frisks would be an excellent name for a high-end cat food.

Lizzy runs into the house and reunites with Jane, who's the only one on hand to greet her. Mr. Bennet's gone off to London, Mary is in her room studying, Kitty is in *her* room coughing, and Mrs. Bennet is in her room, from which she now never ventures, languishing. Her nerves, we're repeatedly told, are so traumatized that she is unable to "exert herself," which affliction almost certainly does not include her mouth.

And sure enough, when Lizzy and the Gardiners are brought before her, she launches into "tears and lamentations of regret, invectives against the villainous conduct of Wickham, and complaints of her own sufferings and ill-usage; blaming everybody but the person to whose ill-judging indulgence the errors of her daughter must be principally owing." This is followed by a rant against the careless Forsters; a presentiment that Mr. Bennet will be killed in a duel and the family summarily kicked out of Longbourn by the rapacious Collinses; and shrill insistence that Lydia and Wickham be *made* to marry as soon as they are discovered. Mr. Gardiner does his best to soothe her, but she keeps heaping him with instructions on how to conduct his time in London, concluding with:

> *"And above all things, keep Mr. Bennet from fighting. Tell him what a dreadful state I am in—that I am frightened out of my very wits; and have such tremblings, such flutterings, all over me, such spasms in my side, and pains in my head, and such beatings at heart, that I can get no rest by night nor by day. And tell my dear Lydia not to give any directions about her clothes till she has seen me, for she does not know which are the best warehouses."*

It's a comic tour de force. Again, I say it's a shame Austen never wrote for the stage; imagine how a decent character actress could turn a speech like this into a bravura set piece, and have the audience collectively falling into the aisles.

Though she'd have some pretty decent competition when Mary took the stage afterwards, as she does here, creeping up to Lizzy and with spectacular smugness whispering in her ear:

> *"Unhappy as the event must be for Lydia, we may draw from it this useful lesson: that loss of virtue in a female is irretrievable—that one false step involves her in endless ruin—that her reputation is no less brittle than it is beautiful—and that she cannot be too much guarded in her behaviour towards the undeserving of the other sex."*

Mary can of course speak with absolute authority on this matter, because she's not likely ever to make a similar mistake. After all, in order to misbehave with the undeserving of the other sex, the other sex has to come within nine yards of you. Girl is *safe*.

A little later, Jane shows Lizzy a letter that Colonel Forster brought them, written by Lydia to his wife to announce her elopement. It's a pretty hilarious piece of work in itself:

> *You need not send them word at Longbourn of my going, if you do not like it, for it will make the surprise the greater when I write to them, and sign my name Lydia Wickham. What a good joke it will be! I can hardly write for laughing. Pray make my excuses to Pratt, for not keeping my engagement and dancing with him tonight. Tell him I hope he will*

> *excuse me when he knows all, and tell him I will dance with him at the next ball we meet, with great pleasure.*

In other words, elopement and marriage are in her mind only a brief hiatus from the hard work of flirting.

Lizzy pities Jane for having had to endure all this ignominy alone, and with a hysterical mother to care for on top of it all. Jane, with the serene stoicism of an autoflagellant saint, protests that she's had plenty of help; Aunt Philips has come by for a few days to sit with Mrs. Bennet, and after she left Lady Lucas came to commiserate with them. Lizzy is appalled by the latter:

> *"She had better have stayed at home...perhaps she meant well, but under such a misfortune as this, one cannot see too little of one's neighbours. Assistance is impossible; condolence, insufferable. Let them triumph over us at a distance, and be satisfied."*

It's right about here that we begin to worry, just a little, about Lizzy. She's starting to sound almost as hard-hearted as Lady Catherine. How soon before, on hearing one more of Jane's airy platitudes, she takes her by the back of her hair and shoves her face-first into a wall...?

Mr. Gardiner sets out for London, but Aunt Gardiner stays behind to help look after Mrs. Bennet. I'm not certain why Mrs. Bennet requires so very much looking after, since she doesn't do anything except lie on her couch all day reciting her litany of woes, but I've noticed that in some families this phenomenon does indeed occur: one completely inert member can be the cause of furious activity in all the others. It's a paradox. And Mrs. Gardiner isn't the only one outside the immediate clan called into service, either:

> *Their other aunt also visited them frequently, and always, as she said, with the design of cheering and heartening them up, though as she never came without reporting some fresh instance of Wickham's extravagance or irregularity, she seldom went away without leaving them more dispirited than she found them.*

In fact all of Meryton is now in active competition to vilify Wickham's name. "He was declared to be in debt to every tradesman in the place, and his intrigues, all honoured with the title of seduction, had been extended into every tradesman's family." And of course everyone who was hiking up their skirts at the sight of him three months ago, now boasts that they'd seen through him all along. Austen reports this gleefully, having no illusions about human nature.

Word of Lydia's fall from grace spreads, and perhaps inevitably there comes a letter (a very *long* letter) from Mr. Collins, which Jane (having been granted permission) opens in her father's absence. It's so full of fatuity and pomposity that really, we can't help missing the big oaf. Its most famous sentiment is, "The death of your daughter would have been a blessing in comparison to this," but the entire text is filled with gasp-inducing delights:

> *...[Y]ou are to be grievously pitied, in which opinion I am not only joined by Mrs. Collins, but likewise by Lady Catherine and her daughter, to whom I have related the affair. They agree with me in apprehending that this false step in one daughter will be injurious to the fortunes of all the others, for who, as Lady Catherine herself condescendingly says, will connect themselves with such a family. And this consideration leads me moreover to reflect with augmented satisfaction on a certain event of last November, for had it been otherwise, I must have been involved in all your sorrow and disgrace.*

Having quite merrily kicked Mr. Bennet while he's down, Mr. Collins now, in his professional capacity, offers him the benefit of his Christian counsel: "Let me advise you, then, my dear sir...to throw off your unworthy child from your affection forever, and leave her to reap the fruits of her own heinous offence." No illusions about the clerical class either, not our J.A.

Once in London, Mr. Gardiner persuades Mr. Bennet to return home; and when this news is conveyed to his wife, who might reasonably be thought to rejoice in it, we get this instead: "What, he is coming home, and without poor Lydia!...Sure he will not leave London before he has found them. Who is to fight Wickham, and make him marry her, if he comes away?"

But come home he does, his shoulders stooped by the weight of his self-reproach. When Lizzy urges him not to be so severe on himself, he redeems himself in our eyes by refusing to consider it: "No, Lizzy, let me once in my life feel how much I have been to blame. I am not afraid of being overpowered by the impression. It will pass away soon enough." This is the kind of subtlety that has earned Austen the honorific of genius; Mr. Bennet, a comic figure, becomes a tragic one before our eyes—because he knows only too well the failings of his own character.

But he still has his old Attic salt, as he proves when Kitty ventures to protest that if *she* were sent to Brighton she'd behave better than Lydia, which launches him into such a salvo of uproarious abuse that Kitty is reduced to tears—and he to uncharacteristic penitence.

> *"Well, well," said he, "do not make yourself unhappy. If you are a good girl for the next ten years, I will take you to a review at the end of them."*

What happens next is a remarkable thing, something that scarcely ever occurs in Austen: a servant speaks—and not only speaks, but is given a name. Hill, the housekeeper, informs Lizzy and Jane that their father has received a letter from Mr. Gardiner. The sisters run off, once again consigning Hill to off-the-page oblivion, her moment in the spotlight over almost before it began.

They find Mr. Bennet out on the grounds looking very concerned. The letter, he tells them, brings good news; Lydia and Wickham are discovered, and though they aren't married ("nor can I find there was any intention of being so," Mr. Gardiner adds), such an arrangement can be made with the simple guarantee of Mr. Bennet settling a small income on Lydia. Jane, of course, is in transports of delight over how well everything has worked out, just as she always knew it would, and she frolics off to sing happy songs and weave daisies into her hair and with any luck fall into a shallow pool and expire. Meanwhile Mr. Bennet confesses his conviction that Mr. Gardiner has taken it upon himself to settle Wickham's massive debts. It's the only possible explanation. "Wickham's a fool if he takes her for a farthing less than ten thousand pounds," he says. "I should be sorry to think so ill of him in the very beginning of our relationship." And thus the reason for Mr. Bennet's consternation: he finds himself suddenly shouldering a crippling obligation to his brother-in-law—one that he can't possibly ever repay.

As he staggers off, a nearly broken man, Jane comes cavorting back, bluebirds circling her head, and enthuses about the new couple:

> *"Their mutual affection will steady them; and I flatter myself they will settle so quietly and live in so rational a manner as may in time make their past imprudence forgotten."*
>
> *"Their conduct has been such," replied Elizabeth, "as neither you, nor I, nor anybody, can ever forget. It is useless to talk of it."*

Word up, Lizbot.

But if Jane's allowed the news to go to her head, Mrs. Bennet lets it go to her feet. Self-exiled to her room during the ordeal, she can now scarcely be contained by the house itself—she longs to go capering off to Meryton to broadcast the news. "She was now in an irritation as violent from delight as she had ever been fidgety from alarm and vexation. To know that her daughter would be married was enough. She was disturbed by no fear for her felicity, nor humbled by any remembrance of her misconduct." Clearly her brain features a rudimentary Click-Undo function, which she is depressing every few seconds, with all the fervor of a hamster in a lab trial.

To bring her to her senses, Jane (yes, *Jane*—Mrs. B. is so far gone that her bliss-ninny eldest daughter is by comparison a pillar of pragmatism) explains that they owe this happy ending almost entirely to the generosity of her brother. But if Jane thinks that will chasten her, she's got another think coming.

> *"Well," cried her mother, "it is all very right; who should do it but her own uncle? If he had not had a family of his own, I and my children must have had all his money you know, and it is the first time we have ever had anything from him, except a few presents."*

And then she's off to the races again, babbling on about Lydia becoming Mrs. Wickham and trying to bolt past her daughters for the stairs. If she makes it to the front door, Mr. Bennet may have to bring her down with a tranq dart. Fortunately, Hill chooses this moment to wander in, perhaps to ask, Beg your pardon, but was that my only line?, and Mrs. Bennet actually addresses her like she's an actual human person: "My dear Hill, have you heard the good news? Miss Lydia is going to be married; and you shall all have a bowl of punch to make merry at her wedding."

But you'll have to drink it off in the margins somewhere, Hill. See, that really *was* your only line. Thank you; you may go now.

CHAPTERS 50-53

Now that Lydia's seduction by Wickham has been massaged from a potential tabloid-scale scandal into a juuust-barely-respectable marriage, Austen pauses to give us the reactions of the various members of the Bennet clan. She starts with the patriarch himself, who is awash in regret that he never "laid by an annual sum for the better provision of his children, and of his wife, if she survived him"—but he never dreamed he'd have to. As a hot young buck, he naturally thought he'd fire off a son or two, to inherit Longbourn and keep the family estate intact. How was he to know he had only X chromosomes in his ammo box...? Five daughters later, he sees the error of his ways. Had he only been prudent, "The satisfaction of prevailing on one of the most worthless young men in Great Britain to be [Lydia's] husband might then have rested in its proper place."

Austen is hard on Mr. B., but consistent. For instance, she tells us that, "When the first transports of rage which had produced his activity in seeking [Lydia] were over, he naturally returned to all his former indolence," wishing only "to have as little trouble in the business as possible"—which is exactly what he'd predicted to Lizzy he'd do, back when she urged him not to take the "business" too much to heart. The only lingering effect of his temporary growth of cojones is an intractable hardness of heart towards Lydia; he writes to Mr. Gardiner regarding the arrangements for the nuptials, but pointedly sends no word to his daughter. Bitch is *dead* to him.

Austen's psychological portrait of Mr. Bennet is an impressively nuanced one. Her portrayal of the townsfolk of Meryton is considerably broader, though equally credible. As word of Lydia and Wickham's impending marriage spreads, the residents, we're told, bear it "with decent philosophy."

> *To be sure it would have been more for the advantage of conversation had Miss Lydia Bennet come upon the town; or, as the happiest alternative, been secluded from the world in some distant farm-house. But there was much to be talked of in marrying her; and the good-natured wishes for her well-doing, which had proceeded before from all the spiteful old ladies in Meryton, lost but little of their spirit in this change of circumstances, because with such an husband, her misery was considered certain.*

No one but an unregenerate misanthrope could write such acid lines. Austen, the dear old winsome auntie of our ignorant age's popular imagining, was a goddamn nasty piece of work when she wanted to be. (This is not a criticism; it's when I like her best.)

As for Mrs. Bennet, she is, as ever, at the far extreme from her husband, thus maintaining the slightly wonky equilibrium of the Bennet household. She's the yin to his yang—or more accurately the whack to his doodle. In any case, we find her "in spirits oppressively high. No sentiment of shame gave a damp to her triumph." She's got both a daughter heading up the aisle, and a sudden case of amnesia about the five-car pile-up that delivered her there. Having long repined in her room upstairs, she now descends for the first time in weeks and rejoins the family at the table, where she gabbles on happily about where Lydia and Wickham might live, like a Century 21 broker thrown back into Century 19. "Haye-Park might do," she says, "if the Gouldings would quit it, or the great house at Stoke, if the drawing room were larger... and as for Purvis Lodge, the attics are dreadful." Mr. Bennet listens to all this with the serene composure of a cobra facing a mongoose, and when the servants depart the room he uncoils and attacks:

> *"Mrs. Bennet, before you take any, or all these houses, for your son and daughter, let us come to a right understanding. Into one house in this neighbourhood they shall never have admittance. I will not encourage the impudence of either by receiving them at Longbourn."*

We're told that a "long dispute" follows this declaration, and in the way of any long dispute that involves Mrs. Bennet, "it soon led to another." For she learns to her horror that the total sum her husband is allowing for Lydia's wedding clothes is exactly zero, zilch, zip, nil, nada. "She was more alive to the disgrace which the want of new clothes must reflect on her daughter's nuptials, than to any sense of shame at her eloping and living with Wickham a fortnight before they took place." She obviously feels that a good solid show of style can more than eradicate any defects in character or degeneracy of behavior, which makes her a spiritual sister to every drag queen who ever drew breath. (We never learn Mrs. Bennet's first name; possibly it's something all fierce and catwalk-y like Ashley, or Maxine, or Tina.)

As for Lizzy...she's got her own regrets to nurse. Now that the fallen Lydia has been dusted off and set on her feet again, she wishes to high holy hell she'd never mentioned the matter to Darcy. Not that she's worried he'll go blabbing it all over the forty-eight counties. "There were few people on whose secrecy she would have more confidently depended; but at the same time, there was no one whose knowledge of a sister's frailty would have mortified her so much." Of course, even if he'd never learned the particulars of Lydia's seduction, its outcome—her marriage to Wickham—would have been enough to put him off any further close encounters of the Lizzy kind.

And it's this sudden loss of Darcy's favor that really twists her innards into knots. "She was humbled, she was grieved; she repented, though she hardly knew of what. She became jealous of his esteem, when she could no longer hope to be benefited by it." Even worse, she imagines him now congratulating himself on having narrowly escaped the taint of marrying into the Bennet family for the second time—like someone who swung over a river filled with snapping alligators, then safely swung right back again. "He was generous, she doubted not, as the most generous of his sex. But while he was mortal, there must be a triumph." And all this occurs to her, just as she becomes fully aware for the first time that "he was exactly the man who, in disposition and talents, would most suit her. His understanding and temper, though unlike her own, would have answered all her wishes."

In other words, *Thanks for nothing, ass-wipe Lydia.* But she can't even work up a nice, shrill longing for revenge against her little sister, because she's only too aware that fate's already got that well in hand. After all, "how little of permanent happiness could belong to a couple who were only brought together because their passions were stronger than their virtue"?

In fact things seem to be going south for Lydia already—or rather, going north, because we now hear that Wickham is to quit the militia and take up an ensigncy much farther upcountry. This is Uncle Gardiner's design; he considers it best to get the two troublemakers as far from the scene of their shame as possible, before they go and do something even more appalling, like fighting in public, or taking lovers, or publishing volumes of verse.

Mrs. Bennet is, typically, as dismayed by Lydia's departure as she is tone-deaf to the cause of it. "She is so fond of Mrs. Forster...it will be quite shocking to send her away! And there are several of the young men, too, that she likes very much. The officers may not be so pleasant in General ———'s regiment." As ever, she has all the delicacy of feeling and subtlety of understanding of a rodeo clown.

But she scores on one front, at least: she persuades Jane and Elizabeth to argue for Lydia being accepted back at Longbourn before her departure, and the two elder sisters urge their father "so rationally and so mildly" (guess which does which) that he relents. Lydia and Wickham arrive after their wedding, with everyone except Mrs. Bennet dreading the initial meeting, since it's bound to be awkward and stilted, with shame and guilt eddying about them all like little radioactive whirlpools.

But they—and we—haven't taken into consideration the invincible cluelessness of Lydia. She strides into Longbourn like a queen post-coronation, dripping with condescension when she can manage to keep a straight face. As for Wickham, who follows her through the door, he's exactly as he ever was: breezy, charming, ready to unlace your pants and have them down around your ankles before you've even got past your hellos.

> *Elizabeth was disgusted; and even Miss Bennet was shocked. Lydia was Lydia still: untamed, unabashed, wild, noisy, and fearless. She turned from sister to sister, demanding their congratulations, and when at length they sat down, looked eagerly round the room, took notice of some little alteration in it, and observed, with a laugh, that it was a great while since she had been there.*

I should note that that single phrase—"from sister to sister"—serves to cover Kitty and Mary, who aren't even mentioned by name in this and the preceding chapter; Austen has all but forgotten about them, and who can blame her, what with Lydia rising up to consume the entire narrative, like a Hanoverian Lady Gaga:

> *"Oh! Mamma, do the people here abouts know I am married to-day? I was afraid they might not; and we overtook William Goulding in his curricle, so I was determined he should know it, and so I let down the side glass next to him, and took off my glove, and let my hand just rest upon the window frame, so that he might see the ring, and then I bowed and smiled like anything."*

Lydia rattles away continuously so that no one else has a chance to speak, which is just as well because no one else could bear to. Jane and Lizzy, as noted above, have basically swallowed their tongues in appalled disbelief, Mary and Kitty have apparently atomized themselves in mortification, and Mr. Bennet keeps staring at Lydia's head as though with sufficient mental energy he might burst it like a melon. Only Mrs. Bennet hangs on Lydia's every word and offers her eager encouragement to divulge every foliage-wilting detail. Not that Lydia requires encouragement; she's so completely self-involved that she'd put on the same performance for the family dog, or the porter, or her favorite chair. And in fact, she goes traipsing off after dinner "to show her ring and boast of being married to Mrs. Hill and the two housemaids," and it's left to us to wonder whether they fawn over her or whether they too regard her with astonished embarrassment; we'll never know because she'll never tell us, if in fact she even remembers any of what passes thirty seconds after turning her backs on them.

Lydia and Wickham are to stay at Longbourn ten days, and much is made of how very short a visit that is, though for those stuck in the house with them I can imagine it feels like ten millennia. Those of us reading about the ordeal, however, still manage to get a kick out of the sheer comic energy of Lydia's relentless self-dramatization. Cornering Lizzy, who till this moment has successfully avoided hearing a blow-by-blow account of the wedding day, Lydia proceeds to punish her with a retelling so interminable it might even make that favorite chair defy all known laws of physics and go clattering out of the room under its own power.

> *"Well, and so we breakfasted at ten as usual; I thought it would never be over; for, by the way, you are to understand, that my uncle and aunt were horrid unpleasant all the time I was with them. If you'll believe me, I did not once put my foot out-of-doors, though I was there a fortnight. Not one party, or scheme, or anything. To be sure London was rather thin, but however the Little Theatre was open."*

But eventually, of course, the law of averages comes into play—i.e. if you insist on spewing forth speech every second of every minute of every hour of every day, sooner or later you're bound to say something you wish you hadn't—and Lydia fatefully puts her foot in it.

> *"Well, and so just as the carriage came to the door, my uncle was called away on business to that horrid man Mr. Stone...Well, I was so frightened I did not know what to do, for my uncle was to give me away; and if we were beyond the hour, we could not be married all day. But, luckily, he came back again in ten minutes time, and then we all set out. However, I recollected afterwards that if he had been prevented going, the wedding need not be put off, for Mr. Darcy might have done as well."*
>
> *"Mr. Darcy!" repeated Elizabeth, in utter amazement.*

Lydia is immediately abashed, because it was supposed to remain a secret, and please don't ask her any more about it because Wickham will be so angry, he'll take her by the hair and slap her about and fling her roughly across the couch and grab her by the wrists and...really, maybe she'd *better* tell Lizzy about it.

But Lizzy, ever mindful of propriety, wouldn't dream of hearing anything not intended for her ear. Not *openly,* of course. But she rushes up to her room and scribbles some lines to Mrs. Gardiner, begging her to reveal what she's honorably able to, all the while telling herself that if her aunt refuses, she is *so* going all ninja-spy-chick to find out.

Fortunately Aunt Gardiner is more than willing to spill everything she knows. In fact she's downright eager. Plucked out of *Pride and Prejudice* and dropped into the oeuvre of Mickey Spillane, she'd make a first-rate stool pigeon. But she prefaces her lengthy explanation by saying how surprised she is that Lizzy's asking for information at all: "Don't think me angry, however, for I only mean to let you know that I had not imagined such inquiries to be necessary on *your* side. If you do not choose to understand me, forgive my impertinence." In other words, she can't believe Lizzy hasn't already heard all this from (ahem) *someone else.* This is the first of several times in the letter that Mrs. G. coyly alludes to Darcy's feelings for Elizabeth.

That done, she tells of how Darcy appeared on their doorstep with the news that he'd discovered Wickham and Lydia. He'd gone in search of them because he felt responsible for having hidden Wickham's true character from those he might have victimized, with the result that one of them is now indeed his victim. For Wickham had taken great delight in making it clear to Darcy that he had no intention at all of marrying Lydia. As for Lydia, he found her "absolutely resolved on remaining where she was. She cared for none of her friends, she wanted no help of his, she would not hear of leaving Wickham. She was sure they should be married sometime or other, and it did not much signify when." I get a mental image of Lydia lounging around, half-dressed, eating chocolates from a box and throwing the wrappers on the floor. Funny, in another novel—say, by Thomas Hardy, or Ford Maddox Ford—I might actually like her; but here...? When she goes on about how she might die from laughing, I find myself wishing she just would already.

Given the couple's obstinacy, Darcy concluded that the only way of salvaging the situation was "to secure and expedite" a marriage, which isn't as simple as it sounds, since Wickham would only wed if it meant an escape from his many, many debts. Darcy accordingly agreed to cover the full amount. Uncle Gardiner protested—to no avail, as Mrs. Gardiner writes:

> *But our visitor was very obstinate. I fancy, Lizzy, that obstinacy is the real defect of his character after all...Nothing was to be done that he did not do himself; though I am sure (and I do not speak it to be thanked, therefore say nothing about it) your uncle would most readily have settled the whole. They battled it together for a long time, which was more than either the gentleman or lady concerned in it deserved.*

And a little later, she adds that "you may rest perfectly assured that your uncle would never have yielded, if we had not given [Darcy] credit for another interest in the affair." Nudge-nudge, wink-wink. If you catch my drift. And in case you don't:

> *Will you be very angry with me, my dear Lizzy, if I take this opportunity of saying (what I was never bold enough to say before) how much I like him. His behaviour to us has in every respect been as pleasing as when we were in Derbyshire. His understanding and opinions all please me; he wants nothing but a little more liveliness, and that, if he marries prudently, his wife may teach him. I thought him very sly; he hardly ever mentioned your name. But slyness seems the fashion.*

Aunt Gardiner is going for the world record in metaphoric tweaks and pinches, here. And she still ain't finished:

> *Pray forgive me if I have been very presuming, or at least do not punish me so far as to exclude me from P. I shall never be quite happy till I have been all round the park. A low phaeton, with a nice little pair of ponies, would be the very thing.*

Covering so many pages with her quill pen constitutes the most she's physically exerted herself since—well, possibly ever, so she now signs off and goes to her room to lie down for the remainder of the novel.

The letter throws Lizzy into "a flutter of spirits, in which it was difficult to determine whether pleasure or pain bore the greatest share." She finds it downright gobsmacking that Darcy condescended to burrow through unsavory London neighborhoods, and forced himself to deal politely with people he despises, all to salvage the reputation of a girl who couldn't wait to throw it away in the first place, and who won't ever bother to thank him for it—though you shudder to think what form her gratitude would take if she did. It's hard to imagine a worse ordeal for Darcy to endure; though possibly a karaoke duet with Mrs. Bennet would do it.

Lizzy's heart "did whisper that he had done it for her. But it was a hope shortly checked by other considerations...Brother-in-law of Wickham! Every kind of pride must revolt from the connection." And when it comes to "every kind of pride," well, Darcy's the man with the complete set, signed and numbered, plus the special display case available only to subscribers. So despite his having placed himself in degrading circumstances for her sake, and having sacrificed both his finer feelings and a good chunk of Darcy change into the bargain, she can't view this evidence of his love for her with anything resembling optimism. He was simply paying a debt of honor by restoring her family's good name; after which, she can't expect him to do more than give her a pat on her rump and send her riding off into her future.

> *Oh! how heartily did she grieve over every ungracious sensation she had ever encouraged, every saucy speech she had ever directed towards him. For herself she was humbled; but she was proud of him. Proud that in a cause of compassion and honour, he had been able to get the better of himself.*

What we have, then, are a pair of would-be lovers who are gradually, painfully, becoming worthy of each other. And as if to prove how far a journey that's been, Lizzy is interrupted now by Wickham, who comes upon her with his perpetual smirk, bringing with him the stink of the past, a regrettable miasma of slyness and self-satisfaction. Well bred thing that she is, she doesn't get up and run from him, or hurl her shoe at him, or hurriedly place her hands over the seat next to her and shout, "Taken! Taken!" No, she gives him a welcoming smile.

Ah, but this is Elizabeth Bennet, remember. A smile on her, is like a smile on a cat. It might be warm and affectionate...or it might be playfully lethal. Since it's Wickham on the receiving end, take a wild guess.

> *"I am afraid I interrupt your solitary ramble, my dear sister?" he said as he joined her.*
>
> *"You certainly do," she replied with a smile; "but it does not follow that the interruption must be unwelcome."*

Right away she's toying with him. Yes, you *are* interrupting me, she says; that doesn't mean it *must* be unwelcome. But notice, she doesn't reassure him that it *isn't* unwelcome.

And so the ensuing scene plays out, as Wickham pathetically tries to reestablish their old bond by the same means as he originally forged it: bemoaning his victimization at Darcy's hands. Lizzy masterfully counters every gambit by supplying the same kind of half-answers she gives above—not quite saying she's onto his duplicity, but leaving the door wide open for him to infer as much. For instance, when hearing that Lizzy has met Darcy's sister, he asks whether she liked her; Lizzy says, "Very much." Frantically, he tries to massage this to his own purpose.

> *"I have heard, indeed, that she is uncommonly improved within this year or two. When I last saw her, she was not very promising. I am very glad you liked her. I hope she will turn out well."*
>
> *"I dare say she will; she has got over the most trying age."*

Hearing Lizzy mention Georgiana's "most trying age" has got to make Wickham's throat go dry; but of course he can't make any comment on it, and she doesn't offer any of her own.

By the time they part, she's basically sliced him to pieces; he's openly hemorrhaging, and tries to hold himself together lest he collapse into a heap of steaming cutlets. But in the final moment, Lizzy takes pity on him: "Come, Mr. Wickham, we are brother and sister, you know. Do not let us quarrel about the past. In future, I hope we shall be always of one mind." And there's little doubt whose mind that will be, is there?

The visit eventually ends, and the newlyweds depart for Wickham's new posting. Mrs. Bennet is distraught at having to part with her favorite child for what may prove a period of years, and begs her to write often. "As often as I can," Lydia replies. "But you know married women have never much time for writing. My sisters may write to *me*. They will have nothing else to do." Not one to waste a single opportunity to get her digs in, that Lydia. She's workin' it right up to the moment she climbs into the coach. If the idea occurs to her, she may order the driver to back up over Lizzy and Jane as a kind of grace note.

When they're gone, Mr. Bennet lets fly with a sarcastic appraisal of Wickham: "He is as fine a fellow...as ever I saw. He simpers and smirks, and makes love to us all. I am prodigiously proud of him. I defy even Sir William Lucas himself to produce a more valuable son-in-law." A bit more anger and toxicity here than we're used to getting from Big B; but considering what Wickham has put him through, perhaps it's understandable.

Mrs. Bennet mopes for a while...but moping isn't her natural state, and she comes flying back to form when she hears that Netherfield is being prepared for the return of its master.

> *"Well, well, and so Mr. Bingley is coming down, sister" (for Mrs. Philips first brought her the news). "Well, so much the better. Not that I care about it, though. He is nothing to us, you know, and I am sure I never want to see him again. But, however, he is very welcome to come to Netherfield, if he likes it. And who knows what may happen? But that is nothing to us. You know, sister, we agreed long ago never to mention a word about it. And so, is it quite certain he is coming?"*

There are so many internal contradictions here, and in such quick succession, it's like Mrs. Bennet has multiple-personality disorder and all her identities suddenly decided to speak at once.

Jane blushes at the news of Bingley's return; but she later tells Lizzy that it wasn't "from any silly cause. I was only confused for the moment, because I felt that I *should* be looked at...Not that I am afraid of *myself,* but I dread other people's remarks." So Jane is suddenly behaving with heroic self-possession and composure; while Lizzy, paradoxically, descends into nervous-nellie fidgets as she wonders whether Bingley is coming back (a) with Darcy's approval, (b) in defiance of Darcy, (c) none of the above, or (d) each of the above, on alternate weekdays and with weekends subject to a coin toss.

Meanwhile, Mrs. Bennet pressures her husband to visit Bingley as soon as he's installed back at Netherfield. But he flatly refuses: "No, no. You forced me into visiting him last year, and promised if I went to see him, he should marry one of my daughters. But it ended in nothing, and I will not be sent on a fool's errand again."

We're back in the territory of the novel's first chapters; everything seems to be a reprise of what happened then, with different orchestral colorings. Bingley's coming...everyone's in a high flutter, wondering when they'll meet him...

...And then he just shows up. Looking out her dressing-room window, Mrs. Bennet spies him riding up the lane, and flies into a panic, arranging her daughters about the room as if art-directing a tableau vivant. Kitty, sneaking a glance out the window, announces that Bingley's not alone, and then gets in an unintentionally hilarious line:

"La!... it looks just like that man that used to be with him before. Mr. what's his name. That tall, proud man."

Yo, Kitty! Welcome back to *Pride and Prejudice.* Where you been, chiquita? You get lost between paragraphs and end up in *The Swiss Family Robinson* for a couple dozen chapters, or what?

But Mrs. Bennet and her Multiple Identities squash Kitty's big moment with an even funnier line: "Good gracious! Mr. Darcy!—and so it does, I vow. Well, any friend of Mr. Bingley's will always be welcome here to be sure; but else I must say that I hate the very sight of him." Possibly she then lifts the sofa over her head and sings an aria from Handel's *Rinaldo;* basically, anything is possible from Mrs. B. at this point.

The gentlemen are admitted, take their seats, and assume their roles as principal audience members at The Mrs. Bennet Show, while Jane and Lizzy tremble on the sidelines. Lizzy has greater reason for discomposure, because she alone knows that Darcy is almost solely responsible for the rescue of Lydia's skinny white ass. And every time Mrs. Bennet snarks on him, Lizzy wants to kill herself. Preferably as part of a murder-suicide.

Eventually the awkwardness between Bingley and Jane melts, and the glow of their old affection returns; but Darcy remains as stone-faced and taciturn as he ever was. It's like someone hit a Rewind button and shuttled him back to Chapter Eight. "But," Lizzy speculates, "perhaps he could not in her mother's presence be what he was before her uncle and aunt. It was a painful, but not an improbable, conjecture." Certainly Mrs. Bennet is giving him plenty of cause to look like he's got something rancid lodged in his teeth. She insists on bringing up Lydia's marriage to Wickham, for one thing:

> *"I suppose you have heard of it; indeed, you must have seen it in the papers. It was in the Times and the Courier, I know; though it was not put in as it ought to be. It was only said, 'Lately, George Wickham, Esq. to Miss Lydia Bennet,' without there being a syllable said of her father, or the place where she lived, or anything. It was my brother Gardiner's drawing up, too, and I wonder how he came to make such an awkward business of it. Did you see it?"*

And all the while Lizzy, in the background, tries in vain to slash her wrists with pinking shears.

Eventually the visit ends and the gentlemen depart. I'm guessing Darcy, his joints locked in place by having remained immobile for so long a time, has to be carried out in a chair. He's barely spoken to Lizzy, scarcely even looked at her; and she's left wondering why the hell he even bothered showing up.

The great romance of Lizzy and Darcy has so far been a lurching, screeching, halting thing; just when you think you've got it pegged, it up-ends itself on you. If I were asking someone to write a romance novel, this is scarcely the formula I'd give them. A screwball comedy, though?...Hell to the yeah. *Pride and Prejudice* is essentially a prototype of the genre. Andrew Sarris defined the screwball comedy as "a sex comedy without the sex." What about a romantic comedy without the romance? Either way, those are the waters we now find ourselves treading.

And speaking of treading water, here comes the great white shark. Come on, you didn't really think Lady Catherine de Bourgh was out of the picture for good, did you...?

CHAPTERS 54-57

Oscar Wilde famously observed that all women become their mothers, and we find the first jarring hint of this in Lizzy as she reflects on Darcy's reappearance at Longbourn, where he comported himself with an air that might accurately be called "funereal" if what we're referring to is the actual corpse. "If he no longer cares for me, why silent?" she asks herself. "Teasing, teasing man! I will think no more about him." Which has all the ringing finality of one of Mrs. Bennet's many resolutions, such as "I have done with you from this day" and "I will never speak of it again."

Meantime, Jane is quite upfront about how much *she's* thinking about Mr. Bingley, though the quantity of her thoughts isn't any guarantee of their quality. "I know my own strength," she tells Lizzy, "and I shall never be embarrassed again by his coming...it will then be publicly seen that, on both sides, we meet only as common and indifferent acquaintances." Lizzy answers this with an admonition to "take care."

> *"My dear Lizzy, you cannot think me so weak as to be in danger now."*
>
> *"I think you are in very great danger of making him as much in love with you as before."*

Well, sweet creeping Jesus, I hope so. If not, we've been a long time in the saddle with nothing to show for it but a sore ass.

But things look pretty much as Lizzy has predicted when a large dinner party assembles at Longbourn, that includes both Bingley and

Darcy. The former makes a beeline for Jane, and within minutes the two have reestablished all their former intimacy; give then another hour and they'll be grooming each other's hair for nits.

Darcy, however, is not so advantageously placed, being "as far from [Lizzy] as the table could divide them," and even worse, seated next to Mrs. Bennet, which is sort of like placing combustible chemicals on the same shelf right next to each other with the caps not entirely screwed on tight. Lizzy "could see how seldom they spoke to each other and how formal and cold was their manner whenever they did." "Formal" and "cold" are qualities already in the Darcy repertoire, but they're new stratagems for Mrs. Bennet, and rather feline ones at that, given that her usual means of expressing her dislike is decidedly canine—i.e., barking a lot and running the full length of the fence.

After dinner, the ladies and the gentlemen part company—that charming old custom, now fallen into disuse since these days so many guests would have trouble deciding which category they fall into. Lizzy endures the interval as best she can while she waits for the men's reappearance—and Darcy's. "If he does not come to me, *then*...I shall give him up forever," she says, still channeling her mother.

But when the moment finally arrives, Lizzy's availability is compromised by an insipid girl who moves in on her, trilling, "The men shan't come and part us, I am determined. We want none of them, do we?" I can't helping thinking that this particular character is taken directly from life, and is based on someone who drew the author's ire in this exact manner. Austen, after all, thrived on male attention; stranded in the company of women for the better part of any given day, she'd have relished any opportunity to bathe herself in some refreshing testosterone. And any fellow female who got in the way of that, is lucky merely to have ended up as a grotesque caricature in the pages of a book, rather than receive an impeccably tailored elbow to the jaw.

Eventually Darcy circles close enough to Lizzy for them to exchange a few banalities—and then he's drawn away from her, "a victim of her mother's rapacity for whist players." And that's it; that's the evening. There's not been as much as a spark of erotic energy between them to reassure the reader that their attraction is still a vital one; all we've had is one awkward pseudo-encounter and a lot of frustrated glancing across furniture.

But while the evening's a dismal failure for Lizzy, her mother chalks it up as a big win. She ticks off its successes afterwards, as though addressing a meeting of shareholders. "The soup was fifty times better than we had at the Lucases' last week," she boasts, "and even Mr. Darcy acknowledged that the partridges were remarkably well done; and I suppose he has two or three French cooks at least." But the chief triumph is that of her eldest daughter:

> *"And, my dear Jane, I never saw you look in greater beauty. Mrs. Long said so too; for I asked whether you did not. And what do you think she said besides? 'Ah, Mrs. Bennet, we shall have her at Netherfield at last.' She did indeed. I do think Mrs. Long is as good a creature as ever lived —and her nieces are very pretty behaved girls, and not at all handsome. I like them prodigiously."*

Lizzy can't but agree; not about Mrs. Long's dog-faced nieces, but about Jane winding up transplanted to Netherfield. She shoots a couple of sly smiles at Jane, which provokes Jane to say stop it, Bingley and I are friends, just friends, you hear me?

> *"I am perfectly satisfied from what his manners now are that he never had any design of engaging my affection. It is only that he is blessed with greater sweetness of address, and a stronger desire of generally pleasing, than any other man."*

...*And* the dreamiest eyes, *and* the most dazzling smile, *and* his breath smells like perfume from France. Yep, that's Mr. Charles Bingley, my totally rad B.F.F.

"You are very cruel," Lizzy replies, echoing our precise sentiments; "you will not let me smile, and are provoking me to it every moment." Later she adds, "We all love to instruct, though we can teach only what is not worth knowing. Forgive me; and if you persist in indifference, do not make *me* your confidante." This, too, smacks of something Austen herself might have uttered—or wished she had, several hours after the exact right moment skittered by. This is one of the great rewards of being a writer: when the perfect, absolutely killer riposte occurs to us too late, *we can still use it.*

Now that Bingley's back in the picture, he starts showing up all the time. His first visit is the very next day, when he throws the household into a tizzy by arriving before anyone's sufficiently dressed to greet him except Kitty, prompting Mrs. Bennet to shriek at Jane, "Oh! hang Kitty! what is she to do with it! Come, be quick, be quick! Where is your sash, my dear?"

A hilarious scene follows in which Mrs. Bennet, seated with her daughters and Bingley, tries to empty the room one person at a time so as to leave Bingley and Jane alone together, with a proposal presumably to follow. The scheme is initially foiled by Kitty's obtuseness; "What is the matter, Mamma?" she asks. "What do you keep winking at me for? What am I to do?" Mrs. B is forced to employ more direct means —which in Lizzy's case almost requires a lariat and a strong horse, because Lizzy, realizing her mother's plan and mortified by its impropriety, is adamant about staying put. Possibly she even grips the chair, making her knuckles go white. But Lizzy is no match for her mother when she's got a potential son-in-law on the hook, and this the proverbial One That Got Away.

Unfortunately, no proposal ensues, though we're told that from this day forward, "Jane said no more of her indifference." But then the proposal *does* come a few days later—it can't help doing so, given the way Mrs. Bennet keeps emptying the house whenever Jane and Bingley get together. She's like a fire-drill warden at a public school; she can evacuate the whole edifice in just under two minutes.

Jane's reaction to the offer is typical: "Oh! Lizzy, to know that what I have to relate will give such pleasure to all my dear family! how shall I bear so much happiness!" Then all the forest animals come and surround her, and turtledoves garland her with flowers while she sings a song about sunshine and specialness.

Lizzy couldn't be more pleased. "And this," she notes contentedly, "is the end of all his friend's anxious circumspection! of all his sister's falsehood and contrivance! the happiest, wisest, most reasonable end!" Incontrovertible evidence that we're basking in the golden twilight of the Enlightenment. Can you imagine any writer from the coming Romantic era validating a match by invoking its reasonableness?

As Jane anticipated, she *does* bring happiness to her family. Kitty, we're told, "simpered and smiled, and hoped her turn was coming soon." As for Mrs. Bennet, "Wickham, Lydia, were all forgotten. Jane was beyond competition her favorite child. At the moment, she cared for no other." And what of the paterfamilias...? He calls his eldest daughter to him and says:

> *"Jane, I congratulate you. You will be a very happy woman. I have not a doubt of your doing very well together. Your tempers are by no means unlike. You are each of you so complying that nothing will ever be resolved on; so easy that every servant will cheat you; and so generous that you will always exceed your income."*

This last remark provokes Mrs. Bennet to remind her husband—possibly in the exact intonations of Robin Leach—that Bingley has "four or five thousand a year, and very likely more." Not a sum to be easily run through, though you can tell Mrs. Bennet would be keen to have a go at trying.

One of the consequences of the engagement is that Jane is now aware of how Caroline Bingley and Mrs. Hurst have deceived her. She understands the impulse that drove them; "But when they see, as I trust they will, that their brother is happy with me, they will learn to be contented, and we shall be on good terms again; though we can never be what we once were to each other." Lizzy approvingly calls this "the most unforgiving speech" she's ever heard Jane utter. Having Caroline finally exposed as the mangy yellow dog she is, must make her just stupidly happy. But Jane wants an even more permanent form of joy for her; she wishes she had her very own Bingley. Lizzy doesn't see the advantage: "If you were to give me forty such men, I never could be so happy as you. Till I have your disposition, your goodness, I can never have your happiness. No, no, let me shift for myself, and perhaps, if I have very good luck, I may meet another Mr. Collins in time."

When the news reaches Meryton, the Bennets are "speedily pronounced to be the luckiest family in the world, though only a few weeks before, when Lydia had run away, they had generally proved to be marked out for misfortune." And then the news spreads *beyond* Meryton, accruing import and implication as it goes; and that brings unexpected consequences about a week later, when there comes the sound of a carriage on the Longbourn drive, despite it being "too early in the morning for visitors, and besides, the equipage did not answer to that of any of their neighbors." Sensing an unwanted intrusion, Bingley leads Jane away to frolic among the foliage, which leaves Lizzy, Kitty, and Mrs. Bennet alone in suspense until the door is "thrown open," and in bursts Lady Catherine de Bourgh, with all the grace and good humor of a Vandal horde.

She takes a seat, and we then get a few hilarious moments of Lady Catherine and Mrs. Bennet interacting. It's like a genre mash-up, where someone combined scenes of Saruman from *The Lord of the Rings* and Kramer from *Seinfeld.*

But amazingly, this isn't the main event. Lady Catherine has business to get down to, and she asks Lizzy to escort her onto the grounds, so as to take them out of earshot of Mrs. Bennet and Kitty. Once there, she goes pretty much postal. "You can be at no loss, Miss Bennet, to understand the reason of my journey hither. Your own heart, your own conscience, must tell you why I've come." In fact Lizzy is utterly stumped. She can only guess that Lady Catherine has brought her a letter from Charlotte; though she knows full well that Lady Catherine going out of her way to do a small favor for any living creature, is about as likely as her stripping down to her bloomers and doing the Dance of the Seven Veils.

But Lizzy won't be kept in suspense for long; because her ladyship is not one to mince words. Oh, no.

> *"My character has ever been celebrated for its sincerity and frankness, and in a cause of such moment as this, I shall certainly not depart from it. A report of a most alarming nature reached me two days ago...that you, that Miss Elizabeth Bennet, would in all likelihood be soon afterwards united to my nephew, my own nephew, Mr. Darcy. Though I know it must be a scandalous falsehood, though I would not injure him so much as to suppose the truth of it possible, I instantly resolved on setting off for this place that I might make my sentiments known to you."*
>
> *"If you believed it impossible to be true," said Elizabeth colouring with astonishment and disdain, "I wonder you took the trouble of coming so far. What could your ladyship propose by it?"*

And so the battle is joined. And it's absolutely goddamn thrilling. Every minute of it crackles with excitement. It's always rousing entertainment to see a nimble, quick-witted, fleet-footed underdog demolish an overbearing, brutish juggernaut—whether it's the English fleet vs. the Spanish Armada, or Popeye vs. Bluto. What gives the Lizzy-Lady Catherine clash an extra dimension is that it's so clearly a product of its time; it couldn't have been written a hundred years earlier. Shakespeare might have pulled it off—but he'd have had Lizzy defeat Lady Catherine with a display of dazzling wordplay; she'd run rings around her with quips, puns, and double entendres. Austen, a daughter of the Englightenment, gives Lizzy the dignity of beating her on level ground. Unimpressed by rank, unmoved by money, Lizzy parries Lady Catherine's threats, demands, and insults with cool, sweet reason; she sidesteps the whole issue of answering for herself, by attacking Lady Catherine's very premises—by turning her own words back on her. Take this exchange:

> *"Let me be rightly understood. This match, to which you have the presumption to aspire, can never take place. No, never. Mr. Darcy is engaged to my daughter. Now, what have you to say?"*
>
> *"Only this: that if he is so, you can have no reason to suppose he will make an offer to me."*

Or this one:

> *"You are to understand, Miss Bennet, that I came here with the determined resolution of carrying my purpose; nor will I be dissuaded from it. I have not been used to submit to any person's whims. I have not been in the habit of brooking disappointment."*
>
> "That *will make your ladyship's situation at present more pitiable, but it will have no effect on* me."

Lady Catherine keeps slugging away, ever more wildly, but she can't connect. It's less a verbal sparring match than a bear-baiting. Imagine Cruella de Vil beset by all 101 Dalmations at once—and each one trained in the Socratic method. That's basically the tone.

> *"You are then resolved to have him?"*
>
> *"I have said no such thing. I am only resolved to act in that manner which will, in my own opinion, constitute my happiness, without reference to you, or to any person so wholly unconnected with me."*

There—right there—you hear it: the death knell of feudalism and the rallying cry of the great humanists—but, as in Voltaire, the cry is leavened with laughter. And unlike Voltaire, it's the laughter of celebration, not of derision. When Lizzy finally banishes Lady Catherine—who by now is pretty much spitting flecks of foam onto her reticule, so maddened is she by her failure to extort even a single concession from her uppity adversary—she's banishing the old world of blood and privilege, and bringing forth a new one of merit and ability—a world in which Lizzy Bennet (and Jane Austen) might conceivably thrive. At one end of the Age of Reason, we have Candide; at the other end, Elizabeth Bennet. This is, in my opinion, a clear case of social progress, if not flat-out evolution.

But when the adrenaline wears off, Lizzy finds herself suffering from "discomposure," largely because she's pretty sure Lady Catherine is going to descend on Netherfield and her nephew, and in her current enraged state she'll nail him to the wall with the eighty gazillion reasons marrying Lizzy would end his happiness, ruin his reputation, tank his credit rating and boost his cholesterol. And given the strange way Darcy's behaved the last few times she's seen him, she's no longer so certain of how he'll react to such a full-frontal assault. "With his notions of dignity, he would probably feel the arguments, which to Elizabeth had appeared weak and ridiculous, contained much good sense and solid reasoning." But before she can worry herself into any silly, Victorian-style handwringing, she remembers who she is: Elizabeth Bennet, goddammit. "If he is satisfied with only regretting me, when he might have obtained my affections and hand, I shall soon cease to regret him at all."

This summoning of intestinal fortitude is put to the test the next morning when her father summons her into his library and says, "I have received a letter this morning that has astonished me exceedingly. I did not know before that I had *two* daughters on the brink of matrimony. Let me congratulate you on a very important conquest...I think I may defy even your sagacity to discover the name of your admirer."

The letter, we learn, is from Mr. Collins, and he's written in a fit of urgency on having heard that Lizzy is the chosen partner of "one of the most illustrious personages in this land," to warn the Bennets "of what evils you may incur by a precipitate closure with this gentleman's proposals, which, of course, you will be inclined to take immediate advantage of."

Mr. Bennet can barely contain himself as he reads this aloud; I picture him rocking back and forth in his chair while emitting small, shrill noises like an animal being stepped on. But Lizzy maintains her poker face and pretends to have no idea, *none,* of whom Mr. Collins is referring to, so that her father is forced to reveal, while basically gasping for breath, that it's "Mr. Darcy, who never looks at any woman but to see a blemish, and who probably never looked at you in his life! It is admirable!" After which he spends a few minutes with his head on the desk, quietly quaking with laughter while Lizzy keeps her gaze resolutely lowered, as though observing microscopic civilizations in her cuticles. When he asks her why she isn't diverted, she insists that she is, really, oh yeah you betcha, and begs him to read on; but the rest of Mr. Collins's letter touches on other subjects (such as his professional opinion on Mr. Bennet's mishandling of Lydia and Wickham after their wedding: "You ought certainly to forgive them as a Christian, but never to admit them in your sight, or allow their names to be mentioned in your hearing"). But a change of topic can't divert Mr. Bennet from the source of so much mirth; he keeps working it like a Catskills comedian: "And pray, Lizzy, what said Lady Catherine about this report? Did she call to refuse her consent?" Lizzy says nothing in reply, but feels a great deal:

> *Her father had most cruelly mortified her by what he said of Mr. Darcy's indifference, and she could do nothing but wonder at such a want of penetration, or fear that perhaps instead of his seeing too* little, *she might have fancied too* much.

Fortunately, she won't have long to wait to discover the truth. We're on the downslope to the finale now, and we'll soon get to see how well everyone has deserved his or her ultimate fate. Am I spoiling it for you if I just say that by the final page, there won't be enough left of Caroline Bingley to blot up with a Handi-Wipe...?

CHAPTERS 58-61

We've reached the point in *Pride and Prejudice* where every chapter seems to open with Mr. Bingley on the Bennets' doorstep, so it's no surprise that that's what happens here. It *is* a surprise, at least to Lizzy, that he's brought Darcy with him, because after Lady Catherine's visit, during which that venomous old reptile did everything but torch the house and sow the soil with salt, Lizzy wasn't sure she'd ever see him again. But here he is, still parading around with his chin in the air, as though on a state visit from Asgard. Bingley, wanting to be alone with Jane, almost immediately suggests a walk—seriously, it's like the door hasn't even shut behind him and he's already yanking Jane back through it—and the others in the party agree. Except for Mrs. Bennet, who is "not in the habit of walking" (which makes it sound like she crawls about on all fours) and Mary, who can "never spare the time" (a titanic intellect being, apparently, a very harsh mistress).

This leaves Bingley and Jane to lead the way, billing and cooing and disporting themselves in arcadian bliss—perhaps Bingley wears a tunic and sandals, and strums a lyre while Jane makes figure-8's in the air with a sash—while behind them follows the more soberly behaved contingent of Darcy, Lizzy, and Kitty...the latter of whom, we're told, is "too much afraid of [Darcy] to talk," and who takes the first opportunity to dart away to Lucas Lodge, possibly to hide under Maria's bed.

With her departure Lizzy and Darcy are basically *a deux*—since by this time Jane and Bingley have frolicked so hard they've gotten half a county ahead—and Lizzy forms a "desperate resolution; and perhaps he might be doing the same." She summons up her courage and blurts out how grateful she is for all of Darcy's kindness to her "poor sister." "Let me thank you again and again, in the name of all my family, for that generous compassion which induced you to...bear so many mortifications, for the sake of discovering them."

> *"If you* will *thank me," he replied, "let it be for yourself alone. That the wish of giving happiness to you might add force to the other inducements which led me on, I shall not attempt to deny. But your* family *owe me nothing. Much as I respect them, I believe, I thought only of you."*

This, being somewhat more pointed than an obligatory "You're welcome" or "Don't mention it," is clearly the run-up to something even more declamatory. And here it comes now:

> *"You are too generous to trifle with me. If your feelings are still what they were last April, tell me so at once.* My *affections and wishes are unchanged, but one word from you will silence me on the subject forever."*

Lizzy doesn't swoon; she doesn't throw herself into his arms, or burst into tears or turn away in an excess of feeling, or any of the other stock responses we've been conditioned to expect by later, more sentimental, and more unashamedly vulgar works. No, Lizzy instead "gave him to understand that her sentiments had undergone so material a change, since the period to which he alluded, as to make her receive with gratitude and pleasure his present assurances."

And *that's* the climactic payoff to the resolution of this seminal "romantic" text. Not "rapture and delirium"...not "ecstasy and abandonment"...but "gratitude and pleasure." Clearly, for Austen, running off at the rails is no way to express ardor; in fact, she openly mocked that kind of thing in her treatment of Lydia. No, for Austen, it's self-command that's sexy; Lizzy and Darcy reach an accord through restraint and understanding, not through the galloping fury of crimson passion. Their muse is Bach, not Beethoven. (Lydia's, I think, is Puccini. Or possibly Amy Winehouse.)

And it's just as well that for this critical moment, this narrative pinnacle, Austen reinforces everything we've learned about her: her economy, her dignity, her witty pragmatism, her stark aversion to melodrama. Because *afterwards*...well, she doesn't *exactly* let down the side, and certainly she never approaches the mind-eroding navel spelunking of today's egregious chick-lit scribes; but she does embark on a lengthy sequence that will very likely prove the hardest for her male readers to get through. It comprises Darcy and Lizzy analyzing, with near surgical zeal, every twist and turn that's brought them to this pass. Granted, all lovers do this (I haven't been immune, myself); no sooner do they enter officially into their coupled state, than they eagerly and earnestly get to work on their very own creation myth, nailing down the dates and the details for a clearly ravenously interested posterity. (For example: Darcy reveals that Lady Catherine *did* come straight to him after leaving Longbourn and *did* relay every syllable of Lizzy's ungrateful obstinacy, which ended up having the opposite effect of that intended; "It taught me to hope," he confesses. And so on and so forth...you get the idea.)

Men, as a rule, aren't often heard asking, "So how'd you two meet?" and our faces can assume a kind of rigid, trapped look when this question is rewarded with a response (especially if it starts with the soul-withering preamble, "You tell it"—"No, *you* tell it so much better" —"No *you,"* etc.). Certainly in this instance, it helps that we've come to be deeply emotionally invested in Lizzy and Darcy breaking on through to the other side; but once they've got there, we menfolk are much less likely to care whether Darcy can "fix on the hour, or the spot, or the look, or the words, which laid the foundation" for his falling in love with Lizzy. And honestly, we get the feeling Lizzy feels pretty much the same; she just likes teasing him—tweaking his pride. "Now be sincere," she tells him; "did you admire me for my impertinence?" He replies, "For the liveliness of your mind, I did"—a reply that would earn him a full afternoon's silent treatment from a self-regarding modern gal. Lizzy, however, totally grooves on it:

> *"You may as well call it impertinence at once. It was very little less. The fact is that you were sick of civility, of deference, of officious attention. You were disgusted with the women who were always speaking and looking and thinking for your approbation alone. I roused, and interested you, because I was so unlike them. Had you not been really amiable you would have hated me for it..."*

She concludes, in one of the novel's more famous lines, "To be sure, you knew no actual good of me—but nobody thinks of that when they fall in love." Which has always struck me as a rather alarming, even Sartrean observation. Again, the readers who get all breathless over it, as though it were some kind of Cole Porter lyric, aren't paying it close enough attention; the only reasonable responses to it are stark terror, or ironic detachment. Lizzy chooses Door Number 2. She even tells Aunt Gardiner: "I am happier even than Jane; she only smiles. I laugh."

Male readers are apt to be much more interested in the reactions of the various other characters to the news of the engagement. Lizzy herself is a little apprehensive about how her family will take it—as well she might be, given that even at the best of times, the Bennets are likely to behave like a band of chimpanzees with indigestion.

Things don't begin well. Lizzy inaugurates her confessions with Jane because she's her principal confidante, and also because Jane's disposition is so incredibly mild, she might actually fade away if you trained a flashlight on her. But even Jane rouses herself to a stunned exclamation:

> *"Oh, Lizzy! It cannot be. I know how much you dislike him."*
>
> *"You know nothing of the matter. That is all to be forgot. Perhaps I did not always love him so well as I do now. But in such cases as these, a good memory is unpardonable. This is the last time I shall ever remember it myself."*

Even so, Jane requires more reassurance, as though half suspicious Lizzy is pulling her leg; maybe as a preamble to locking her in the closet, or pushing her into the coal shed. She begs Lizzy to "do anything rather than marry without affection," and asks if she's double, triple, cherry-on-top *sure* she loves him. Which causes Lizzy to confess the ultimate convincer: "that I love him better than I do Bingley. I am afraid you will be angry."

And when Jane, still trying to wrap her mind around all this, asks how *long* she's loved him, Lizzy responds, "It has been coming on so gradually that I hardly know when it began. But I believe I must date it from my first seeing his beautiful grounds at Pemberley." Jane entreats her please to be serious. Um, Jane, sweetheart...if she were any more serious, this would be goddamn Chekhov.

The time then comes when Darcy beards Mr. Bennet in his library to ask for Lizzy's hand, a meeting from which the elder man emerges visibly shaken, as if Darcy has used the opportunity to forcibly take his wallet and watch fob as well. He calls Lizzy in for a private conference, and their conversation is one of the more deeply felt in the novel. "Lizzy," he says, "what are you doing? Are you out of your senses to be accepting this man? Have you not always hated him?" Lizzy attempts to reassure him that her state of mind on the subject of Darcy has done a regular one-eighty, but with little success.

> *"Lizzy," said her father, "I have given him my consent. He is the kind of man, indeed, to whom I should never dare refuse anything which he condescended to ask. I now give it to* you, *if you are resolved on having him. But let me advise you to think better of it. I know your disposition, Lizzy. I know that you could be neither happy nor respectable, unless you truly esteemed your husband, unless you looked up to him as a superior. Your lively talents would place you in the greatest danger in an unequal marriage. You could scarcely escape discredit and misery. My child, let me not have the grief of seeing* you *unable to respect your partner in life."*

This is possibly the saddest speech in all of Austen; but it does a lot to redeem Mr. Bennet's many prior failings as a father, if not as a husband.

Lizzy eventually wins him over by revealing Darcy's role in Lydia's rescue from ruin. When Mr. Bennet recovers from the shock, he draws himself up and says, "I shall offer to pay him to-morrow; he will rant and storm about his love for you, and there will be an end of the matter." As she leaves the room, he tells her, "If any young men come for Mary or Kitty, send them in, for I am quite at leisure." So we've had our little catharsis, and now Mr. B is back to normal, which is a relief. This may be my *second* favorite scene in the novel; it shimmers with humanity.

Finally, the news is broken to Mrs. Bennet, and the thunderous effect it has on her is best conveyed by the single sentence, "Mrs. Bennet sat quite still and unable to utter a syllable." Of course, this near miraculous state of being can't endure, and she soon rouses herself to a condition of wonder, agitation, and only intermittently coherent prattle.

> *"Good gracious! Lord bless me! Only think! dear me! Mr. Darcy! Who would have thought it! And is it really true? Oh, my sweetest Lizzy! how rich and great you will be! What pin-money, what jewels, what carriages you will have! Jane is nothing to it—nothing at all. I am so pleased—so happy. Such a charming man!—so handsome! so tall!—Oh, my dear Lizzy! pray apologize for my have disliked him so much before. I hope he will overlook it. Dear, dear Lizzy! A house in town! Everything that is charming! Three daughters married! Ten thousand a year! Oh, Lord! What will become of me? I shall go distracted."*

Mrs. Bennet saying "I shall go distracted" is like Aquaman saying "I shall get wet."

Lady Catherine's reaction to the news is so violent that it sends Charlotte scampering all the way back to Hertfordshire, like Dorothy trying to outrace the twister. So Lizzy's best friend presumably gets to be present at her wedding. Which gives her a leg up on us. Austen does not devote even a single line to describing the ceremony. There's only this glancing reference: "Happy for all her maternal feelings was the day on which Mrs. Bennet got rid of her two most deserving daughters"—which seems to imply that Jane and Lizzy shared the same wedding day, and probably the same wedding service. Possibly this is a narrative nod to the sisters' closeness; I think it more likely Austen's means of dispatching both nuptials with one flick of her pen. Weddings bore her. Romance bores her. Passionate emotion makes her snort in derisive laughter.

What interests the author of *Pride and Prejudice* is character, and integrity, and decorum. Her world is emphatically not a realm of romance, not a sphere in which tender feeling reigns supreme and lovers are exalted above all others; in fact it is a cesspool of social Darwinism, a merry hell ruled by arrogant monsters and staffed by oily sycophants. It's a world in which indulgence leads to ruin, and every kind of appetite is self-destructive—even Mary's gluttony for books and learning is mocked. Lovers are not so much rewarded as are their persecutors brought low; Caroline Bingley must smile and bow and scrape to those she has worked like a demoness to subvert, and her greatest punishment—a fate far worse than death—is that, rather than lose access to Pemberley, she must pay off "every arrear of civility to Elizabeth." I'm guessing she takes to drink. Lady Catherine, with greater resources at her command, holds out for significantly longer, but in the end is compelled to extend an olive branch to her nemesis, if only to satisfy her burning curiosity about how she's managing as mistress of Pemberley. I picture her striding angrily through every room and gallery, her eagle eye picking out each minute failing of housekeeping or taste, and clicking her tongue in disgust; unable to admit, even to herself, that she is an utterly failed creature—all her criticisms mean nothing, because she has had to make herself contrite. She has, by her own standard of measure, diminished herself. And y'know what?...Couldn't happen to a nicer battle-axe.

Every time I read *Pride and Prejudice,* I laugh. It's the laughter of philosophy; the clear, cold laughter of those who reside in the abyss but are untouched by its sweat-soaked, writhing tumult. We laugh, because Austen lifts us above the fray and nimbly escorts us to a farther shore, where there are kindred spirits waiting. We can't stay there long; but we can return whenever we like...again, and again, and again, and again.

PART THREE
MANSFIELD PARK

CHAPTERS 1-3

Is there anyone who *doesn't* have a problem with *Mansfield Park?...* Having just given the world one of its most irresistible literary characters, Jane Austen faced the same dilemma as a bowler returning to the lanes for the first time after scoring ten straight strikes: How the hell do you follow a perfect game? Most probable answer: You choke.

Though of course we're taking literature, not tenpins, so the reality is likely to be more complicated. My own take is that Austen was feeling a little guilty after *Pride and Prejudice;* in creating Elizabeth Bennet, she'd shamelessly pulled out all the stops, loading her character with every imaginable attraction, from sparkling impertinence to righteous recklessness. There's nuance in Lizzy, but it's all brightly lit; everything about her is incandescent. Here is a character pitched to reach the galleries, and successfully so; two hundred years later, we're still hanging on her every word, our jaws parted in readiness for adoring laughter.

So perhaps Austen thought, *this* time I won't make it so easy for myself. *This* time I'll try to construct a heroine with more shade—someone whose charm will be of the hidden variety, as opposed to the wagging-her-tail-and-doing-tricks kind. Possibly she even thought of this as artistic atonement; and if so, she took it too far, like those 14th century saints who scourged themselves with whips and licked the open wounds of lepers, because what she came up with was Fanny Price, a creature famously described by the great Kingsley Amis as "a monster of complacency and pride...under a cloak of cringing self-abasement." And it *is* more than a little maddening that everything

Fanny gains (and over the course of the novel she gains a *lot)* is obtained by withholding, withdrawal, refusal. She embodies negation. Her default setting is Off.

Mansfield Park begins with the usual dollop of Austenian backstory, here concerning three sisters, all beauties, the eldest of whom marries a baronet ("All Huntingdon exclaimed on the greatness of the match, and her uncle, the lawyer, himself, allowed her to be at least three thousand pounds short of any equitable claim to it"), the second of whom marries respectably (a clergyman), and the youngest of whom marries, "in the common phrase, to disoblige her family, and by fixing on a Lieutenant of Marines, without education, fortune, or connections, did it very thoroughly."

This latter match results in a breach between the sisters. The eldest, Lady Bertram, being "easy and indolent," would be content with "merely giving up her sister, and thinking no more of the matter;" but the middle sister, Mrs. Norris, is far more Type A, and can't rest till she's written a thundering *"J'accuse!"* to the newly minted Mrs. Price, essentially condemning her to hellfire and brimstone and...well, even more hellfire. To which Mrs. Price replies, essentially, You are not the bosses of me so you can both go suck the same egg. With which epithet Mrs. Norris scampers to Lady Bertram, forcing Lady Bertram to raise her ire, which is the only actual exertion she'll undertake during the entirety of the novel.

I love that Austen introduces Mrs. Norris as possessing "a spirit of activity," which is apparently Regency code for "highly developed sociopathic egocentrism," or if you like, 100% see-you-next-Tuesday. Mrs. Norris is a compendium of the worst traits of every Austen villain up till now: she comprises Lady Catherine de Bourgh's bullying, Caroline Bingley's smugness, Mr. Collins's shameless sycophancy, Mrs. Bennet's delusions of humility, and Fanny Dashwood's martyr complex. And to these she adds a fault all her own: triumphal miserliness. By rights she should be a kind of Frankenstein monster, a mangle of elements that don't mesh at all, but in fact she works beautifully, all these ghastly attributes integrating like cogs in an infernal machine, interlocking with each other and keeping them in perpetual motion.

One of the most delightful things about her is the way she always has her eye on the main chance. As we've seen, she was the one who basically orchestrated the breach with Mrs. Price (because, what did she *think* that lady was going to do, faced with all her scorn and derision? Write back with, "Yes, of course, you're right, I'm so sorry"?), which gave her several years' bragging rights at being the one who exposed the true depths of her sister's perverseness and ingratitude. But eventually Mrs. Price writes to mend the breach, having in the ensuing decade been humbled by a career of serial pregnancy, on top of "an husband disabled for active service, but not the less equal to company and good liquor." The newly contrite sister asks whether there isn't something her grander relatives can do to promote the fortunes of one or two of her approximately eighty-six children. Mrs. Norris, sensing that righteous indignation, enjoyable as it is, has about exhausted itself in her repertoire, hits upon the scheme of responding instead with forgiveness and largesse—and thus convinces Sir Thomas and Lady Bertram that it would be an excellent idea to take one of Mrs. Price's daughters off her hands.

Sir Thomas is initially wary of the idea, thinking "of his own four children—of cousins in love, &c.," but Mrs. Norris, fixed now on setting herself up as an icon of magnanimity, talks him through that particular worry.

> *"You are thinking of your sons—but do not you know that of all things upon earth that is the least likely to happen; brought up, as they would be, always together like brothers and sisters? It is morally impossible. I never knew an instance of it. It is, in fact, the only sure way of providing against the connection."*

She carries the day, and puts the seal on her sanctity by assuring him that "I will write to my poor sister to-morrow, and make the proposal; and, as soon as matters are settled, I will engage to get the child to Mansfield; you shall have no trouble about it. My own trouble, you know, I never regard."

Since this plan has been from the start hers and hers alone, Mrs. Norris might be supposed to be the one to take responsibility for the mail-order niece; after all, she has no children of her own, so a helpmeet of this kind would be just the thing. But oh, no.

> *...Mrs. Norris had not the least intention of being at any expense whatever in her maintenance. As far as walking, talking and contriving*

> *reached, she was thoroughly benevolent, and nobody knew better how to dictate liberality to others; but her love of money was equal to her love of directing, and she knew quite as well how to save her own as to spend that of her friends...though perhaps she might so little know herself, as to walk home to the Parsonage after this conversation, in the happy belief of being the most liberal-minded sister and aunt in the world.*

And so it's settled that the child will reside in the magnificence of Mansfield Park with Sir Thomas and Lady Bertram and their brood; though Sir Thomas observes that they must strive "to preserve in the minds of my daughters the consciousness of what they are, without making them think too lowly of their cousin." Mmmmm-hm. *That'll* happen. No one in the narrative has yet twigged to the fact that they've set up the perfect conditions for a classic Wicked Stepsisters scenario. Wicked Stepmother, too, except for Lady Bertram's invincible inertia; you might as well ask for a Wicked Sofa, or a Wicked Daybed.

But never mind, Aunt Norris is quite happy to play the role instead. "I only wish I could more useful," she says obligingly; "but you see I do all in my power." What we see, actually, is that she desires—demands—the thanks of a grateful nation, and she wants it just for showing up. This is the kind of woman who, on a good day, can inflict on you a lifetime of indebtedness for allowing you to serve her a cup of decaf.

Yeah, it's pretty easy to tell who my favorite character is, going into this baby.

Young Fanny Price now enters the novel, being met at Northampton by her Aunt Norris, "who thus regaled in the credit of being foremost to welcome her, and in the importance of leading her in to the others, and recommending her to their kindness." Because, see, otherwise they might have just tied her to a post out by the burn pit.

Fanny at this point is ten years old and not much to look at, though certainly possessed of "nothing to disgust her relations." Austen is fond of this gambit: introducing her heroines by laying a stress on how unremarkable they are, though this is usually followed by the gradual amplification of their attractions by wit, courage, or integrity. Not so with Fanny, who will remain a small, cringing, flinching thing for pretty much the full span of the story. Even after she gets over her initial terror of Sir Thomas and Lady Bertram and her awe at her cousins, she still seems to scurry along the baseboards like a mouse.

She spends a good part of these early chapters curled up in secluded dark corners, crying. Eventually, the law of averages being what it is, someone eventually trips over her while she's in the throes of one of these sob fests. Fortunately it's her cousin Edmund, the kindly second son. The elder brother, Tom, is inclined to poke her with the toe of his shoe and taunt her, as though trying to turn her into a fear-biter, while the Bertram girls can't get over how thick-headed she is for not possessing such basic knowledge as "the Roman emperors as low as Severus" (these days it would be the Zodiac signs of the Jonas Brothers). So yes, it's lucky indeed that Edmund is the one to find her in distress on the attic stairs, and not one of the other children or, God forbid, the adults (though of course the only way Lady Bertram would come near the attic stairs is if someone lit dynamite beneath her chaise longue).

Edmund is kind to Fanny, and draws her out of her sorrow by asking her about the family she left behind, who he's sharp enough to realize she must miss; and by this means he discovers her special affection for her brother William, whose absence she feels most keenly. When Edmund observes that surely William will write to her, Fanny agrees, but alas he's instructed *her* to write first to *him.*

> *"And when shall you do it?" She hung her head and answered, hesitatingly, "she did not know; she had not any paper."*

We all know, or have known, someone like this: someone who always has an excuse for inaction, for inertia, for failure, and is only too ready to produce it. Never mind that it's a good excuse; it still grates on our nerves. And here we have it in Fanny; her pattern is set from this moment.

Edmund takes her into the breakfast-room where he not only supplies her with paper but rules her lines for her, "with all the good will that her brother could himself have felt, and probably with somewhat more exactness." Those of us who have read *Sense and Sensibility* and *Pride and Prejudice* now realize exactly where *this* is headed, and are free to settle back and wait for Mrs. Norris to push her way back into the narrative.

It doesn't take long. The lady is taking her duties as Wicked Step-aunt seriously, and we find her encouraging the worst character traits of the Wicked Stepsisters, answering their reports of Fanny's stupidity with the assurance that, "though you know (owing to me) your papa and mama are so good as to bring her up with you, it is not at all necessary that she should be as accomplished as you are;—on the contrary, it is much more desirable that there should be a difference." In other words, let Fanny's dullness and dumpiness make you look all the more hawt by comparison. Which is just the kind of advice these girls gobble up like mixed nuts. The author then notes:

> *...[I]t is not very wonderful that with all their promising talents and early information, they should be entirely deficient in the less common acquirements of self-knowledge, generosity, and humility. In every thing but disposition, they were admirably taught.*

In Austenspeak, this is some *serious* slammin'.

Meanwhile, Edmund takes on Fanny's education, and of course she's a willing pupil; she responds to every kindness like a dog that's spent its whole life being kicked. He "recommended the books which charmed her leisure hours, he encouraged her taste, and corrected her judgment; he made reading useful by talking to her of what she read, and heightened its attraction by judicious praise." Maybe it's too harsh to say that he's building his own personal Stepford Wife, but dang, *isn't* he?...If there were one recorded instance of Fanny exhibiting independent thinking—daring to disagree with him on some matter, and thereby proving that what he'd made of her mind was more than just a reflection of his own—I'd be contented. But what we get instead is what we'll be getting for the foreseeable future: grateful Fanny... unworthy Fanny...grateful, unworthy, grateful, unworthy.

You have to wonder what Austen was thinking here; what, exactly, she made of her new heroine. The Austen I know and love—the keenly intelligent, fiercely independent, poison-tongued mock-maker —would have had Fanny Price for breakfast. In fact, I'm sure she must have met many such girls at dances and balls, and at the sight of these dutiful, humble little dormice she must have sharpened her metaphorical knives, and had a simply wonderful evening carving them into ribbons. Yet here, she's giving us this quivering blancmange as our presumed point of reference. Jane, honey...you got some *issues* you wanna tell us about?

Anyway, we come to our next plot point. Mrs. Norris's husband expires (dying just as he lived: behind the scenes), which leaves his living vacant. Edmund, who's meant for the clergy, was intended to have it, but his older brother Tom has run up so many gaming debts that Sir Thomas has to sell the living to another candidate to make up for it, leaving Edmund without any prospects. Sir Thomas, deeply feeling the injustice to Edmund, rips Tom a new one over this, but alas, his son's the kind of charming rogue who has a built-in bounce-back feature.

> *Tom listened with some shame and some sorrow; but escaping as quickly as possible, could soon with cheerful selfishness reflect, 1st, that he had not been half so much in debt as some of his friends; 2dly, that his father had made a most tiresome piece of work of it; and 3dly, that the future incumbent, whoever he might be, would, in all probability, die very soon.*

When the living eventually goes to one Dr. Grant, his being "a hearty man of forty-five" seems at first to negate Tom's third point; but no—"he was a short-neck'd, apoplectic sort of fellow, and, plied well with good things, would soon pop off."

Impossible not to like Tom, though I know we're not supposed to.

Another repercussion of Mr. Norris's demise, is the general expectation that Fanny will now leave Mansfield Park to live with his widow. Her chief objection to taking Fanny in the first place had been Mr. Norris's poor health, which couldn't stand the activity and noise of a young girl in the house (because you know, Fanny is such a *hellion*), but now that he is beyond the reach of teenage torment, the way is clear for Fanny finally to join her aunt in her new household. Fanny spends several pages panicking over the idea, to the point that even Edmund can't comfort her; but she might've spared herself. Because Aunt Norris again reveals herself to be a strategist of almost Napoleonic wiliness:

> *...Mrs. Norris had not the smallest intention of taking her. It had never occurred to her, on the present occasion, but as a thing to be carefully avoided. To prevent its being expected, she had fixed on the smallest habi-*

> *tation which could rank as genteel among the buildings of Mansfield parish; the White house being only just large enough to receive herself and her servants, and allow a spare room for a friend, of which she made a very particular point;—the spare-rooms at the parsonage had never been wanted, but the absolute necessity of a spare-room for a friend was now never forgotten.*

Outmaneuvered, the Bertrams resign themselves to keeping Fanny, despite the waning of their fortunes—which, we learn, isn't due only to Tom's recklessness, but also to troubles on Sir Thomas's estates in Antigua, from whence most of his income derives. His wife has one last go at her sister, commenting that anyone would think Mrs. Norris would be glad of some young company and household help, which provokes an absolutely hilarious outpouring of self-styled victimhood, in which Mrs. Norris—whose will and energy might be sufficient to shift the entire foundation of London by thirty degrees if she thought it might earn her a few pence—paints herself as too broken in spirits and in health to look after a robust teen. She concludes in high style:

> *"Dear Lady Bertram! what am I fit for but solitude? Now and then I shall hope to have a friend in my little cottage (I shall always have a bed for a friend); but the most part of my future days will be spent in utter seclusion. If I can but make both ends meet, that's all I ask for."*

Mrs. Norris has scored a victory over her relations, but she doesn't have long to enjoy it; because when Dr. Grant moves into the parsonage, it soon becomes evident that his wife is a very liberal housekeeper. She "gave her cook as high wages as they did at Mansfield Park, and was scarcely ever seen in her offices. Mrs. Norris could not speak with any temper of such grievances, nor of the quantity of butter and eggs that were regularly consumed in the house." She complains bitterly about this prodigal behavior to her sister, but Lady Bertram has her own reasons to resent Mrs. Grant:

> *She could not enter into the wrongs of an economist, but she felt all the injuries of beauty in Mrs. Grant's being so well settled in life without being handsome, and expressed her astonishment on that point as often, though not so diffusely, as Mrs. Norris discussed the other.*

For a brief, exhilarating moment we get a feeling we're being set up for a venerable English comedy of manners—a tug-of-war for supremacy between three indomitable ladies. Sort of like *Mapp and Lucia* with special guest-star Lady Bracknell. Then we remember we've still got Fanny hanging onto the narrative, like a wad of gum to the sole of a shoe, and there goes that.

Then, unexpectedly, a sliver of genuine darkness descends.

> *Sir Thomas found it expedient to go to Antigua himself, for the better arrangement of his affairs, and he took his eldest son with him in the hope of detaching him from some bad connections at home. They left England with the probability of being nearly a twelvemonth absent.*

There's a narrative reason for taking Sir Thomas offstage at this point. His daughters have grown about as horrible as they can, given the restraint his presence imposes on them; with him gone—and with no compensating authority in their somnambulant mother, and with an aunt who so far from checking their arrogance, actively encourages it—they can now become really worthy foils to Fanny Pureheart. Austen is just taking Aunt Norris's principle and reversing it: for Fanny to look even more angelic, all that's required is for her cousins to go completely Moll Flanders.

And, given that Sir Thomas has to go, it seems only natural that he be dispatched in a manner consistent with gentlemen of his time and place. Many among the aristocracy of 18th century England grew rich from trade in sugar, coffee and tobacco plantations in the West Indies; Austen would surely have known that. It must have seemed to her the most natural thing in the world, that Sir Thomas Bertram would have such an interest, and be called on to manage it.

But what's less clear is the extent to which Austen understood how such operations were run. She may have known, and in fact almost certainly did know, of the slave trade that supplied the labor for such places; but did she know—could she even have conceived—of the appalling brutality of the conditions forced on those human beings kept there in servitude against their will? Austen, like most of polite Regency society, is silent on the issue; slavery was, to a great extent, the elephant in the room for her contemporaries in what was then the emerging imperial power in western Christendom. I'd like to think that

Austen—the chaste daughter of a provincial nobody—had never encountered anything that would allow her to grasp even the minutest horror of the inhumanity suffered by the people "owned" by Sir Thomas Bertram's real-world corollaries.

But *we* can grasp it. *We* know full well what the lives of these people were like; and their endless wretchedness, the shrieking injustice of their condition, reverberates down the centuries. We can't *not* know it; there's no excuse for ignorance of it—the hideous details are only a point-click away. When Sir Thomas Bertram departs England for Antigua to address the problems plaguing his enterprise there, we modern readers are immediately assailed by appalling images: of slave uprisings, violent reprisals, corporal punishments. From this moment on, it's difficult for us to feel any warmth or sympathy for Sir Thomas; he's become deeply, criminally suspect in our eyes. Worse, it's become equally difficult—almost impossible—to think of Mansfield Park itself with any of the romantic longing we allow ourselves when we contemplate, say, Pemberley; because we know that the great house sits on a foundation of human blood and bone. This, as much as Fanny Price's insipidity, is the reason so many of us just can't warm to *Mansfield Park*.

However...I will try. My aim in this treatise is to document the development of Jane Austen's prowess as a social satirist on the level of Swift and Voltaire. To that end, I'll give her the benefit of the doubt; I'll presume (as indeed I do anyway) that she writes in ignorance of the horrific excesses of the slave economy that allowed landed gentry like Sir Thomas Bertram to flourish; I'll assume that for her, persistent troubles in Antigua are merely a convenience for her narrative. And I'll keep my focus where I think she would've wanted it: on the frictions, frissons, and fireworks that occur between her cast of characters.

And when Sir Thomas does eventually reenter the narrative, I will attempt to take him at face value as well. This current chapter is to be my only foray into the economic underpinnings of *Mansfield Park;* in any case, they've been written about much more piercingly elsewhere. But while I may be setting them aside for this *particular* endeavor ...let me just assert that, in general, they shouldn't be set aside at all. We owe those who suffered at least that much.

CHAPTERS 4-6

We now find a denuded family in residence at Mansfield Park, Sir Thomas and his eldest son having been carried off to Antigua on a wave of Manifest Destiny. Lady Bertram, far from dissolving into the helpless histrionics of her heirs in Victorian fiction, discovers she gets along just swimmingly without her principal menfolk, and you get the impression that just a few weeks will find her staring perplexedly at their portraits in her locket, unable to recall which is which.

But where for Lady Bertram out of sight really does mean out of mind, for Mrs. Norris the world beyond Mansfield is a place of hazards and perils, all of which she contemplates with the satisfaction of a genuine sadist, or a reality-show addict. In fact she's whipped herself into a wonderful certainty of some lethal fate befalling both father and son.

> *...[A]nd as she depended on being the first person made acquainted with any fatal catastrophe, she had already arranged the manner of breaking it to all the others, when Sir Thomas's assurances of their both being alive and well, made it necessary to lay by her agitation and affectionate preparatory speeches for a while.*

Love that "for a while".

Winter comes and goes without incident—in fact, almost without punctuation—and then the social season begins, which is the Bertram daughters' opportunity to make a big splash. And with their Aunt Norris's tireless help they do just that, so much so that their reputation as the crème de la crème is pretty soon cemented in the neighborhood. In one of Austen's subtler (and therefore funniest) passages, she remarks on its effect on the girls:

> *Their vanity was in such good order, that they seemed to be quite free from it, and gave themselves no airs; while the praises attending such behaviour, secured, and brought round by their aunt, served to strengthen them in believing they had no faults.*

Lady Bertram doesn't venture out to witness her daughters' triumphs, because that would require things like listening to other people speak, not being in the supine, and a pulse. Seriously, at this point I doubt her ankles even work anymore. When she dangles her feet over the edge of her chaise, I imagine they just drape there, like Salvador Dali's clocks. But never mind, Aunt Norris is only too keen to take her place. Hell, she's such a team player she'd wear a BERTRAM GIRLS sweatshirt and duckbill cap, given the chance. She also relishes "the means it afforded her of mixing in society without having horses to hire."

This leaves Fanny to stay at home and keep Lady Bertram company, which has got to be a fairly easy task, given that Lady Bertram mainly passes the time by making mouth bubbles. "As to her cousins' gaieties," we're told, "[Fanny] loved to hear an account of them...but thought too lowly of her own situation to imagine she should ever be admitted to the same, and listened therefore without an idea of any nearer concern in them." Seriously, if she were a dog, you'd just shoot her and call it a mercy.

Then Fanny's old grey pony dies. She's soon feeling "the loss in her health as well as her affections," because no effort is made to replace him. Now, here you do have to feel a slight tremor of pity, because if Fanny's only exercise has consisted of going out on an old grey pony... well, for God's sake. How old is she, ninety? The most strenuous thing about the whole endeavor must have been staying awake so as not to fall out of the saddle. If Fanny really wanted exercise, she could have taken up something more vigorous, like counting the chairs in the dining room, or whistling, or jumping to conclusions.

When Edmund gets wind of Fanny's deprivation, he's instantly on the case. "Fanny must have a horse," he insists, in the face of arguments against it by both his mother and aunt. It's the only reply he bothers giving them; he keeps repeating it over and over, like a 19th century Rain Man. Eventually he takes it upon himself to act, and exchanges one of his own three mounts for one able to "carry a woman," the criteria for which we aren't given, but which presumably involve a daintier step, a calmer demeanor, and a coat complementary to her fashion season. (Fanny is pretty much sure to be a Winter. In fact, a Nuclear Winter.)

You can guess Fanny's reaction to this kindness; her feelings for Edmund, already earnest, now expand into the downright cringe-worthy. "She regarded her cousin as an example of every thing good and great, as possessing worth, which no one but herself could ever appreciate"—basically, she's so abjectly devoted to him she'd throw her cloak over a puddle for him to tread on. With her still in it.

Word now comes that Sir Thomas's homecoming, long anticipated, is to be delayed. "Unfavorable circumstances had suddenly arisen...and the very great uncertainty in which every thing was then involved, determined him on sending home his son." Austen always understates matters of high moment (she will, for instance, refer to soul-shredding grief as "severe distress"), so those phrases "unfavorable circumstances" and "very great uncertainty" carry a chill. They conjure up sounds of gunfire and screams of terror, the crackle of flames and the cracking of whips.

Aunt Norris apparently agrees with me, because after hearing this news "she could not help feeling dreadful presentiments; and as the long evenings of autumn came on, was so terribly haunted by these ideas, in the sad solitariness of her cottage, as to be obliged to take daily refuge in the dining room of the park." This is acid, knife-edge stuff right here; the bitch in the bonnet at her most scaldingly, hilariously misanthropic. How do people manage to gloss over this, or worse, bury it beneath cozy, dozy images plucked from Austen's pastoral milieu—a milieu she never chose, but with which she was stuck, and uncomfortably so? It just lays me flat.

Anyway, Mrs. Norris is now pretty much on hand 24/7, so she's there for the debut at the park of Mr. Rushworth, a staggeringly rich and even more staggeringly stupid neighbor who sets his cap at the eldest Bertram girl, Maria. Aunt Norris does everything she can to promote the match, short of actually cinching the couple together in a lariat, but Maria doesn't really need encouraging; "as marriage with Mr. Rushworth would give her the enjoyment of a larger income than her father's, as well as ensure her a house in town, which was now a prime object, it became, by the same rule of moral obligation, her evident duty to marry Mr. Rushworth if she could."

Which of course she can. Mr. Rushworth is such an incredible sap, he could probably be persuaded to swallow his own fist without too much trouble; so when Maria makes half an effort to dazzle him, he is obligingly dazzled. An engagement soon follows, and though it will be several months before Sir Thomas's consent can be had, everyone is so sure of his approval that there's no other attempt at secrecy "than Mrs. Norris's talking of it every where as a matter not to be talked of at present."

Then, as though it's Christmas or something, we're treated to two *more* additions to the cast: Mary Crawford, the adored younger sister of Mrs. Grant, comes to live at the parsonage for a while, and their dashing brother Henry accompanies her. The Crawfords are worldly young people, and Mrs. Grant worries that they might find Mansfield too rustic or boring; but in fact the pair of them are utterly feline in nature, and plunked down amidst the Northamptonshire country folk, are less appalled by any lack of fashion or manners, than they are giddy at the preponderance of plump, scurrying natives for them to torture and ultimately eat.

Mary hasn't even got her boots unlaced before she's decided her chief game will be Tom Bertram. "Matrimony was her object, provided she could marry well, and having seen Mr. Bertram in town, she knew that objection could no more be made to his person than to his situation in life. While she treated it as a joke, therefore, she did not forget to think of it seriously." That last line has so modern a sheen to it, it almost knocks you right out of the Regency; and in fact Henry and Mary Crawford are Austen's most forward-looking creations. They're basically Noël Coward characters air-dropped into an Austen novel, and bring with them all the sarcasm, insouciance, and casual irreverence we've come to associate with heroes and heroines of the past hundred years. Perhaps understandably, then, they're not the hero and heroine here; quite the opposite. This world isn't ready for their brand of topsy-turvy social satire; though it's slowly becoming so. Even Edmund, who never met a caprice he couldn't cow with a scowl, will succumb to Mary's coy contrariness before ultimately coming to his senses and settling down with Fanny, who has all the wit, charm, and sex appeal of an exceptionally loyal Labrador.

As for me…well, it should be pretty clear I'm crazy about the Crawfords. In order to hear one muttered aside from Mary, I'd push Fanny into oncoming traffic.

The Crawfords and the Bertrams hit it off beautifully. We're told that "Miss Crawford's beauty did her no disservice with the Miss Bertrams. They were too handsome themselves to dislike any woman for being so too," which is a nice change from what we'd expect—the usual catty jealousies you get in stories of beautiful women (invariably written by men). Mr. Crawford, not quite as hot as his sister, at first makes no strong impression; but his charm and insinuating manner soon win over the Bertram girls big time, and though Maria's engagement "made him in equity the property of Julia," Maria is queasy at the idea of just handing him over. She takes one look at him standing next to Mr. Rushworth, and knows the sinking feeling of having chosen too soon, like a woman who buys a pair of party pumps at Payless, then wanders past the window at Jimmy Choo.

As for Henry Crawford himself, he doesn't see why he shouldn't flirt with both sisters. "He did not want to die of love; but with sense and temper which ought to have made him judge and feel better, he allowed himself great latitude on such points." There's that feline nature again.

Mrs. Grant tries to head off any trouble by making certain Henry prefers Julia. He tells her, "Miss Bertram is certainly the handsomest, and I have found her the most agreeable, but I shall always like Julia best, because you order me." Understandably finding this less than reassuring, she reminds him that Maria is engaged, and Henry replies:

> *"Yes, and I like her the better for it. An engaged woman is always more agreeable than a disengaged. She is satisfied with herself. Her cares are over, and she feels that she may exert all her powers of pleasing without suspicion. All is safe with a lady engaged; no harm can be done."*

And he says this to the wife of a *clergyman*. I think this is why I'm so fond of him, where I loathed Willoughby and Wickham; he hides nothing, engages in no subterfuge. He's selfish, hedonistic, and utterly amoral, but he admits it right up front, with a great big dazzling grin. As for Mrs. Grant, she too is completely seduced; neither young, nor beautiful, nor clever herself, she hero-worships her younger siblings to the point of laughing off their shocking morals. And her husband is equally content to have them around, "a talking pretty young woman like Miss Crawford" being "always pleasant society to an indolent, stay-at-home man; and Mr. Crawford's being his guest was an excuse for drinking claret every day."

As for Mary's pursuit of Tom: that goes well, too. While she finds both Bertram brothers pretty fly, Tom has "more liveliness and gallantry than Edmund...She had felt an early presentiment that she *should* like the eldest best. She knew it was her way." Every once in a while Austen drops some small line or phrase that utterly reveals her genius; "She knew it was her way" is one of them. It instantly tells us volumes about Mary: we now know that she isn't just self-centered, she's self-aware. This kind of complexity—so lightly dispensed, as though there were nothing really difficult in it—is one of the reasons people compare Austen to Shakespeare. The perversity of *Mansfield Park* is that Austen eventually decides she must punish herself for this sublime creation—and punish the creation too, and us for responding to her.

Pleased with Tom's optics, Mary, no swooning romantic, turns her attention to his other attractions.

> *She looked about her with due consideration, and found almost every thing in his favour, a park, a real park five miles round, a spacious modern-built house, so well placed and well screened as to deserve to be in any collection of engravings of gentlemen's seats in the kingdom, and wanting only to be completely new furnished—pleasant sisters, a quiet mother, and an agreeable man himself—with the advantage of being tied up from much gaming at present, by a promise to his father, and of being Sir Thomas hereafter.*

Are we supposed to despise her for this bit of calculation? Austen has by this time made more than a few references to Mary Crawford's harrowing upbringing—orphaned young, brought up by an uncle "of vicious conduct" until forced out by the installation of the man's mistress—so we can all too easily understand Mary's longing for property, stability, and harmonious surroundings. We can also infer that at least some of her impudence and spiky wit are well-worn survival mechanisms. Austen seems deeply conflicted here; she continually prompts us to dislike Mary, while providing us ample reasons not to.

Chief among these, is that when push comes to shove, Mary can't even act on her calculations. She ends up tumbling instead for the sober solidity of the second son—succumbing to the same qualities that Fanny herself rolls over on her back for, though confusing herself in the process so that she can't help mocking the very things that endear her. We find the first inklings of this mutual attraction in a sparkling conversation between the two during an otherwise unremarkable walk about the park. The other young people are all along (except of course Fanny, who, being a little mole creature, isn't disposed to traveling in a pack), but Mary and Edmund seem to be the only ones doing much talking. Their subject, strangely enough, is Fanny herself. "Pray, is she out, or is she not?" Mary asks. "I am puzzled.—She dined at the parsonage, with the rest of you, which seemed like being *out;* and yet she says so little, that I can hardly suppose she *is.*"

Edmund, whose head is perpetually up his trousers seat, can only give her an equivocal answer. "My cousin is grown up. She has the age and sense of a woman, but the outs and not outs are beyond me." This sets Mary off on a dazzling stand-up routine about how easy it is to tell whether a girl is out or not out—and how the process of coming out itself is often transformative in the worst sense.

> *"They sometimes pass in such very little time from reserve to quite the opposite—to confidence! That is the faulty part of the present system. One does not like to see a girl of eighteen or nineteen so immediately up to every thing—and perhaps when one has seen her hardly able to speak the year before. Mr. Bertram, I dare say you have sometimes met with such changes."*

As it happens, he has; in fact he was once deeply embarrassed by the young sister of a friend, who as a child had practically hidden behind the furniture from him, as though afraid rays from his eyes might set her shoes on fire. When he met her again after her coming out, she bounded over to him, attached herself to him like a lamprey, and proceeded to pummel him with talk, oblivious to the fact that he had no idea who the hell she was. Edmund is convinced Mary has heard this story and is teasing him about it. Mary protests her innocence, but a little half-heartedly. Austen never says, but I'm pretty sure Mary *has* heard the story and is deliberately using it to tweak Edmund, knowing his dignity is his sore spot. (Again with that feline batting-about of helpless prey.)

This leads to a long discussion of proper and improper feminine behavior, notable because Tom steps in to share a couple of juicy Girls Gone Wild anecdotes from his own experience; he, like Mary, is obviously an avid trash-talker. Edmund retires from the conversation till Mary brings it back around to Fanny: "Does she go to balls? Does she dine out every where, as well as at my sister's?"

> *"No," replied Edmund, "I do not think she has ever been to a ball. My mother seldom goes into company herself, and dines no where but with Mrs. Grant, and Fanny stays at home with her."*
>
> *"Oh! then the point is clear. Miss Price is not out."*

And with that, Mary seems to dismiss Fanny from any of her future calculations; certainly the girl can't pose any kind of threat to her. (Nor, in an ideal world—or novel—would she.)

Fanny appears at the next gathering, a dinner party at the park which Mary rather dreads, because Tom won't be there, having gone off to race one of his horses. Even worse from Mary's point of view, Mr. Rushworth *is* there, and he brutalizes everyone by droning on and on about his scheme to improve his property. No one else can get a word in, and as you may have inferred by now, if Mary must be in a room where someone is talking incessantly, she prefers it to be herself. But she's met her match in Mr. Rushworth. Seriously, you could base a college drinking game on how many times he says the word "improvement."

> *The subject had been already handled in the drawing-room; it was revived in the dining-parlour. Miss Bertram's attention and opinion was evidently his chief aim; and though her deportment showed rather conscious superiority than any solicitude to oblige him, the mention of Sotherton Court, and the ideas attached to it, gave her a feeling of complacency, which prevented her from being very ungracious.*

Again, love that "very."

Aunt Norris is also present, engaging in two of her favorite pastimes, encouraging others to spend money and eating food she hasn't paid for. When Mr. Rushworth mentions an architect whose terms are five guineas a day, she lashes into him. "Well, and if they were *ten*...I am sure *you* need not regard it. The expense need not be any impediment. If I were you, I should not think of the expense. I would have every thing done in the best style, and madc as nice as possible."

She then goes on at length about the few meager but wonderful improvements she herself managed to make to the parsonage, in particular an apricot tree she had planted, that she seems to feel Dr. Grant, its inheritor, ought to get down on his knees and thank her for. When Dr. Grant, quite to the contrary, disparages the blandness of the fruit as rendering it "little worth the trouble of gathering," Mrs. Norris draws herself up in indignation, and possibly levitates half an inch out of her chair. "Sir, it is a moor park, we bought it as a moor park, and it cost us—that is, it was a present from Sir Thomas, but I saw the bill, and I know it cost seven shillings, and was charged as a moor park."

Dr. Grant isn't impressed; he essentially tells her she wuz robbed—"[T]hese potatoes have as much the flavor of a moor park apricot"—and Mrs. Grant has to insert herself and play peacemaker before Mrs. Norris hurls a plate or something. You gotta love Jane Austen dinner parties. They're always such riotous set pieces.

But inevitably (sigh) Fanny speaks up, and immediately all the air goes out of the room, the candles sputter and die, and the wine goes flat. "I should like to see Sotherton before it is cut down," she says, "to see the place as it is now, in its old state; but I do not suppose I shall." You almost have to admire her; she turns passive-aggressiveness into an art form.

Edmund, not quite her equal in this, yet takes up the gauntlet and gives it a shot.

> *"I do not wish to influence Mr. Rushworth...but had I a place to new fashion, I should not put myself into the hands of an improver. I would rather have an inferior degree of beauty, of my own choice, and acquired progressively. I would rather abide by my own blunders than his."*

Mary Crawford, unimpressed, skillfully—almost unnoticeably—manages to turn this into a discussion about herself; she's an artist of a different sort. Other Austen characters have been in the habit of bending any topic of conversation their way, but Mary is unique in that she does it so deftly, without any hint of arrogance; and also in that her experiences and point of view really are invariably more interesting than what she's steering the conversation away from.

Soon she's informing Edmund on the whereabouts of one of her prized possessions:

> *"Mr. Bertram...I have tidings of my harp at last. I am assured that it is safe at Northampton; and there it has probably been these ten days, in spite of the solemn assurances we have so often received to the contrary... The truth is, that our inquiries were too direct; we sent a servant, we went ourselves: this will not do seventy miles from London—but this morning we heard of it the right way. It was seen by some farmer, and he told the miller, and the miller told the butcher, and the butcher's son-in-law left word at the shop."*

This is so giddily subversive, it might be lifted right out of *The Importance of Being Earnest.* Mary continues in this bubbly, delightfully mocking vein for several effervescent pages, interrupted only occasionally by Fanny saying something about how she should dearly love to be within fifty miles of a harp someday, or wondering aloud whether if everybody's now had seconds she might humbly presume to have firsts.

But alas, even Mary Crawford eventually has to take a breath, and as soon as she does Mr. Rushworth blurts "Improvement!" and regains the ground he'd lost. Everyone is again forced to discuss the improvement of his estate, and soon Henry Crawford is volunteered to come and stay at his house and advise him, Henry's taste being presumably impeccable. Aunt Norris, who realizes that this scheme will necessarily remove Henry from Julia's clutches for God knows how long—a week at least; Julia will be a haggard old maid by the end of it—is emboldened to ask, "[B]ut why should not more of us go?—Why should not we make a little party? Here are many that would be interested in your improvements, my dear Mr. Rushworth, and that would like to hear Mr. Crawford's opinion on the spot"—excepting of course Fanny, whose longing to see the place before its alteration has fallen on ears not deaf, but hostile. Fanny could offer to crawl to Sotherton on a road of glass shards strewn with mousetraps, and Mrs. Norris would still forbid her.

Even I'm not that cruel. I'd certainly grant the request. Why, I'd prime the mousetraps myself.

CHAPTERS 7-9

In my analysis of *Pride and Prejudice* I observed that the triangulations of, and repartee between, Lizzy and Darcy anticipate the conventions of romantic comedy. We now come to a chapter of *Mansfield Park* that seems to anticipate another modern genre: the "cringe comedies" that have become all the rage lately (and of which *Curb Your Enthusiasm* may be the standard bearer). It's comedy as blood sport, with a flawed protagonist, incapable of ever learning anything, trying to get through a day with some measure of dignity, but continually bringing the same shit storm of humiliation down on himself. And so we have Fanny Price in chapter 7, stubbornly sounding her passive-aggressive gong again and again and again, with results degenerating from utter disregard to the utterly disastrous.

The only problem with this analysis is, I don't think Austen means it to be funny. I think she intends us to lament the injustice of a world that keeps snapping a wet towel in poor Fanny's face. I can't help it if my reaction is the opposite.

We begin on the morning after the dinner party at the park, with Edmund asking Fanny's opinion of Mary Crawford's conduct. Sensing that Edmund is impressed with Mary, and of course always wanting to agree with him, she readily offers that Mary is a heckuva gal, both witty and pretty. "It is her countenance that is so attractive," Edmund agrees. "She has a wonderful play of feature! But was there nothing in her conversation that struck you, Fanny, as not quite right?"

Fanny immediately twigs that she hasn't given him the correct answer, and so hastily switches gears, criticizing the way Mary spoke slightingly of her uncle. Edmund now smiles and commends her judgment, and possibly tosses her a small fish as a reward; which emboldens her to add that Mary's conduct was also ungrateful. Uh-oh—Edward frowns again! Bad Fanny!

> *"Ungrateful is a strong word. I do not know that her uncle as any claim to her* gratitude*; his wife certainly had; and it is the warmth of her respect for her aunt's memory which misleads her here. She is awkwardly circumstanced. With such warm feelings and lively spirits it must be difficult to do justice to her affection for Mrs. Crawford, without throwing a shade on the admiral...I do not censure her opinions; but there certainly is impropriety in making them public."*

Fanny's now completely confused; do we like Mary Crawford, or don't we? Testing the waters, she remarks that Mary was out of line for using Henry's skimpy letter-writing as blanket proof that no brother can spare more than a few dashed-off lines to his sister. Her brother William certainly wouldn't fit that mold, if he ever got around to writing her. "And what right had she to suppose," she adds, "that *you* would not write long letters when you were absent?" She looks up eagerly, expecting approval; but oh dear.

> *"The right of a lively mind, Fanny, seizing whatever may contribute to its own amusement or that of others; perfectly allowable, when untinctured by ill humour or roughness; and there is not a shadow of either in the countenance or manner of Miss Crawford..."*

So Fanny has just blown it again. But never mind, she lets Edward have the last word, so that he's ultimately satisfied with the way she rolls over and claps her fins and honks the little horns to play "Danny Boy." "I am glad you saw it all as I did," he says in conclusion, which even Austen is forced to comment on with a well, duh:

> *Having formed her mind and gained her affections, he had a good chance of her thinking like him; though at this period, and on this subject, there began now to be some danger of dissimilarity, for he was in line of admi-*

> *ration of Miss Crawford, which might lead him where she could not follow.*

Mary Crawford is juuust beginning to chap Fanny's ass. Which condition soon worsens, as Mary's much-longed-for harp finally arrives, and she skillfully employs it not only as a musical instrument but as a devastating fashion accessory:

> *A young woman, pretty, lively, with a harp as elegant as herself; and both placed near a window, cut down to the ground, and opening on a little lawn, surrounded by shrubs in the rich foliage of summer, was enough to catch any man's heart. The season, the scene, the air, were all favourable to tenderness and sentiment. Mrs. Grant and her tambour frame were not without their use; it was all in harmony; and as every thing will turn to account when love is once set going, even the sandwich tray, and Dr. Grant doing the honours of it, were worth looking at.*

Okay, maybe Austen *does* mean for us to laugh; but I doubt she intends our laughter to be so thoroughly at Fanny's expense. But that's exactly the scenario she's given us. The great yacht Mary Crawford has sailed into harbor, leaving the dinghy Fanny Price to bob perilously in her wake...whoops! there she goes, capsized. Anyone got a life preserver? Oh never mind, I'm sure she floats.

Edmund and Mary are now "a good deal in love," which is a bit of a mystery to Mary; "for he was not pleasant by any common rule, he talked no nonsense, he paid no compliments, his opinions were unbending, his attentions tranquil and simple." But she doesn't let it bother her: "[H]e pleased her for the present; she liked to have him near her; it was enough." Like a cat luxuriating in a patch of sunlight, she's content just to enjoy it.

But with Edmund sprinting over to the parsonage every morning to render Mary all weak-kneed with his tranquility and compliments-withholding, Fanny finds herself missing his presence at the park. "[I]f Edmund were not there to mix the wine and water for her, [she] would rather go without it than not." Which is Fanny in a nutshell, right there. I'm pretty sure that, in a similar situation, Mary would be thinking, *Edmund's not here to mix my wine and water?...Thank God, I can finally drink it straight.*

And you can just guess what happens when Mary takes a look around and sees all the ladies on horseback but her. She drops a coy hint about wanting to learn to ride, and Edmund is ready to strap on a saddle himself to accommodate her. Fortunately, calmer heads prevail and he decides instead to borrow the horse he'd only recently given Fanny. Fanny, for her part, is "almost overpowered with gratitude that he should be asking her leave for it," not pausing to consider what he might do if she actually said no. I'm pretty sure the result would be Mary 1, Fanny 0.

Mary's riding time is supposed to conclude early enough to allow Fanny to have hers; and her first day out, it does. But alas, "The second day's trial was not so guiltless. Miss Crawford's enjoyment of riding was such, that she did not know how to leave off." Which leaves Fanny "ready and waiting and Mrs. Norris was beginning to scold her for not being gone." There's something almost metaphysically significant about being scolded for "not being gone." Fanny really just *cannot* win.

Fanny goes out looking for Edmund and Mary, and has the exquisite agony or spotting them from afar, riding with Henry, Dr. Grant, and Mrs. Grant, and having a grand old time of it. "[S]he wondered that Edmund should forget her, and felt a pang. She could not turn her eyes from the meadow, and could not help watching all that passed"—no surprise, Fanny is a self-torturer.

When Mary finally returns the horse, she gaily says, "My dear Miss Price...I am come to make my own apologies for keeping you waiting—but I have nothing in the world to say for myself—I knew it was very late, and that I was behaving extremely ill; and therefore, if you please, you must forgive me. Selfishness must always be forgiven, you know, because there is no hope of a cure." Fanny's answer, we're told, is "extremely civil." When charm meets civility, guess which wins?... Actually, don't bother guessing. Just look at Edmund's face.

Edmund excuses Mary's lateness by observing that it's actually been a *favor* to Fanny, because the clouds are moving in now, so that Fanny will have escaped riding in the heat. And if that weren't indignity enough, Edmund then escorts Mary away, leaving Fanny to be partnered by the old coachman—whose company is made even more hilariously awful when he can't stop talking about Mary, who he declares a natural horsewoman. "I never see one sit a horse better...Very different from you, miss, when you first began...Lord bless me! How you did tremble when Sir Thomas first had you put on!"

These sentiments are echoed by the Bertram sisters later that day; they praise Mary's figure, form, and energy of character. "I cannot but think that good horsemanship has a great deal to do with mind." Really, if someone mistakenly threw Fanny into the fire in place of a log, it couldn't get worse than this.

But she absolutely brings it on herself. When Edmund asks her whether she means to ride the next day, she maddeningly replies "No, I do not know, not if you want the mare." When he reassures her that Mary's enjoyment must always be secondary to hers, Fanny goes for the gold in the passive-aggressive Olympics and says she has no plans to ride for the foreseeable future.

Edward, unsurprisingly, is delighted to hear it (what did she expect? That he'd beg her to reconsider?) and the next few days find the young couple galloping all over the county together, with Fanny left behind to indulge in menial labor of the Cinderella variety—only she's at the mercy of two wicked stepmothers, not one. (Though really, Lady Bertram is more witless than wicked.) She's made, for instance, to cut roses in the heat of the sun, which leaves her sick with a headache—and when Edmund finds out about it, and about the other tasks she's had to perform, like ping-ponging between the park and Mrs. Norris's house, he basically Hulks out. (Well...the Edmund equivalent, anyway. Which means standing in the middle of the room and frowning *very, very hard.*)

Mrs. Norris, realizing she's been busted for working Fanny like pharaoh worked the Jews, goes into panicked spin-control mode.

> *"I am sure I do not know how it was to have been done better...unless I had gone myself indeed; but I cannot be in two places at once; and I was talking to Mr. Green at that very time about your mother's dairymaid, by her desire, and had promised John Groom to write to Mrs. Jeffries about his son, and the poor fellow was waiting for me half an hour. I think nobody can justly accuse me of sparing myself upon any occasion, but really I cannot do every thing at once. And as for Fanny's just stepping down to my house for me, it is not much above a quarter of a mile, I cannot think it was unreasonable to ask it. How often do I pace it three*

times a-day, early and late, ay and in all weathers too, and say nothing about it."

In other words, I didn't do it, it's not my fault, I'm not even here, I left twenty minutes ago, oh look! a bat!, hey who wants cake?

But in fact Edmund's ire is principally directed at himself, because he's the one who abandoned Fanny to this fate. He makes up for it by giving her a soothing glass of madeira, while shooting his aunt and mother a *Not. One. Word.* look. Fanny, being Fanny, "wished to be able to decline it; but the tears which a variety of feelings created, made it easier to swallow than to speak."

Seriously: confronted with Fanny Price, Lizzy Bennet would roll her eyes so hard they might actually leap out of her head.

After this satisfying feast of Fanny-mortification, what comes next is necessarily anticlimactic; it's one of those switching-gears chapters all novelists must eventually rely on, and thus is heavy on getting things done, with a lighter hand on the hilarity. Mr. Rushworth revives the idea of welcoming a party to his house, and there's a lot of talk along the lines of oh what fun and shall we take only the carriage or also the barouche, and who's going to sit with Lady Bertram and watch her stare at molecules while we're gone, Fanny of course, no Fanny must come so I will instead, no Edmund you must come too, okay I will sit with her then, thanks Mrs. Grant you're swell. You may find your attention drifting a bit during all this, though Mrs. Norris has a couple of sterling moments. You could pretty much stuff Mrs. Norris into a cupboard bound and gagged, and she'd still find a way to entertain.

The only plot point of significance here is that, come the day of the expedition, when everyone gathers to pile into the carriages, there's a question of who will be the lucky gal who gets to sit up in the barouche box with dreamy Henry Crawford. Julia wins, and Maria doesn't take it well. In fact, if there were a blunt instrument somewhere within reach, Julia's brains might have ended up dashed all over the drive-way. Instead, Maria must be satisfied with sulking and stewing and trying to blow up the entire planet with her mutant mind powers...at least until the carriage reaches the perimeter of the Sotherton estate, when she can stop simmering over Henry and start showing off to Mary everything that will very soon be hers, hers, *hers*. Austen puts it beautifully: "She had Rushworth-feelings and Crawford-feelings, and in the vicinity of Sotherton, the former had considerable effect."

Mary, however, is more interested in keeping tabs on Edmund, who follows on horseback; as is Fanny, who has more time to devote to this endeavor since no one bothers talking to her. Austen pauses to compare the two women, and one passage particularly intrigues me:

> *[Mary] had none of Fanny's delicacy of taste, of mind, of feeling; she saw nature, inanimate nature, with little observation; her attention was all for men and women, her talents for the light and lively.*

Pardon me, but doesn't that sound like Austen describing herself?... I've posited before that Mansfield Park may be some kind of rehabilitative therapy on Austen's part, perhaps religiously motivated, in which she tries to exorcise the merrier, more earthly, sensual side of her nature and exalt her more neglected spiritual and empathic qualities (which may have been less apparent to her than they are to us); but it's a doomed business, and when the final judgment comes down, it will feel forced and unhappy.

How much better when the two sides can be allowed to coexist, if not in perfect equanimity at least in perfect accord, as in this charming passage:

> *In looking back after Edmund...when there was any stretch of road behind them, or when he gained on them in ascending a considerable hill, [Mary and Fanny] were united, and a "there he is" broke at the same moment from them both, more than once.*

The party is welcomed into Sotherton Court, "where a collation was prepared with abundance and elegance. Much was said, and much was ate," but nothing is described—as ever, Austen is largely indifferent to food. In that respect, certainly, she's innocent of excessive sensuality. Then Mr. Rushworth's mother gives her guests a tour of the premises.

> *...Miss Crawford, who had seen scores of great houses, and cared for none of them, had only the appearance of civilly listening, while Fanny, to whom every thing was almost as interesting as it was new, attended with*

> *unaffected earnestness...delighted to connect any thing with history already known, or warm her imagination with scenes of the past.*

Once more, Austen seems to be building up her heroine with virtues she thinks she *ought* to embrace more than those she actually does. Try a little thought experiment, here: you're in the entrance hall of a great country house. To your left, there's a small knot of fashionable people chatting, gossiping, laughing. To your right, an old woman blathers on about the family portraits hanging over the staircase. You've got Jane Austen straining on a leash; when you unhook her, in which direction does she go?...Well?

Eventually Mrs. Rushworth leads her guests to the family chapel, and Fanny whispers her disappointment to Edmund: "This is not my idea of a chapel. There is nothing awful here, nothing melancholy, nothing grand. Here are no aisles, no arches, no inscriptions, no banners. No banners, cousin, to be 'blown by the night wind of Heaven.' No signs that a 'Scottish monarch sleeps below.'"

This is like an early glimpse of Catherine Morland, the heroine of *Northanger Abbey,* whose swooning, hyper-imaginative romanticism leads her to look for gothic awfulness in every conceivable corner. We have a moment of hope that Fanny might be afflicted with some similarly entertaining folly; but alas, Edmund tells her to stop being so silly, and she stops being so silly.

Mary Crawford wanders up just as Edmund and Fanny are shaking their heads over the sad way family chapels have fallen into disuse. You can just imagine Mary's opinion on *that* score. Far from envying the Rushworth ancestors who used to gather here to worship, she's convinced that "...if the good people who used to kneel and gape in that gallery could have foreseen that the time would ever come when men and women might lie another ten minutes in bed, when they woke with a headach, without danger of reprobation, because chapel was missed, they would have jumped with joy and envy."

Fanny is roused to anger by Mary bringing her brand of glib irreverence into a place designed specifically *for* reverence, but even now Edmund strives to excuse her, saying, "Your lively mind can hardly be serious even on serious subjects." They go on to debate the merits of public versus private worship, with Mary defending the latter in the airy manner of someone whose moments of prayer can probably be measured with an egg-timer. They're so immersed in this animated exchange that they don't even notice Henry and Maria Bertram flirting madly by the altar, which behavior is certainly a damn sight more irreverent than dispensing a few lilting witticisms.

Julia doesn't see the sparks flying between Henry and Maria either; she's too wrapped up in a dizzy little conceit she's come up with, that this would be the *perfect* opportunity, right here, right now, for Maria and Mr. Rushworth to actually tie the knot, "If Edmund were but in orders!" On hearing this, Mary Crawford's jaw hangs open like a rural mailbox as she realizes she's just been arguing the irrelevancy of the clergy with...a soon-to-be clergyman. She pulls herself sufficiently together to apologize, then beats a hasty retreat.

Mrs. Rushworth leads them out of the chapel and is just considering the best way she might show them the grounds, when they come upon an outer door opening onto a flight of steps, and all the young people just plunge right through it. "Suppose we turn down here for the present," Mrs. Rushworth belatedly calls after them. It's one of the best gags in the novel; I bark out a laugh every time.

The party quickly divides into thirds. Mr. Rushworth and Mr. Crawford go on a fault-finding mission accompanied by Maria; Edmund, Fanny, and Mary Crawford "seemed as naturally to unite"; and bringing up the rear, we find Julia sadly saddled with the old women, Mrs. Rushworth and Mrs. Norris.

> *Poor Julia, the only one out of the nine not tolerably satisfied with their lot, was now in a state of complete penance, and as different from the Julia of the barouche-box as could well be imagined. The politeness which she had been brought up to practise as a duty, made it impossible for her to escape; while the want of that higher species of self-command, that just consideration of others, that knowledge of her own heart, that principle of right which had not formed any essential part of her education, made her miserable under it.*

If I may quote *The Simpsons*' Nelson Muntz: *Haaaa-ha!*

Edmund, Fanny, and Mary take refuge from the heat in a little enclosed wilderness, where Mary, having rallied her spirits, seizes the opportunity to get back to teasing Edmund—but this time with a slight edge of desperation to her tone. He can't *really* mean to be a clergyman, can he? "I thought *that* was always the lot of the youngest, where there were many to choose before him." Edmund, stung, shoots back, "Do you think the church itself never chosen then?" Mary backpedals, but just a hair: "*Never* is a black word. But yes, in the *never* of conversation which means *not very often,* I do think. For what is to be done in the church? Men love to distinguish themselves, and in either of the other lines, distinction may be gained, but not in the church."

Edmund is accordingly prompted to give a defense of his calling—the defense I wanted to hear someone, anyone, provide in *Sense and Sensibility,* when Edward Ferrars's choice of the collar was being so roundly mocked. Well, it's finally arrived, and it's worth waiting for, as much for the vindication of the profession as for an insight into how Austen herself must view it:

> *"A clergyman cannot be high in state or fashion. He must not head mobs, or set the ton in dress. But I cannot call that situation nothing, which has the charge of all that is of the first importance to mankind, individually or collectively considered, temporally and eternally—which has the guardianship of religion and morals, and consequently of the manners which result from their influence. No one here can call the* office *nothing. If the man who holds it is so, it is by the neglect of his duty, by foregoing its just importance, and stepping out of his place to appear what he ought not to appear."*

Take *that*, Mr. Collins.

But Mary isn't having it. "You really are fit for something better," she tells him. "Come, do change your mind. It is not too late. Go into the law."

> *"Go into the law! with as much ease as I was told to go into this wilderness."*
>
> *"Now you are going to say something about law being the worst wilderness of the two, but I forestall you; remember I have forestalled you."*
>
> *"You need not hurry when the object is only to prevent my saying a bon-mot, for there is not the least wit in my nature. I am a very matter of fact, plain spoken being, and may blunder on the borders of repartee for half an hour together without striking it out."*
>
> *A general silence succeeded.*

Yeah, I'll *bet* it did.

Fanny now announces that she's tired; undoubtedly from the rigors of touring the house and grounds, but also probably from having whipped her head back and forth following Edmund and Fanny's verbal tennis match. Everyone agrees to sit and rest for a spell, but Mary's shapely booty hasn't even warmed the bench before she springs to her feet again. "I must move," she says, "resting fatigues me"—a wonderfully apt summation of her entire character. Edmund gets up to accompany her, ostensibly on some further exploration of the wilderness, but really to explore whether their compatability, already fragile, has been irrevocably shattered. He forbids Fanny to come along as well, even though she protests she's fine now, really fine, all rested up and full o' pep and hey look, she can even kick up her heels and... whoops, did anyone see where her shoe went?

So Fanny stays behind, all alone and no doubt forgotten the moment Edmund and Mary turn their backs on her. And you think, heart full of hope, that maybe no one will remember to come and fetch her, and she'll just stay there till the 19th century heads into its downslope, when some intrepid Victorian botanist will stumble across her bones while seeking out interesting fungi. But in fact fate—and Austen—have other plans for Fanny. Which we'll discover next chapter.

CHAPTERS 10-12

We find Fanny as we left her, alone on the grounds of Sotherton. The wilderness that surrounds her evokes Shakespeare, and indeed lovers and would-be lovers now come and go before us, so that we might indeed be in the forest of Arden, or the Athenian wood. The exception, of course, being Fanny, who takes no part in any such frolics; she's immobile, inert—once again, a pillar of negation around whom life, in all its turbulent, awful, wonderful variety, swirls.

First to arrive are Maria, Mr. Rushworth, and Henry Crawford. Maria is enjoying herself thoroughly, reveling in her power over the two men, the first of whom she's engaged to marry, the latter with whom she's engaged in a flirtation. The three of them briefly remark on stumbling across Fanny, the way you might say, "Oh look, here's where the dog got to," then proceed to ignore her entirely.

Maria notices an iron gate, and half a mile beyond it a knoll from which the entire party might enjoy a better view of the estate. She declares this will aid them in their continuing discussion of Mr. Crawford's proposed improvements, and the gentlemen of course agree—in this company, Maria could suggest they all clamber up a tree and swing about like gibbons and they'd be all "Yes, yes, the very thing"—but unfortunately the gate is locked. Uh-oh. Cue a screeching halt to the good times. And everyone knows whose fault it is.

> *Mr. Rushworth wished he had brought the key; he had been very near thinking whether he should not bring the key; he was determined he would*

> *never come without the key again; but still this did not remove the present evil.*

We've all been in this spot, and we can feel for Mr. Rushworth, who's spent the whole morning in a kind of confused cloud, wondering why he feels so unsettled, such a third wheel here with his fiancée and his helpful friend. He's not the sharpest tool in the shed, poor sod, but in this instance at least he knows exactly what he has to do: run all the way back to the house (and I do mean run) and get that damned key.

As soon as he's gone Maria and Mr. Crawford start flirting more brazenly, as though Fanny really *were* a dog, or some kind of illiterate deaf-mute who could only ever convey her knowledge of their indiscretions by drawing stick figures in the dirt. Maria, in the tone of a wounded woman, accuses Henry of having had too much fun with her sister: "You seemed to enjoy your drive here very much this morning ...You and Julia were laughing the whole way." But he's a polished seducer and knows how to mollify her with flattery:

> *"Were we? Yes, I believe we were; but I have not the least recollection at what. Oh! I believe I was relating to her some ridiculous stories of an old Irish groom of my uncle's. Your sister loves to laugh."*
>
> *"You think her more light-hearted than I am."*
>
> *"More easily amused," he replied, "consequently you know," smiling, "better company. I could not have hoped to entertain* you *with Irish anecdotes during a ten miles' drive."*

Now it's his turn to needle *her,* by observing that if she really wanted to get beyond the gate she might juuuuust be able to squeeze round its post, but of course she'd never *think* of proceeding "without Mr. Rushworth's authority and protection." This has exactly the desired effect, as Maria launches to her feet and starts shimmying around the gate like a Rockette in a conga line. Mr. Crawford follows, after deputizing Fanny to tell Mr. Rushworth they've gone on ahead, but Fanny is scandalized by this development, and calls after Maria to stop. She knows her cousin well enough to understand that an appeal to propriety won't halt her, so she ingeniously warns her that she'll harm herself or, worse, her outfit. Alas, by the time she gets the words out Maria is already on the other side, and tosses her an acid, "Thank you, my dear Fanny, but I and my gown are alive and well, and so good bye."

Soon she and Henry are lost to view, and Fanny's alone again...but not for long, as a few minutes later Julia descends on her like the Allies onto the beach at Normandy, demanding to know where everyone's got to. She's just met Mr. Rushworth, who was "posting away as if upon life and death, and could but just spare time to tell us his errand, and where you all were." Except now that she's arrived, she finds only Fanny, which is just a hair better than finding no one at all.

Fanny explains where Mr. Crawford and Maria have gone, and how, which of course prompts Julia to execute the very same stunt; and just as before, Fanny attempts to stop her, begging her to wait for Mr. Rushworth's return. But Julia refuses, saying as she wriggles past the gate:

> *"I have had enough of the family for one morning. Why child, I have but this moment escaped from his horrible mother. Such a penance as I have been enduring, while you were sitting here so composed and so happy! It might have been as well, perhaps, if you had been in my place, but you always contrive to keep out of these scrapes."*

Fanny feels this as an "unjust reflection"—doesn't anyone realize how hard her lot is? How much effort it requires to stay perfectly still and never speak, never stir, never dare, never hope?...Oh, she is so *very* misunderstood.

But give her credit: it's not principally for herself that she's upset. She's well aware of how mortified Mr. Rushworth will be when he returns and finds everyone but her long gone. And here he comes now —huffing and puffing and holding onto his hat (an unkinder author would give him a pratfall)—and it's Fanny's unappy duty to tell him what's occurred. "At first," we're told, "he scarcely said any thing; his looks only expressed his extreme surprise and vexation, and he walked to the gate and stood there, without seeming to know what to do."

> *After an interval of silence, "I think they might as well have staid for me," said he.*
>
> *"Miss Bertram thought you would follow her."*
>
> *"I should not have had to follow her if she had staid."*

Well. Can't argue that one.

Mr. Rushworth then reveals he's not quite as stupid as everyone thinks he is, by delving right to the heart of his troubles: "Pray, Miss Price, are you such a great admirer of this Mr. Crawford as some people are? For my part, I can see nothing in him." When Fanny attempts to answer diplomatically, he waves it aside. "In my opinion, these Crawfords are no addition at all. We did very well without them." And if that isn't surprise enough, he proudly decides against any further scurrying after Maria, until Fanny manages to persuade him to it—I mean, otherwise the whole hundred-yard-dash for the key was all for nothing, right?

This sudden glimmer of dignity—wounded dignity, to be sure, but dignity just the same—isn't what we expect from one of Jane Austen's buffoons. Her powers are expanding, deepening; becoming more what we might today consider traditionally literary. And this throws another light on why *Mansfield Park* fails to satisfy: Austen's earlier novels were thick with monsters and freaks of the most appalling and hilarious kind; *Mansfield Park* has thus far had almost none to speak of—just Mrs. Norris, carrying the entire weight of Austenian absurdity on her bony back (and admittedly, doing a bang-up job of it). Mr. Rushworth has been a figure of fun up to this point; but now that we've seen him as a man of feeling—a man, *period*—it won't be so easy to laugh at him anymore (of course, we will; but not without guilt). Similarly, his mother, whom Julia calls "horrible," isn't horrible at all by Austen standards; she's a bit of a snob, but she exhibits a self-deprecating wit.

We can feel, then, that Austen is striving for something new here, and not just in her heroine; she's reaching for a greater verisimilitude, a sense of her secondary characters as actual human beings as opposed to broadly drawn burlesques. With her next novel, *Emma,* she'll grandly achieve everything she aims for here: a heroine of genuine complexity and shading, and supporting characters, like Miss Bates, who manage to be knee-slappingly funny while still coming across as fully developed personae. But for the moment, we're here in *Mansfield Park,* and she hasn't quite found her footing yet.

Anyway, back to Fanny—who, perhaps suffocating in the miasma of humiliation Mr. Rushworth has left in his wake, is finally roused to action. She goes in search of Edmund and Mary, and finds them pleasurably whiling away the time on the very avenue she's been trumpeting her desire to see for the past seven hundred years or so. Once again she's soaked through with mortification; Edmund protests that they've missed her, of course, but it's clear they didn't miss her all that freaking much. Abashed by how badly his thoughtlessness has injured Fanny, he suggests returning to the house, where they find everyone else in a pretty similar funk; all the running-after-but-continually-missing-each-other that produces such magical results in Shakespeare has here resulted only in sour tempers and wounded egos. With the exception, as always, of Aunt Norris, who's had an absolutely ripping day, getting to know the gardener and the cook and all the other major players on the household staff, and coming away with armloads of Sotherton swag.

When Aunt Norris tries to make it a perfect day all around by dumping a barrowful of indebtedness into Fanny's lap ("Well, Fanny, this has been a fine day for you, upon my word!...I am sure you ought to be very much obliged to your aunt Bertram and me, for contriving to let you go. A pretty good day's amusement you have had!"), Maria is sufficiently irritable to say, "I think *you* have done pretty well yourself, ma'am," and then go on to accuse her of "spunging." You can imagine how well *that* goes over. Mrs. Norris spends the remainder of the carriage ride declaring that the bounty was *forced* onto her by her new friends, who *insisted* she take it all despite her adamant refusals. That's Aunt Norris for you: always the victim, even in prosperity.

If the Bertram sisters think the Sotherton outing was a wash, they soon discover they have worse awaiting them, when the learn their dear old dad is coming home—"November was the black month fixed for his return." Maria and Julia have been pretty much getting away with murder while he's been away, tearing around the neighborhood like a biker gang, but all that's bound to come to a screeching halt when Sir Thomas gets wind of it. Maria in particular is distressed because she knows that once her old man's home, there'll be no more reason to delay her wedding, and she's no longer a hundred percent sure she *wants* to get married so soon...if at all. At least, not to Mr. Rushworth. She decides to deal with the anxiety in the time-honored manner of teenage girls: by just not thinking about it.

> *It was a gloomy prospect, and all that she could do was to throw a mist over it, and hope when the mist cleared away, she should see something*

> *else. It would hardly be* early *in November, there were generally delays, a bad passage or* something*; that favouring something which everybody who shuts their eyes while they look, or their understandings while they reason, feels the comfort of. It would probably be the middle of November at least; the middle of November was three months off. Three months comprised thirteen weeks. Much might happen in thirteen weeks.*

We've all done this, haven't we?...And yes, we know just how swimmingly it usually works out.

Mary Crawford isn't any more keen to see Sir Thomas back home, because that will also be the cue for his son to be ordained. "Don't be affronted," she says, laughing; "but it does put me in mind of some of the old heathen heroes, who after performing great exploits in a foreign land, offered sacrifices to the gods on their safe return." Edmund corrects her: there's no sacrifice involved—his taking orders is "quite as voluntary" as Maria's marrying.

But Mary can't see it; to her, a religious life is a sentence, not a calling, and she can't wrap her mind around anyone willingly embracing it. She can only assume Edmund is taking it on because he's to be given a living by his father—in other words, it's the path of least resistance. Fanny now comes to Edmund's defense, as though he's being picked on by the schoolyard bully, observing that this isn't any different from the way the son of an admiral will choose the navy, or the son of a general the army. "Nobody wonders that they should prefer the line where their friends can serve them best."

But Mary can easily understand why the army or navy might be chosen on its own merits, given that the enlistee can go on to cover himself in glory (and in shiny medals—accessories always being a high motivator in Mary-land). A clergyman, by contrast, is essentially a well-connected couch potato.

> *"It is indolence, Mr. Bertram, indeed. Indolence and love of ease—a want of all laudable ambition, of taste for good company, or of inclination to take the trouble of being agreeable, which make men clergymen. A clergyman has nothing to do but be slovenly and selfish—read the newspaper, watch the weather, and quarrel with his wife. His curate does all the work, and the business of his own life is to dine."*

Edmund is able lightly to dismiss all this, because he knows Mary hasn't ever really known any clergyman; only her admittedly unspectacular brother-in-law, and him only recently. Her prejudices have been formed by hearsay; "You are speaking," he tells her, "what you have been told at your uncle's table." But she's adamant: "I speak what appears to me the genuine opinion; and where an opinion is general, it is usually correct." Yeah, I've been hearing that reasoning a lot around election time.

Mary's continuing—and increasingly harsh—attacks on Edmund's chosen profession are muted by our understanding of what's behind them, which is simple, desperate selfishness. It's not that she can't see Edmund as a vicar; it's that she can't see herself as a vicar's wife. She's in love with him, but can't bring herself to acknowledge that she can't have him without giving up some essential part of herself—that part which longs for wealth and rank and society. We forgive her for it, because we know, simply by the fact of her making the case over and over again, that she's being slowly worn down; if her choices are to give up Emund, or take him on and become a rural Mrs. Nobody like her sister, well then, all right, fine, Door Number 2 please. She just has to go through this flailing period first—this battering herself against the iron wall of fate. When she's finaly exhausted herself, she'll be ready. It's a very nuanced portrait Austen gives us here, and she relies on us to read it as she intends; and we do.

Fanny, however, doesn't, and continues defending Edmund; which might annoy or irk Mary, had she not already decided Fanny presented no kind of threat to her. Instead she's come to see her as Edmund's devoted little pet, and in just the way we might compliment the loyalty of a good friend's hound, Mary now openly admires Fanny. When Edmund echoes the sentiments, Mary—perhaps noticing a blush creep over Fanny's cheek, or perhaps Fanny endeavouring to crawl under the settee—adds, "I fancy Miss Price has been more used to deserve praise than to hear it"—and might go on to offer more in the same vein, were she not now summoned to the piano, "earnestly invited by the Miss Bertrams to join in a glee":

> *[She] tripped off to the instrument, leaving Edmund looking after her in an ecstacy of admiration of all her many virtues, from her obliging manners down to her light and graceful tread.*

Girl knows how to *bring* it.

But while Edmund may effuse over her, he pointedly remains by the window with Fanny, gazing with her out at the "solemn and soothing" unclouded night, which inspires Fanny to some rather prosaic raptures:

> *"Here's harmony!" said she. "Here's repose! Here's what may leave all painting and music behind, and what poetry only can attempt to describe. Here's what may tranquilize every care, and lift the heart to rapture! When I look out on such a night as this, I feel as if there could be neither wickedness nor sorrow in the world; and there certainly would be less of both if the sublimity of Nature were more attended to, and people were carried more out of themselves by contemplating such a scene."*

Again, I get the impression Austen is using her heroine to lecture herself—to try to re-form her own attitudes and behaviors by exalting those of her idealized heroine's; because I'm pretty goddamn sure that were she herself on hand, in this scene she's invented, she'd be over at that glee like white on rice. And frankly, so would I.

And so, it turns out, would Edmund. The charms of the window are apparently insufficient to transfix him for long—Fanny, by contrast, would be happy to pull up a chair and settle down with a bowl of popcorn—and eventually he drifts over to the piano, where Maria, Julia and Mary are now performing the Regency equivalent to "Stop! In the Name of Love," with Miss Crawford as Miss Ross. Leaving poor Fanny to sigh "alone at the window till scolded away by Mrs. Norris's threats of catching cold."

So our score at the chapter's end is Gloaming 0, Glee 4. Extra points for the latter should Fanny really come down with the sniffles.

Jump-cut to November, and Tom Bertram arriving home...

> *...to be gay, agreeable, and gallant again as occasion served, or Miss Crawford demanded, to tell of races and Weymouth, and parties and friends, to which she might have listened six weeks before with some interest, and altogether to give her the fullest conviction, by the power of actual comparison, of her preferring his younger brother.*
>
> *It was very vexatious, and she was heartily sorry for it; but so it was; and so far from now meaning to marry the elder, she did not even want to attract him beyond what the simplest claims of conscious beauty required*

> *...were he now to step forth the owner of Mansfield park, the Sir Thomas complete, which he was to be in time, she did not believe she could accept him.*

Mary functions as the heroine's rival in this novel, the way Lucy Steele and Caroline Bingley did in Austen's earlier works; but she's cut from decidedly different cloth than those calculating, viperish villains. Mary is more finely etched; she has impulses, good and bad, and has a harder time accommodating the former than the latter. But she perseveres; she's self-aware to an uncomfortable degree; and we see the strain of her efforts beneath her veneer of breezy, cheeky charm. It's absolutely impossible, at least for a modern reader, not to like her; certainly she engages our sympathies much more actively than Fanny, who remains virtually inanimate throughout the novel.

Thus we can view Mary's character both as clear evidence of the growth of Austen's powers—she is no longer content to treat her antagonists as outsize cartoons—and as an indication of how far she has yet to go; for, while succeeding in turning Mary into a three-dimensional character, she diminishes her capacity to fill the role set out for her. Mary as adversary...? To herself, maybe; no one else.

While Mary languishes at center-stage, her brother bows out of the narrative completely, if temporarily; leaving the Bertram sisters to pine for him, and to stew in their jealousy of each other. And here's where we can see how far Mary has pulled ahead of him, since their introduction as a pair of lip-smacking libertines not so many chapters back. For, so far from allowing any genuine feeling to ripple the placid surface of his self-regard, Henry sails on untroubled:

> *[It was] a fortnight of sufficient leisure in the intervals of shooting and sleeping, to have convinced the gentleman that he ought to keep longer away, had he been more in the habit of examining his own motives, and of reflecting to what the indulgence of his idle vanity was tending; but, thoughtless and selfish from prosperity and bad example, he would not look beyond the present moment. The sisters, handsome, clever, and encouraging, were an amusement to his sated mind; and finding nothing in Norfolk to equal the social pleasures of Mansfield, he gladly returned to it at the time appointed, and was welcomed thither quite as gladly by those whom he came to trifle with farther.*

In other words: the car's barreling towards a brick wall, but everyone inside it is having a hella good time.

Fanny is the only one who sees the danger, but of course she doesn't say anything; she has no confidence in her own opinion. The most she can manage is to drop heavy hints when Edmund's around —things like, Isn't it strange that Mr. Crawford came back so early from his journey, or How fond both your sisters are of Mr. Crawford, how *very very* fond, or My goodness how odd it was that we should discover Mr. Crawford with his entire forearm down Maria's bodice front.

Edmund, oblivious lump of granite that he is, dismisses all these insinuations. On the subject of Henry being too attentive to Maria, for instance, he lectures Fanny: "I believe it often happens, that a man, before he has quite made up his own mind, will distinguish the sister or intimate friend of the woman he is really thinking of, more than the woman herself." Which makes you wonder exactly how much time Edmund spends watching the Disney Channel.

He's not the only one with blinders on. Mrs. Norris, too, sees just what she wants to see—as on the occasion of a ball held by the Rushworths. We get the incident from Fanny's point of view, because amazingy enough, she's on hand to overhear it. (It's her first ball, and she's only been allowed to come because there was a place to fill for which anyone with more vigor than a potted plant would be acceptable.) Watching Maria dance with Mr. Rushworth, her face distorted with affected smiles and spraying machine-gun laughter every time they chance to whirl by Henry Crawford and Julia, Mrs. Norris has only this to say: "[D]ear Maria has such a strict sense of propriety, so much of that true delicacy which one seldom meets with now-a-days, Mrs. Rushworth, that wish of avoiding particularity!"

Mm-hm. Maria avoids particularity like Sarah Palin avoids publicity.

Anyway, while Fanny is languishing against the wall, her cousin Tom descends on her, and her little heart goes all a-flutter because she's *sure* he's going to ask her to dance, but instead he pulls up a chair, and proceeds to give her "an account of the present state of a sick horse, and the opinion of the groom, from whom he had just parted." After which, he "took a newspaper from the table, and looking over it said in a languid way, 'If you want to dance, Fanny, I will stand up with you.'" Fanny "with more than equal civility" declines, and Tom sighs in relief. "I am glad of it...for I am tired to death. I only wonder how the good people can keep it up so long." Honestly, are we supposed to be mortified for Fanny here? Because...sorry. Can't. Too busy making the kind of clubbed-baby-seal noises that frighten my dogs out of the room.

Tom then goes on to indulge in some nice, juicy trash-talking, including some gossip about Dr. Grant, only to realize that Dr. Grant is pretty much right at his elbow, so that he has to snap himself into some serious damage control. "A strange business this in America, Dr. Grant!—I always come to you to know what I am to think of public matters." But it's grim going, and when Mrs. Norris comes over to co-opt both gentlemen for a game of bridge with her and Mrs. Rushworth, Tom decides the least worst choice open to him is to grab Fanny and make for the dance floor.

> *"A pretty modest request upon my word!" he indignantly exclaimed as they walked away. "To want to nail me to a card table for the next two hours with herself and Dr. Grant, who are always quarrelling, and that poking old woman, who knows no more of whist than of algebra...It raises my spleen more than any thing, to have the pretence of being asked, and of being given a choice, and at the same time addressed in such a way as to oblige one to do the very thing—whatever it be! If I had not luckily thought of standing up with you, I could not have got out of it."*

It's right about here that we experience our first twinge of regret that Mary Crawford hasn't kept up her campaign for Tom. Imagine the two of them going off together, and taking the novel with them, and all of us getting to listen to them chatter away to each other like this, for hundreds and hundreds of pages. What the hell...I can dream, can't I?

CHAPTERS 13-15

The Honourable John Yates, a new friend of Tom's who's been lurking at the margins for a while (you could almost hear him clearing his throat, trying to get our attention), now finds his way into the plot proper. It seems he's just come from a "large party assembled for gaiety at the house of another friend," which broke up unexpectedly when a death in the family put a pall over the proceedings, as a death in the family usually will. Thus Mr. Yates has arrived in Mansfield "on the wings of disappointment, and with his head full of acting, for it had been a theatrical party," organized to put on Elizabeth Inchbald's *Lovers' Vows* "at Ecclesford, the seat of the Right Hon. Lord Ravenshaw, in Cornwall, which would have immortalized the whole party for at least a twelvemonth!"

So disappointed is Mr. Yates that he can't stop ruminating on his bum luck at never getting a chance to shine on the stage, and reiterating how wonderful he would have been and how astonished the audience and damn damn damn and the world is so unfair and do you want to hear his speeches? Oh. Well, do you want to hear them again?

Rather than running from such a drum-beating bore, or hiding behind the Chinese screens at the first trumpeting of his voice in the hall, the Bertrams sit on the edge of their seats and hang raptly on every word. "From the first casting of the parts, to the epilogue, it was all bewitching, and there were few who did not wish to have been a party concerned, or would have hesitated to try their skill." Austen doesn't tell us who those few were, but we don't need telling. We can already see Edmund looming over the group, glaring at them with a great fiery eye like Sauron on Mount Doom; and where Edmund disapproves, so must Fanny, though from a greater distance—say, the other side of the room, next to an open window so that if anyone looks askance at her she can just noiselessly fling herself through it.

But Austen is less concerned with her nominal heroine—and if Fanny can't hold *her* interest, I don't know how she expects her to hold ours—than she is with the follies and foibles of the pro-theatre crew, who spend the rest of the chapter puffing up their own egos in a way that makes you sorry Austen didn't live long enough to get to know actual theatre folk in London, because *damn* if she couldn't have delivered a real acid bath to the whole profession. But we'll have to settle for what we have here, which is not inconsiderable. There is, for instance, the endless, self-pitying whingeing of Mr. Yates:

> *"It is not worth complaining about, but to be sure the poor old dowager could not have died at a worse time; and it is impossible to help wishing, that the news could have been suppressed for just the three days we wanted. It was but three days; and being only a grandmother, and all happening two hundred miles off, I think there would have been no great harm..."*

Then there's the irreverent glibness of Tom, who's constitutionally incapable of taking anything seriously: "An after-piece instead of a comedy," he quips, like a Noël Coward character (all he needs is a tumbler of gin in one hand); "Lovers' Vows were at an end, and Lord and Lady Ravenshaw left to act My Grandmother by themselves."

Then, after the Mansfield pack decides—as of course you knew they would—to take up the mantle themselves (though not in a theatre, in the privacy of their house), Austen masterfully charts the escalation of the plan, degree by degree, till suddenly we've got Tom all but knocking down walls and turning his absent father's billiards room into the Folies-Bergère. When Edmund—who's begun to snark like a self-righteous thirteen-year-old whom no one will listen to—cautions Tom to have a care with how he handles the house, Tom replies that, ahem, as the heir to whole estate he has perhaps a *tad* more reason than Edmund to care about the condition of the place, so why not trust him to look after it, there's a good little sourpuss. When Edmund says he's sure their father wouldn't approve, Tom just contends the opposite. Never mind, Edmund keeps coming up with reasons to cease and desist—Maria's status as a wife-to-be, Julia's status as a single woman, the obligations of their class and the standards of the community—and Tom breezily counters with Maria's and Julia's ability to think for themselves, and hey how about the obligations and standards of shut the fuck up.

But then Tom oversteps himself, by arguing:

> *"And as to my father's being absent, it is so far from an objection, that I consider it rather as a motive; for the expectation of his return must be a very anxious period to my mother, and if we can be the means of amusing that anxiety, and keeping her spirits for the next few weeks, I shall think our time very well spent, and so I am sure will he.—It is a very anxious period for her."*

Cut immediately to Lady Bertram sprawled out on her chaise, snoring lightly, a little drool running down the side of her mouth. Anyone else might be abashed at having so baldly overstated his case, but Tom just laughs aloud and admits, Okay, maybe not so much, and shrugs it off. (Seriously, *how much* do we love Tom? Show of hands?...Thought so.)

But Edmund won't leave off; he's like a little terrier, tugging at Tom's pants leg and yipping at everyone else. We've all known this type, haven't we; the sanctimonious do-righter, who stands on the sidelines while everyone else is reveling in the energy and excitement of some new endeavor, forging a community and—well, *living life*—and pestering them with a continual chorus of "You guys are in *soooo* much trouble. Man, I would *not* want to be you when Dad gets home." I mean, yeah, of course he's right. That just makes him all the more despicable. (If Austen were herself, and not laboring under some kind of pentitential delusion, she'd agree.) Eventually Tom has had enough, and throws down the gauntlet: "Don't act yourself, if you do not like it, but don't expect to govern every body else."

Edmund says he'd rather have root canal surgery than act—no, kidney-stone surgery—no wait, all his limbs amputated—but oops, never mind, Tom's already walked away. Edmund retreats to where Fanny still sits by the window, knowing she'll always take his side (of course she will, he programmed her himself). He doesn't adopt her suggestion of shoring up his side of the argument by enlisting Aunt Norris, saying, "Family squabling is the greatest evil of all, and we had better do any thing than be altogether by the ears." In other words: No thanks, I'd rather make a great show of sulking.

But even that pleasure is denied him when a new arrival bursts in (perhaps finally sending Fanny over the sill and down into the hedgerow):

> *...Henry Crawford entered the room, fresh from the Parsonage, calling out, "No want of hands in our Theatre, Miss Bertram. No want of under strappers—My sister desires her love, and hopes to be admitted into the company, and will be happy to take the part of any old Duenna or tame Confidante, that you may not like to do yourselves."*

Maria shoots Edmund a gloating look, because if Mary Crawford is in favor of the theatricals, Edmund can't make too big a stink about it. And in fact Mary's approval does turn his mind a bit: "[He] was obliged to acknowledge that the charm of acting might well carry fascination to the mind of genius; and with the ingenuity of love, to dwell more on the obliging, accommodating purport of the message than on any thing else."

I think Austen wants us to fear for Edmund here; we're meant to see him as a man of principle, succumbing to the charms of a vivacious but amoral temptress. But seriously...Mary just brims with the life-force; Tom too. That Edmund pits himself against them, only mars him in our eyes. And the way he gives up his assault on the theatricals the minute he hears of Mary's participation, makes him look cynical as well. Or weak. Or both. Edmund is a straw man, who pretends to have a spine of iron. He, not Mr. Yates, is the bore in this business.

In a rare shaft of perception, Fanny assures Edmund that the whole enterprise may founder on the selection of material, because with all the egos variously at work, it's unlikely they'll ever find a play to satisfy every desire for stardom. And so it falls out, as the company proves unable even to decide whether to go for drama or comedy, with Tom for the latter and everyone else the former. Austen has great fun describing them tearing through the western canon, discarding great works of art like gristle from a chicken:

> *"...That* might *do, perhaps, but for the low parts—If I* must *give my opinion, I have always thought it the most insipid play in the English language—*I *do not wish to make objections, I shall be happy to be of any use, but I think we could not choose worse."*

Without knowing it, Austen is speaking directly to her readers of two centuries hence, who have suffered through many a business meeting in which exactly this dynamic plays out. Were she alive now, she'd be a wizard at corporate satire. She even has Tom Bertram step in to play the role every such meeting inevitably delivers up: the self-appointed mediator, who makes a great show of heroically taking the first step towards necessary compromise:

> *"This will never do...We are wasting time most abominably. Something must be fixed on. No matter what, so that something is chosen. We must not be so nice. A few characters too many, must not frighten us. We must* double *them. We must descend a little. If a part is insignificant, the greater our credit in making any thing of it. From this moment on,* I *make no difficulties. I take any part you choose to give me, so as it be comic. Let it but be comic, I condition for nothing more."*

In other words: I graciously and humbly agree to accept whatever the rest of you choose, as long as it's exactly what I suggested in the first place.

Eventually they do settle on a play: *Lovers' Vows,* the very piece Mr. Yates's party had been engaged in before that selfish old grandmother had to put the kibosh on it by dying. You might have thought they would've just chosen this piece at the outset, by default—I mean, Mr. Yates already knows it backwards and forwards. Indeed, someone even says, "How came it never to be thought of before? It strikes me as if it would do exactly." So, in terms of plot, pretty much everything in the preceding pages might be cut—all the negotiating and posturing and grandstanding—and I'll lay down a wager those scenes are missing from the Reader's Digest Condensed version. This is the danger of concentrating solely on plot; because the meat of Jane Austen is character, and the reason we love her—the reason she's immortal—is the absolute sureness of touch with which she renders her cast's vanity, venality, hypocrisy, and greed. To wit:

Mr. Yates was particularly pleased; he had been sighing and longing to do the Baron at Ecclesford, and had grudged every rant of Lord Ravenshaw's, and had been forced to re-rant it all in his own room.

Take out passages like this, and you essentially gut Jane Austen with a Bowie knife. And what you've got left is pretty people in their waistcoats and pelisses, gliding about being photogenic. Which is, believe it or not, exactly what some people want from Austen. Seriously. I've met them. What they crave is less Jane Austen than The Jane Austen Catalog, with chapeaus and gloves and china cups you can imagine wantonly Adding To Cart.

Austen continues with her show-biz psychodrama, as the Bertram sisters—already rivals over Henry Crawford—try to edge each other out for the plum female role. "Each sister looked anxious; for each felt the best claim to Agatha, and was hoping to have it pressed on her by the rest." Mr. Crawford himself is the chief agent of appeal; and he chooses Maria, but again proves to be the most polished of silver-tongued devils, by doing so in terms designed to flatter Julia right out of her knickers.

"I must entreat Miss Julia *Bertram...not to engage in the part of Agatha, or it will be the ruin of all my solemnity. You must not, indeed you must not...I could not stand your countenance dressed up in woe and paleness. The many laughs we have had together would infallibly come across me, and Frederick and his knapsack would be obliged to run away."*

But Julia's no fool; she steals a glance at Maria, and seeing the "smile of triumph" on her face just confirms "the injury to herself." And if she's on the fence as to how to react—whether graciously, or in a temper—Tom tips the scales for the latter by chiming in:

"Oh! yes, Maria must be Agatha. Maria will be the best Agatha. Though Julia fancies she prefers tragedy, I would not trust her in it. There is nothing of tragedy about her. She has not the look of it. Her features are not tragic features, and she walks too quick, and speaks too quick, and would not keep her countenance. She had better do the old countrywoman; the Cottager's wife; you had, indeed, Julia."

Mr. Yates is astonished, declaring the Cottage's wife "an insult...At Ecclesford the governess was to have done it," and proposes the second female role, Amelia, instead; but Tom Bertram has Mary Crawford in mind for that ("Amelia should be a small, light, girlish, skipping figure. It is fit for Miss Crawford and Miss Crawford only") and won't budge. There's more wheedling, pettiness, and desperate flattery—not to mention more maddeningly satisfied smiles from Maria—before Julia decides which role she's going to play, and it's that of To Hell With the Whole Lot Of You, I'm Audi. And with a big violent rustle of fabric, she storms off.

This leaves Maria all clear for *her* preferred role, which is Most Misunderstood Of All God's Lonely Creatures, as she whimpers to Mr. Crawford, "I am sure I would give up the part to Julia most willingly, but that though I shall probably do it very ill, I feel persuaded *she* would do it worse," which elicits all sorts of there-there-you-poor-suffering-angel's from Henry. And maybe another smile of triumph from Maria. Smiling in triumph seems to be her default mode.

When the party breaks up, Fanny—who's remained on the fringes this whole time, watching and listening like a spaniel who's been ordered into a sit-stay and is taking special pride in holding it even when no one's looking—sneaks over to the table where the copy of *Lovers' Vows* lies open, and gives it a skim—presumably gleaning enough to understand that it deals with illicit sex and an illegitimate birth. Within moments she drops it as through she'd inadvertently picked up the latest issue of *Screw*. She comes away shocked, *shocked* that her cousins would even consider putting on this carnival of debauchery.

Of course, Fanny's dismay and disapproval mean exactly flap all to anybody else, so the plan continues apace. Mr. Rushworth is drawn into the production and is highly flattered by the attention and by the consequence it seems to give him in Maria's eyes—though he can't understand why her character and his aren't allowed any scenes together; apparently he thinks the company is writing the play as well as acting it. But any moping on his part is preempted by "pointing out the necessity of his being very much dressed, and choosing his colours...[he] liked the idea of his finery very well, though affecting to despise it, and was too much engaged with what his own appearance would be, to think of the others, or draw any of those conclusions, or feel any of that displeasure, which Maria had been half prepared for." Indeed, when Edmund returns after a morning out, Mr. Rushworth greets him with an enthusiasm bordering on molestation:

> *"We have got a play," said he.—"It is to be Lovers' Vows; and I am to be Count Cassel, and am to come in first with a blue dress, and a pink satin cloak, and afterwards am to have another fine fancy suit by way of a shooting dress.—I do not know how I shall like it."*

From here on in, this is his role in every scene: to boast of the glories of his part, then tag a disclaimer on the end of it. In sitcoms, many a character has made shtick no meatier than this play out for entire seasons. Mr. Rushworth certainly plays out his for all it's worth.

> *"I come in three times, and have two and forty speeches. That's something, is not it?—But I do not much like the idea of being so fine.—I shall hardly know myself in a blue dress, and a pink satin cloak."*

A few more recurrences of this and whaddaya know, he's even got a catchphrase—and you might find yourself wishing for a t-shirt that reads, not THAT'S WHAT SHE SAID, or WORST. EPISODE. EVER, but I HAVE TWO AND FORTY SPEECHES.

Edmund, whose errand this morning was apparently to refuel his depleting tank of outrage, now rips into Maria over the choice of that *scandalous* play. He challenges her to "Read only the first Act aloud, to either your mother or aunt, and see how you can approve it." I actually think Maria should take him up on this; after all, Lady Bertram would smile and nod dreamily through a reading of *Oh! Calcutta!,* while Mrs. Norris would just delight in Maria's impeccable aspirates and vowel sounds.

Edmund has better luck appealing to her vanity ("*You* must set the example.—If others have blundered, it is your place to put them right, and shew them what true delicacy is.—In all points of decorum, *your* conduct must be law to the rest of the party"). But at the last moment Maria realizes that if she withdraws from the play, Julia will just step in and take her part, and there goes that.

Aunt Norris interrupts with a long, hilarious speech on the misbehaviors of some neighbors ("the Jacksons are very encroaching, I have always said so,—just the sort of people to get all they can") which demonstrates, once again, that Austen understands the principle of projection and is all too happy to use it for comic effect. (Remember Mrs. Bennet's endless harangues about Lady Lucas's pushiness and arrogance?) By the time she rambles to a conclusion, tempers have cooled, and Edmund finds "that to have endeavoured to set them right must be his only satisfaction," though he's been such a remarkable killjoy that no one now dares to speak of the project in his presence—even Tom, who up to now has seemed pretty immune to Edmund's Catholic-nun censoriousness.

Mary Crawford now shows up and, reading the currents instantly, attempts to assuage Tom's wounded pride by speaking, not to him, but to his mother in his hearing, complimenting her on the fortitude with which she's bearing all the noise and silliness of the players. We know this can't really be meant for Lady Bertram because the woman has the fortitude of your average sea-dwelling invertebrate, and also because several times during the address Mary glances "half fearfully, half slily, beyond Fanny to Edmund." I love that added detail of having to look past Fanny—or possibly through her.

Mary is then welcomed into the company and brought up to speed (Mr. Rushworth informs her of his two and forty speeches), and everyone gets down to business. But dang if they don't run into a hitch right off the bat: there are a couple of roles still uncast. Mary, adopting her most flirtatious manner—she all but gets up and cavorts around his chair—tries to get Edmund to take the bait by reverse-psychology. She tells him she understands he refuses to act, but what then would he advise the company to do about the role of Anhalt? Edmund, not falling for such guile, says, Change the play.

Mary, not giving up, decides on a more direct approach, noting that, "If *any* part could tempt you to act, I suppose it would be Anhalt...for he is a clergyman, you know." Edmund replies that this would actually *prevent* him from taking the part, because he'd "be sorry to make the character ridiculous by bad acting." This is a pretty lame excuse, and very far from the blistering outrage we expect from him (i.e. "No role could tempt me to enlist in an enterprise so certain to expose my sister and others to opprobrium and shame"). It's clear he can't summon up that much ire with Mary seated before him—Mary in the firelight, no less (because, canny creature, she's seated herself right before the hearth, so that the flames can dance over her skin).

Jane Austen helped invent the conventions of courtship comedies, so we can't exactly accuse her of cheating us here; this is just shy of the midpoint of her career, and she was still perfecting her craft, trying new things. But after a few more scenes like these, we're going to *feel* pretty damn cheated anyway. We've been taught, time and time again, in the two centuries since *Mansfield Park*, that couples whose attraction for each other is at odds with their moral, ethical, or political differences, will always end up happily setting aside the world and finding contentment only in each other. And we've learned to like it that way. What we don't want, is to have the differences win; we don't want lovers to turn away from each other over belief systems or class discrepancies. And I can't believe Austen does, either. Maybe that's why *Mansfield Park* ultimately feels like a betrayal; Austen was betraying herself.

Just look at what happens now, when the novel's professed heroine, Fanny, is called on to take the part of the Cottager's Wife. She refuses; despite all entreaties (and there are a *lot* of entreaties, plus a few veiled threats), she holds firm and keeps repeating: I cannot act, you must excuse me, I cannot act, you must excuse me. Obviously we're meant to see this as some kind of heroism on her part, some clinging fast to a higher principle. But we understand instinctively that it's just another example of Fanny's all-consuming negativity; she is an abyss, into which all potential, all hope, irrevocably disappears.

Whereas Mary—Mary is quicksilver; she's alive to the ebb and flow, to shifts in power; she can see when persuasion edges into persecution. She witnesses Fanny's tears, and mistaking them for evidence of girlish shyness (how is someone like Mary to understand that Fanny's real distress is at being pressed to choose action over inaction, presence over absence? How can a life force comprehend a vacuum?), she *takes Fanny's side*. She rescues her from her tormentors; she *comforts* her.

Mary Crawford, ladies and gentlemen. Let's give her full props, and while we're at it, the keys to the Chevy and the title of Prom Queen in Heaven. Because she won't get a happily-ever-after from anyone else but us. I'm just sayin'.

CHAPTERS 16-18

The Fanny Problem becomes, in these chapters, exacerbated by the essential absence at her core. When we left her, she had just refused to act in *Lovers' Vows*—refused even against the exhortation and outright coercion of the entire theatrical party (they did everything but pinch and poke at her)—and had done so both adamantly and inarticulately. She refused, but- wouldn't say why; or rather, *couldn't* say why. For Fanny, the word "no" is its own justification.

Up in the East Room—the former schoolroom of the Bertram girls, which Fanny has subsequently claimed, inch by inch, kudzu-style—she is free to reflect on her misery. Being essentially morbid by nature, she of course wallows in reliving every horrifying moment of her trial:

> *To be called into notice in such a manner, to hear that it was but the prelude to something so infinitely worse, to be told that she must do what was so impossible as to act; and then to have the charge of obstinacy and ingratitude follow it, enforced with such a hint at the dependence of her situation, had been too distressing at the time, to make the remembrance when alone less so,—especially with the superadded dread of what the morrow might produce in continuation of the subject.*

She lurches around the room in a ferment, eventually pausing before a portrait of Edmund to see "if she could catch any of his counsel," which works about as well as that kind of thing usually does. I suppose we should be grateful she doesn't sit cross-legged before it, burning incense and playing finger-cymbals. Instead she continues her coyote-like pacing of the room's perimeter, which forces her, by presenting her with a grand tour of all the gifts and tokens she's received from her cousins over the years, to wonder whether her obstinacy is, in fact, justifiable by any measure. "Was she right in refusing what was so warmly asked, so strongly wished for? What might be so essential to a scheme on which some of those to whom she owed the greatest complaisance, had set their hearts? Was it not ill-nature—selfishness—and a fear of exposing herself?"

Well?...*Was it?*...This is the question—the BIG one—we've been waiting for Fanny to confront. She's on the precipice of a breakthrough, here—a recognition that maybe, just maybe, her kneejerk reaction of saying no to everything in the entire world, cosmos, and universe might be doing her no favors, and in fact might constitute a form of passive-aggressiveness bordering on the truly sociopathic.

But before she can quiiiite reach this blessed epiphany, there's a tap on the door, and "her gentle 'come in,' was answered by the appearance of one, before whom all her doubts were wont to be laid. Her eyes brightened at the sight of Edmund." *Her* eyes, anyway; ours are more likely to roll right up into our craniums. All hope of Fanny reaching a new understanding evaporates as her hero, idol, and chief enabler enters, to reinforce all her worst character traits.

Or does he?...In fact, Edmund has come to astonish her. Alarmed by Tom's efforts to find someone to take one of the uncast roles—which apparently involve riding around the countryside petitioning every male who can stand upright in his boots without wetting himself—Edmund is moved to drastic measures: to save his sister and Miss Crawford from excessive familiarity with a stranger (because in Edmund's view, reciting ribald lines from a playscript is pretty much third base), he has made up his mind to take the role himself. Well, you could knock Fanny over with a feather. (Actually, you can probably knock Fanny over with a feather at the best of times. But let it pass.)

Edmund desires her approval, which she isn't ready to give (though she doesn't quite refuse it, either; bold, decisive girl). She says how sorry she is that Edmund's complete 180 will give "such a triumph to the others," which he's forced to admit it will; but he must bear all their smug smiles and fist-pumping and high-fives and focus on the power he will then have to keep the production from going completely off the rails.

> *"As I am now, I have no influence, and they will not hear me; but when I have put them in good humour by this concession, I am not without hopes of persuading them to confine the representation within a much smaller circle than they are now in the high road for. This will be a material gain. My object is to confine it to Mrs. Rushworth and the Grants. Will that not be worth gaining?"*

Of course it is, and Fanny knows it. But still she withholds her assent, because that's what Fanny does best: she withholds, withdraws, refuses. It doesn't help, of course, that Edmund keeps harping away on the danger to Mary Crawford, as though trying to convince himself that this is really his motive, and that there's no appeal, none at all do you hear, in the idea of murmuring salaciously wicked couplets in Mary's lovely ear. He even scolds Fanny for not being more sensible to Mary's certain relief at having him rescue her this way, especially after Mary rescued her just a few hours earlier—not realizing that with every word he's further damning Mary in Fanny's eyes. At this point, if Mary were clinging for dear life off the white cliffs of Dover, Fanny would so far make an exception to her rule of complete and total inertia, as to stamp ever so lightly on Mary's pretty fingers.

Fanny manages to mumble enough evasive but agreeable-sounding syllables to convince Edmund that she does indeed give him her blessing, and the interview winds down. Edmund, in a little spate of amiable chatter before he departs, makes it clear that despite her being a creature of his own creation, he has absolutely no idea who she is.

> *"How does Lord Macartney go on?—(opening a volume on the table and then taking up some others.) And here are Crabbe's Tales, and the Idler, at hand to relieve you, if you tire of your great book. I admire your little establishment exceedingly; and as soon as I am gone, you will empty your head of all this nonsense of acting, and sit comfortably down to your table."*

He may be the most clueless hero in all of Austen—and he doesn't exactly make up for it with boatloads of charm. (Unless he's around

Mary, who manages to elicit something winsome and sweet out of him, the way hummingbirds use their long beaks to draw nectar from deep within a flower.)

As you might have guessed, Fanny's prediction comes to pass, and the theatrical party *do* exult over Edmund's submission. Like there was ever any doubt. Maria is constitutionally incapable of *not* exulting when she gets her way. If she tried, the effort might blow the top of her scalp right off—with a tiny mushroom cloud as a grace note. We're told that they all "congratulated each other in private on the jealous weakness to which they attributed the change...he was to act, and he was driven to it by the force of selfish inclinations only"—meaning, they're perfectly aware of the part Mary Crawford played in changing his mind. He has, therefore, lost all moral standing in their eyes, which pretty much torpedoes his chances of setting them on a less self-exposing course of action. At this point, if a runaway carriage were barreling towards them, and Edmund strongly advised moving out of its path, they might take this as sufficient reason for standing firm till they really thought it over.

But to his face, of course, they're completely congenial and collegial. "It was all good humour and encouragement. Mrs. Norris offered to contrive his dress, Mr. Yates assured him that Anhalt's last scene with the Baron admitted a good deal of action and emphasis, and Mr. Rushworth underook to count his speeches."

There's a danger to Fanny, though, that the party, emboldened by its victory over Edmund, might renew its assault on her to join the cast; but she's saved by Mrs. Grant agreeing to take the part earlier offered to her. You'd think this would be unalloyed joy for Fanny, but no, because Mrs. Grant has signed on at the urging of Mary Crawford (though it can't have taken *much* urging. You get the impression Mrs. Grant could be persuaded to bungee-jump off Tower Bridge by a single hint dropped two rooms away). Thus it's due to Mary's intervention that Fanny is spared from further attack. She is even *more* indebted to her, and she doesn't like it. Not. One. Bit.

Even worse, Fanny's black hole of inertia now seems to have lost its negative power over the household.

> *Every body around her was gay and busy, prosperous and important, each had their object of interest, their part, their dress, their favourite scene, their friends and confederates, all were finding employment in consulta-*

> *tions and comparisons, or diversion in the playful conceits they suggested. She alone was sad and insignificant; she had no share in any thing; she might go or stay, she might be in the midst of their noise, or retreat from it to the solitude of the East room, without being seen or missed.*

In other words, Fanny can't take any pleasure in being inert anymore, if she's not also sucking the life out of every room she enters. What good is her power of denial, if everybody around her is just thoughtlessly taking up whatever they want anyway, without even considering her?...It's here we really begin to see the "monster of complacency and pride...under a cloak of cringing self-abasement" that Kinglsey Amis declared her to be.

"She could almost think any thing would have been preferable" to her new irrelevancy in the household, but despite this "she could never have been easy in joining a scheme which, considering only her uncle, she must condemn altogether." But she's *not* considering only her uncle; she'd already decided the play itself is beyond the pale. She therefore has *two* pillars of moral support for holding herself apart from the theatricals.

Fanny's not alone in languishing on the fringes of the *Lovers's Vows* enterprise. Julia, too, exists in a state of irrelevancy. Henry Crawford, in plainly favoring her sister, has wounded her so deeply that she "either sat in gloomy silence, wrapt in such gravity as nothing could subdue... or allowing the attentions of Mr. Yates, was talking with forced gaiety to him alone, and ridiculing the acting of the others." In other words, it's either Notice me, I'm sulking, or Notice me, I'm perfectly happy without you and your stupid play. Either one of those tacks might have worked, but when you use them together, they kinda cancel each other out.

Even worse for Julia, she makes the tactical mistake of rebuffing Henry's attempts to conciliate her, which just persuades him to give up the matter entirely. He's thus emboldened to go openly sniffing and pawing around Maria as though she were a bitch in high heat, which can't possibly escape the notice (and the alarm) of everybody else. Julia is forced to watch from the sidelines as the man she apparently does in fact love, makes a spectacle of himself over the sister "who was now her greatest enemy." Julia's only comfort is in selfishly hoping for a scandal that will disgrace both. Never mind that it would mean the ruin of her family and the wreck of her household; her *feelings* are hurt, dammit. *Scourge the whole damn planet, if that's what it takes.*

You'd think Fanny and Julia, as the two outcasts from theatrical paradise, might make common cause, or at least come together to commiserate, but "there was no outward fellowship between them. Julia made no communication, and Fanny took no liberties." Of course not. It's her nature to *refuse,* not to *take.* She could no more extend a sympathetic hand to Julia, than she could climb the walls like a spider and scamper across the ceiling.

But Fanny and Julia aren't to be alone in their discontent for long. For Edmund's submission has marked the high point of the proceedings; only a short while later, we find all the harmony and high spirits dissipated. "Every body began to have their vexation..."

> *Fanny, being always a very courteous listener, and often the only listener at hand, came in for the complaints and distresses of most of them. She knew that Mr. Yates was in general thought to rant dreadfully, that Mr. Yates was disappointed in Henry Crawford, that Tom Bertram spoke so quick he would be unintelligible, that Mrs. Grant spoilt every thing by laughing, that Edmund was behind-hand with his part, and that it was a misery to have any thing to do with Mr. Rushworth, who was wanting a prompter through every speech...Every body had a part either too long or too short;—nobody would attend as they ought, nobody would remember on which side they were to come in—nobody but the complainer would observe any directions.*

I could happily read stuff like this all day long, and can't help wishing Austen had just turned her attention in this direction instead of continually wresting it back onto old Misery Guts.

Speaking of whom, is it surprising to you that she ends up being the mother confessor to the whole cast, given her antipathy to the play and her staunch moral stand against its being undertaken in Sir Thomas's absence?...Well, get a load of this:

> *Fanny believed herself to derive as much innocent enjoyment from the play as any of them;—Henry Crawford acted well, and it was a pleasure to her to creep into the theatre and attend the rehearsal of the first act—in spite of the feelings it excited in some speeches for Maria.—Maria she*

> *also thought acted well—too well;—and after the first rehearsal or two, Fanny began to be their only audience, and—sometimes as prompter, sometimes as spectator—was often very useful.*

WTF?!? Hello, hypocritical much? Either the play is immoral, or it isn't; either the production is a breach of decorum, or it isn't. Fanny appears to want to have it both ways: standing aloof in her black cloak of disapproval, and yet fluttering on in for a couple hits of sensation whenever the fancy strikes her.

In fact this is where Fanny and I part company, for good. Her hollow core is finally revealed for the moral and spiritual abyss it is. She has no ballast, no bottom; she's a thin, dry reed, a stick-thing, propped up by the cold wind of pride, though her roots are utterly dead. Never mind the Jane Austen horror mash-ups that are flooding the market these days; Austen herself anticipated them. In Fanny Price, she has given us a perfectly creditable vampire.

Denied the power to suck the life out of the entire endeavor, Fanny has been reduced to darting about its perimeter like a ghoul, sipping when she can from the torrents of emotion that flow there (notably wild jealousy of Henry Crawford's superior acting skills) and helping Aunt Norris with all the needlework the production requires. "[Fanny's] gloom of her first anticipations was proved to have been unfounded. She was occasionally useful to all; she was perhaps as much at peace as any." This is one of Austen's subtler jibes, because none of them is at anything close to peace—Fanny the succubus least of all.

Fanny's chief cause for anxiety is a scene—soon to be rehearsed—between Edmund and Mary Crawford, "the whole subject of [which] was love—a marriage of love was to be described by the gentleman, and very little short of a declaration of love be made by the lady." Heady stuff, apparently; the Regency equivalent of a money shot.

> *[Fanny] had read, and read the scene again with many painful, many wondering emotions, and looked forward to their representation of it as a circumstance almost too interesting. She did not* believe *they had yet rehearsed it, even in private.*

As it happens, she's right about that; and confirmation arrives in the form of Mary Crawford herself, who intrudes upon Fanny in the frigid confines of East Room (henceforth to be known alternately as Castle Dracula) with an unusual request.

> *"I came here today intending to rehearse [the third act] with Edmund—by ourselves—against the evening, but he is not in the way; and if he* were, *I do not think I could go through it with* him, *till I have hardened myself a little, for really there* is *a speech or two...There, look at* that *speech, and* that, *and* that. *How am I ever to look him in the face and say such things? Could you do it? But then he is your cousin, which makes all the difference. You must rehearse it with me, that I may fancy you him, and get on by degrees. You* have *a look of his sometimes."*

Mary's motives deserve some consideration, here. Because where Austen can't seem to bring Fanny to life in the way she desires, she never puts a foot wrong with Mary. So we have to take Mary at face value; she's never once shown even the slightest impulse for dissembling. If anything, her habit is to be excessively truthful, and to delight in the gasps and blushes that follow. So if she says she's too shy to rehearse these romantically charged scenes with Edmund, we have to believe her. In fact it's endearing; Mary, who wouldn't think twice about reciting an obscene limerick for the Archbishop of Canterbury (possibly while pole-dancing on his crosier), is nervous about exchanging some suggestive lines with Edmund. Why?...Because they may reflect on her own true feelings; and while Mary may happily flout convention, that kind of nakedness is enough to give her pause.

And yet...I think there's a dual purpose to her prevailing on Fanny this way. Yes, she wants to build up her courage for the rehearsal by running through the lines in advance with the one person on whom she can depend to help her do so; but she also recognizes that that very person is someone whose palpable feelings for Edmund (which Mary alone can see—because she's the only person who's actually bothered to *look* at Fanny) might cause some sort of trouble or disruption down the road. That pointed reference to Edmund being Fanny's cousin, and therefore beyond the reach of any embarrassment at acting the lover with him, is Mary's subtle way of reminding Fanny of the hopelessness (if not the silliness) of any tenderness she may feel for him. This isn't, I'm convinced, a case of Lucy Steele-type cattiness on Mary's part;

quite the opposite—she's more likely to be trying to save Fanny from disappointment and heartbreak, than to forestall her becoming a rival.

Her point made, Mary—aware that she may have mortified Fanny by her observation—goes to great lengths to comfort her in the manner Mary knows best: through gossip. She draws up two chairs and settles into a cozy little chin-wag about all the others, as in this anecdote (which, incidentally, again reveals Mary's essentially perceptive and generous nature) about "those indefatigable rehearsers," Maria and Henry:

> *"If* they *are not perfect, I shall be surprised...I looked in upon them five minutes ago, and it happened to be exactly at one of the times when they were trying not to embrace, and Mr. Rushworth was with me. I thought he began to look a little queer, so I turned it off as well as I could, by whispering to him, 'We shall have an excellent Agatha, there is something so* maternal *in her manner, so completely* maternal *in her voice and countenance.' Was not that well done of me? He brightened up directly."*

Go ahead, try to despise this woman. Try, even, not to love her to pieces. And try, just go ahead and try, to prefer the gaping void in the chair opposite.

At Mary's behest, Fanny begins to read the scene with her—again, leaping right into those incendiary lines that had previously so shocked her she'd utterly refused to have anything to do with them—and it's all going swimmingly until there's another knock on the door, and Edmund enters. (Let me just say again, it's a shame Austen never wrote for the stage; her theatrical instincts are infallible. Even in a novel in which she heaps opprobrium on the whole concept of theatricals.)

Edmund has, of course, come to Castle Dracula for the same reason Mary did: to run through his lines with Fanny before daring to attempt them with Mary. (Since, it goes without saying, no possible embarrassment could accompany reciting them before Fanny; he might just as comfortably try them out in a mirror. Or on the family dog. Or on a moderate-sized piece of masonry.)

Once the awkwardness of the coincidence has passed, the two colleagues figure they might as well seize the opportunity and read their lines together here and now, and ask Fanny "to prompt and observe them."

> *She was invested, indeed, with the office of judge and critic, and earnestly desired to exercise it and tell them all their faults; but from doing so every feeling within her shrank, she could not, would not, dared not attempt it...*

We begin to see a pattern here. Fanny is more than willing to set aside her lofty standards and affronted morals at the request of a single supplicant, whether this means helping Mr. Rushworth learn his lines, or Mrs. Norris run up the costumes. Indeed, she's all but giddy to lend a hand. But when two or more of them appeal jointly to her, suddenly she draws herself up and cloaks herself in No. In other words, when there's something before her that can conceivably be termed an audience, she—what else can you call it?—puts on an front. She acts.

I repeat: hypocrite.

In this case, however, she's pretty much forced to give in; she can't resort to her usual tactic—fleeing to the East Room—because they're already *in* the East Room. And it's clear Edmund and Mary aren't going to budge from it till they've got what they came for. In fact, they'd probably just forge ahead whether Fanny was with them or not, so the whole point of Fanny's refusal is rendered moot. She finds herself sitting and listening to them, and witnesses "the increasing spirit of Edmund's manner," and we're supposed to feel the depths of her suffering. Again, not so much.

Now that Edmund and Mary have cut their teeth on their big emotional scene, we're ready for the first regular rehearsal, which takes place that very evening. Everyone's in high spirits, milling about the makeshift theater, eager to get started; they're just awaiting the arrival of the Crawfords and Mrs. Grant. But alas, the Crawfords arrive alone. Mrs. Grant has had to stay behind due to her husband suffering an "indisposition" after having *not* having eaten dinner, which just makes no sense. Unless he turned away the dinner because he'd already gobbled up the downstairs parlor maid.

Without Mrs. Grant the rehearsal can't proceed. *Unless*...all turn as one to Fanny. "If Miss Price would be so good as to *read* the part," someone says, with the emphasis on *read* as opposed to *act,* which everyone knows Fanny would rather hurl herself into quicksand than agree to. Fanny, who's already given way on so many other little issues connected with the production, is on far less secure ethical footing now, and even Edmund urges her: "Do Fanny, if it is not *very* disagreeable to you."

> *"You have only to* read *the part," said Henry Crawford with renewed entreaty.*
>
> *"And I do believe she can say every word of it," added Maria, "for she could put Mrs. Grant right the other day in twenty places. Fanny, I am sure you know the part."*

Fanny's falseness and hypocrisy have finally trapped her; and, in the manner of sinners and criminals everywhere, she seems almost glad of it. In a way, it will be a relief to shed the burden of so much negativity; to join at last in fellowship, to embrace activity openly and without conditions. She is, we realize, once again on the point of salvation: this could be the very moment at which she's drawn out of the cold isolation of her cycle of refusals, and into the warm embrace of the country of Yes. Her heart pounds...her mouth goes dry...but she's ready to do it. She's ready...she's willing. She *will* do it. She says as much. She'll help them—and she'll be free.

> *They [began]—and being too much engaged in their own noise, to be struck by unusual noise in the other part of the house, had proceeded some way, when the door of the room was thrown open, and Julia appeared at it, with a face all aghast, exclaimed, "My father is come! He is in the hall at this moment!"*

The candles snuff; the casements slam shut. And Fanny Price pulls her shroud tight about her, and slips gratefully back into her tomb.

CHAPTERS 19-21

"How is the consternation of the party to be described?" the author asks, with regard to the unexpected arrival of Sir Thomas on the premises. The answer is simple: it's to be described with flat-out, balls-to-the-wall hilarity, with the cast darting about like characters in a French bedroom farce, in search of some screen or settee they might hide behind.

The exceptions are Maria and Henry Crawford, who, at the moment of the fateful announcement, are rehearsing a passionate scene between Frederick and Agatha in which the former presses the hand of the latter against his heart. That Henry does not, on hearing the news of Sir Thomas's presence in the house, relinquish that hand, but keeps it fast in place, enabling Maria to continue copping a feel of his studly pecs, gives her a thrill of conquest. "She hailed it as an earnest of the most serious determination, and was equal even to encounter her father."

When the Bertram siblings finally file out, no doubt dragging their feet like a chain gang, to welcome their returning sire (with Mr. Rushworth fluttering behind them, piping "Shall I go too?—Had not I better go too?—Will not it be right for me to go too?"), Fanny stays behind with the Crawfords and Mr. Yates.

> *She had been quite overlooked by her cousins; and as her own opinion of her claims on Sir Thomas's affection was much too humble to give her any idea of classifying herself with his children, she was glad to remain behind and gain a little breathing time...She was nearly fainting; all her former*

> *habitual dread of her uncle was returning, and with it compassion for him and for almost every one of the party on the development before him...She had found a seat; where in excessive trembling she was enduring all these fearful thoughts...*

We look for certain things in an Austen heroine, especially one placed under duress; "excessive trembling" is not among them.

While Fanny rattles and quakes, the Crawfords and Mr. Yates damn the luck that has brought the lord of the manor home at this precise juncture. The Crawfords realize it means the abrupt end of their theatrical experiment, but Mr. Yates—who is rapidly turning into a first-rate Austen idiot, a self-obsessed babbler who sees nothing beyond the tip of his nose—considers it only "a temporary interruption, a disaster for the evening." And when the Crawfords, understanding that in these circumstances retreat is the better part of valor, slink off home to the parsonage and advise Mr. Yates to likewise vamoose, he refuses. He "preferred remaining where he was that he might pay his respects to the old gentleman handsomely since he was come; and besides, he did not think it would be fair by the others to have every body run away."

Mr. Yates has all the social instincts of a howler monkey. But wait, he gets even better.

Fanny, meanwhile, has by some means—possibly a strong wind, or a minor earthquake—got herself to the drawing-room door, outside of which she pauses "for what she knew would not come, for a courage which the outside of no door had ever supplied her," and really, if her will to live can't withstand an encounter with a door, it's hard to hold out much hope for her.

As it happens, she enters the room just as Sir Thomas is enquiring after her ("But where is Fanny?—Why do I not see my little Fanny?" —the last bit of which, I'm sorry, my inner seven-year-old cannot read without a snort). And when she presents herself, he's so sweet and solicitous that it throws her into a confusion. For a moment she doesn't know whether to faint, or weep, or sink her teeth into his arm. Ultimately affection for him wins out, especially when she sees that he "was grown thinner and had the burnt, fagged, worn look of a hot climate," which suggests that in the movie version he be played by Donatella Versace.

Returned to his ancestral homestead and with his family gathered around him, Sir Thomas is in fine spirits, and he even takes a liking to his future son-in-law, Mr. Rushworth, a gentleman not famous for making a positive first impression. (Or a second, or a third, for that matter.) He gathers his clan around him to bask in their affection, and his wife is so moved by joy that "she had been *almost* fluttered for a few minutes," and actually moves her needlework and her pug aside to make room on the couch for him—which is the Lady Bertram equivalent of serenading him beneath a window, or launching a thousand ships to sail on Troy.

Aunt Norris, however, is pretty p.o.'ed at her brother-in-law's sudden return—because he has surprised her as fully as the others, leaving her not one damn thing to do.

> *Mrs. Norris felt herself defrauded of an office on which she had always depended, whether his arrival or his death were to be the thing unfolded; and was now trying to be in a bustle without having any thing to bustle about, and labouring to be important where nothing was wanted but tranquillity and silence.*

She's at her riotous best in these scenes of Sir Thomas attempting to relate his adventures to his family; as, for instance, "in the most interesting moment of his passage to England, when the alarm of a French privateer was at the height, she burst through his recital with a proposal of soup." He gently refuses all her entreaties, to the point you half expect her to sneak off and set fire to the dining room, just so she can be seen to be the one who puts it out.

Eventually Lady Bertram, in her Olympian cluelessness, says, "How do you think the young people have been amusing themselves lately, Sir Thomas? They have been acting." Which prompts all the young'uns to clear their throats and hastily say things like Only a little, just a few lines here and there, nothing substantial, pay no attention, is that a bear at the window, tell us again about the French privateer, and hey, how *about* some soup?

This successfully derails Sir Thomas from the subject until he decides he can't "be any longer in the house without just looking into his own dear room," and is so quickly off to do just that, that no one has time to stick a leg out to trip him or throw a burning log in his path.

Tom is the first to recover his wits, and he hurries after his father, reaching him just as he is standing in astonishment—not only at the transformation of his billiard room into a candlelit playhouse, but at the presence there of "a ranting young man, who appeared likely to knock him down backwards." Mr. Yates, interrupted in the midst of running through his lines, is no less astonished, and gives "perhaps the very best start he had ever given in the whole course of his rehearsal." People who think Jane Austen didn't write physical comedy, need to think again.

Despite the harrowing peril this puts him in, Tom can't help finding the funny side (which is, of course, why we love Tom):

> *His father's looks of solemnity and amazement on this his first appearance on any stage, and the gradual metamorphosis of the impassioned Baron Wildenhaim into the well-bred and easy Mr. Yates, making his bow and apology to Sir Thomas Bertram, was such an exhibition, such a piece of true acting as he would not have lost on any account. It would be the last—in all probability the last scene on that stage; but he was sure there could not be a finer. The house would close with the greatest éclat.*

Tom steps in to make a formal introduction, which doesn't help matters, as Sir Thomas is apparently familiar with Mr. Yates's family, and not in a way that promises ski weekends together. And it doesn't help that Mr. Yates's "easy indifference and volubility in the course of the first five minutes seemed to mark him as the most at home of the two." The three gentlemen return to the drawing room, "Sir Thomas with an increase of gravity which was not lost on all."

It is, however, entirely lost on Mr. Yates, who proceeds to yammer away for the remainder of the evening on the history of the endeavor, how it originated in the ill-fated production at Ecclesford, how it subsequently took root here, and every single detail of how it has proceeded since that day, short of the actual number of drop-stitches Mrs. Norris worked into Mr. Rushworth's pink satin cloak.

> *[He related] every thing with so blind an interest as made him not only totally unconscious of the uneasy movements of many of his friends as they sat, the change of countenance, the fidget, the hem! of unquietness, but prevented him even from seeing the expression of the face on which his own*

> *eyes were fixed—from seeing Sir Thomas's dark brow contract as he looked with inquiring earnestness at his daughters and Edmund...*

Fanny, however, doesn't miss those harsh glances thrown at Edmund. "She knelt in spirit to her uncle, and her bosom swelled to utter, 'Oh! not to him. Look so to all the others, but not to him!"

Kneeling in spirit: another trait we very much *don't* look for in an Austen heroine.

When Mr. Yates's monologue finally runs out of steam—it happens somewhere around the autumn of 1907—Sir Thomas makes a visible attempt to keep his temper on an even keel, and condescends to change the subject by asking about the Mr. and Miss Crawford whom he has heard mentioned in several letters. Tom, "being entirely without particular regard for either...could speak very handsomely of both" (brilliant!) and commends them to his father as "a most pleasant gentleman-like man;—his sister a sweet, pretty, elegant girl." Which provokes Mr. Rushworth—jealous as he is of Henry Crawford (and possibly jealous, too, of Mr. Yates having just having spectacularly stolen his title as the novel's champion boor), wildly interjects:

> *"I do not say he is not gentleman-like, considering; but you should tell your father he is not above five feet eight, or he will be expecting a well-looking man."*
>
> *Sir Thomas did not quite understand this, and looked with some surprize at the speaker.*

Fortunately, Mr. Rushworth then redeems himself by saying how tired he is of acting anyway, and how he thinks "we are a great deal better employed, sitting comfortably here among ourselves, and doing nothing." Doing nothing being, in all likelihood, Mr. Rushworth's favorite hobby. Sir Thomas, "aware that he must not expect a genius in Mr. Rushworth," is thus satisfied to find him a "well-judging steady young man" (this judgment may founder a bit when he learns about the pink satin cape), and Mr. Rushworth is "most exceedingly pleased with Sir Thomas's good opinion, and saying scarcely any thing, he did his best towards preserving that good opinion a little longer."

By now it's pretty clear that *Lovers' Vows* is about to be replaced by *Hell To Pay*. Edmund, not willing to wait around to play the part assigned to him, beards his father in his den the next morning and makes a full confession of his own culpability in the matter of the theatricals, with humble regrets inserted where appropriate.

> *"We have all been more or less to blame," said he, "every one of us, excepting Fanny. Fanny is the only one who has judged rightly throughout, who has been consistent.* Her *feelings have been steadily against it from first to last. She never ceased to think of what was due to you."*

This is clearly a load of crap. Fanny was an active participant in every aspect of the production, except the acting of it. And even there, while unwilling to take a role herself, she was more than ready to help the others learn their lines, and to prompt them during rehearsals. Possibly Edmund, who can't but see Fanny as his own creation, is unable to discern this clear hypocrisy. And Austen, as Edmund's creator as well as Fanny's, seems saddled by the same impairment.

Sir Thomas is sufficiently mollified by Edmund's manful blame-taking, that "He did not enter into any remonstrance with his other children: he was more willing to believe that they felt their error, than to run the risk of investigation," which makes him at least more self-aware than his son. Edmund is congenitally blind to Fanny's faults; Sir Thomas makes a conscious decision not to see those of his offspring.

He does, however, see quite clearly Mrs. Norris's guilt in the matter, and doesn't let her off so lightly. The children are young and, with the exception of Edmund, "he believed of unsteady characters" (which is a nice way of saying they're completely deranged hyena people); but Mrs. Norris, as a grown woman, ought to have exercised better judgment. When he confronts her on the matter, she gives one of her best comic performances—a real tour de force. Realizing she can't possibly excuse or even mitigate her role in advancing the theatricals, she makes a panicked, desperate case for herself by enumerating at length (and this being Mrs. Norris, the term "at length" is no mere figure of speech), the many, many, many, many other services she provided the Bertram family in Sir Thomas's absence. "Her greatest support and glory was in having formed the connection with the Rushworths," which has resulted in Maria's engagement. *"There* she was impregnable."

And to hear her tell it, her efforts on that score were no less than herculean; for example, she gives an account of how she managed to dislodge Lady Bertram from her sofa and haul her all the way across the county to meet Mrs. Rushworth. "You know the distance to Sotherton," she says; "it was in the middle of winter, and the roads almost impassable, but I did persuade her." Sir Thomas keeps valiantly trying to derail her with a series of Yes-but's, which she plows right through, building the story of the journey to Sotherton into an adventure more fraught with incident than Sir Thomas's encounter with the French privateer.

> *"My heart quite ached for [the coachman] at every jolt, and when we got into the rough lanes about Stoke, where what with frost and snow upon beds of stones, it was worse than anything you can imagine, I was quite in an agony about him. And then the poor horses too!—To see them straining away! You know how I always feel for the horses. And when we got to the bottom of Sandcroft Hill, what do you think I did? You will laugh at me—but I got out and walked up. I did indeed. It might not be saving them much, but it was something, and I could not bear to sit at my ease, and be dragged up at the expense of those noble animals. I caught a dreadful cold, but that I did not regard. My object was accomplished in the visit."*

If allowed to run on longer, she might also claim to have dug the coach out of a sudden rockslide, and warded off a pack of ravenous wolves. Unfortunately, Sir Thomas chooses this moment to give in to her—she's exhausted all the sternness right out of him—and the interview ends there. Still, it's one of the funniest scenes in the whole Austen canon, and makes one regret yet again that Austen never wrote for the stage. Just imagine the meal a good character actress could have made out of a scene like this one. Even the most dour audience member might have wound up needing of oxygen.

Sir Thomas then turns his hand to clearing out every last atom of evidence that *Lovers' Vows* ever infiltrated his hallowed halls. Essentially he tilts the entire house up forty-five degrees, and just shakes all the offending elements right out the door and windows. When the place is thus disinfected, the damage seems minimal: "The scene painter was gone, having spoilt only the floor of one room, ruined all the coachman's sponges, and made five of the under-servants idle and dissatisfied," and sweet Jesus, if we must, if we absolutely *must* suffer a deluge of modern novels attempting to flesh out or continue Austen's originals, can't someone at least have the ingenuity to turn his or her mind to the story of those five under-servants? (Ply me with enough single-malt scotch and I may just do the damn job myself.)

The sole exception to Sir Thomas's *Lovers' Vows* housecleaning is, of course, Mr. Yates, who manages to cling like a barnacle to the floorboards when the shaking is going on. He's such a sublime idiot that he's only just now twigging to the fact that the play might not be going forward as planned, and his thought process on hearing this confirmed is worth examining:

> *To be a second time disappointed in the same way was an instance of very severe ill-luck; and his indignation was such, that had it not been for the delicacy towards his friend and his friend's youngest sister, he believed he should certainly attack the Baronet on the absurdity of his proceedings, and argue him into a little more rationality...but there was a something in Sir Thomas, when they sat around the same table, which made Mr. Yates think it wiser to let him pursue his own way, and feel the folly of it without opposition...He was not a man to be endured but for his children's sake, and he might be thankful to his fair daughter Julia that Mr. Yates did yet mean to stay a few days longer under his roof.*

Masterful stuff—another example of Austen's genius at its pithiest, most acerbic, and most psychologically devastating. Mr. Yates has been stripped naked and flayed alive before our eyes, and though it takes us a moment to appreciate this, we realize—to our delight—that *he* still hasn't. How she manages to toss off these lethal little character bits, so glibly that you almost don't feel the knife going in till the final punctuation, is a perpetual mystery to me.

We now turn our attention to Maria, who's growing increasingly frantic because her father's reappearance has set the wheels of her marriage to Mr. Rushworth in motion. But Henry Crawford, whom she hasn't seen since the moment their rehearsal was interrupted, has yet to arrive to rescue her from this fate. "It was of the utmost consequence to her that Crawford should now lose no time in declaring himself, and she was disturbed that even a day should be gone by without seeming to advance the point." At least she doesn't have to suffer Mr. Rushworth's clumsy attentions in the meantime; he "had set off early with the great news for Sotherton; and she had fondly hoped for such an immediate eclaircissement as might save him the trouble of ever coming back again."

Eventually Henry does reappear, in the company of Dr. Grant, both come to pay their respects to the returned Sir Thomas, and "Maria saw with delight and agitation the introduction of the man she loved to her father." But alas, mere moments later Henry takes a chair near Tom, and Maria is jolted out of her raptures by overhearing him say that "he was going away immediately, being to meet his uncle at Bath without delay, but if there were any prospect of a renewal of 'Lovers' Vows,' he should hold himself positively engaged...The play should not be lost by *his* absence." He soon turns to Maria and gives her the same piece of news, "with only a softened air and stronger expressions of regret."

> *But what availed his expressions or his air?—He was going—and if not voluntarily going, voluntarily intending to stay away; for, excepting what might be due to his uncle, his engagements were all self-imposed.—He might talk of necessity, but she knew his independence.—The hand which had so pressed her's to his heart!—The hand and the heart were alike motionless and passive now!*

And then, just like that, Henry is gone—"gone from the house, and within two hours afterwards from the parish; and so ended all the hopes his selfish vanity had raised in Maria and Julia Bertram." We're still disposed to like Henry; and since Maria and Julia have never shown themselves to be anything but spoiled narcissists, we don't take much account of their wounded feelings. But suddenly Austen surprises us by rendering the sisters more human—reminding us that, in this novel, she's making a conscious effort to paint her villains, as well as her heroes, in more subtle hues:

> *Julia could rejoice that he was gone—His presence was beginning to be odious to her; and if Maria gained him not, she was now cool enough to dispense with any other revenge.—She did not want exposure to be added to desertion.—Henry Crawford was gone, she could even pity her sister.*

A few days later, Sir Thomas finally succeeds in dislodging Mr. Yates as well (possibly with the aid of his hounds and a loaded shotgun), and with that preening gasbag out of the picture there is, finally, nothing left in his field of vision to remind him that *Lovers' Vows* ever existed, even as a concept.

Before Austen closes the chapter, she gives the final bow to our favorite player:

> *Mrs. Norris contrived to remove one article from [Sir Thomas's] sight that might have distressed him. The curtain over which she had presided with such talent and such success, went off with her to her cottage, where she happened to be particularly in want of green baize.*

So Aunt Norris has outfoxed Sir Thomas, virtually getting away with, if not quite murder, at least an armful of top-quality textiles. You gotta imagine she's sleeping well tonight.

Everyone else, though, not so much. Sir Thomas's return to Mansfield has meant not just the crash and burn of *Lovers' Vows,* but the end of the revolving door of guests and revelers. Mansfield House goes into total lockdown: no one comes in, no one goes out. Sir Thomas wants to spend quiet evenings alone with his family, and goddammit, that's what he's going to do.

This comes as quite a shock to us as well, after the last few rollicking chapters. And in the sudden, deafening quiet—we can almost hear the ticking of the hall clock echoing through the house like a series of tiny thunderclaps—who should emerge from the shadows, but the character we've all but forgotten in the recent tumult: Fanny. She creeps noiselessly back into the narrative, where everyone is bemoaning the loss of all company, and tries to talk Edmund into happy submission to the new regimen. Of course she does; a vacuum is the thing Fanny likes best. When Edmund laments that even Dr. and Mrs. Grant are now shut out, and that they would "enliven us, and make our evenings pass away with more enjoyment to my father," Fanny counters:

> *"Do you think so?...In my opinion, my uncle would not like any addition ...And it does not appear to me that we are more serious than we used to be; I mean, before my uncle went abroad. As well as I can recollect, it was always much the same. There was never much laughing in his presence; or,*

> *if there was any difference, it was not more I think than such an absence has a tendency to produce at first."*

In other words, everyone was happy sitting around staring at their cuticles before; soon, we all will be again!

Fanny then observes, "I suppose I am graver than other people." Gosh, ya *think?* Girl is graver than most *graves.* (Gravity being, need I say it, another quality we absolutely don't look for in an Austen heroine). She goes on to comment on how much she loves listening to her uncle's stories of the West Indies. "It entertains *me* more than many other things have done—but then I am unlike other people I dare say." Which, give her credit, is a slam-dunk.

Edmund informs Fanny that the compliment is returned—that Sir Thomas enjoys her company as well; though at this point his enjoyment is largely due to Fanny having (ahem) filled out in all the right places.

> *"Your complexion is so improved!—and you have gained so much countenance!—and your figure—Nay, Fanny, do not turn away about it. It is but an uncle. If you cannot bear an uncle's admiration what is to become of you? You must really begin to harden yourself to the idea of being worth looking at.—You must try not to mind growing up into a pretty woman."*
>
> *"Oh! don't talk so, don't talk so," cried Fanny, distressed by more feeling than he was aware of...*

Hooo boy.

This tendency of Fanny's—to escape, to flee, to lurk in the margins—seems to have its effect on her creator as well, as we can almost sense Austen having to remind herself to bring Fanny forward. Not a difficulty she suffered with any of her other protagonists.

And indeed we're on the brink of losing Fanny again for a significant chunk of the narrative, as we segue into developments on the Maria-and-Mr. Rushworth front. The male Bertrams are to dine at Sotherton, and Fanny hopes Sir Thomas's initial good opinion of Mr. Rushworth will survive the occasion. Edmund won't bet money on it.

> *"That is impossible, Fanny. He must like him less after to-morrow's visit, for we shall be five hours in his company. I should dread the stupidity of the day, if there were not a much greater evil to follow—the impression it must leave on Sir Thomas. He cannot much longer deceive himself. I am sorry for them all, and would give something that Rushworth and Maria had never met."*

So much for Mrs. Norris's much-trumpeted credit in arranging the match. Can't wait to see this flung back at her, right? (I'm not being cruel here. It's just that, as we've seen, a cornered Aunt Norris is a very entertaining Aunt Norris.)

And it all goes down just as Edmund predicted. Sir Thomas spends an evening experiencing Mr. Rushworth in all his glory—perhaps showing off his favorite pair of house slippers, and reciting the alphabet all the way up to "G"—and comes away convinced that his son-in-law-to-be has less active grey matter than his nine-month-old Irish setter, and considerably less humility. He then makes a point of observing how his daughter behaves towards him, and notes—as we've seen illustrated all too clearly over the last hundred pages—that Maria now treats Rushworth as something like a human compost heap.

And here's where Sir Thomas shows himself, in spite of everything, to be a pretty standup guy. He decides to give Maria an out. If she wants to end the relationship, he'll back her up on it.

> *Advantageous as would be the alliance, and long standing and public as was the engagement, her happiness must not be sacrificed to it. Mr. Rushworth had perhaps been accepted on too short an acquaintance...[he] assured her that every inconvenience should be braved, and the connection entirely given up, if she felt herself unhappy in the prospect of it.*

We expect her to jump at the chance, because we know full well that Henry Crawford has forever soiled Mr. Rushworth in her eyes. Ah, but we forget who we're dealing with: Maria Bertram, whose thoughts never stray farther ahead than the next ninety seconds. Rather than consider how a marriage to Foghorn Leghorn will fundamentally impinge on her freedom, her character, her very identity, all she cares about is "not giving Crawford the triumph of governing her actions, and destroying her prospects." In other words, it's not her future happiness that concerns her, it's her current fit of pique. So far from wanting out, Maria wants to hurry on the nuptials:

> *In all the important preparations of the mind she was complete; being prepared for matrimony by an hatred of home, restraint, and tranquilllity; by the misery of disappointed affection, and contempt of the man she was to marry. The rest might wait. The preparations of new carriages and furniture might wait for London and spring, when her own taste could have fairer play.*

Only a first-rank misanthrope could so breezily write such unremittingly bleak lines.

The marriage accordingly takes place within the month, and we finally get—for the very first time in Austen!—an actual description of a wedding ceremony. Here it is, in all its sumptuous, rapturous, dizzying chick-lit splendor:

> *It was a very proper wedding. The bride was elegantly dressed—the two bridesmaids were duly inferior—her father gave her away—her mother stood with salts in her hand, expecting to be agitated—her aunt tried to cry—and the service was impressively read by Dr. Grant. Nothing could be objected to when it came under the discussion of the neighborhood, except that the carriage which conveyed the bride and bridegroom and Julia from the church door to Sotherton, was the same chaise which Mr. Rushworth had used for a twelvemonth before. In every thing else the etiquette of the day might stand the strictest investigation.*

Seriously, the marquis de Sade has more romance in him than Jane Austen. (This is not a criticism.)

Mrs. Norris exults in having played matchmaker so well, "and no one would have supposed, from her confident triumph, that she had ever heard of conjugal infelicity in her life, or could have the smallest insight into the disposition of the niece who had been brought up under her eye." Meantime, the newylweds head to Brighton for their honeymoon, and Julia with them, since "Some other companion than Mr. Rushworth was of the first consequence to his lady". The greatly depleted family circle at Mansfield can't but feel their absence, and

Austen remembers in the nick of time to add that oh yeah, Fanny misses them, too.

CHAPTERS 22-24

With the Bertram girls now gone off to wreak havoc on the larger world, Fanny is left as the only specimen of female nubility at Mansfield Park (barring any sleek bitches in Sir Thomas's hunting pack). This makes her for the first time a novelty in the house, meaning that "it was impossible for her not to be more looked at, more thought of and attended to, than she had ever been before; and 'where is Fanny?' became no uncommon question, even without her being wanted for any one's convenience." In other words, welcome to Fanny hell.

And it's not just at home; she's suddenly flavor of the month at the parsonage, too—"that house which she had hardly entered twice since Mr. Norris's death." This comes about by accident, when Fanny, on an errand for Aunt Norris, is caught by a sudden downpour and takes refuge beneath a tree visible from the parsonage windows. She is of course invited to come into the house and of course refuses, until Dr. Grant himself comes out with an umbrella to entreat her. This is classic Fanny: once again she's used her power of denial to throw an entire household into disarray. You find yourself wishing the Grants would just say, "She'd *rather* stay in the rain?...Hooo-kay. Her call."

But in this instance that's not an option, because the parsonage is home to Mary Crawford, and on a long, wet day Mary would lasso the Apocalypse Beast himself across her threshold just for the few hours' break from boredom he would supply. Actually, the Apocalypse Beast might make for more diverting company that Fanny, whose résumé isn't long on turning monotony into novelty. More the reverse. But ah, we're reckoning without the ingenuity of Mary, who immediately forces Fanny out of her wet clothes and into some of her own dry ones—Austen's subtle way of telegraphing that Mary's going to make Fanny over into the kind of companion she requires (or die trying).

And things do go well initially, though not without the usual depressing caveats from our heroine:

> *...Fanny might have enjoyed her visit could she have believed herself not in the way, and could she have foreseen that the weather would certainly clear at the end of the hour, and save her from the shame of having Dr. Grant's carriage and horses to take her home, with which she was threatened.*

She should look at the bright side; possibly Dr. Grant might choose instead to kick her downhill all the way home, thus preserving her humility.

Then Mary learns, to her astonishment, that Fanny has never heard her play the harp—and, "calling to mind an early-expressed wish on the subject, was concerned at her own neglect." (Again: *this* is the rival we're meant to hate? This thoughtful charmer? This *snookums*?) She gets right down to business, sitting down at the instrument and running through her entire repertoire for her harp-starved neighbor—though Fanny's eyes inevitably stray to the window, because she's worried that someone, somewhere might be wanting to yell at her about now, and what will they do if she's not there? Mary can only keep her from bolting by promising next to play Edmund's favorite piece. Of *course* Fanny will stay for that. Fanny would stay to be shown the stain on the carpet where Edmund threw up his picked herring.

Anyway, from this moment on, Mary and Fanny become kinda-sorta BFF's.

> *Fanny went to her every two or three days; it seemed a kind of fascination; she could not be easy without going, and yet it was without loving her, without ever thinking like her, without any sense of obligation for being sought after now when nobody else was to be had; and deriving no higher pleasure from her conversation than occasional amusement, and that often at the expense of her judgment, when it was raised by pleasantry on people or subjects which she wished to be respected.*

There's no mystery, really; Fanny's just in the thrall of a stronger, more vital, more vibrant personality. Her puny little scruples are no match for Mary's star power. It's harder to see what's in it for Mary, other than an audience (no mean thing, for someone of her persuasion).

The two friends spend most of their time taking long walks, during which Fanny is given to "ejaculations" of delight on the subject of nature's awesomeness:

> *"The evergreen!—How beautiful, how welcome, how wonderful the evergreen!—When one thinks of it, how astonishing a variety of nature! —In some countries we know the tree that sheds its leaf is the variety, but that does not make it less amazing, that the same soil and the same sun should nurture plants differing in the first rule and law of their existence. You will think me rhapsodizing; but when I am out of doors, especially when I am sitting out of doors, I am very apt to get into this sort of wondering strain. One cannot fix one's eyes on the commonest natural production without finding food for a rambling fancy."*

Austen is trying rather hard to make us like Fanny here (especially when immediately contrasted with Mary's admission that "I see no wonder in this shrubbery equal to seeing myself in it"), but it doesn't work for me. It just makes me ask questions. I mean, these women spend two or three days a week together. Does Fanny extol the foliage every goddamn time?

Mary might be immune to nature's variety, but when pressed she admits that the pastoral life doesn't completely lack its charms, and that she "can even suppose it pleasant to spend *half* the year in the country, under certain circumstances." She then amplifies in a way that once again fixes her as a precursor to the witty, sardonic heroines of Wilde and Coward:

> *"An elegant, moderate-sized house in the centre of family connections—continual engagements among them—commanding the first society in the neighborhood—looked-up to perhaps as leading it even more than those of larger fortune, and turning from the cheerful round of such amusements to nothing worse than a tête-à-tête with the person one feels most agreeable in*

the world. There is nothing frightful in such a picture, is there, Miss Price?"

Miss Price has probably gone into cardiac arrest by now, but never mind.

This segues into a discussion of Maria's marriage and Mary's expectation that "we shall be all very much at Sotherton another year...for the first pleasures of Mr. Rushworth's wife must be to fill her house, and give the best balls in the country." And *then* comes one of those moments where Austen gives a bravura example of her psychological brilliance; for Mary exclaims, "Ah! here he is"—but it's not Mr. Rushworth she means, it's Edmund, who hasn't been mentioned by name for several pages, but who Mary clearly invoked when describing "the person one feels most agreeable in the world." Edmund's presence, summoned forth in this manner, is so much stronger than that of Mr. Rushworth, even when the latter is being openly discussed, that "Here he is" can only mean the former—at least for these two women. And they know it; they know it about each other, too. It's an unspoken thing between them...but we get the feeling Mary views it as a bond, while for Fanny it's more of a threat.

Edmund, accompanied by Mrs. Grant, joins the young ladies, and several pages of sparkling badinage ensue (in which Fanny, predictably, takes no part at all; not that anyone actively excludes her—she willingly sidelines herself). Eventually Mary and Edmund get around to tormenting each other in that special way they have, which begins with Mary proclaiming that she means to be a rich woman, since "A large income is the best recipe for happiness I ever heard of."

"You intend to be very rich," said Edmund with a look which, to Fanny's eye, had a great deal of serious meaning.

"To be sure. Do not you?—Do not we all?"

"I cannot intend any thing which it must be so completely beyond my power to command. Miss Crawford may chuse her degree of wealth. She has only to fix on her number of thousands a year, and there can be no doubt of their coming. My intentions are only not to be poor."

They're still trying to negotiate some kind of a future together—but since Mary is too fearful of failure to attempt any other approach but a teasing one, and Edmund too earnest to give way even an inch, they wind up as emotionally bollixed as ever. Even when Edmund, by doggedly insisting that she define her terms, maneuvers Mary into a corner where it seems she'll be forced to concede him a point, she masterfully gets the better of him by saying, "Oh!...You ought to be in parliament"—in other words, his very skill at making a case for his clerical calling is just evidence he should be a politician instead. Mary's quicksilver that way, maddening and delightful. How can her creator not have been crazy about her?—How, in fact, can she ultimately slight her in favor of the drippy sourpuss who's been lurking at the edge of all this incandescent, heart-stopping talk? It's the insoluble mystery of *Mansfield Park*.

The chapter ends with Mrs. Grant inviting Fanny to dine at the parsonage. Fanny of course declines, claiming that accepting "would not be in her power," and this is true, because her power is exclusively one of refusal. Edmund, however, accepts for her, which kind of screws the pooch, because her only other constant, besides negation, is the principle that Edmund Totally Rules.

When Lady Bertram hears about the invitation she's absolutely gobsmacked—"But why should Mrs. Grant ask Fanny?" she keeps repeating, over and over again, as though that lady had done something entirely incomprehensible, like cutting off all her hair and running naked through the town with her breasts painted blue. Edmund tries to explain the simple civility of the gesture, but Lady Bertram still can't wrap her mind around the idea of Fanny at an actual dinner party; you get the impression that at home they feed her from a ceramic bowl on the floor of the kitchen.

Eventually Edmund suggests that Lady Bertram appeal to her husband for his opinion on the matter, but this takes a while to accomplish, because it involves waiting for Sir Thomas to come within hailing range of Lady Bertram's couch. (The novel would go in an entirely different direction if anyone had the genius to affix the piece of furniture in question with wheels.) When the consultation does take place, Fanny has to sneak out of the room...

> *...for to hear herself the subject of any discussion with her uncle, was more than her nerves could bear. She was anxious, she knew—more anxious perhaps than she ought to be—for what was it after all whether she went*

> *or staid?—but if her uncle were to be a great while considering and deciding, and with very grave looks, and those grave looks directed to her, and at last decide against her, she might not be able to appear properly submissive and indifferent.*

Anyone else really, really missing Lizzy Bennet right about now?... Hm? Show of hands?

Sir Thomas naturally decrees that Fanny can go to dinner at the Grants'—in fact he doesn't understand why he's been appealed to on the matter at all. Are we not having a civilization here, or what? "The only surprize I can feel," he says, "is that this should be the *first* time of [such notice] being paid." Mrs. Norris, it's decided, will come and take Fanny's place so that Lady Bertram will have someone on hand to make her tea, without which, it is strongly implied, she will fall into a swift decline and immediately perish.

When Aunt Norris gets wind of the extraordinary favor being shown to Fanny, she works herself into such a fit of furious indignation that it takes several pages of scaldingly hilarious invective to work herself out of it again. It's probably her best sustained monologue in the book. She hovers over the trembling Fanny, who's trying to get herself ready for the dinner, and hammers her with verbal abuse; she even manages to weave in a reminder of her jealous hatred of Mrs. Grant (remember that?):

> *"...I must observe, that five is the very awkwardest of all possible numbers to sit down to table; and I cannot but be surprised that such an* elegant *lady as Mrs. Grant should not contrive better! And round their enormous great wide table too, which fills up the room so dreadfully! Had the Doctor been contented to take my dinner table when I came away, as any body in their senses would have done, instead of having that absurd new one of his own, which is wider, literally wider than the dinner table here —how infinitely better it would have been! and how much more he would have been respected! for people are never respected when they step out of their proper sphere. Remember* that, *Fanny. Five, only five to be sitting round that table! However, you will have dinner enough on it for ten I dare say."*

Then occurs this wonderful line: "Mrs. Norris fetched breath and went on again." How I'd love to see that line on every third page of *Mansfield Park*.

This remarkable performance eventually concludes with Aunt Norris telling Fanny that even though it's almost certain to rain again, she'd better not get any ideas of *riding* home, as though she were Maria or Julia or the Empress of Russia or something, but should make whatever preparations she must for a walk home in inclement weather. This is immediately followed by Sir Thomas poking his head in the door and saying, "Fanny, at what time would you have the carriage come round?"—and if you read this passage without barking out a laugh, you must be clinically dead or something. It's a simple comic turn, but Austen's epic set-up (two-and-a-half pages of Mrs. Norris's vitriolic harangue) is what makes the payoff so deliciously sidesplitting.

Fanny, unfortunately, not only can't bring herself to triumph over Aunt Norris; she can't quite *not* triumph over her, either. In fact she slinks out the room on Sir Thomas's heels specifically to avoid the issue altogether. Mrs. Norris is left to sputter and fume and put the best face on it she can: "Quite unnecessary!—a great deal too kind! But Edmund goes;—true—it is upon Edmund's account. I observe he was hoarse on Thursday night."

Fanny has donned the white dress Sir Thomas bought her for Maria's wedding, which she hopes isn't too fine. Edmund thinks it's just right, and I only wish we were able to watch the play of her features as he reassures her with these words:

> *"A woman can never be too fine while she is all in white. No, I see no finery about you; nothing but what is perfectly proper. Your gown seems very pretty. I like these glossy spots. Has not Miss Crawford a gown something the same?"*

I admit it: I barked a laugh again. That's twice in three pages. Austen's clearly on a roll here.

When Edmund and Fanny arrive at the parsonage, they spot Henry Crawford's barouche outside. Edmund is glad to have his friend returned; Fanny not so much. "There was no occasion, there was no time for Fanny to say how very differently she felt; but the idea of having such another to observe her, was a great increase of the trepidation with which she performed the very aweful ceremony of walking into the drawing-room."

We last saw Fanny nearly thwarted by a door; now her difficulty is in only in entering a room. I suppose that's progress.

Once she's accomplished this daredevil feat, Fanny realizes that Crawford's unexpected arrival might be to her benefit, because "every addition to the party must rather forward her favourite indulgence of being suffered to sit silent and unattended to"—and indeed there is "such a happy flow of conversation prevailing in which she was not required to take any part" that we suspect we might be allowed *our* favourite indulgence of being suffered to forget she's in the novel at all.

But no...for in fact Fanny actually, really, honest-to-God-I-ain't-lyin' adds a layer to her eggshell veneer in this chapter. She becomes—wait for it—an avatar of female outrage. A very, very small and wholly ineffective one, granted, but even the faintest flourish of personality is a welcome relief from the nullity she's been up to now.

The inspiration for this change—the smirking cad who galvanizes her into actual strong feeling—is Crawford, who behaves in his usual blithe, careless manner, showing not only no penitence, but not even any awareness of what a completely amoral douchebag he was in his treatment of both Julia and (especially) Maria. Fanny is so offended by him that Austen resorts to the word "hate"—the strongest reaction we've ever had from Fanny about anything, anywhere, ever.

As she listens to Henry prattle on about what a golden age the *Lovers' Vows* rehearsals were for them all and how alive and energized they'd all been, Fanny is appalled by his "corrupted mind" (conveniently forgetting that she'd snuck in to watch his rehearsals with Maria for a little energizing of her own). And then Henry, emboldened by her silence—which he of course takes for tacit agreement—goes too far:

> *"I think if we had had the disposal of events—if Mansfield Park had had the government of the winds just for a week or two about the equinox, there would have been a difference. Not that we would have endangered [Sir Thomas's] safety by any tremendous weather—but only by a steady contrary wind, or a calm. I think, Miss Price, we would have indulged ourselves with a week's calm in the Atlantic at that season."*

Fanny—"with a firmer tone than usual"—replies, "As far as I am concerned, sir, I would not have delayed his return for a day. My uncle disapproved it all so entirely when he did arrive, that in my opinion, every thing had gone quite far enough." Crawford is surprised by this admonitory blast from meek little Fanny, and is chastened by it—though more than a little charmed as well. It's like when a kitten surprises you by giving you a good, sharp swipe with its claws; you know you'll be more careful of it in future, but damn if that wasn't cute.

Having "trembled and blushed at her own daring," Fanny has pretty much exhausted herself with this display and so sits out the rest of the chapter, possibly even indulging in a restorative nap. Focus turns to the after-dinner conversations in the parlour, where Henry Crawford shocks his sister by revealing to her that Edmund is soon to take orders—and adding that he will "not have less than seven hundred a year," which in his opinion isn't so bad for a younger brother, especially since he'll still be living at home and "a sermon at Christmas and Easter, I suppose, will be the sum total of his sacrifice."

> *His sister tried to laugh off her feelings by saying, "Nothing amuses me more than the easy manner with which every body settles the abundance of those who have a good deal less than themselves. You would look rather blank, Henry, if your menus plaisirs were to be limited to seven hundred a year."*

She's wounded to the quick, but refuses to show it—refuses to feel it, even. Instead, she puts on a front of blasé amusement. Later, when the others sit down to cards, she takes refuge in her harp (being "too much vexed by what had passed to be in a humor for any thing but music").

> *She was very angry with [Edmund]. She had thought her influence more. She* had *begun to think of him—she felt that she had—with the greatest regard, with almost decided intentions; but she would now meet him with his own cool feelings. It was plain that he could have no serious views, no true attachment, by fixing himself in a situation which he must know she would never stoop to. She would learn to match him in his indifference. She would henceforth admit his attentions without any idea beyond imme-*

> *diate amusement. If* he *could so command his affections,* her's *should do her no harm.*

Because, y'know, *that* always works.

While Mary is making up her mind to resist Edmund from now on, her brother is making up *his* mind to do something quite the opposite. Speaking the next morning of the two weeks he means to spend at Mansfield, he tells her: "And how do you think I mean to amuse myself, Mary, on the days that I do not hunt? I am grown too old to go out more than three times a week; but I have a plan for the intermediate days...to make Fanny Price fall in love with me."

Mary scoffs, and tells him he "ought to be satisfied with her two cousins." But nobody ever gained a point by telling Henry Crawford what he ought to do, and sure enough he sails right past it, waxing eloquent about the "wonderful improvement" Fanny has undergone since last he saw her. Mary points out, quite correctly, that the wonderful improvement he speaks of is that she's now the only girl for five miles in any direction—"and you must have a somebody" (wonderful line). She continues:

> *"[I]f you do set about this flirtation with her, you will never persuade me that it is in compliment to her beauty, or that it proceeds from any thing but your own idleness and folly."*
>
> *Her brother gave only a smile to this accusation, and soon afterwards said, "I do not quite know what to make of Miss Fanny. I do not understand her. I could not tell what she would be at yesterday. What is her character?—Is she solemn?—Is she queer?—Is she prudish?"*

Yes, yes, and yes. Or rather: she's not joyful—she's not conventional—she's not earthy. (It's always best to define Fanny by negatives.)

Mary knows Henry too well, and mocks him for targeting Fanny solely because of her coldness and sharpness to him; she represents a challenge to his charms. "I do desire that you will not be making her really unhappy; a little love perhaps may animate and do her good, but I will not have you plunge her deep, for she is as good a little creature as ever lived, and has a great deal of feeling."

Personally, I can't but view this as another mark in Mary's favor. She knows full well she can't lure her brother off the prowl now that he's got Fanny's scent; but she might be able to minimize the angle of his descent on her. And frankly, if Fanny were any sort of normal human being, a decent flirtation *would* do her good. But how could someone like Mary—active, curious, adventurous—ever begin to suspect the engine of entropy that is Fanny Price?

But her brother is deaf to Mary's pleas.

> *"It can be but for a fortnight," said Henry, "and if a fortnight can kill her, she must have a constitution which nothing can save. No, I will not do her any harm, dear little soul! I only want her to look kindly on me, to give me smiles as well as blushes, to keep a chair for me by herself wherever we are, and be all animation when I take it and talk to her; to think as I think, be interested in all my possessions and pleasures, try to keep me longer at Mansfield, and feel when I go away that she shall be never happy again. I want nothing more."*

Sometimes even Noël Coward wasn't quite this Noël Coward.

Yes, Henry's a cad; yes, he's got the moral bearings of a virus. But he's easy and warm and knows himself, and *laughs* at himself, and this can't help disarming any disapproval we might feel. Possibly the reason *Mansfield Park*—and *Mansfield Park* alone of Austen's major novels—fails to cohere is that she really sets herself too difficult a task. Maybe she felt she was up to it; if so, she learned her lesson afterward, to her immense benefit (as we'll discuss later, in our summation). In Fanny Price, she's created a heroine who's inert; in Mary Crawford, a rival who beguiles; in Edmund, a hero without passion; and in Henry Crawford, a gigolo who can't help being his own victim. We have to give her credit for trying to work with greater shade and complexity—it would have been so easy to give us two more hissing cretins, in the Lucy Steele-George Wickham mode—but she goes too far in the opposite direction, granting her villains more earnest humanity (and gallons more charm) than her heroes. The narrative, thrown out of balance, never recovers, and our affections, once they've splashed outside the receptacle intended for them, can't be tipped back.

And so we watch with an interest entirely at odds with the author's as Henry begins to wear down the reserve of his chosen prey. "She had by no means forgotten the past, and she thought as ill of him as ever; but she felt his powers; he was entertaining, and his manners were so improved, so polite, so seriously and blamelessly polite, that it was impossible not to be civil to him in return."

In fact, we *want* her to succumb. We have a feeling it'd be good for both of them. And that feeling only deepens when Fanny's beloved brother William re-enters the narrative, the ship on which he serves having come home to dock at Portsmouth.

William isn't one of Austen's great creations. Like most fictional characters, he was invented to serve the narrative—in this case, by providing a means for those who think well of Fanny (Edmund, Sir Thomas, Henry) to make their regard apparent to her. (Since any favor to herself only horrifies her, there has to be another to whom a favor shown will make her go all melty.) Most fictional characters manage to accrue flesh and blood while serving their function in the narrative (as witness Mrs. Norris; her sole purpose is to blunt Fanny's self-esteem, but she quickly develops into a comic creation of Falstaffian proportions). William never does; he remains a cipher. When he and Fanny are reunited, Austen tells us that "it was some time...before the disappointment inseparable from the alteration of person had vanished, and she could see in him the same William as before," but she doesn't tell us how he's been altered; and in fact to our eyes, he appears exactly the same (in every bland particular) as he did on his first appearance, many chapters back. And the scenes he and Fanny share are generalized to the point of near meaninglessness:

> *Fanny had never known so much felicity in her life, as in this unchecked, equal, fearless intercourse with the brother and friend, who was opening all his heart to her, telling her all his hopes and fears, plans, and solicitudes...*

You get the drift. My point is, William hasn't been brought back to the narrative for his own sake, but to serve as a means by which Henry Crawford can see Fanny exhibit the kind of warmth and openness of affection he's been trying to charm out of her—and to realize, with a kind of shock, that he now wants it for its own sake; that he sees a value in her affection beyond the mere validation of his powers of seduction. It's been a long while (the opening chapters of *Sense and Sensibility*, in fact) since the narrative scaffolding of an Austen novel has poked through the storytelling this way, and as it's the only time it happens in all of *Mansfield Park,* let's just give our gal a pass.

What we're left with, then, is a changed Henry Crawford—a Henry who considers that "it would be something to be loved by such a girl, to excite the first ardours of her young, unsophisticated mind! She interested him more than he had foreseen. A fortnight was not enough. His stay became indefinite."

Welllll...okay. But only because we can't wait to see how Aunt Norris reacts to *this.*

CHAPTERS 25-27

Last time, we saw the addition of William Price to the clan at Mansfield, and the return of Henry Crawford to the pack at the parsonage. The presence of these good-humored young bucks provides just the added sense of occasion required for Sir Thomas to lower his own personal Homeland Security Alert from orange to mellow yellow, resulting in his "more than toleration" of increasing face-time with his neighbors.

It's during his first dinner party at the parsonage that Sir Thomas notices Henry's attentions to Fanny—or rather, he *would* notice them if he were the kind of man who noticed such things; but in a brilliant flourish, which tells us so much about the character in so few wonderfully deliberate strokes, Austen gives us this:.

> *[I]t was in the course of that very visit, that he first began to think, that any one in the habit of such idle observations* would have thought *that Mr. Crawford was the admirer of Fanny Price.*

In other words, Sir Thomas doesn't draw inferences of his own, he anticipates what inferences other, lesser people might draw if they were confronted with the same evidence as he. He's so lofty, he might literally have his head in the clouds. A low-flying plane would shear it right off his neck.

The dinner, we're told, is "generally felt to be a pleasant one, being composed in a good proportion of those who would talk and those who would listen," which makes us think immediately, *Mrs. Norris and Fanny,* who are sort of the Platonic illustrations of both those states of being. But it turns out, alas, that Aunt Norris doesn't have much to say on this particular occasion, because her indignation at everything she sees at the parsonage is so titanically great that it just stops her throat right up. All she can do is quietly sputter.

> *[She] could never behold either the wide table or the number of dishes on it with patience, and...did always contrive to experience some evil from the passing of the servants behind her chair, and to bring away some fresh conviction of its being impossible among so many dishes but that some must be cold.*

Afterwards the party takes up cards, with one table devoted to Whist and another to a less demanding game. Lady Bertram, in her characteristic bewilderment, can't decide between them. "What shall I do, Sir Thomas?" she asks her husband. "Whist and Speculation; which will amuse me most?" Without skipping a beat he steers her towards the latter, for "He was a Whist player himself, and perhaps might feel that it would not much amuse him to have her as a partner."

So it's Speculation for her ladyship; the only remaining issue being that she doesn't know how to play it, so of course "Fanny must teach me." But Fanny knows as little about it as she does. (Shocking; but too late to send her back, I suppose.) Enter Henry Crawford to the rescue; he agrees to sit between them and give them both instruction.

And so we're geared up for another of Austen's bravura set pieces, with Sir Thomas, Mrs. Norris, and Dr. and Mrs. Grant "being seated at the table of prime intellectual state and dignity," while the five younger people are off on their own, free to chatter and flirt on the pretext of playing cards, encumbered only by Lady Bertram, who's really no encumbrance at all; in fact they may have to tether her to a table leg lest she float right on out the window.

Henry Crawford is of course the star of the scene. He plays both Fanny's and Lady Bertram's hands for them, as well as his own, all the while keeping up a running commentary designed to seduce the metaphorical panties off everyone else at the table. There's also a great running joke in which he continually interrupts himself with asides to

Lady Bertram, forbidding her to look at her cards (because what possible good can come of *that*?).

Fanny, however, is annoyed by him, because it takes her all of three minutes to learn the rules, despite which he continues to hover and cluck over her, telling her what to do with the cards she's dealt. He takes it on himself to "inspirit her play, sharpen her avarice, and harden her heart, which, especially in any competition with William, was a work of some difficulty"—because, yes, that's the kind of woman Fanny is: she will *play to lose.* Here's where we most clearly see the "monster of complacency and pride...under a cloak of cringing self-abasement" that Kingsley Amis declared her to be; because there's just no other way to slice it: someone who works to undermine herself so that you can win a competition, is quite clearly of the belief that if she didn't, you wouldn't. In other words, she sees victory as hers to relinquish. Look me in the eye and tell me that's not cap-A arrogance.

Henry Crawford, who's got both Fanny and Lady Bertram comfortably in his sphere of influence, now turns his baby blues on Edmund, and says, "Bertram...I have never told you what happened to me yesterday in my ride home." Apparently the two had been out hunting together, but Henry had been obliged to give it up after his horse threw a shoe. Edmund had gone on alone, leaving Henry to find his way back, or rather to lose his way "because I can never bear to ask" directions (apparently certain masculine traits are just plain immutable). He soon stumbled upon a small church and its attendant parsonage house, which he immediately concluded to be Thornton Lacey. Edmund isn't quite persuaded:

> *"You inquired then?"*
>
> *"No, I never inquire. But I* told *a man mending a hedge that it was Thornton Lacey, and he agreed to it."*

All right, fine. Big Henry fan, here. So sue me.

Austen is very nimble in the passage that follows, telling us that "Thornton Lacey was the name of [Edmund's] impending living, as Miss Crawford well knew; and her interest in a negociation for William Price's knave increased." Meanwhile, Henry Crawford launches into an appraisal of the property for his friend that begins, "You are a lucky fellow. There will be work for five summers at least before the place is livable." He continues with a detailed plan of what must be done to make the place habitable, which falls just short of disassembling the entire edifice and rebuilding it brick by brick to an entirely new blueprint. And don't let's even get into his ideas for improving the grounds. You get the feeling, if Henry had his way, Edmund would find himself plunked down in the middle of a kind of Regency-era Graceland.

When he finally runs out of steam, Edmund tells him that alas "very little of your plan for Thornton Lacey will ever be put in practice...I must be satisfied with rather less ornament and beauty. I think that the house and premises may be made comfortable, and given the air of a gentleman's residence without any very heavy expense, and that must suffice me; and I hope may suffice all who care about me."

This couldn't be more obviously aimed at Mary if he wrote it out on a sheet of paper, wrapped it around a stone, and lobbed it at her head; and Mary herself—after "securing [William's] knave at an exorbitant rate," exclaims:

> *"There, I will stake my last like a woman of spirit. No cold prudence for me. I am not born to sit still and do nothing. If I lose the game, it shall not be from not striving for it."*

The way these two manage to score direct hits while still talking past each other makes for giddy, page-turning fun. How Austen could put them through all this and then wrest them apart at the end of it, is a kind of betrayal—the only significant one in her entire body of work, and as we've seen (and are seeing now), one attended by a whole caravan of other delights, so we forgive her...conditionally. The condition being that she never do it again. Which she not only honors, but even couches in the form of a sly apology in her next novel...but I'm getting ahead of myself.

Henry isn't giving up on his vision for Thornton Lacey. He waxes long and enthusiastic about its possibilities, interrupted only by an occasional aside (such as "Let me see, Mary; Lady Bertram bids a dozen for that queen; no, no, a dozen is more than it is worth. Lady Bertram does *not* bid a dozen. She will have nothing to say to it. Go on, go on"). His final argument is that for the mere "expenditure of a few hundreds a year," Edmund may transform it into—well, into the kind of place a man like Henry Crawford would be proud to live.

> *"You may raise it into a* place. *From being the mere gentleman's residence, it becomes, by judicious improvement, the residence of a man of education, taste, modern manners, good connections. All this may be stamped on it; and that house receive such an air as to make its owner be set down as the great land-holder of the parish; especially as there is no real squire's house to dispute the point..."*

He then whirls unexpectedly on Fanny, and asks whether she doesn't see it exactly as he does; which is a bit of a risk—I mean, taking Fanny by surprise, especially at such close quarters. If he startles her sufficiently he really could end up losing a finger, or the tip of his nose.

Fortunately Henry's appendages are saved by the interjection of Mary, who—perhaps sensing that Edmund must surely be weakening now that Henry's been browbeating him without pause for what seems like a month and change—now leaps in to add the weight of her own opinion, which is that Edmund, rather than dismissing her brother out of hand, ought to remember all the wonderful ideas he had for improving Sotherton.

And here's where we learn that Henry isn't so self-involved that he can't see beyond his own irresistible charm. He's learned enough about Fanny—*discerned* enough about her, from having observed and considered and *listened* to her, which is more than Edmund's ever done—to know that by bringing up that day at Sotherton, Mary hasn't done him any favors in her eyes. So, "in a low voice directed solely at Fanny," he says, "I should be sorry to have my powers of *planning* judged of by the day at Sotherton. I see things very differently now. Do not think of me as I appeared then."

Fanny is spared the trouble of replying, because Aunt Norris has overheard the word "Sotherton" and—"being just then in the happy leisure which followed securing the odd trick by Sir Thomas's capital play and her own," she takes great, luxurious relish in assuring William what a rare, once-in-a-lifetime treat he missed by not having been on hand for the day of the expedition to that magnificent pile of bricks—not to mention the transporting joy of having been in the company of Maria and Julia. But now that she thinks of it, he might call on them in Brighton; they'd certainly condescend to see him, being the gracious, magnanimous, sweet-smelling paragons of super-specialness that they are, and plus?—also?—completely and totally by coincidence?—"I could send a little parcel by you that I want to get conveyed to your cousins."

God love Aunt Norris; she never, ever disappoints. But in this case, alas, her transparent little gambit to save a few cents on postage fails her, as Sir Thomas advises William against going so far when he'll have other opportunities to meet Maria and Julia closer to home. So Mrs. Norris has been nice to William for nothing, which has got to gall her just about as much as the size of Mrs. Grant's table.

Henry Crawford then turns the topic of conversation back to himself (and really, given the company, who can blame him). He confesses a "scheme" to rent a house in the neighborhood the following winter.

> *[H]e had set his heart upon having a something there that he could come to at any time, a little homestall at his command where all the holidays of his year might be spent, and he might find himself continuing, improving, and* perfecting *that friendship and intimacy with the Mansfield Park family which was increasing in value to him.*

We realize at once that Henry's primary motive is almost certainly the establishment of a bachelor pad into which he might entice Fanny for glass or two of bubbly, a little Montavani on the stereo, and maybe an hour or six of sweet monkey lovin'. But either Fanny herself is ignorant of this, or is just too mortified to react, because, "She said little, assented only here and there, and betrayed no inclination either of appropriating any part of the compliment to herself or of strengthening his views in favour of Northamptonshire."

Sir Thomas certainly sees nothing objectionable in Henry's plan, except for his choice of Thornton Lacey as the house in question. Yeah, that's right, Henry has been trying to convince Edmund to make the place over so that *he himself* can live there. This is the kind of brass-balled arrogance that's so completely over the top you can't even be offended by it; you can only laugh. Henry may be a man after the main chance, but he's so completely upfront about it that you can't scorn him for it. Might as well scorn a dog for running off with your Frisbee.

But unfortunately for Henry, it seems Edmund has plans to live in the house himself, which is something Henry hadn't counted on; he'd naturally presumed Edmund would remain at Mansfield Park and just swing over to his living every week or two for christenings or funerals or whatever else was on the docket. But Sir Thomas, obviously proud of his son, sets him straight: Edmund "knows that human nature needs more lessons than a weekly sermon can convey, and that if he does not live among his parishioners and prove himself by constant attention their well-wisher and friend, he does very little either for their good or his own."

We're told that "Mr. Crawford bowed his acquiescence," but I'm guessing the whole speech turned into Tagalog as soon as it reached his ears.

Mary Crawford, however, has heard every word of it, and not happily. She'd been listening to her brother's airy suggestions for Thornton Lacey's improvement and had allowed herself to imagine inhabiting such a place, whose improvements would "shut out the church, sink the clergyman, and see only the respectable, elegant, modernized, and occasional residence of a man of independent fortune"—and now she was "considering Sir Thomas, with decided ill-will, as the destroyer of all this", though without, of course, "daring to relieve herself by a single attempt at throwing ridicule on his cause."

The paradox here is that I like Mary a great deal, yet I enjoy seeing her writhe in anxiety and even anguish; the more Austen torments her, the more lovable she appears. And while I generally disdain Fanny, I can't stand it when Austen torments *her*. Maybe this is due to the nature of the torments. Mary is plagued by a sinking inevitability that, in order to be with the man she loves, she'll have to give up everything she now prizes; she's thus being made more human—being brought, by degrees, to a reluctant acceptance of sacrifice.

Whereas Fanny's torments always hinge on being forced from passivity to activity—even so passive an activity as merely being noticed. This is what happens now, when her brother William asks Sir Thomas, "Is not Fanny a very good dancer, sir?"

> *Fanny, in dismay at such an unprecedented question, did not know which way to look, or how to be prepared for the answer. Some very grave reproof, or at least the coldest expression of indifference must be coming to distress her brother, and sink her into the ground.*

If only she *would* sink into the ground. But of course she's given no cause; quite the opposite. Sir Thomas has now spent several chapters being uniformly kind to and solicitous of her, yet she still acts like if he notices she's in the room, he might just unhinge his jaws and devour her whole, like a snake swallowing a rat.

Henry, having taken the trouble to look at Fanny as a human being, sees this, and accordingly declines to join the discussion of Fanny's terpsichorean skills because, "There is *one* person in company who does not like to have Miss Price spoken of," that being of course Miss Price, and so would everyone please just knock it off for her sake. And yet, of course, he's still Henry Crawford:

> *True enough, he had once seen Fanny dance; and it was equally true that he would now have answered for her gliding about with quiet, light elegance, and in admirable time, but in fact he could not for the life of him recall what her dancing had been, and rather took it for granted that she had been present than remembered any thing about her.*

This is exactly the kind of inattention she asks for, so again, can you blame him?

But Fanny's dancing won't remain a subject for speculation for much longer, because Sir Thomas—that horrible ogre who strikes perpetual fear into Fanny's cringing heart—decides that William's desire to see his sister dance must be gratified; and he alone is the man who can gratify it. And so the next morning at breakfast, he tells William:

> *"It would give me pleasure to see you both dance. You spoke of the balls at Northampton. Your cousins have occasionally attended them; but they would not altogether suit us now...I believe, we must not think of a Northampton ball. A dance at home would be more eligible, and if—"*
>
> *"Ah! my dear Sir Thomas," interrupted Mrs. Norris, "I knew what was coming. I knew what you were going to say. If dear Julia were at home, or dearest Mrs. Rushworth at Sotherton...if* they *were at home to grace the ball, a ball you would have this very Christmas. Thank your uncle, William, thank your uncle."*

This is classic Aunt Norris: barging in, presupposing, and berating a poor relation into expressing gratitude for having had nothing whatsoever done for him.

But in fact Sir Thomas, "gravely interposing," corrects her assumption that without his daughters at hand there's insufficient reason for a ball. "Could we be all assembled, our satisfaction would undoubtedly be more complete, but the absence of some is not to debar the others of amusement."

Chided, Mrs. Norris eventually takes comfort in knowing that with Lady Bertram being about as useful as a beached beluga, she'll have to step in and be the hostess for the evening. Accordingly, she's soon "ready with her suggestions as to the rooms he would think fittest to be used" and the date most suited for the event, but finds to her dismay that Sir Thomas has already settled these things on his own. Happily, here's a case where no paradox creeps in to unsettle me: I cheerfully despise Aunt Norris, and love, love, *love* to watch Austen poke and prick and mortify her.

As the event draws near, Austen gives us a brief survey of some of the others in the household. Fanny has worked herself up into a dithering state over what to wear, her chief concern being that she has no chain on which to hang an amber cross William has given her. Should she wear it with a ribbon then, despite the ball's formality? Or should she not wear it at all, and risk hurting William's feelings...? This is a bit of a tempest in a teapot, and you find yourself wondering why Austen devotes such a quantity of narrative space to it; but she has her reasons, which we'll discover soon.

Meanwhile, over to Edmund, whose mind is less on the ball than on what follows swiftly on its heels: his ordination. Everything is set for the commencement of his career as a clergyman...everything but the question of the wife who will be the partner of his labors. There's really only one candidate, of course; and while Mary has certainly shown him in every conceivable way that she's fond of him, she's also been equally definitive in expressing her complete disdain for the clerical life; so that he scarcely knows whether she's the kind of woman who would happily inhabit a vicarage or who would more happily burn it to the ground.

> *The issue of all depended on one question. Did she love him well enough to forego what had used to be essential points—did she love him well enough to make them no longer essential? And this question, which he was continually repeating to himself, though oftenest answered with a "Yes," had sometimes its "No."*

Of course the surest way to discover this is simply to ask her; but it seems Edmund hasn't quite worked up the stones to do that yet. And so he sets his sights a little lower than that for the present: "To engage her early for the two first dances, was all the command of individual happiness which he felt in his power, and the only preparation for the ball which he could enter into, in spite of all that was passing around him on the subject, from morning to night."

While Edmund broods over Mary, she's on Fanny's mind as well. Still uncertain about how to dress for the ball, Fanny decides to seek out Mary's advice, and heads over to the parsonage to see her—only to meet her halfway, coming the opposite direction and carrying a parcel. They return to the parsonage where Mary "proposed their going up into her room, where they might have a comfortable coze, without disturbing Dr. and Mrs. Grant" (what *they're* doing that requires such privacy is, thankfully, not mentioned) and there Mary, who's totally a proto-fashionista, "gave her all her best judgment and taste, made every thing easy by her suggestions, and tried to make every thing agreeable by her encouragement."

When Mary asks whether Fanny will be wearing her brother's cross, Fanny admits she has nothing to hang it by; and here we discover why Austen made such an issue of this lack earlier on. For Mary now unwraps the parcel she'd been carrying, producing a trinket box containing several gold chains and necklaces, "and in the kindest manner she now urged Fanny's taking one for the cross and to keep for her sake"—which of course Fanny, one of the world's most tireless self-deniers, refuses "with a look of horror", as though Mary were offering her a nipple clamp, or earrings made of human teeth. But Mary presses her hard: "You see what a collection I have...more by half than I ever use or think of. I do not offer them as new. I offer nothing but an old necklace. You must forgive the liberty and oblige me."

Eventually Fanny "found herself obliged to yield that she might not be accused of pride or indifference, or some other littleness"—and note, please, the wording there: she yields not out of fear that she might be *guilty* of pride or indifference, but that she might be *accused* of them.

Fanny pores over the offerings, "longing to know which might be least valuable"—presumably to *seem* humble rather than be it—and eventually settles on a certain necklace that Fanny keeps bringing to her attention over all the others, in the hopes that she is thus "chusing what Miss Crawford least wished to keep." Mary does indeed seem pleased with Fanny's choice, immediately jettisoning the others and insisting on affixing this one to Fanny's neck before she changes her mind.

> *Fanny had not a word to say against its becomingness, and excepting what remained of her scruples, was exceedingly pleased with an acquisition so very apropos. She would rather perhaps have been obliged to some other person. But this was an unworthy feeling. Miss Crawford had anticipated her wants with a kindness which proved her a real friend.*

How difficult is it to not hate Fanny here?...I can't answer, because I can't manage it. Smug, proud, judgmental little twit; she has the sheer gall to seek out Mary's help, discover Mary already on the case and ready to answer with more than was asked for—and yet Fanny would rather be "obliged to some other person." I suppose we're meant to forgive this ignoble behavior because Fanny herself recognizes that it's unworthy; but hey, as long as she doesn't *appear* unworthy, what's it to her?

She gets what she deserves in the immediate aftermath, when Mary reveals that the necklace in question was one that had been given to her by her brother Henry. Fanny rips it from her throat—really, she couldn't be more nakedly scornful if she stamped and spat on it—but "Miss Crawford thought she had never seen a prettier consciousness," which tells us only that Mary still thinks she's dealing with a shy, uncertain innocent, and hasn't yet seen the acres of scorched earth behind Fanny's demurely downcast gaze.

It takes all of Mary's considerable powers of persuasion to get Fanny to take up the necklace again, though she does so with considerably less willingness before, "for there was an expression in Miss Crawford's eyes which she could not be satisfied with." Oh, for the love of God. *What* expression? And then there's this:

> *It was impossible for [Fanny] to be insensible of Mr. Crawford's change of manners...He evidently tried to please her—he was gallant—he was attentive—he was something like what he had been to her cousins; he wanted, she supposed, to cheat her of her tranquility as he had cheated*

> *them; and whether he might not have some concern in this necklace!—She could not be convinced that he had not, for Miss Crawford, complaisant as a sister, was careless as a woman and a friend.*

What Austen is inviting us to do here—whether she knows it or not—is to suspect Mary of aiding Henry in a conspiracy of rape; whether actual or metaphorical, it amounts to the same thing. It's absolutely jarring—it doesn't tally a jot with anything we've been led to feel for or about Mary—or Henry either, for that matter—but from this point on, it's what drives the plot. As I've said, it's Austen's only real failure in her entire body of work; but it is, alas, a massive one, and from here on in, *Mansfield Park* becomes heavy going because of it.

In fact, we plunge right on in to one of the most distressing chapters in all of Austen. Fanny hurries back home and goes up to her room intending to deposit "this doubtful good of a necklace" in a box, and when she opens the door she finds Edmund there, at her writing table. "Such a sight having never occurred before, was almost as wonderful as it was welcome."

He's come, we learn, to give her a chain for William's cross, which he would have given her earlier but for blah blah blah (Edmund's dialogue, like Edmund himself, does not sparkle) but here it is now and no don't thank me, now I must rush off before your torrent of rapture submerges and drowns me. Except Fanny—who's thrilled not only by the simpler taste of Edmund's chain, but by the excuse it now gives her to forego Mary's necklace—implores him to stay and advise her on the best way to return the gift to Mary.

Edmund, hearing of Mary's largesse, predictably goes all moony over her perfection in having foreseen Fanny's need, and offers her the opposite counsel to the one being sought: rather than offend her friend, Fanny must wear Mary's necklace:

> *'For one night, Fanny, for only one night, if it be a sacrifice...wear the necklace, as you are engaged to do tomorrow evening, and let the chain, which was not ordered with any reference to the ball, be kept for commoner occasions. That is my advice. I would not have the shadow of a coolness between the two...in whose characters there is so much general resemblance in true generosity and natural delicacy as to make the few*

> *slight differences, resulting principally from situation, no reasonable hindrance to a perfect friendship."*

No, I don't know what drugs Edmund has been taking, but I sure wish I knew where to score some.

He then goes on to refer to Mary and Fanny as "the two dearest objects I have on earth," which sends Fanny into a little tailspin of happy-sad: "She was one of his two dearest—that must support her. But the other!—the first!...Could she believe Miss Crawford to deserve him, it would be—how far more tolerable! But he was deceived in her; he gave her merits which she had not; her faults were what they had ever been, but he saw them no longer."

All right, maybe we can chalk up this rank ingratitude to understandable dismay at her realization that Edmund is going to wed Mary and that any kinda-sorta-sometimes-under-the-covers-at-night hopes she herself might have had in that direction were "an insanity". But then comes the real cray-cray: Fanny greedily scoops up the note Edmund had been writing to her and reads over its single unfinished sentence with little gasps of ecstasy.

> *Two lines more prized had never fallen from the pen of the most distinguished author—never more completely blessed the researches of the fondest biographer. The enthusiasm of a woman's love is even beyond the biographer's. To her, the hand-writing itself, independent of any thing it may convey, is a blessedness. Never were such characters cut by any other human being, as Edmund's commonest hand-writing gave! This specimen, written in haste as it was, had not a fault; and there was a felicity in the flow of the first four words, in the arrangement of "My very dear Fanny," which she could have looked at for ever.*

If you had shown me this passage out of context and asked me to guess its author, Jane Austen is just about the last name I'd have given you. Pretty much everyone else in the western canon would have come before it. Thackeray, Dickens, George Eliot...what the hell, Jean-Paul Sartre, H.P. Lovecraft, Mickey Spillane. But Austen? This is exactly the kind of archness, the kind of preciousness—the kind of flat-out romantic fetishism—that our girl typically mocks. (The brazenly irreverent juvenile Jane would have gone even further: she'd have had Fanny actually *try* to stare at those four words forever, and waste away from hunger in the process.) I don't know exactly what happened to Austen here, but you want to avert your eyes and pretend not to notice, like when someone you love farts in a church.

Thankfully, these turgid passages come to an end in a swift onrush of minor incident; but then, just as swiftly, we arrive at the night of the ball, when Fanny, on her way upstairs to make herself ready, reflects that yesterday "it had been about the same hour that she had found Edmund in the east room", and "in a fond indulgence of fancy" she wonders whether she'll find him there again—only to have Edmund appear right there before her on the stairs. You blink once, then twice, and you wonder: *What the hell has happened to Jane Austen?* This...this is a Barbara Cartland moment.

It continues in this chest-heaving vein. Edmund, who looks seriously beat down, tells Fanny he's just come from the parsonage, and "You may guess my errand there, Fanny." She of course presumes he's popped the question, and begins quietly steeling herself, until he says, "I wished to engage Miss Crawford for the first two dances," and then sunshine and lollipops, Fanny is *so* relieved, and if I had hair I would tear it out right at the roots.

But while Mary has agreed to honor Edmund's request, "she says it is the last time that she will ever dance with me...She never has danced with a clergyman, she says, and she never *will*." Edmund then prevails on Fanny's sterling qualities as a listener to bear with him as he tears down Mary's character—yes, *Mary,* who mere pages before he was rhapsodizing as the pinnacle of sweetness and consideration and delicacy—as being no different in essentials than Fanny herself—and of course Fanny is only too happy to listen, and in her Fanny way encourage him with silence...agreeing by withholding agreement. Not that Edmund needs encouragement or agreement; like an eighth-grader who's been rejected by the popular girl, he intends to salve his pride by sullying the reputation of the one who wounded it. Suddenly and miraculously, he's able to point to all sorts of subtle indications that Mary's not *really* a quality human being at all, and...

...and, you know what? Enough, already. I can't bear it anymore. We'll get into the actual ball next time, but right now I need a good stiff drink. A tumbler of Glenfiddich ought to do it.

Actually, better make that a double.

CHAPTERS 28-30

And so we come to the night of the ball...and we re-settle ourselves in our seats, because we've learned by now that when Austen brings all her characters together for these great occasions, she's going to treat us to a series of riotously funny set pieces. But, alas, it doesn't work out that way this time, for a number of reasons. First, Austen has moved the majority of her most entertaining boors offstage (Tom, the Rushworths, Mr. Yates), and with the exception of Mrs. Norris—who isn't nearly up to her usual roaring awfulness for reasons we'll soon discuss—no one else can be counted on for the kind of misbehavior we require from an Austen gathering. The Crawfords *frère et soeur* are supposedly our villains, but in fact, they keep giving us reasons to adore rather than abjure them.

And then there's Fanny, who is the central figure here, and hence (what a surprise) the central problem. She edges nearer to being likable in this chapter than she does anywhere else in the novel—because she actually, if tentatively, embraces activity over passivity, motion over stillness—but ultimately she remains entirely inner-directed. We see the ball almost exclusively through her eyes, and her observations are nearly always of the selfish variety. With the exception of Edmund and William, at whom she stares moonily all evening, she regards no one with any curiosity or interest, only with an eye to evading their notice. Her humility is entirely reactive and self-defeating. A genuinely humble person—someone's who's actively good rather than good by default—will inspire good in others; will have, in a quiet way, *influence.* Think of

Dickens's Little Dorrit—as I often do when reading *Mansfield Park. Her* effect on those who encounter her is, in the end, spiritually stimulating; Fanny has no such effect. Even Sir Thomas's sudden kindly interest in her seems inspired more by the improvement in her looks than in anything that might be called her character.

And so we pass the night of the ball stuck within her tenuous, tremulous point of view—alternately febrile and faint-hearted—and the effect is not beguiling. By the third page you're positively willing her to overindulge at the punchbowl—*anything* to drop the curtain on the frightened-rabbit act she's playing into the ground.

The evening starts promisingly enough, with an exchange between Sir Thomas and Aunt Norris in which the former remarks on how very well Fanny looks. The latter can't leave *that* alone any more than a stray dog could pass up a ham hock, so she leaps in with six-guns a-firin':

> *"Look well! Oh yes...she has good reason to look well with all her advantages: brought up in this family as she has been, with all the benefit of her cousins' manners before her. Only think, my dear Sir Thomas, what extraordinary advantages you and I have been the means of giving her. The very gown you have been taking notice of, is your own present to her when dear Mrs. Rushworth married. What would she have been if we had not taken her by the hand?"*

This is meat and drink to us by now, and we look forward to a whole lot more of Aunt Norris paradoxically claiming authorship of any improvement Fanny may exhibit, while simultaneously striving to discredit that improvement in the process. But instead Aunt Norris recedes quickly in the background...we only catch glimpses of her later, as when Fanny dares to practice her dance steps in the drawing room despite Mrs. Norris being there (possibly the most charming thing she's done in all 280-plus pages thus far), and Mrs. Norris ignores her because she is "entirely taken up at first in fresh arranging and injuring the noble fire which the butler had prepared." Even at her most glowingly successful, Fanny can't hold her principal antagonist's interest long enough to inspire her to undertake a sustained campaign to ruin her happiness, which you'd think would be the kind of thing that would make Mrs. Norris's whole night. But no, Fanny remains affectless...a nullity...in short, just not worth it.

Henry Crawford arrives and secures Fanny's promise of the first dance; and Fanny knows she *ought* to be grateful, because "she so little understood her own claims as to think, if Mr. Crawford had not asked her, she must have been the last to be sought after, and should have received a partner only through a series of inquiry, and bustle...which would have been terrible"—and yet at the same moment "there was a pointedness in his manner of asking her, which she did not like," and she ends up goddamn *resenting* the guy for rescuing her.

This is a thematic replay of the scene we covered in the last chapter, in which Fanny *went out of her way* to appeal to Mary Crawford for help in dressing for the ball, only to end up disrespecting Mary's advice and begrudging her any thanks for having so willingly supplied it. And here she is at it again—"there was a pointedness in his manner," my skinny white ass. Fanny is very, very hard to like here; where exactly does someone so supposedly abject in her humility—to the point of being unwilling to lead the first dance of the evening (because oh! oh! she should be *looked* at!)—dredge up this kind of lofty pomposity?... Disdaining Mary and Henry on the basis of gestures—of inflections—of *style?*

And while we're still reeling over this, Mary herself enters the scene, and Fanny, "anxious to get the story over, hastened to give the explanation of the second necklace"—the one Edmund gave her, on which she's hung William's cross instead of the chain Mary herself supplied.

And Mary's reaction: what do you think? Hurt? Pique? Sly remarks about Fanny's fealty as a friend? No, nothing remotely so self-regarding. Instead, she's bowled over by Edmund's generosity; "her eyes, bright as they had been before, shewing they could yet be brighter, she exclaimed with eager pleasure, 'Did he? Did Edmund? That was like himself. No other man would have thought of it. I honour him beyond expression.'"

Oh, but wait. There's more. The ball begins, and Fanny and Henry lead the first dance. And what is Mary's immediate inclination? To scoff, to make mock, to subvert the occasion, to head for the buffet and tuck in? Oh no. Mary makes a point of *increasing everyone's enjoyment of the moment.* She starts with her host:

> *Miss Crawford saw much of Sir Thomas's thoughts as he stood, and in spite of all his wrongs towards her, a general prevailing desire of recom-*

> *mending herself to him, took an opportunity of stepping aside to say something agreeable of Fanny. Her praise was warm, and he received it as she could wish, joining in it as far as discretion, and politeness, and slowness of speech would allow...*

Granted, this isn't entirely selfless; there's that "prevailing desire of recommending herself to him," though what she hopes to gain by it is unclear (possibly even to herself). But she then goes and repeats the performance with Lady Bertram, whose opinion of her, for good or ill, can't possibly benefit her in any way imaginable; presuming an opinion could even be formed in a mind so entirely clouded by white noise.

Lady Bertram's reply to Mary's paean to Fanny is, by the way, the capstone to a running joke in which her ladyship has spent the entire party bragging that she sent her maid Chapman to help Fanny dress, which is funny because we've just seen that Chapman arrived too late to lift a finger on the girl's behalf. And now Austen brings the joke home with rimshot-worthy brio:

> *"Yes, she does look very well," was Lady Bertram's placid reply. "Chapman helped her dress. I sent Chapman to her." Not but that she was really pleased to have Fanny admired; but she was so much more struck with her own kindness in sending Chapman to her, that she could not get it out of her head.*

Mary then goes to Mrs. Norris—thassright, *Mrs. Norris*—and knowing her "too well to think of gratifying *her* by commendation of Fanny," she instead sighs, "Ah! ma'am, how much we want dear Mrs. Rushworth and Julia to-night!" which of course just slathers the marzipan on Aunt Norris's gingerbread. Now, that is pure, flat-out selflessness. But then Mary's campaign of amplifying the happiness of everyone present runs aground when she takes it to...guess who? Take a wild, flailing, stab in the dark.

> *Miss Crawford blundered most towards Fanny herself, in her intentions to please. She meant to be giving her little heart a happy flutter, and filling her with sensations of delightful self-consequence...and misinterpreting Fanny's blushes, still thought she must be doing so.*

Mary's great offense?...Implying that Fanny would know why Henry is going to town the following morning; and when Fanny protests her ignorance, concluding, "I must suppose it to be purely for the pleasure of conveying your brother and talking of you by the way." Yeah, man, what a *bitch.*

Similarly, Henry Crawford's attentions make Fanny "feel that she was the object of all," and "though she could not say that it was unpleasantly done...there was indelicacy or ostentation in his manner" —really, she *thinks* this. Who, I ask you, *who* is the unregenerate lout here: the woman doing her best to spread joy wherever she goes, or the one trying to evade all notice, and quietly deriding the only friends she has in the world for not being exactly one-hundred-percent-and-change what she thinks they ought to be?

Then Edmund comes to claim a dance with Fanny, and listen to *this*:

> *"I am worn out with civility," said he. "I have been talking incessantly all night, and with nothing to say. But with you, Fanny, there may be peace. You will not want to be talked to. Let us have the luxury of silence."*

So they dance without saying a word. Right, let's just review here: Henry Crawford gets sneered at because he happens to grin a bit too knowingly as he fawns all over Fanny and treats her like the goddamn queen of Sheba...but then Edmund basically tells her, "Let's dance, sure, but for God's sake let's not talk," and she eats it up with a spoon and asks for seconds. THE. HELL.

I'd love love *love* for some of the self-professed Austenites out there to have their own boyfriends or spouses say something similar to *them* as they're being led onto the dance floor. Oh yeah, they'd comply, all right...in fact, they'd give the sons of bitches the silent treatment for about two full *weeks.*

Finally—thank the sweet lawd baby Jebus in his cradle—Sir Thomas decides Fanny has had enough excitement for one night and sends her on up to bed. But she has one more cringe-inducing scene to play: she begs to be allowed to get up and take breakfast with William before he sets off to rejoin his ship...then goes into a passive-aggressive snit when Henry Crawford inserts himself into the party as well. Henry Crawford, *who is providing William with transportation at his own expense.*

The woman is just a menace. A *menace.*

Luckily, the disappointment of the ball is ameliorated by the following chapter, which sneaks up and takes us by surprise; it's one of the most affecting in the novel.

William and Henry depart after breakfast, and after seeing them off Fanny returns to the breakfast room to enjoy a good wallow.

> *...and there her uncle kindly left her to cry in peace, conceiving perhaps that the deserted chair of each young man might exercise her tender enthusiasm, and that the remaining cold pork bones and mustard in William's plate, might but divide her feelings with the broken egg-shells in Mr. Crawford's.*

Referenced just to remind us that, yes godammit, we're dealing with a *writer* here.

We follow Fanny through a "heavy, melancholy day" in which even the pleasure of reliving the ball is denied her, because the only other soul on hand is Lady Bertram, who might as well have passed the whole evening underwater.

> *"She could not recollect what it was that she had heard about one of the Miss Maddoxes, or what it was that Lady Prescott had noticed in Fanny; she was not sure whether Colonel Harrison had been talking of Mr. Crawford or of William, when he said he was the finest young man in the room; somebody had whispered something to her, she had forgot to ask Sir Thomas what it could be."*

Love that detail of her needing her husband to tell her what had been *whispered* to her. Lady Bertram has her moments; few and far between, but worth waiting for.

To make matters even more melancholy, Sir Thomas takes Fanny by surprise with a valedictory remark about Edmund, who has gone off as well, to visit a friend of his, a certain Mr. Owen; "[W]e must learn to do without him. This will be the last winter of his belonging to us, as he has done." Meaning, he'll soon take orders and assume residence at Thornton Lacey. Fanny wrestles with this for a while, but of course self-abnegation is her daily diet, so she soon comes to a calm acceptance of Edmund's departure from her life.

However, what "was tranquility and comfort to Fanny was tediousness and vexation to Mary."

> *To Fanny's mind, Edmund's absence was really in its cause and its tendency a relief. To Mary it was in every way painful. She felt the want of his society every day, almost every hour...Angry as she was with Edmund for adhering to his own notions and acting on them in defiance of her...she could not help thinking of him continually when absent, dwelling on his merit and affection, and longing again for the almost daily meetings they lately had.*

Even more remarkably:

> *Then she began to blame herself. She wished she had not spoken so warmly in their last conversation. She was afraid she had used some strong—some contemptuous expressions in speaking of the clergy, and that should not have been. It was ill-bred—it was wrong. She wished such words unsaid with all her heart.*

And into this roiling stew of heady emotion—anger, longing, regret—something entirely unexpected gets stirred in: jealousy. "His friend Mr. Owen had sisters—He might find them attractive." The mixture proves combustible; it launches Mary right out of her chair, as though she's been unwittingly sitting on an anti-aircraft missile. "She could not live any longer in such solitary wretchedness; and she made her way to the Park, through difficulties of walking which she had deemed unconquerable a week before, for the chance of hearing a little in addition, for the sake of at least hearing his name."

To a modern reader, this is ravishing stuff. Our sympathies are absolutely with the woman in torment, repenting of her glibness and sharp tongue and repining for the man she so casually tossed aside; to our sensibilities, she's much worthier of our pity than the passive little nonentity who's willing to let him go with a couple of watery sighs.

When Mary gets Fanny alone, she tries to affect a casual, offhand manner, but her anguish comes spilling out with every word:

> *"[Edmund] is a very—a very pleasing young man himself, and I cannot help being rather concerned at not seeing him again before I go to London,*

> *as will now undoubtedly be the case.—I am looking for Henry every day, and as soon as he comes there will be nothing to detain me at Mansfield. I should like to have seen him once more, I confess. But you must give my compliments to him. Yes—I think it must be compliments. Is not there something wanted, Miss Price, in our language—a something between compliments and—and love—to suit the sort of friendly acquaintance we have had together?—So many months acquaintance!—But compliments may be sufficient here.—Was his letter a long one?—Does he give you much account of what he is doing?—Is it Christmas gaieties that he is staying for?"*

This is, quite simply, heartbreaking.

Eventually Mary rallies, and her conversation regains its usual Nöel Coward brilliancy; she does a little riff on the Owens sisters that sparkles like diamond:

> *"[F]or one knows, without being told, exactly what they are—all very accomplished and pleasing, and one very pretty. There is a beauty in every family.—It is a regular thing. Two play on the piano-forte, and one on the harp—and all sing—or would sing if they were taught—or sing all the better for not being taught—or something like it."*

Fanny brings this to a crashing halt by bluntly stating, "I know nothing of the Miss Owens." Once a buzzkill...

Fanny *does* attempt—but only because she feels "obliged to speak" —to assuage Mary's feelings to the extent of saying she'll be missed when she's gone. But Mary waves this away. "Oh! yes, missed as every noisy evil is missed when it is taken away; that is, there is a great difference felt. But I am not fishing; don't compliment me. If I am missed, it will appear. I may be discovered by those who want to see me. I shall not be in any doubtful, or distant, or unapproachable region."

Two hundred years after these words were written, they're utterly familiar to us, because the tone and tenor of them has been repeated in more romantic comedies than can be counted on a bank of supercomputers; and in every one of those confections, the warring, wounding, ever-at-odds hero and heroine come at the end to a blissful détente—or an equally felicitous mutual defeat—and collapse into each other's arms, their defenses lying in rubble at their feet. Austen didn't invent this genre (as I've noted before, she had Beatrice and Benedick, among others, to harken back to) but she did formalize and popularize it as no one else before or since. That she, to our eyes, betrays the genre in *Mansfield Park* by violating this prime tenet, is certainly troublesome; and seeing Mary in actual torment in this chapter only increases our discomfort, since we know the relief the genre demands for her isn't coming.

But we do need to keep in mind that it wasn't *yet* a genre when Austen was penning this tale; and that she was clearly challenging herself to do something different than she'd done before. And that what she learned from the failed experiment of *Mansfield Park,* yielded dazzling benefits in what came after. Just keep telling yourself this; increasingly, you'll need it as consolation.

Especially because now, Austen really starts piling it on. The succeeding chapter is basically an extended dialogue between Henry and Mary, in which Henry—having no sooner arrived back at the parsonage than high-tailed it to the Park to pay his respects—returns after an hour and a half virtually pinwheeling with excitement. "I am quite determined, Mary. My mind is entirely made up. Will it astonish you? No—You must be aware that I am quite determined to marry Fanny Price."

It *does* astonish Mary, who hadn't a clue that her brother's fancy had taken him so far; the last she'd heard of it, he'd planned only to make a play for Fanny's affections as a kind of hedge against boredom, the way another man might, say, take up gardening. That the scheme has gone so cattywampus as to make *Henry's* the affections that get trussed up for slow-roasting, absolutely gobsmacks Mary. What it does *not* do—could anything? ever?—is render her speechless.

> *"Lucky, lucky girl!...what a match for her! My dearest Henry, this must be my first feeling; but my second, which you shall have as sincerely, is that I approve your choice from my soul, and foresee your happiness as heartily as I wish and desire it. You will have a sweet little wife; all gratitude and devotion. Exactly what you deserve. What an amazing match for her! Mrs. Norris often talks of her luck; what will she say now? The delight of all the family indeed! And she has some* true *friends in it. How they will rejoice! But tell me all about it. Talk to me for ever."*

Henry doesn't remark, as he might, that he can't talk forever because Mary just has; in fact he happily takes up the challenge and the two of them go riding off at a conversational gallop. What impresses us chiefly is that Henry's feeling for Fanny seems largely to have rehabilitated him, in the way that Mary's for Edmund has improved her—made her more compassionate, more selfless, less able to hide her feelings behind a mask of coy insouciance. Henry now, too, seems chiefly excited by the joy he thinks he'll be giving Fanny, rather than the happiness she'll bring to him.

There are, of course, lapses—or, rather, what Austen must mean us to see as lapses. For instance, when Mary compares Henry's match to the miserable union of their late aunt to the hideous Admiral:

> *"Henry, I think so highly of Fanny Price, that if I could suppose the next Mrs. Crawford would have half the reason which my poor ill used aunt had to abhor the very name, I would prevent the marriage, if possible; but I know you, I know that a wife you loved would be the happiest of women, and that even when you ceased to love, she would yet find in you the liberality and good-breeding of a gentleman."*

Henry of course launches into a soliloquy on "the impossibility...of ceasing to love Fanny Price," and I suppose we're meant to feel Mary's indelicacy in even bringing up the idea; but instead it just impresses us with her maturity (if not her timing). Marital ardor *does* often ebb away; we know it as well as Mary—and furthermore Austen knows it too; she invented Mr. and Mrs. Bennet, remember?

Then, in Henry's exaltation of Fanny, he praises her at the expense of Lady Bertram, remarking on how she attended "with such ineffable sweetness and patience, to all the demands of her aunt's stupidity... then returning to her seat to finish a note which she was previously engaged in writing for that stupid woman's service". Again, I think we're meant to be shocked by Henry's excessive candor, and to disapprove it (and him); but he *is* talking to his sister, and I doubt Austen herself observed conversational niceties when in intimate chat with *her* siblings (in fact, in some of her surviving letters to her sister Cassandra, she uses terms that make Henry Crawford sound downright euphemistic).

Plus?...Hey, Lady Bertram *is* stupid. It's pretty much her sole defining attribute (other than immobility).

Henry is so far reformed that when Mary asks him what Mrs. Rushworth and Julia will have to say at the news, he replies, "They will be angry...Mrs. Rushworth will be very angry. It will be a bitter pill to her; that is, like other bitter pills, it will have two moments ill-flavour, and then be swallowed and forgotten; for I am not such a coxcomb as to suppose her feelings more lasting than other women's, though *I* was the object of them."

Yes, he has *that much* self-awareness...just as we've repeatedly seen Mary does. Certainly every Austen novel must have a cad, to imperil the heroine's affections, and a rival, to threaten to entrap the hero. And we can appreciate that in *Mansfield Park* Austen is attempting to work her characters in subtler shades, presumably for a more deeply resonant and literary effect; but when the cad and the rival are allowed so much subtlety and shade that they become actually *preferable* to the hero and heroine—when arid, chalky Edmund and dour, po-faced Fanny come to seem like *they're* the cad and the rival—then the trains are all on the wrong tracks, and we're headed towards a tremendous smack-up.

Fasten your seatbelts: it's a-comin' on fast.

CHAPTERS 31-33

We now arrive now at a stretch of the narrative that's actually difficult to read without cringing. Henry Crawford—brash, impulsive, confident to the point of arrogance—launches a full-scale charm offensive against Fanny. And .despite the many ways in which he missteps and offends, it's hard to feel other than pity for him; because he's a man of action—frenetic, indiscriminate action—and in his campaign to win Fanny's heart he happily seizes on any weapon at hand and batters away at her tirelessly, talking all the while—or if not talking winking, gesturing, or clearing his throat across a crowded room at her.

And she?...Of course she does nothing. She withdraws ever further into her tortoise shell of refusal, and seems ready, willing, and able to just wait out the storm of attention. It's very much a case of irresistible force meeting immovable object, though in this instance the irresistible force is at a disadvantage, because it's fueled merely by a young man's fancy, while Fanny Price is fueled by the universe-devouring power of entropy.

Henry starts well, arriving at Mansfield Park with a coup in his pocket. He finds Fanny with Lady Bertram in the breakfast room, but by a stroke of luck, the latter is "on the very point of quitting it as he entered."

> *She was almost at the door, and not chusing by any means to take so much trouble in vain, she still went out, after a civil reception, a short*

> *sentence about being waited for, and a "Let Sir Thomas know," to the servant.*

Clearly, on the rare occasions when Lady Bertram is forced from her usual state of inertia to one of actual locomotion, she's not about to allow anything like good manners or hospitality interrupt her single-minded trek towards the next place she can sit down.

Henry, "overjoyed to have her go," now plops himself down next to Fanny and with barely a preamble—hell, with barely a hello—he flourishes some letters in her face and crows in triumph.

> *"Knowing as I do what your feelings as a sister are, I could hardly have borne that any one in the house should share with you in the first knowledge of the news I bring. He is made. Your brother is a Lieutenant. I have the infinite satisfaction of congratulating you on your brother's promotion. Here are the letters which announce it, this moment come to hand. You will, perhaps, like to see them."*

He drops them into her lap, then gets up and pimp-walks around the room, pausing only to slam-dunk a few invisible hoops. Because Henry—as Fanny discovers when she reads the letters with darting, rabbity eyes—is the man responsible for her beloved brother's promotion. It turns out that *this* was the nature of his clandestine mission in town a few chapters back: to introduce William to his uncle, the much-maligned Admiral, and see what the old reprobate might do for him. Which, as it turns out, is quite a bit.

"I will not talk of my own happiness...great as it is, for I think only of yours," Henry says, just before launching into an almost epic-length discourse on his own happiness. "How impatient, how anxious, how wild I have been on the subject, I will not attempt to describe," he says of his endeavors on William's behalf, right before describing in explicit detail exactly how important, how anxious, and how wild he has been in pursuit of them. It's hard to blame him, as Fanny all but eggs him on, asking him repeatedly for clarification in a way that leads us to believe she might not be the sharpest pin in the cushion: "Has this been all *your* doing, then?...Good Heaven! how very, very kind! Have you really—was it by *your* desire—I beg your pardon, but I am bewildered. Did Admiral Crawford apply?—how was it?—I am stupefied."

Henry is "most happy to make it more intelligible," and his eagerness gets the better of him because he's soon larding his narration with some heavily dropped hints—using "such strong expression...so abounding in the *deepest interest,* in *two-fold motives,* in *views and wishes more than could be told,* that Fanny could not have remained insensible of his drift, had she been able to attend," but alas she's too busy plucking her lower lip and staring at the letters, and asking him to wait, wait, start over again: *you* did this?

Eventually she twigs to the whole story (possibly the first buds of spring have made their appearance by this time), and overcome by emotion she jumps up—we think, to throw herself into Henry's arms, which come on, is what he's been angling for and no less than he deserves—but no, she sprints immediately for the door, announcing her eagerness to tell her uncle the good news.

And here's where Henry screws the pooch; he doesn't let her go. Which is how we can tell the poor lad's really smitten. The *old* Henry—the Henry who played Maria and Julia Bertram like mice in a maze, getting them to turn whichever way he wanted by strategically batting his bedroom eyes—that Henry is gone, and in his place is this headlong creature who is too impatient to allow Fanny time to dwell on his kindness to William—to allow her heart to soften by degrees. It's like he's got every Broadway show-tune ever written clanging away in his ears, so that he's driven to stake everything on a wild throw of the dice. He blocks her escape, asking for five minutes more; and when she balks at that, he ups the ante and asks for the entire rest of her life. Not a shy one, our Henry. And of course, while Fanny is still reeling—possibly literally, like a top—he moves in for the kill. "He pressed her for an answer," Austen tells us, and you get the idea she's maybe speaking literally; like, he pins her behind a door, or under a sofa cushion, and refuses to let her loose until she says yes, yes, I'll marry you, please, I can't breathe.

Fanny responds, as Fanny always does, with a grapeshot spray of concealment, refusal, denial, and flight.

> *"No, no, no," she cried, hiding her face. "This is all nonsense. Do not distress me. I can hear no more of this. Your kindness to William makes*

> *me more obliged to you than words can express; but I do not want, I cannot bear, I must not listen to such—No, no, don't think of me. But you are not thinking of me. I know it is all nothing."*

I could write a dissertation on this paragraph alone. It's the most archetypal of all Fanny's speeches in the book.

Henry, unfortunately, is congenitally immune to the word "no"—I doubt he even hears it; it turns to butterflies before it reaches his ear—so of course he pursues her, but has the bad luck to run into Sir Thomas, and so must stop and pay his respects—"though to part with her at a moment when her modesty alone seemed to his sanguine and pre-assured mind to stand in the way of the happiness he sought, was a cruel necessity." Meantime, Fanny squirrels herself away in the East Room and reflects on the turn of events.

> *It was all beyond belief! He was inexcusable, incomprehensible!—But such were his habits, that he could do nothing without a mixture of evil. He had previously made her the happiest of human beings, and now he had insulted—she knew not what to say—how to class or how to regard it. She would not have him be serious, and yet what could excuse the use of such words and offers, if they meant but to trifle?*

This is about as much effort as she'll ever take towards trying to understand Henry's declaration—to considering Henry as a person at all. Granted, he made a bad first impression by the callous way he toyed with Maria and Julia; but Fanny seems unwilling to recognize any change in him—any *possibility* of change—even though she herself is its apparent catalyst.

This is a misstep on Austen's part...at least in our eyes. Popular culture has conditioned us—has virtually *indoctrinated* us—to look approvingly on rogues rehabilitated by love; in fact, to *expect* that bad boys will become good men through the agency of a patient, loving woman. We've learned to like this story, and to enjoy seeing it played out over and over again, in only slightly modified variations. You might argue that Austen is literature, not popular culture, and that we should allow for more complexity in her works than we find in a Lifetime Original Movie; and that's a valid point. But I'd argue that Austen is both literature *and* popular culture, and that with her novels she played a critical part in the *invention* of popular culture. Many of the genre conventions we associate with romantic comedy and social satire, stem from her; so when she herself appears to violate them, it jars. Our modern, humanist sensibilities enjoy seeing the charmingly caustic, laconically cynical Henry Crawford turn into a slobbery golden retriever in pursuit of Fanny—and we resent Fanny for not enjoying it as well, and rewarding him for it.

This brings us to a crucial point that we'll be discussing further as the plot deepens. Our ethical sympathies will remain with Fanny as she's increasingly pushed toward accepting Henry against her will; after all, one of the foundations of liberal democracy is the right to self-determination, and as a society we abhor all forms of coercion. Yet at the same time we can't help being impatient with her as well; like those who will try to strong-arm her into accepting Henry as a husband, we're annoyed that she won't even take a goddamn *look* at the guy. It's especially perverse behavior for someone whose entire life is devoted to her own self-abasement; what, *now* she's suddenly too good for someone?

As it happens, I've been rereading Robert Graves's *Claudius The God* concurrently with *Mansfield Park,* and there's a section early on in which Graves has Claudius define certain men as being "always true to a single extreme character," and then divide these men into four categories: scoundrels with stony hearts, virtuous men with stony hearts, virtuous men with golden hearts, and—"most rarely found"— scoundrels with golden hearts. These character types (expanded to include women) tally neatly with the cast of *Mansfield Park.* Aunt Norris, for instance, is obviously a scoundrel with a stony heart; and Edmund, while admittedly a dry old stick, is unarguably a virtuous man with a golden heart.

More revelatory is the recognition of Fanny as a virtuous woman with a stony heart (unlike Edmund's, her heart never yields to persuasion, nor bends to supplication), which helps explain nearly all of her inherent contradictions. And then there's Henry Crawford, who provides a classic example of the scoundrel with a golden heart. There's no question that in our day we vastly prefer the golden-hearted scoundrels to the stony-hearted saints; but I've seen enough 18th century literature to venture an educated guess that this was true in Austen's time as well. So again we're left a-wonderin'.

Fanny hides in the East Room all day to avoid risking a further encounter with Henry, but uh-oh, he's been invited to dinner, and so she's forced to go down and face him. Or rather, to *not* face him—to engage instead in an almost Pac-Man like game of shuttling around the room in avoidance of him, while he chugs along alternate routes trying to intersect her and, presumably, gobble her up.

To add to Fanny's discomfort, when he finally does catch her in an unguarded moment, he hands her a note from his sister that's full of congratulations and best wishes and smiley faces and i's dotted with hearts. And while we can excuse Henry for not yet having twigged to Fanny's refusal (because he's never been refused before, and does not understand this strange new concept), for him to have gone ahead and filled in the blank with actual acceptance when relating the story to his sister, is more than a tad boorish. So yeah, we can spare some pity for Fanny, pummeled by all those x's and o's from Mary's machine gun of sisterly love. But worse is coming.

First, though, there's a wonderful interlude with Aunt Norris, who's been far too infrequent a presence in these recent chapters. William's promotion is not the kind of news designed to delight her, since her principal aim, with regard to her Price nieces and nephews, is to make certain that they're kept firmly in their humble place; the idea being, presumably, that *she* can't be the poor relation while there are poorer still to point to.

And yet she surprises us: William's promotion has her positively bubbly...because it removes him from any further claim on her generosity. Not, of course, that she begrudges him her previous endowments. "She was very glad that she had given William what she did at parting, very glad indeed that it had been in her power, without material inconvenience just at that time, to give him something rather considerable"—which leads to this side-splitting exchange:

> *"I am glad you gave him something considerable," said Lady Bertram, with most unsuspicious calmness—"for* I *gave him only 10*l*."*
>
> *"Indeed!" cried Mrs. Norris, reddening. "Upon my word, he must have gone off with his pockets well lined! and at no expense for his journey to London either!"*
>
> *"Sir Thomas told me 10*l*. would be enough."*

> *Mrs. Norris being not at all inclined to question its sufficiency, began to take the matter in another point.*

Fanny meanwhile is still trying to force reality to fit her preferred reading of it. Mr. Crawford "once or twice" forces a look on her "which she did not know how to class among the common meaning; in any other man at least, she would have said that it meant something very earnest, very pointed. But she still tried to believe it no more than what he might often have expressed towards her cousins and fifty other women." Faced with something, she must reduce it to nothing. Faced with a presence, she must render it an absence. After "she carefully refused him every opportunity" of speaking with her, Mr. Crawford is forced finally to ask whether she will, at the very least, reply to his sister's note...?

Breeding demands that she do at least that, and so, "wishing not to appear to think any thing really intended" between herself and Henry, she pens a few evasive lines, concluding with, "I do not know what I write, but it would be a great favour of you never to mention the subject again." Everything she expresses in these chapters is just bathed in negation. When she opens her mouth, you hear the sound of doors slamming shut, one after another, after another, after another.

Having dismissed Henry with as little actual human contact as possible—she'd have returned the note to him through an airlock, if she could've managed it—she awakens the next day with him still on her mind, though "not less sanguine," as if sanguine is a word that could ever apply to Fanny Price. You might as well call her "frisky," or "rambunctious."

> *If Mr. Crawford would but go away!—That was what she most earnestly desired;—go and take his sister with him, as he was to do, and as he returned to Mansfield on purpose to do. And why it was not done already, she could not devise, for Miss Crawford certainly wanted no delay.*

Keep in mind that Henry and Mary Crawford are pretty much Fanny's only friends in the world—almost the only people she knows at all, outside her family circle. She's spent the entire novel disdaining their affection for her, and now fervently wishes they'd just hit the bloody road already. See what I'm sayin'? Heart. Of. Stone.

She's certain that her note to Mary must have put the kibosh on the whole marry-me-sweetheart business, so she's gobsmacked when she spies Henry skipping up the drive again. She bravely scurries back to her bolt hole, like a rodent evading a flashlight beam, and there she hunkers down to wait out Henry's visit—which she's sure can't *possibly* have anything to do with her, because—well, *because.* Fanny logic.

Eventually there's a tread on the stair, and Fanny, at her most devoted-canine, recognizes it as Sir Thomas's, and suddenly there he is at the door, begging permission to come in. When she admits him (all a-tremble, again, *because*), he notices that she has no fire in the hearth, and questions her on this rather glaring lack; because it's the dead of winter, and hello, your fingernails are blue. Surely Lady Bertram can't be aware of this alarmingly Spartan state of affairs. Fanny—being virtuous (if stony-hearted)—has no wish to play stool pigeon, "but being obliged to speak, she could not forbear, in justice to the aunt she loved best, from saying something in which the words 'my aunt Norris' were distinguishable."

Sir Thomas heaves a page-long sigh in which he basically says, in the most refined phrases imaginable, I know your aunt Norris is a screaming bitch-queen from the black pit of tarnation, but for God's sake don't hate her for it or you'll turn out the same way and one of you is quite enough, thanks. Well, really, just listen to a little sampling from *his* version and imagine what a world it would be if we could all express our furious annoyance so with such mellifluous civility:

> *"I know what her sentiments have always been. The principle was good in itself, but it may have been, and I believe has been carried too far in your case.—I am aware that there has been sometimes, in some points, a misplaced distinction; but I think too well of you, Fanny, to suppose you will ever harbour resentment on that account...and of this you may be assured, that every advantage of affluence will be doubled by the little privations and restrictions that may have been imposed."*

Sir Thomas Bertram and his amazing silver tongue, ladies and gentlemen! He's here all week. Tip your waitress. Try the Chicken Kiev.

Now down to the business of his remarkable appearance in Fanny's private lair. He's just had a visit from Henry Crawford, whose "errand you may probably conjecture." Yep, he's gone ahead and applied to Sir

Thomas for Fanny's hand, and "done it all so well, so openly, so liberally, so properly," that Sir Thomas, who seems a tad smitten himself by Henry's dash and gallantry (you can almost sense the hot flush in his cheeks as he describes him), "was exceedingly happy to give the particulars of their conversation—and, little aware of what was passing in his niece's mind, conceived that by such details he must be gratifying her far more than himself." He concludes by entreating her to come downstairs and give her answer to Mr. Crawford in person.

You don't need to be told Fanny's reply. Hell, you could probably write it yourself. In fact, I'm thinking of designing a smart-phone app which will supply an appropriate Fanny Price response to any conceivable question. It'll be easy. I'll just program in the following words:

IMPOSSIBLE CANNOT UNWORTHY UNTHINKABLE
INCONCEIVABLE MISTAKEN UNBEARABLE UNABLE
NO NOT NEVER NOTHING

You'll press a button, and the words will reshuffle themselves with a few pronouns, verbs, and articles thrown in, and there you'll have it: *iFanny*!

In this case she uses all the negatives in her command and several more besides. For his part, Sir Thomas is astonished to the point of anger, like a Taylor Lautner fan confronted with a nonbeliever.

> *"There is something in this which my comprehension does not reach. Here is a young man wishing to pay his addresses to you, with every thing to recommend him; not merely situation in life, fortune, and character, but with more than common agreeableness, with address and conversation pleasing to every body. And he is not an acquaintance of to-day, you have now known him some time. His sister, moreover, is your intimate friend, and he has been doing* that *for your brother, which I should suppose would have been almost sufficient recommendation to you, had there been no other...You must have been...some time aware of a particularity in Mr. Crawford's manners to you. This cannot have taken you by surprise. You must have observed his attentions; and though you always received them very properly, (I have no accusation to make on that head,) I never perceived them to be unpleasant to you. I am half inclined to think, Fanny, that you do not quite know your own feelings."*

She replies with another reshuffling of the Fanny app...and so it goes, with Sir Thomas bearing down on her with reason, authority, and a gentle but firm claim on both her gratitude and indebtedness, and Fanny shooting back with more CANNOT UNTHINKABLE IMPOSSIBLE NEVER, until Sir Thomas is about as red-faced as a pomegranate, and Fanny is reduced to tears. You'd cry too, if he turned his admirable vowel sounds on you with this kind of opprobrium behind them:

> *"I had thought you peculiarly free from willfulness of temper, self-conceit, and every tendency to that independence of spirit, which prevails so much in modern days, even in young women, and which in young women is offensive and disgusting beyond all common offense. But you have now shewn me that you can be willful and perverse, that you can and will decide for yourself, without any consideration or deference for those who have surely some right to guide you—without even asking their advice."*

Fanny has a trump card, which is the disclosure of Henry's character as it revealed itself during the whole *Lovers' Vows* imbroglio; but we're told she doesn't dare play it, because Julia and especially Maria are "so closely implicated in Mr. Crawford's misconduct, that she could not give his character, such as she believed it, without betraying them." I can respect that; and might be more inclined to do so, did Fanny not sully her own integrity a few paragraphs earlier, by willfully misleading Sir Thomas when he inquires—in the most delicate terms imaginable—whether her refusal of Mr. Crawford stems from another affection directed elsewhere (i.e. "Are you hot to trot for my son Edmund?"). "She would rather die than own the truth, and she hoped by a little reflection to fortify herself beyond betraying it." Mm-*hmmm.*

Reassured on this point, Sir Thomas backs off a bit; and being a kindly, fair-minded man—seriously, the trash that gets talked about him in this novel is completely alien to what we see of him; slave-owner aside, the guy's a goddamn pussycat—he decides that a strategic retreat might be the very thing to salvage this whole fiasco.

> *He knew her to be very timid, and exceedingly nervous; and thought it not improbable that her mind might be in such a state, as a little time, a little pressing, a little patience, and a little impatience, a judicious mixture of all on the lover's side, might work their usual effect. If the gentleman*

> *would but persevere, if he had but love enough to persevere*—Sir Thomas *began to have hopes...*

Not much doubt on that score, is there? Golden-hearted Henry has more the enough love to persevere...even after Fanny flatly, steadfastly, and—I think—rudely refuses Sir Thomas's reasonable request to come down and give him the bad news herself. (I have to wonder what might happen if Sir Thomas insisted; how far would Fanny resist? Would he finally realize that what he takes for timidity is actually a stasis field, a powerful column of impenetrable inertia? If he dared place a hand on her to force her, would it wither right off his arm?) Sir Thomas manfully undertakes to deliver the blow himself, then comes back to report that Henry, when told of Fanny's unwillingness even to see him, "behaved in the most gentleman-like and generous manner...Upon my representation of what you were suffering, he immediately, and with the greatest delicacy, ceased to urge to see you for the present." *For the present,* mind, so don't think you're off scot-free, chiquita.

Sir Thomas concludes by saying, "I shall make no mention below of what has passed; I shall not even tell your aunt Bertram. There is no occasion for spreading the disappointment; say nothing about it yourself." Fanny is only too happy to comply, nothing being her most favorite thing of all to say. Sir Thomas follows this kindness with another—encouraging Fanny to go out for a walk to clear her mind—and yet another—having a fire waiting for her when she returns to the East Room. Apparently, we have another Virtuous Man With a Golden Heart on our hands. Who knew?

Ah, but what of the Scoundrel With a Heart of Stone?...Well, when *she* hears that Fanny's been out walking, she goes into a snit, railing away that if she'd *known* Fanny was going out she could have recruited her to take some orders to her household staff, since "It would have made no difference to you, I suppose, whether you had walked in the shrubbery, or gone to my house." And not even Sir Thomas's interjection that it was he who recommended the shrubbery can put Mrs. Norris's nose back in joint. It's one of her minor performances, but given the steaming mass of emotional carnage we've just been through, it's refreshing to dip into some cold, clear cruelty. And she doesn't relent, either, continuing to snarl at Fanny through the rest of the evening, despite Sir Thomas's increasingly obvious attempts to change the subject. "Mrs. Norris had not discernment enough to perceive, either now, or at any other time, to what degree he thought well of his niece, or how very far he was from wishing to have his own children's merits set off by the depreciation of hers. She was talking *at* Fanny, and resenting this private walk half through the dinner."

Sir Thomas's kindnesses lead Fanny to conclude hopefully (and as we know, wrongfully) that he's coming to terms with her refusal of Henry's proposal. But Sir Thomas still insists that Mr. Crawford has a right to hear that refusal from her own pinched lips. So the after the next day's tea, when the butler appears to summon Fanny to her uncle's office, she knows exactly what's going down. Aunt Norris, however, doesn't, and delivers up a really wonderful symphony of self aggrandizement:

> *"Stay, stay, Fanny! what are you about?—where are you going?—don't be in such a hurry. Depend upon it, it is not you that are wanted; depend upon it it is me...but you are so very eager to put yourself forward. What should Sir Thomas want you for? It is me, Baddeley, you mean; I am coming this moment. You mean me, Baddeley, I am sure; Sir Thomas wants me, not Miss Price."*
>
> *But Baddeley was stout. "No, Ma'am, it is Miss Price, I am certain of it being Miss Price." And there was a half smile with the words which meant, "I do not think you would answer to the purpose at all."*

Suddenly—as almost never happens in Jane Austen—a servant is not only brought to the fore as an individual character, and given an actual name; but we're allowed as well a glimpse into his private thoughts, and it's a wonderful moment indeed. What I wouldn't give to hear what Baddeley and his colleagues say about Mrs. Norris below stairs. (Or about Fanny, for that matter.) *There's* meat for an Austen "sequel" I'd actually *want* to read.

And so Fanny is finally forced to face her wooer, in a "conference [that] was neither so short, nor so conclusive, as the lady had designed." Because while she may be an earthly avatar of nullity and negation, it appears that Henry Crawford is her opposite principle: the incarnation of positivity and possibility. You could make a smart-phone app for him, too, using words like CERTAINLY, INEVITABLY, UNDOUBTEDLY, INDEED, and ABSO-FRACKIN'-LUTELY-ARE-YOU-KID-

DING-ME? His way of thinking makes Fanny's "affection appear of greater consequence, because it was withheld, and determined him to have the glory, as well as the felicity, of forcing her to love him."

> *He would not despair: he would not desist. He had every well-grounded reason for solid attachment; he knew her to have all the worth that could justify the warmest hopes of lasting happiness with her...He knew not that he had a pre-engaged heart to attack. Of that, he had no suspicion. He considered her rather as one who had never thought on the subject enough to be in danger...*

I suppose it could be argued, that just as I've derided Fanny for not being willing to look past her prejudices to see Henry as he really is, Henry too isn't seeing past his own idealized view of Fanny. But there's a difference: Henry is completely open and artless—even at his worst, he's never hidden his character from view—whereas Fanny is an active practitioner of every kind of concealment. Of course he can't see the kind of woman she really is. No one can; not even Edmund.

As delightful and sympathetic as we may find Henry, we can foresee trouble ahead; Austen may have made some serious miscalculations at the conceptual level in *Mansfield Park,* but she still shows why she's a match for Shakespeare at conveying the complexity of human psychology. Take this passage: "A little difficulty to be overcome, was not evil to Henry Crawford. He rather derived spirits from it. He had been apt to gain hearts too easily. His situation was new and animating." We read this and we begin to suspect the sustainability of his high emotion; and that concluding statement troubles us as well, as it implies that novelty may be the chief attraction of his heroic resolve. In which case, despair and aggrievement might prove "new and animating" too. We may like Henry well enough—I'm pretty clearly crazy about him—but Austen, while failing to paint him as a despicable rogue, does convey his essential unsteadiness. Against which, I suppose, Edmund is meant to look all the better; but alas, his plodding dependability still pales beside Henry's glamour and vivacity.

Fanny, of course, meets Henry's professions and pledges with repeated choruses of her whole NEVER UNTHINKABLE IMPOSSIBLE repertoire, to absolutely no effect. "Her manner was incurably gentle, and she was not aware how much it concealed the sternness of her purpose. Her diffidence, gratitude, and softness, made every expression of indifference seem almost an effort of self-denial; seem at least, to be giving nearly as much pain to herself as to him."

This is richly ironic; Fanny's so accustomed to concealment that she doesn't know how to appear genuine when she actually *is* finally speaking her mind. In fact, her performance is so unconvincing it even causes her to waffle a bit herself—to wonder whether "here were claims which could not but operate;" but no, her stony heart remains impenetrable, and she ends up angry and resentful "at a perseverance so selfish and ungenerous. Here was again a want of delicacy and regard for others which formerly so struck and disgusted her...Had her own affections been as free—as perhaps they ought to have been—he never could have engaged them." For her, then, virtue isn't an oasis to which she can gently draw those whose spirits respond to hers; rather it's a promontory from which she can look down in judgment at those who don't meet her standards. *Heart. Of. Stone.*

Sir Thomas is disappointed to hear of the lack of progress in the meeting, but cheered by Henry's continued enthusiasm—by the tail-wagging way he's willing to chase that stick every time Fanny hurls it away. He praises him to Fanny: "He is a most extraordinary young man, and whatever be the event, you must feel that you have created an attachment of no common character," and further says if she had more experience of "the unsteady nature of love, as it generally exists," she'd be knocked on her namesake by Henry's doggedness in the face of defeat. When Fanny tries once again to explain herself by not explaining herself, he shuts her down, saying, "There is nothing more to be said or done. From this hour, the subject is never to be revived between us."

But as we know by now, anytime someone in an Austen novel says that, you can count on several more pages filled with nothing *but* the subject never to be revived between them. And sure enough, Sir Thomas is forced to introduce the matter again, because his earlier promise not to mention it to the rest of the family has been rendered moot by Henry himself, who has not the smallest intention of being quiet about it—as previously noted, his is not the kind of character inclined to hide *anything*—and whose chivalric quest to win the heart of his lady fair is already pretty much his sole topic of conversation at the parsonage, and, we can guess, likewise with his barber, his tailor, his saddler, and any stray dogs he takes by surprise in the streets. If he had a Twitter account, the story would be global.

So Sir Thomas feels he'd better inform his wife and sister-in-law before they hear of it from other quarters, though he actively dreads telling the latter. "Sir Thomas, indeed, was, by this time, not very far from classing Mrs. Norris as one of those well-meaning people, who are always doing mistaken and very disagreeable things." Which is just more evidence in favor of Sir Thomas's heart being golden. I mean, *"not very far"* from classing Mrs. Norris this way?...What would she have to do to really convince him? Ritually slaughter and disembowel Fanny, and dance around a pentacle with the entrails? Also, excuse me, but Mrs. Norris is "one of those well-meaning people" only in the way that, say, Hitler was damn well meaning to invade Poland and pity anyone who got in his way.

Such is Sir Thomas's authority, however, that when he follows the delivery of the news with an injunction for "the strictest forbearance and silence" towards Fanny, Aunt Norris is compelled to obey.

> *She only looked her increased ill-will. Angry she was, bitterly angry; but she was more angry with Fanny for having received such an offer, than for refusing it. It was an injury and affront to Julia, who ought to have been Mr. Crawford's choice; and, independently of that, she disliked Fanny, because she had neglected her; and she would have grudged such an elevation to one whom she had been always trying to depress.*

I love imagining Aunt Norris as she "only looked her increased ill-will". I picture her face as a virtual Kabuki mask of rage, contorting in quiet fury as she concentrates on stopping Fanny's heart from beating through sheer force of malevolent will, like a homicidal Uri Geller.

Lady Bertram's reaction is entirely opposite—and apposite.

> *She had been a beauty, and a prosperous beauty, all her life; and beauty and wealth were all that excited her respect. To know Fanny to be sought in marriage by a man of fortune, raised her, therefore, very much in her opinion. By convincing her that Fanny was very pretty, which she had been doubting about before...it made her feel a sort of credit in calling her niece.*

And of course, she herself takes a large part of the credit for drawing Mr. Crawford's attentions to Fanny because—possibly you haven't heard—on the night of the ball? She sent Chapman to dress her. Never mind if you missed it, she mentions it twice more here...which effectively clinches it as the novel's newest catch-phrase. So you can retire your I HAVE TWO-AND-FORTY SPEECHES t-shirt, and replace it with one saying I SENT CHAPMAN TO DRESS HER.

I wear a Medium, if anyone's feeling generous.

CHAPTERS 34-36

As I write this, Hurricane Irene is hammering the east coast, providing the obvious (if rather prosaic) analogy for the state in which we find Fanny Price: deluged on all sides by encouragement, expectations, and exhortations that she marry Henry Crawford, who has, in a fit of romantic fervor bordering on (if not edging into) flat-out insanity, pledged her his troth. The newest battering ram to attempt to breach Fanny's Citadel Of No is Edmund, who has returned to Mansfield belatedly—"His absence had been extended beyond a fortnight purposely to avoid Miss Crawford"—only to find, to his surprise, that Miss Crawford is still hanging around. Which is just fine, because the closer he drew to Mansfield, the more he repented of deliberately missing her. And when he arrives and finds her not only still there but once more the flirtatious little minx she used to be—and when he learns that the *reason* she's still there and suddenly so coquettish, is her brother's pursuit of Fanny's chilly hand—well, you better *believe* he gets on the Henry-Fanny bandwagon.

But after his first dinner at home, Sir Thomas takes him aside and gives him the whole sorry story of how the Henry-Fanny bandwagon has gotten mired in some serious mud flats. Fanny, who sees the two men go off together, deduces instantly that she's to be their object of discussion, and as usual she dies about a million deaths at the idea of being noticed by anyone, anytime, anywhere, ever.

When Edmund returns from the interview, he sits beside her and takes her hand in his and presses it kindly; and Fanny takes this as a sign that he understands her, he supports her, he's her champion, her stalwart, her BMOC.

Except...um, not so much.

> *He was not intending...by such action, to be conveying to her that unqualified approbation and encouragement which her hopes drew from it...He was, in fact, entirely on his father's side of the question...Sir Thomas could not regard the connection as more desirable than he did. It had every recommendation to him, and while honouring her for what she had done under the influence of her present indifference...he was most earnest in hoping, and sanguine in believing, that it would be a match at last...*

Up to now Edmund has been Fanny's lodestar, whose supreme authority has directed her every move; so we can imagine his confusion when now, seemingly out of nowhere, she's suddenly all you-are-not-the-boss-of-me. And yet give him credit: while he doesn't understand it, he at least knows Fanny well enough to hit on the exact right course of action. He "saw enough of [her] embarrassment to make him scrupulously guard against exciting it a second time, by any word, or look, or movement." This is also excellent advice for training skittish animals, with the difference that skittish animals are usually worth the trouble.

Fanny, of course, is only resisting his blandishments because she's secretly in love with him; unbeknownst to him, the only thing he can't command her to do, is take another man in his place.

And yet...let me just bring this to the table. Jane Austen is no stranger to romantic and even erotic tension. We actively feel Colonel Brandon's stabbing pangs every time Marianne Dashwood enters a room. We could cut with a butter knife the thick haze of longing, duty and grief that fills any given space between Elinor Dashwood and Edward Ferrars. And even with their claws out (maybe *especially* with their claws out), we can feel the entire universe around Lizzy Bennet and Fitzwilliam Darcy, contracting into a small, cozy cocoon of inevitability.

And yet I don't for a moment feel anything between Fanny and Edmund. Between Edmund and Mary Crawford, oh *hell* yes...and between Henry and Fanny—well, on Henry's part, at least, it's strong enough to lift me momentarily out of my seat, like when your car sails over a speed bump. But Fanny's professed feelings for Edmund?... Austen tells me they're there, and I'm forced to believe her for the sake of the narrative, but it's a purely intellectual exercise. It doesn't register in my chest or twinge in my thighs, or set my toes a-thrumming the way her other matches do. Fanny has always seemed, and continues to seem, like an emotional nihilist, her displays of feeling no more than involuntary muscle spasms.

To be fair, possibly the same might be said of Henry, because when he now returns to Mansfield Park to continue wooing Fanny, Edmund has his first chance to observe him in the act, and to see how Fanny rewards him...which as we all know is with the sort of enthusiasm most of us exhibit for imminent periodontal surgery.

> *[Edmund] was almost ready to wonder at his friend's perseverance.—Fanny was worth it all; he held to her to be worth every effort of patience, every exertion of mind—but he did not think he could have gone on himself with any woman breathing, without something more to warm his courage than his eyes could discern in hers.*

So we have to wonder whether Henry is in fact genuine in his feelings; possibly he's got one eye in a mirror, and is enjoying his performance as the ardent lover, more than he's actually feeling ardent love. I'm not saying this to disrespect him; all romantic love begins somewhere—in lust, or in laughter, or in a particularly intense shared experience—and it's only time and familiarity that galvanize it into genuine, lasting affection. Henry Crawford is absolutely capable of becoming, from these beginnings, the kind of man Fanny Price deserves. (Quite a bit better than she deserves, I'd say.) But he can't do it alone; and without Fanny's help and direction, he's bound sooner or later to come to wreck on the shoals.

Her refusal to acknowledge any good in him at all is made even more maddening by an episode immediately following, in which he and Edmund come across Fanny and Lady Bertram seated together quietly. Lady Bertram informs them that Fanny has just been reading to her from a volume of Shakespeare ("she was in the middle of a very fine speech of that man's—What's his name, Fanny?—when we heard your footsteps"), but had hastily put the book down. Because, see, if they caught her reading, they would look at her, and listen to her, and just generally be aware of her presence on planet Earth. Can't have *that.*

Henry, being a bit of a grandstander (in the nicest possible way—and I mean, seriously, if any novel ever *needed* a grandstander, it's this one), plucks up the book and asks if anyone would mind him continuing where Fanny left off. Lady Bertram wouldn't mind at all, and as for Fanny, she doesn't even reply; she's facing the opposite direction, apparently using her telescopic vision to minutely observe the travails of a community of rice harvesters in Japan. (The girl is by far the rudest of all Austen's heroines. Possibly all Austen's villainesses, too.)

So Henry plunges in. The very fine speech, we learn, is one of Cardinal Wolsey's from *Henry VIII,* and when it concludes Henry just keeps on going with the rest of the play. And though Fanny does her best to pretend not to listen, burrowing her head down into her needlework so closely that she's in danger of sewing a button on her nostril, she can't help herself.

> *She could not abstract her mind five minutes; she was forced to listen; his reading was capital, and her pleasure in good reading extreme. To good reading, however, she had been long used; her uncle read well—her cousins all—Edmund very well; but in Mr. Crawford's reading there was a variety of excellence beyond what she had ever met with. The King, the Queen, Buckingham, Wolsey, Cromwell, all were given in turn; for with the happiest knack, the happiest power of jumping and guessing, he could always light, at will, on the best scene, or the best speeches of each; and whether it were dignity or pride, or tenderness or remorse, or whatever were to be expressed, he could do it with equal beauty.—It was truly dramatic.*

Edmund watches Fanny with interest, seeing how "she gradually slackened in her needle-work...and at last, how the eyes which had appeared so studiously to avoid him throughout the day, were turned and fixed on Crawford." Unfortunately, *Henry VIII* eventually comes to an end, and since neither Shakespeare nor the Tudor dynasty was sufficiently thoughtful to provide us with a *Henry IX*, Crawford is forced to close the book, and just like that the spell is broken. Fanny becomes self-aware again, and curls up into a ball like a chinoiserie possum.

Edmund hurriedly tries to keep Fanny's admiration from flagging by prompting it with his own. "That play must be a favorite with you," he tells Henry; "You read as if you knew it well."

> *"It will be a favourite I believe from this hour," replied Crawford; "—but I do not think I have had a volume of Shakespeare in my hand before, since I was fifteen—I once saw Henry the 8th acted.—Or I have heard of it from somebody who did—I am not certain which."*

To hell with Fanny Price...*I'll* marry this guy.

There follows a page of two of praise for Shakespeare, interlaced with praise for Henry Crawford, and if you're not paying close attention you might lose track of which is being praised when. Lady Bertram, roused to dizzying heights of admiration, is moved to declare, "You have a great turn for acting, I am sure, Mr. Crawford...and I will tell you what, I think you will have a theatre, some time or other, at your house in Norfolk. I mean when you are settled there. I do, indeed. I think you will fit up a theatre at your house in Norfolk." And Henry says in response:

> *"No, no, that will never be. Your Ladyship is quite mistaken. No theatre at Everingham! Oh! no."—And he looked at Fanny with an expressive smile, which evidently meant, "that lady will never allow a theatre at Everingham."*

Now, if he pulled that on Elinor Dashwood, she'd give him a glare that would sink him right through the floorboards. Marianne would snark on him so hard, he'd topple over in his chair. And Lizzy Bennet would say something so artfully devastating that it wouldn't be till later, when he tried to get up, that he'd see she's sheared his legs clean off. But Fanny? Fanny just...withdraws. I heard nothing, he said nothing, I'm not listening, I'm not here.

Edmund goes on to lament the dearth of good reading in his own profession, which amazingly excites some interest from Henry (possibly he's faking it for effect; but come on, isn't that the basis of all good manners?). He peppers Edmund with questions about his ordination and his hopes of success...questions asked "with the vivacity of friendly interest and quick taste—without any touch of that spirit of banter and levity which Edmund knew to be most offensive to Fanny..."

> *...and when Crawford proceeded to ask his opinion and give his own as to the properest manner in which particular passages in the service should be delivered, shewing it to be a subject on which he had thought before, and thought with judgment, Edmund was still more and more pleased. This would be the way to Fanny's heart.*

Fanny's heart. Send out a search party.

At one point Henry pauses in the midst of a mildly self-effacing spiel and, sensing a reaction from Fanny, turns to her and says, "Did you speak?" and when she insists she didn't, he won't let go: "Are you sure you did not speak? I saw your lips move. I fancied you might be going to tell me I *ought* to be more attentive, and not *allow* my thoughts to wander. Are you not going to tell me so?" Fanny makes the mistake of beginning a reply to the contrary—something beyond her usual monosyllabic bleat—and then she realizes, uh-oh, she's walked into his trap. She has allowed herself to *engage the enemy.* "She stopped, felt herself getting into a puzzle, and could not be prevailed on to add another word, not by dint of several minutes of supplication and waiting. He then returned to his former station, and went on as if there had been no such tender interruption."

So we've reached the point at which our nominal heroine is interrupting the flow of the narrative, *in her own novel.* And she does it again a page later, shaking her head in disapproval at something Henry says, so that he's immediately by her side asking What, what, tell me what I said to displease you, and she does everything but take up her needle and stitch her mouth shut. But eventually Henry wears down her resistance —yes, he really *does* it; it's a superhuman effort and anyone who's made it this far is going to need a nap afterwards, possibly preceded by a good stiff drink—but he actually pokes and prods and pesters Fanny to the point that she's provoked into honestly saying something...into admitting that yeah, it's nice Henry's such a stand-up guy now, what a shame he wasn't *always* that way.

Henry is delighted at having got Fanny to reveal the root of her problem with him: she still holds it very much against him that he stirred up such a sexual hornet's nest on his first arrival in Mansfield.

And he attacks this perception with all the rhetorical ability at his command, which is, let me tell you, *a lot* of rhetorical ability. What it boils down to is, I've changed, and you *will* see that I've changed, and you *will* see that I am worthy of you. He's so confident, you expect him to slap a ten-pound note on the table and make it an outright wager.

Fanny has nothing left in her arsenal of denial except the weapon of last resort: flight. And she's actually considering it—she's on the point of hiking her skirt above her ankles and making a runner for the door —when Baddeley, clearly not content with his supporting role in the last chapter, comes barging in with the tea things. The spotlight immediately shifts to him (he may well seize the opportunity to execute a few soft-shoe moves and crack a joke). Fanny is saved...but even so is left gasping for air. She's in trouble, and she knows it.

And in fact, the next assault on her defenses is soon under way. The day for the Crawfords' departure from Mansfield is fixed, and as it draws nearer, Sir Thomas decides he can't let that dreamy Henry get away without at least one more encounter with Fanny, "that all his professions and vows of unshaken attachment might have as much hope to sustain them as possible." Clearly Sir Thomas hasn't been watching Fanny too carefully, or he'd have noticed that the mere mention of Henry's name is enough for her to make like that cartoon character who hides by jumping into a hole and pulling the hole in after him. But in another respect, he's pretty canny: "Sir Thomas was most cordially anxious for the perfection of Mr. Crawford's character in that point. He wished him to be a model of constancy; and fancied the best means of effecting it would be by not trying him too long."

This is the first laugh we've had in God knows how many pages. It reminds us of what we read Austen for in the first place, and we wonder if maybe, God willing, she's finally getting back to it.

But first we have another excruciating scene between Edmund and Fanny. The former is enlisted by his father to massage Fanny's rigor-mortis grip on the word "no" sufficiently to allow for one last meeting with Henry. Edmund agrees, but being a noble sort, he undertakes it more for Fanny's sake than anyone else's, for "he must be of service to her, whom else had she to open her heart to? If she did not need counsel, she must need the comfort of communication." All right, I admit it, I do like Edmund; he'll never top my list of longed-for dinner guests, but he'd be just the guy to have beside you in a pinch.

Fanny's spirits are so woefully depleted that she's skittish of Edmund when he comes upon her in the garden; he essentially has to coax her out of her wariness, like she's an untrusting dog who won't come out from under the bed. But Edmund, alas, has only words to work with, Kibble not yet having been invented.

He does the best he can, by first telling her, "[Y]ou have done exactly as you ought in refusing [Mr. Crawford]. Can there be any disagreement between us here?" Fanny, emerging tentatively from her thicket of thorns, admits there isn't. Edmund, sensing the road to success, piles it on, adding, "How could you imagine me an advocate for marriage without love?" and "You did not love him—nothing could have justified your accepting him."

Fanny, we're told, "had not felt so comfortable for days and days." Edmund's got her on her back, wiggling to have her tummy scratched. And that's when he lowers the boom.

> *"Crawford's is no common attachment; he perseveres, with the hope of creating that regard which had not been created before. This, we know, must be a work of time. But (with an affectionate smile), let him succeed at last, Fanny, let him succeed at last. You have proved yourself upright and disinterested, prove yourself grateful and tender-hearted; and then you will be the perfect model of a woman, which I have always believed you born for."*

And Fanny's back up on her feet, hackles raised and snarling. "Oh! never, never, never; he will never succeed with me."

Right, I get it; she loves Edmund...so it's repugnant to have Edmund himself urge her on another man she can't (ahem, *won't*) esteem. But I'm reminded again of Elinor Dashwood, who stood stoically aside rather than tempt the man *she* loved away from honoring his youthful commitment to a woman more reptile than human. The circumstances aren't analogous except in the sense that Elinor held herself to a higher standard; to an ideal. Fanny refuses to do the same. She recognizes the claims of authority, gratitude, and obedience that the Bertram family have on her; she just refuses to honor them.

Even worse, she still insists on hiding her real reason for refusing Henry: that he isn't Edmund. Fine, maybe she can't openly admit this, but there's something cringeworthy about the way she *actively* tries to hide it, claiming the reason she can't love Henry is that "we are so very, very different in all our inclinations...We have not one taste in common." Which Edmund immediately calls out as bullshit—citing Shakespeare right off the top of his head.

Edmund does admit that their temperaments are different, but this, he says, is an advantage rather than the opposite. "It is your disposition to be easily dejected, and to fancy difficulties greater than they are. His cheerfulness will counteract this. He sees difficulties no where; and his pleasantness and gaiety will be a constant support to you." He goes on a bit too long in this vein, however, and Fanny soon twigs that he's speaking less of her and Henry, than of himself and Mary. So, nnnnot exactly helpful.

Fanny has only one card left to play: the one she's so nobly held to her breast till now. But she's cornered, dammit, so to hell with morality ...and thus she finally throws her cousins under the bus, telling Edmund that she can never think well of Henry because of the way he willfully, improperly, and gleefully incited Maria and Julia into acting like contestants on *Flavor of Love.* But alas, she's waited too long, and the trump card no longer trumps. As far as Edmund is concerned, the statute of limitations has long since kicked in for *that* particular misadventure.

> *"My dear Fanny," replied Edmund, scarcely hearing her to the end, "let us not, any of us, be judged by what we appeared at that period of general folly. The time of the play is a time which I hate to recollect. Maria was wrong, Crawford was wrong, we were all wrong together; but none so wrong as myself. Compared with me, all the rest were blameless. I was playing the fool with my eyes open."*

Is there anything so satisfying as having a tattletale put in her place...? Edmund then follows through with the logic most of us have already landed on sixty-whatever pages earlier, which is that Henry's former bad behavior is put in the shade by his subsequent reformation and by his ability not only to recognize but to love Fanny's finer qualities: "It does him the highest honour; it shews his proper estimation of the blessing of domestic happiness, and pure attachment. It proves him unspoilt by his uncle. It proves him, in short, everything I had been used to wish to believe him, and feared he was not."

Fanny testily counters, "I am persuaded that he does not think as he ought, on serious subjects." Which Edmund again excuses, because, hello, given the virtual brothel he grew up in, how can he be expected to have thought on serious subjects *at all?* But his heart's in the right place, and Fanny can help guide him to a more substantial manhood. "He will make you happy, Fanny, I know he will make you happy; but you will make him every thing."

This is a distinctly Christian appeal; but Fanny's Christianity is of the moralizing, judgmental variety, not the self-sacrificing, soul-saving kind. She begs off rescuing Henry Crawford because it is "such an office of high responsibility"—but Edmund shoots that down too. He isn't just generally interested in Henry's happiness; he has a *very specific* investment in the Crawford family's felicity. You do *know* that, right, Fanny?...I mean, come *on.*

And just like that he's off on another recitation of the many, many things that make Mary Crawford just oh so superfine. And shame on Fanny for having shunted her aside, at this moment when she's just bursting with sisterly love for both Henry *and* Fanny. "She is hurt, as you be would be for William; but she loves and esteems you with all her heart."

And so it goes, for many pages more, with Edmund hitting Fanny with wave after wave of reason, duty, filial entreaties, and borderline exasperation, and Fanny emerging after each dousing, coughing and spitting and still saying no, no, no, no, no. Finally Edmund mortifies her by revealing that her unflinching reticence has become a kind of joke, even among the Crawfords themselves: "Miss Crawford made us laugh by her plans of encouragement for her brother. She meant to urge him to persevere in the hope of being loved in time, and of having his addresses most kindly received at the end of about ten years' happy marriage!"

We laugh at this. (And we love Mary all the more for it, too. Girl's a Hanoverian Dorothy Parker.) But you can imagine Fanny's reaction. For someone with a morbid, almost pathological loathing of being noticed, how much worse to know she's not just being talked about behind her back, but *laughed at?* "[T]o have Miss Crawford's liveliness repeated to her at such a moment, and on such a subject, was a bitter aggravation."

Seeing the look of Saharan desolation that now dims Fanny's eyes, Edmund realizes he's gone far enough: he'd better lay off before he drives her right out of *Mansfield Park* and into *Tess of the d'Urbervilles* or something. But he does confirm that the Crawfords are leaving after the weekend, so both he and Fanny will be sure to see them for a final goodbye on Sunday. "They really go on Monday!" he sighs. "[A]nd I was within a trifle of being persuaded to stay at Lessingby till that very day! I had almost promised it. What a difference it might have made. Those five or six days more at Lessingby might have been felt all my life." Yes, Edmund is once again crushing hard on Mary Crawford. Hey, I get it; my only criticism is that he ever stopped.

When Sunday arrives, Fanny predictably faces it with all the upright moral courage of a small scavenging rodent. "The promised visit from her 'friend,' as Edmund called Miss Crawford"—ahem, may I just pause here to object to those snarky quotation marks? If Mary isn't Fanny's friend, then Fanny doesn't have one—"was a formidable threat to Fanny, and she lived in continual terror of it," and sure enough we see her clinging like a barnacle to Lady Bertram lest Mary arrive and catch her alone; she all but hides herself under Lady B's voluminous petticoat.

When Mary arrives, however, she's undaunted by Lady Bertram's presence (which even on its best days is hard to distinguish from an absence), and after a few minutes of paying her respects she just comes right out and insists on seeing Fanny alone. "Denial was impossible," we're told, though I don't see why, Fanny has spent the entire novel denying far more to far greater numbers. Fanny trudges on up to the East Room—no condemned wife of Henry VIII ever went to the block dragging her heels more desolately—while behind her Mary says, "Sad, sad girl! I do not know when I shall have done scolding you."

But as soon as Mary is once again admitted to Fanny's little bolt-hole, she's taken aback by an unexpected bout of nostalgia; she hasn't been here since that day during the *Lovers' Vows* rehearsal when she and Edmund both showed up separately and ended up seated in this very spot, trading suggestive lines with each other while Fanny looked on, trying to make Mary's chair collapse through telekinesis. All the anger floods out of Mary, as she luxuriates in the renewed sensations of that afternoon, and of all the days that preceded it.

> *"If I had the power of recalling any one week of my existence, it should that week, that acting week. Say what you would, Fanny, it should be* that*; for I never knew such exquisite happiness in any other. His sturdy spirit to bend as it did! Oh! it was sweet beyond expression. But alas! that very evening destroyed it all...Yet, Fanny, do not imagine I would speak disrespectfully of Sir Thomas, though I certainly did hate him for many a week. No, I do him justice now. He is just what the head of such a family should be. Nay, in sober sadness, I believe I now love you all."*

So says Fanny's "friend."

To be fair, Fanny is affected by this speech, and by those that follow, in which Mary elaborates on her unconcealed fondness for her and her regret at leaving her. But Fanny is unable to respond in kind. She merely listens, her withered, stunted, crabbed little spirit jerking spasmodically at the pricks and prods Mary's lightning storm of emotion delivers it, without being inspired to anything equally grand or forgiving; as ever, Fanny remains utterly immune to transcendence.

With her "little fit", as she merrily calls it, now concluded, Mary eases back into the kind of breezy, cheeky, sophisticated prattle we originally loved her for, and which reminds us—and by this time, sweet creeping Jesus, we need reminding—that we're reading a Jane Austen novel. Unfortunately, one of the gossipy stories she tells—about a friend of hers, a certain Janet Fraser who married a rich man and has been regretting it ever since—doesn't do her any favors in her current company:

> *"Poor Janet has been sadly taken in; and yet there was nothing improper on her side; she did not run into the match inconsiderately, there was no want of foresight. She took three days to consider of his proposals; and during those three days asked the advice of every body connected with her, whose opinion was worth having...This seems as if nothing were a security for matrimonial comfort!"*

You can almost feel the grim satisfaction Fanny takes from this story, and the strength it gives her to hold out against the entire god-damn world, if necessary. She won't make the same mistake as Janet Fraser. The Risen Christ could come forth and command her to marry Henry, and she'd shoot him down like a game hen.

Mary commits another tactical error by revealing that the necklace she had given Fanny for William's pendant—a necklace Fanny was later horrified to learn had been a gift from Henry himself—was actually intended for Fanny by both sister *and* brother. They'd conspired to get it around her neck. And so it ends up being Fanny who scolds Mary, rather than the reverse:

> *"I will not say...that I was not half afraid at the time, of its being so; for there was something in your look that frightened me—but not at first—I was as unsuspicious of it at first!—indeed, indeed I was. It is as true as that I sit here. And had I had an idea of it, nothing would have induced me to accept the necklace."*

That "frightening" look in Mary's eye...possibly it was the sparkle of her earnest desire to give joy and happiness to her friend. Excuse me, "friend." If this is really Austen's gambit to build a case against Mary before the final shoe drops, she's just not convincing me. She's an ambitious writer, we know this, we've seen her astonishing development over a mere three novels—I can well believe she's trying to challenge herself, to make Mary vastly more complex a rival than her usual shrill harridan—but there's a whiplash feeling to the whole endeavor, as when Mary suddenly admits that Fanny's right, Henry was out of line in the way he carried on with Maria.

> *"I do not defend him. I leave him entirely to your mercy; and when he has got you at Everingham, I do not care how much you lecture him. But this I will say, this his fault, the liking to make girls a little in love with him, is not half so dangerous to a wife's happiness, as a tendency to fall in love himself, which he has never been addicted to. And I do seriously and truly believe that he is attached to you in a way he never was to any woman before...If any man ever loved a woman for ever, I think Henry will do as much for you."*

Fanny, of course, has only heard the first part of this speech; the rest is just waa waa waaah. Her moment of being affected by Mary's honest love for her and her family, is gone; she's back to being her coal-hearted self, a vengeful vessel for Old Testament intransigence.

Mary takes her leave of Fanny with more warm expressions of affection and enduring friendship, and asks only two favors of her: first that she write to her, and second that she "often call on Mrs. Grant and make her amends for my being gone."

> *The first, at least, of these favours Fanny would rather not have been asked; but it was impossible for her to refuse the correspondence: it was impossible for her even not to accede to it more readily than her own judgment authorized. There was no resisting so much apparent affection.*

"Apparent" affection. Fanny just will not give Mary a break here—but when does she ever give anyone a break? When Henry comes to sit with her before he too departs (that's what we're told—he "came and sat"—so I'm guessing he's already given up trying to lure her into a conversation), Fanny's heart is sufficiently softened "because he really seemed to feel...He was evidently oppressed, and Fanny must grieve for him, though hoping she might never see him again till he were the husband of some other woman." Hey, I'm with her on that one. Though for his sake, not hers.

And so the Crawfords—twin whirlwinds of laughter and chatter and joy and cheerfulness and mischief and incaution and, well, *life*—are swept out of the narrative, leaving Fanny Price at long last free to... what, exactly? The heroine of *Mansfield Park,* the central figure of this story and the supposed repository of all our hopes and fantasies...she's now free to do—exactly *what?*

CHAPTERS 37-39

With the removal of the Crawfords, Austen has cleared her stage of virtually all its vital, percolating characters, leaving only the tepid quartet of Fanny, Edmund, Sir Thomas, and Lady Bertram. Aunt Norris is still lurking on the perimeter but only occasionally intrudes on the narrative, like a sudden but temporary rash; and the Grants are technically still in residence at the parsonage, but Austen seems to have utterly forgotten them. They might as well have fallen down a well, or been eaten by wolverines.

In other words, the novel desperately needs an injection of comic energy. And wouldn't you know it, Austen is about to mainline some high-grade mama smack.

But first we've got to get through some introspective dithering among our somnambulant foursome. This involves Sir Thomas watching Fanny in the days following Henry Crawford's departure, looking for signs that she may be missing him. Mm-hmm. Luck with that.

> *He watched her with this idea—but he could hardly tell with what success. He hardly knew whether there were any difference in her spirits or not. She was always so gentle and retiring, that her emotions were beyond his discrimination.*

I like to picture Sir Thomas surreptitiously slipping a mirror under her nose to confirm that she has not, in fact, actually expired.

Sir Thomas asks Edmund what he thinks on the matter, given his better knowledge of Fanny's mysterious ways, but Edmund "did not discern any symptoms of regret, and thought his father a little unreasonable in supposing the first three or four days could produce any." Three or four decades, maybe. Or three or four geologic ages, if you want to be absolutely safe. But what *does* strike Edmund is that Fanny shows no sign of missing Mary Crawford either, which is inconceivable to him, now that he's back on his Mary Rules 4 Evah kick.

Fanny of course is only too aware of the rekindled urge to merge between Edmund and Mary. "On his side, the inclination was stronger, on hers less equivocal. His objections, the scruples of his integrity, seemed all done away—nobody could tell how; and the doubts and hesitations of her ambition were equally got over—and equally without apparent reason." Austen may have been a provincial spinster, but she understood that powerful attraction often—always?—trumps common sense. It's just that in this novel, she'll ultimately try to fix that—implement a course correction, and steer Like towards Like, shunting Unlike aside. She's laying the groundwork even now, as witness Fanny reflecting on Mary's essential unworthiness:

> *In their very last conversation, Miss Crawford, in spite of some amiable sensations, and much personal kindness, had still been Miss Crawford, still shewn a mind led astray and bewildered, and without any suspicion of being so; darkened, yet fancying itself light. She might love, but she did not deserve Edmund by any other sentiment.*

I might rewrite that to read, "In their last conversation, Miss Price, in spite of some tender sensations, and much personal forbearance, had still been Miss Price, still shewn a mind unyielding and judgmental, and without any suspicion of being so; cold, yet fancying itself warmth. She might love, but she did not deserve Edmund by any other sentiment."

Anyway, that's where we stand at Mansfield—checkmate all around —when Austen decides to mix things up a bit by bringing William Price back into the picture. William still strikes me as more a plot device than an actual character...we never really feel we know him very well; he's a standup guy, sure, but never anything *more* than a standup guy. In any case, he's got ten days' leave of absence and has come to spend them with his sister, his only regret being that he can't show off his naval uniform to her, as "cruel custom prohibited its appearance except on duty."

This prompts a minor brainstorm on Sir Thomas's part. "This scheme was that [Fanny] should accompany her brother back to Portsmouth, and spend a little time with her own family"—which would not only allow her to see William all pimped out in his lieutenant's duds, but reconnect her with the parents and siblings from whom she's been so long removed. Though the impulse for the plan, we soon learn, isn't quite so nakedly charitable.

> *[Sir Thomas's] prime motive in sending her away, had very little to do with the propriety of seeing her parents again, and nothing at all with any idea of making her happy. He certainly wished her to go willingly, but he as certainly wished her to be heartily sick of home before her visit ended; and that a little abstinence from the elegancies and luxuries of Mansfield Park, would bring her mind into a sober state, and incline her to a juster estimate of the value of that home of greater permanence, and equal comfort, of which she had the offer.*

In other words, give her a few weeks in Portsmouth, and she'll crawl back on all fours begging to be Mrs. Henry Crawford.

The subject of this experiment, unaware of how she's being manipulated, approves the idea. In fact, "Had Fanny been at all addicted to raptures, she must have had a strong attack of them, when she first understood what was intended"—though if Fanny were at all addicted to raptures, this novel would have taken an entirely different course starting at about page 40.

She's eager to see her family again and wallows a bit in uncharacteristic nostalgia; but just a bit. She also appreciates that two months away from Edmund "(and perhaps she might be allowed to make her absence three)" will help her get over her moony-eyed crush on him, and face up to his imminent engagement to Mary. "What might have been hard to bear at Mansfield, was to become a slight evil at Portsmouth."

The only impediment to the plan is that Fanny's absence will leave no one to sit with Lady Bertram and watch her nod off every four-and-a-half minutes, a service her ladyship simply cannot do without. Enter Aunt Norris, eager as ever to be of service—and equally eager to prove that nobody really needs Fanny anyway. She almost vaults onto the scene, waving her arms and crying, *I can do it! I can do it! Me! Me! Over here!*

That seems settled, then; and Fanny and William begin looking ahead to their big adventure. But then Mrs. Norris changes her mind, after realizing that all her arguments for economy to the contrary, Sir Thomas means to send his niece and nephew to Porstmouth by post.

> *[W]hen she saw Sir Thomas actually give William notes for the purpose, she was struck with the idea of there being room for a third in the carriage, and suddenly seized with a strong inclination to go with them...it would be such an indulgence to her; she had not seen her poor dear sister Price for more than twenty years; and it would be a help to the young people in their journey to have her older head to manage for them; and she could not help thinking her poor dear sister Price would feel it very unkind of her not to come by such an opportunity.*

William and Fanny "were horror-struck at the idea," as can easily be imagined. Stuck in a coach with Mrs. Norris is the kind of punishment Dante might have inflicted on the sixth or seventh circle of Hell, if he weren't such an old softie. But never mind, the youngsters don't have to live long in dread, for it soon occurs to their would-be tormentor that "though taken to Portsmouth for nothing, it would be hardly possible for her to avoid paying her own expenses back again. So, her poor dear sister Price was left to all the disappointment of her missing such an opportunity; and another twenty years' absence, perhaps, begun."

Edmund had intended to go to London at about this time, but has changed his plans so as not to leave his parents completely devoid of younger company; he has "delayed for a week or two longer a journey which he was looking forward to, with the hope of its fixing his happiness for ever." He tells Fanny as much, and she "was the more affected from feeling it to be the last time in which Miss Crawford's name would ever be mentioned between them with any remains of liberty." He promises to write to her when he has (wink, wink) news, and Fanny immediately starts dreading the day she receives that letter, and at this point all the passive emotional undercurrents are starting to make us feel tired and cranky, like we've been sitting in the bath too long and can we just get out now, please.

And then...relief. We find ourselves on the open road with the Price siblings. "Every thing supplied an amusement to the high glee of William's mind, and he was full of frolic and joke, in the intervals of their higher-toned subjects, all of which ended, if they did not begin, in praise of the Thrush," so obviously they weren't all *that* high-toned. We get a small hint of William's capacity for snark when he describes for Fanny "schemes for an action with some superior force...(supposing the first lieutenant out of the way—and William was not very merciful to the first lieutenant)" which is the first time I've actually wanted to hear more of what William had to say.

What they very much do *not* discuss is Henry Crawford. That's a touchy subject, given that William owes basically everything plus change to Henry, while Fanny has treated this paragon like last week's tekka maki. Mary Crawford isn't discussed either, though she's constantly on Fanny's mind. We're told that Fanny has heard "repeatedly" from Mary in the three weeks since her departure from Mansfield. "It was a correspondence which Fanny found quite as unpleasant as she had feared. Miss Crawford's style of writing, lively and affectionate, was itself an evil"; presumably Mary never bothers to wax rhapsodic on the miracle of shrubbery. But even worse, from Fanny's point of view, is the addition of several adoring lines from Henry in each missive...not to mention that Edmund has insisted on having all of Mary's letters read to him, after which Fanny "had to listen to his admiration of her language, and the warmth of her attachments."

In fact, there's so much in the letters that seems designed for Edmund's ears rather than hers, that Fanny begins to suspect she's being used as a kind of epistolary go-between. She takes consolation in thinking that, once she's in Portsmouth and far from Edmund, Mary will have no reason to write to her anymore, and "their correspondence would dwindle into nothing."

But Fanny is forced to abandon her fantasies of a perfect Fanny world in which her only friend never writes to her, because she and William have arrived in Portsmouth and now draw up before the door of a small house on a narrow street, the very abode in which Fanny once lived. "The moment they stopt, a trollopy-looking maidservant, seemingly in wait for them at the door, stept forward, and more intent on telling the news, than giving any help," begins to inform them that the Thrush has gone out of harbor and that William is wanted, before she's shoved aside by a boy who's launched himself out of the house like a sock monkey from a cannon, intent on delivering this vital news himself. Both the trollopy maid and the slingshot boy come as shocks to our system after so many pages of furtive glances, hushed asides, and arched eyebrows. One or the other of these newcomers would have been welcome on his own, but to have them both in one scene, colliding off each other like billiard balls, is Austen's way of telling us the status quo has just gone ass-over-teakettle. We're off-balance, and she means us to stay that way.

Ladies and gentlemen, the Prices are in the building!

William—now agitated by the news of the Thrush's movement—hustles Fanny to the threshold, where she's greeted by her mother and about forty more brothers and sisters, all of whom can barely be bothered to do more than spend a few seconds sizing her up. "She was then taken into a parlour, so small that her first conviction was of its being only a passage-room to something better, and she stood for a moment expecting to be invited on"—and right about here, you have to pause between snorts of laughter to wonder if maybe Sir Thomas hasn't got this thing nailed up tight after all.

And then comes the wonderful moment Fanny's mother opens her mouth. In the space of two pages she manages to fill the narrative with more sheer talk than has taken place at Mansfield in the space of two hundred. On and on she goes, blathering away while the Price children cavort behind her, like a cross between circus acrobats and a demolition crew. Occasionally she turns to fling some watery orders at them, only to have defiance flung back at her—to Fanny's great shock and dismay.

It's true: at long last, Austen has decided to bestow on us one of her epic talkers...my personal favorite in her arsenal of character types. But, wait—wait—can it be? Is Austen rewarding us for having endured the almost Ingmar Bergmanesque astringency of the novel up to now, by heaping upon us more sheer revivifying vulgarity than we can possibly stand?...Because Fanny's father now enters, and—overlooking her the way he'd ignore a stray cat who wandered into the house—begins bawling out a monologue that makes his wife's elaborate bleatings appear as concise as Rousseauvian aphorisms.

> *"But by G—, you lost a fine sight by not being here in the morning to see the Thrush go out of harbour. I would not have been out of the way for a thousand pounds. Old Scholey ran in at breakfast time, to say that she had slipped her moorings and was coming out. I jumped up, and made but two steps to the platform. If ever there was a perfect beauty afloat, she is one; and there she lays at Spithead, and anybody in England would take her for an eight-and-twenty. I was upon the platform two hours this afternoon, looking at her. She lays close to the Endymion, between her and the Cleopatra, just to the eastward of the sheer hulk."*

This salty gush is all addressed to William, who for Mr. Price's purposes is the only person of interest in the room. When he finally runs out of breath, Fanny intrudes on the corner of his eye like a fleck of ash, and he suddenly remembers her; "and, having given her a cordial hug, and observed that she was grown into a woman, and he supposed would be wanting a husband soon, seemed very much inclined to forget her again."

Fanny "shrunk back to her seat, with feelings sadly pained by his language and his smell of spirits"; in all likelihood she then tries to cloak the house with her disapproval until everyone in it is trapped like butterflies beneath a net, after which everything will be nice and still and inert the way Fanny likes it. But she's met her match this time. She may be an abyss, but even an abyss has limits on how much it can swallow, and the Price family produce enough sheer clanging chaos to clog up any void as swiftly as a double cheeseburger in the arteries of a lifelong vegan. Fanny can't even manage to cast her torpid spell over the youngest and most impressionable of the clan.

> *Both [boys] were kissed very tenderly, but Tom she wanted to keep by her, to try to trace the features of the baby she had loved, and talk to him of his infant preference of herself. Tom, however, had no mind for such treatment; he came home, not to stand and be talked to, but to run about and make a noise; and both boys had soon burst away from her, and slammed the parlour door till her temples ached.*

This is followed by more glorious turbulence: accusations, confrontations, rows, more popping in and out of doors than in a game of Whac-a-Mole—and at the center of it all, Mrs. Price, the kind of woman who spends so much time pivoting around in confusion that there's always a loose strand of hair stuck in her mouth. I could happily stay in these Portsmouth chapters forever. Again, I'm left wondering at the way Austen works at cross-purposes to herself in *Mansfield Park*; in her previous novels, she's shown an evident preference for noisy gabblers over taciturn stuffed-shirts, but it's clear we're meant to be appalled by the garrulous Prices, especially in comparison to the starchy Bertrams; but I feel just the opposite. It's like I've just taken a plunge into a cold, clear pool, after having languished too long in an overheated room.

Fanny, thwarted, sits in the parlour now, ignored by the only other person remaining there—her father, who's engrossed in his (borrowed) newspaper and hogging the only available candle—and she succumbs to "bewildered, broken, sorrowful contemplation." But even this is too much emotion for Fanny, whose preferred state of being is arid desolation, so she packs up the sloppy self-pity by deciding she doesn't warrant any special treatment from her kin, anyway. "What right had she to be of importance to her family? She could have none, so long lost sight of!" And yet she still smarts over being so *completely* overlooked. Really, this girl is a prime candidate for an analyst's chair.

It doesn't take too long for her to find a few consolations. Her sister Susan—at fourteen, on the impressionable cusp of womanhood—has "an open, sensible countenance; she was like William—and Fanny hoped to find her like him in disposition and good will towards herself." And speaking of William, he now enters the room (preceded by a tumble of several young Price children, snarling and snapping like dogs).

> *He, complete in his Lieutenant's uniform, looking and moving all the taller, firmer, and more graceful for it, and with the happiest smile over his face, walked up directly to Fanny—who, rising from her seat, looked at him for a moment in speechless admiration, and then threw her arms round his neck to sob out her various emotions of pain and pleasure.*

So much for keeping those sloppy emotions suppressed. Give her enough time in the bosom of her family, and we'll yet see Fanny hurling plates across the room. (I can dream, can't I?)

When William finally departs to be rowed out to the Thrush, something like quiet descends over the house (though it's really just a temporary spell of exhaustion) and Fanny's mother can finally sit and have a chat with her. But she makes only one enquiry about her relations at Mansfield—"How did her sister Bertram manage about her servants?" —before she's off on a rambling monologue about "her own domestic grievances; and the shocking character of all the Portsmouth servants, of whom she believed her own two were the very worst".

You know what I'd like to see?...A one-act play: The three sisters—Lady Bertram, Aunt Norris, Mrs. Price—trapped in an elevator for 40 minutes. It would virtually write itself.

Fanny then takes a longer look at her sister Betsey, who was born after she left Portsmouth for Northamptonshire; she's reminded of another sister, Mary, who was about the same age at that time, and who has since died—the news of which, when it reached Fanny, left her "for a short time...quite afflicted" (one of the few inklings in Austen of the period's high child mortality rate—with that "for a short time" providing evidence of how thick-skinned society had to be about it to survive). Fanny notices that Betsey is "holding out something to catch her eyes, meaning to screen it at the same time from Susan's." Fanny asks to see it; it's revealed as a silver knife.

> *Up jumped Susan, claiming it as her own, and trying to get it away; but the child ran to her mother's protection, and Susan could only reproach, which she did very warmly, and evidently hoping to interest Fanny on her side... "It was very hard that she was not to have her own knife; it was her own knife; little sister Mary had left it to her on her death-bed, and she ought to have had it to keep herself long ago. But mamma kept it from her, and was always letting Betsey get hold of it..."*

I'm sure this is all meant to impress us with the lack of discipline and authority in the Price house, but it just makes me wonder what in God's name a bunch of little girls are doing tussling over a knife in the first place. Let's give Austen the benefit of the doubt and assume it's a butter knife or something, and not the Regency equivalent to a switchblade. Though this is Portsmouth, so who can say.

The effect of all this on Fanny is predictable. She's "quite shocked. Every feeling of duty, honour, and tenderness was wounded by her sister's speech and her mother's reply"—which is to defend Betsey against the attack, and justify it on the basis that the knife was the gift of Mary's godmother, a certain Mrs. Admiral Maxwell, just a few weeks before her death. "My own Betsey, (fondling her), *you* have not the luck of such a good godmother. Aunt Norris lives too far off, to think of such little people as you." This segues into a pleasant surprise: Mrs. Norris may be left behind in Mansfield, but she can still make hilarious incursions into the narrative. To wit:

> *Fanny had indeed nothing to convey from aunt Norris...There had been at one moment a slight murmur in the drawing-room at Mansfield Park, about sending [Betsey] a Prayer-book; but no second sound had been heard of such a purpose. Mrs. Norris, however, had gone home and taken down two old Prayer-books of her husband, with that idea, but upon examination, the ardour of generosity went off. One was found to have too small a print for a child's eyes, and the other to be too cumbersome for her to carry about.*

Fanny is installed in a room she'll share with Susan, which is apparently not quite half the size "of her own little attic at Mansfield Park, in that house reckoned too small for anyone's comfort." All this constriction, chaos, and cacophony take their toll. "Could [Sir Thomas] have seen only half that she felt before the end of a week, he would have thought Mr. Crawford sure of her, and been delighted in his own sagacity." Even William is taken away from her; the Thrush has had its orders and sailed, and William's visits ashore—few and brief as they were—now cease entirely.

And so Fanny is left stranded in a home "the very reverse of what she could have wished. It was the abode of noise, disorder, and impropriety. Nobody was in their right place, nothing was done as it ought to be." She finds her father "dirty and gross...he scarcely ever noticed her, but to make her the object of a coarse joke." (Is it wrong of me that I'd like to hear some of them?)

In spite of this, Fanny's "disappointment in her mother was greater; *there* she had hoped much, and found almost nothing. Every flattering scheme of being of consequence to her soon fell to the ground... [Fanny] never met with greater kindness from her than the first day of her arrival...Her daughters never had been much to her. She was fond of her sons, especially of William, but Betsey was the first of her girls whom she had ever much regarded."

> *Her days were spent in a kind of slow bustle; always busy without getting on, always behindhand and lamenting it, without altering her ways; wishing to be an economist, without contrivance or regularity; dissatisfied with her servants, without skill to make them better, and whether helping, or reprimanding, or indulging them, without any power of engaging their respect.*

Austen's humanity comes through here, damning Mrs. Price in swift, precise strokes, yet somehow managing to leaven the attack (how does she do it?) with a hint of pity. Then there's this:

> *[Fanny] might scruple to make use of the words, but she must and did feel that her mother was a partial, ill-judging parent, a dawdle, a slattern, who neither taught nor restrained her children, whose house was the scene of mismanagement and discomfort from beginning to end, and who had no talent, no conversation, no affection towards herself; no curiosity to know her better, no desire of her friendship, and no inclination of her company that could lessen her sense of such feelings.*

Notice that when Austen switches to Fanny's point of view, that lingering whiff of sympathy evaporates entirely: only condemnation remains. I'm guessing this is because, whatever else she may be, Mrs. Price is *funny*; and for that reason Austen can't bring herself to vilify her entirely. Her heroine, however, has no use for humor of any kind, in any form. We never see Fanny laugh; we barely ever see her smile. And I'm betting that smile could crack a slab of concrete in two.

There's more opprobrium to be heaped: on Betsey ("a spoilt child, trained up to think the alphabet her greatest enemy, left to be with the servants at her pleasure, and then encouraged to report any evil of them"), and of Susan ("her continual disagreements with her mother, her rash squabbles with Tom and Charles, and petulance with Betsey, were at least so distressing to Fanny...she feared the disposition that could push them to such length must be far from amiable"), so that Fanny, far from putting Mansfield from her mind, now can't help thinking dreamily back on the place, with its "elegance, propriety, regularity, harmony—and most of all, the peace and tranquillity" of the house and its environs.

> *At Mansfield, no sounds of contention, no raised voice, no abrupt bursts, no tread of violence was ever heard; all proceeded in a regular course of cheerful orderliness...and as to the little irritations, sometimes introduced by aunt Norris, they were short, they were trifling, they were as a drop of water to the ocean, compared to the ceaseless tumult of her present abode.*

Alas for Fanny, ceaseless tumult makes for better comedy than cheerful orderliness, and I can't imagine any reader being eager to see her escape the snapping jaws of Portsmouth for the blissful shades of Mansfield, where the most stirring event of any given day is when Lady Bertram rises from her chaise longue and makes glacially for the settee. We'd much rather the rest of the cast came down and joined Fanny here.

And as a matter of fact, we'll get a bit of that next time. I won't spoil it by telling you *which* member of the cast; but here's a big hint: from Fanny's point of view? *Worst. Choice. Possible.*

CHAPTERS 40-42

In each of her first three novels, Austen shakes up the status quo by implementing major shifts in locale. In *Sense and Sensibility*, it was from Devonshire to London; in *Pride and Prejudice,* from Hertfordshire to Derbyshire. She's recently moved *Mansfield Park* from bucolic Northamptonshire to the noisy, bustling, seemingly anarchic city of Portsmouth, which is exactly the kind of blast furnace of humanity in which a delicate flower like Fanny Price can't long survive. And in fact we now witness Fanny's systematic humbling. It does seem odd, even to me, to speak of "humbling" Fanny, since she's very pointedly worn a cloak of humility throughout the entirety of the novel; but by this time we've more than twigged to the steely, iron-willed pride that cloak conceals.

Now, however, the cloak has unraveled and spooled uselessly about her feet. She's so exposed, so powerless, so *reduced* from her former state of inflexible disapprobation, that she actually regrets being right about Mary Crawford's correspondence tapering off once she's no longer at Mansfield. In fact, when a letter from Mary *does* arrive from London, Fanny pounces on it like some ravenous alley cat. "In her present exile from good society, and distance from every thing that had been wont to interest her, a letter from one belonging to the set where her heart lived, written with affection, and some degree of elegance, was thoroughly acceptable." You read that right, she's grooving on Mary's *affection* now, after having so often sneered at her easy familiarity.

But even with this "strange revolution of mind," Fanny still can't be half as happy to hear from Mary as we are. And Mary doesn't disappoint; her letter sparkles with wit and energy. Take this passage, about her first encounter with the Bertram sisters after the news of Fanny's offer from their favorite boy-toy, Henry, has become public:

> *"I have seen your cousins, 'dear Julia and dearest Mrs. Rushworth'; they found me at home yesterday, and we were glad to see each other again. We* seemed very *glad to see each other, and I do really think we were a little.—We had a vast deal to say.—Shall I tell you how Mrs. Rushworth looked when your name was mentioned? I did not use to think her wanting in self possession, but she had not quite enough for the demands of yesterday."*

As for the other Bertram sister, it seems she has an extra cushion of distraction against such high emotion:

> *"From all that I hear and guess, Baron Wildenhaim's attentions to Julia continue, but I do not know that he has any serious encouragement. She ought to do better. A poor honourable is no catch, and I cannot imagine any liking in the case, for take away his rants, and the poor Baron has nothing. What a difference a vowel makes!—if his rents were but equal to his rants!"*

This is almost exactly the tone you find in Austen's own letters. Once again, you can't help wondering what game she thinks she's playing here—setting up her own doppelgänger as the bad girl, and heaping all her praises on a joyless little Pharisee instead.

Mary's letter continues: "Your cousin Edmund moves slowly; detained, perchance, by parish duties. There may be some old woman at Thornton Lacey to be converted. I am unwilling to fancy myself neglected for a *young* one." Fanny, who dreads the inevitable news of Edmund and Mary's engagement, finds both comfort and discomfort in this (though, being Fanny, chiefly the latter). Even so, she "would have been glad to have been sure of such a letter every week"—oh yes, Fanny's *humbled,* all right. The question is...how far?

Not very, as we quickly learn. Her judgments on her new family and their circle are typically harsh—"she saw nobody in whose favour she could wish to overcome her own shyness and reserve"—and as a result she quickly gains the reputation of a snob...and, worse, a poseur. "The young ladies who approached her at first with some respect in consideration of her coming from a Baronet's family, were soon offended by what they termed 'airs'—for as she neither played on the piano-forte nor wore fine pelisses, they could, on farther observation, admit no right of superiority."

Does anyone have the slightest doubt that if Mary Crawford were dropped into this exact same circle, they'd all be tripping over themselves in adoration of her before the first week was up? Hell, the first *meal?*

Fanny does find one ray of hope in this land of the lost: her young sister. Though Susan's combativeness and pride have shocked her up to now, she begins to see that the girl has simply been using what limited resources she has—her sense of justice and the force of her own personality—to try to improve her lot, and her family's. "That a girl of fourteen, acting only on her own unassisted reason, should err in the method of reform was not wonderful; and Fanny soon became more disposed to admire the natural light of the mind which could so early distinguish justly, than to censure severely the faults of conduct to which it led." And amazingly, Fanny perceives that Susan's noisy flailings *have* made things better, by checking the worst abuses of her careless parents.

And why shouldn't she act as she does? She has nothing to lose. For, poignantly, it turns out Susan is unloved. "The blind fondness which was for ever producing evil around her, *she* had never known. There was no gratitude for affection past or present, to make her better bear with its excesses to the others." Another one of those miraculous character sketches, so brief and so incisive and startling, that catapult Austen to the rank of genius.

So Fanny begins to view her sister "as an object of mingled compassion and respect", and "new as it was to imagine herself capable of guiding or informing anyone," she resolves to start dropping hints as to how properly to behave, which based on what we know of Fanny, means teaching Susan to be passive-aggressive instead of aggressive-aggressive. She even resolves to make up for the lack of affection in Susan's life by replacing the goddamn silver knife everyone keeps battling over, though Fanny is "so wholly unused to confer favours, except on the very poor, so unpractised in removing evils, or bestowing kindnesses among her equals, and so fearful of appearing to elevate herself as a great lady at home," that she's almost mummified by her own interal red tape before she can make it to the silversmith. But eventually the gift is bestowed and Susan is appropriately gratified and newly attuned to Fanny's favor.

Fanny thus begins reshaping her sister into Fanny Mk II. Since books play such a significant role in that transformation, Fanny amends the household's lack of improving literature—hell, of *any* reading matter (even Mr. Price's borrowed newspaper has to be returned)—by means of a circulating library. "She became a subscriber—amazed at being any thing *in propria persona,* amazed at her doings in every way; to be a renter, a chuser of books!" What she's feeling, in short, is the heady rush that comes with *activity*—with doing something as opposed to nothing. It's her first tentative step out of the stasis field in which she's not only lived till now, but into which she's tried her damnedest to drag everyone else within a ten-mile radius. This ought to be cause for rejoicing, but for God's sake, we're on page 414. Too little, too late. This should've happened on page 75.

Time passes, and Fanny hears no news about Edmund and Mary, despite his having had plenty of time to arrive in town; which can either mean "his going had been again delayed, or he had yet procured no opportunity of seeing Miss Crawford alone—or, he was too happy for letter writing!" But her uncertainty on the subject doesn't need to torment her further, because someone actually arrives on her doorstep who can tell her everything she wants to know. Austen, with absolutely rock-solid theatrical instincts, wastes not a word in bringing him onstage:

> *It was a gentleman's voice; it was a voice that Fanny was just turning pale about, when Mr. Crawford walked into the room.*

He thus takes us by surprise as surely as he does Fanny. A lesser writer would have tried to load the moment with suspense—put off the reveal while prolonging the anxiety, teasing the consequences—but these are cheap tricks; kitsch; soft-core porn. None of that for Austen; she's the real deal.

Fanny's "good sense" gets her through the introduction to her parents, even to the point of remembering to refer to him as "William's friend," but once everyone is seated she plunges quickly into Fannyness and "fancied herself on the point of fainting away," though for all the times Fanny has felt so inclined, I can't recall a single instance when she's ever actually done so. Frankly, it's time to put up or shut up, chiquita; I will no longer believe how close to swooning you are, till I see you hit the floor at least *once.*

As for Henry...remember a few paragraphs ago when I said, imagine Mary with this crowd, they'd be putty in her hands?...Well, her brother Henry sorta kinda proves my point. Yes, he's male and therefore immediately of more consequence than any mere woman, and yes, he enters the house already beatified by virtue of his favors to William... but even so, it takes him approximately ninety seconds before every member of the Price family is on his or her back, offering their tummies for him to rub. He does this—as Mary would as well—as any person of breeding would—by simply not seeing, or pretending not to see, that he has in fact entered the primate house and is surrounded by shrieking gibbons for whom his sudden appearance is just barely sufficient cause to interrupt them flinging feces at each other. Where Fanny, in this situation, cringed and winced and frowned and withdrew, Henry smiles and bows and charms and flatters.

And whaddaya know, it doesn't just win over his audience...it inspires them to meet him at his own level. "Warmed by the sight of such a friend to her son, and regulated by the wish of appearing to advantage before him, [Mrs. Price] was overflowing with gratitude, artless, maternal gratitude, which could not be unpleasing." Her husband is out, which she regrets very much, but Fanny doesn't regret it, not one bit; "for to her many other sources of uneasiness was added the severe one of shame for the home in which he found her...and she would have been yet more ashamed of her father, than of all the rest."

After a certain interval, "it was not unreasonable to suppose, that Fanny might be looked at and spoken to," and Henry now does so, giving her the rundown on his recent whereabouts; which chatter—amiable, breezy, and (he thinks) inconsequential—includes the riveting intel that he hasn't seen Edmund, but knows him now to be in town. Which makes Fanny think, "then by this time it is all settled," and we don't need to be told what *that* means.

Henry starts dropping hints about what a beautiful day it is and what a lovely thing it would be to go out for a walk, but since subtlety is a thing unknown in the Price household—Henry might as well write his desire on a slip of paper, in French, then tear it up and blow the pieces in Mrs. Price's face for all the impression it makes—he's forced to do something just shy of tucking Fanny up under his arm and carrying her out bodily. Oh, and Susan too, because the way she's been down on all fours, sniffing at his pants leg, makes it pretty clear there's no getting rid of her.

And darn the luck, wouldn't you know they no sooner reach the High Street than they bump into Mr. Price, who is apparently projectile-vomiting on a bush or something by the way Fanny recoils from the sight of him. And here's where we come up against some interesting and I think noteworthy female psychology; for Fanny realizes that Henry must be appalled by her father.

> *He must be ashamed and disgusted altogether. He must soon give her up, and cease to have the smallest inclination for the match; and yet, though she had been so much wanting his affection to be cured, this was a sort of cure that would be almost as bad as the complaint; and I believe, there is scarcely a young lady in the united kingdoms, who would not rather put up with the misfortune of being sought by a clever, agreeable man, than have him driven away by the vulgarity of her nearest relations.*

Really?...*This* is the way women think? *This?*..."Please, please, anything to keep this lothario from imposing his awful attentions on me...but *God forbid he should no longer want me?* Let him leave me alone—but *not* because he's horrified by my family? I only ask that he stay far, far away from me, for the rest of his life—but still desire and long for me? Let me never see him again—but *let him always suffer for my lack?" That's* it? *Really?*

Because that is the most monumentally selfish, contemptible, outrageous feat of brazen egoism I've heard in quite some time.

When I first read *Mansfield Park,* this is where I had to put the book down and just walk away for a while. By which I mean, for a week or so...I needed a long, clear space of time in which to cleanse myself of the oozing, gummy, self-dramatizing, self-regarding leakage that is Fanny Price's train of thought. The idea that it might be something she shares with all females is, frankly, terrifying.

And I can't believe it is. I mean, imagine Elinor Dashwood in this same situation. I'm willing to bet her reaction would be something wry and ironic, like, *I never thought to find myself grateful for my father's want of social graces.* She'd be *glad* to have Dad scare the bozo away.

But as it happens, despite Fanny's fears, the encounter with Mr. Price goes just as swimmingly as the one with his better half. If Henry *is* in fact appalled by what he sees before him, he doesn't show it; and Mr. Price responds to Henry's gentlemanly bonhomie with a refinement in his own manners, which, "though not polished, were more than passable; they were grateful, animated, manly; his expressions were those of an attached father, and a sensible man;—his loud tones did very well in the open air, and there was not a single oath to be heard." In short, Henry and Mr. Price charm the pants off each other, which is a good thing, because at least in Mr. Price's case those pants could almost certainly use a good washing, if not burning at the end of a stick.

Mr. Price offers to show Henry the dockyard, and Henry accepts the favor, "though he had seen the dock-yard again and again". But his acceptance is contingent on the Price sisters not being "afraid of the fatigue; and as it was somehow or other ascertained, or inferred, or at least acted upon, that they were not at all afraid, to the dock-yard they were all to go"—this being one of those quietly hilarious, unmistakably English passages that make me sorry for people who read Austen in translation; there's no way for its proto-absurdist charm to survive conversion to, say, Swedish.

Mr. Price is wonderfully neglectful of his daughters, who it seems have a certain pace they just can't exceed, as though simple locomotion is something they've only added to their physical repertoire yesterday. He strides swiftly ahead, leaving them to struggle on behind; occasionally he looks over his shoulder and bellows down the lane to hurry them. Never mind, Henry Crawford gallantly stays with them, strolling at their side and pointedly not asking excuse me, but by chance do you have turtles strapped to your feet instead of shoes? Really, the man is a pillar of courtesy.

At the dockyard they run into a "brother lounger" of Mr. Price's (and *dang* do I love that term), and the two go off together to discuss "matters of equal and never-failing interest," which leaves the young people to stop and rest for a moment or two or forty-six.

> *Crawford could not have wished [Fanny] more fatigued or more ready to sit down; but he could have wished her sister away. A quick looking girl of Susan's age was the very worst third in the world—totally different from Lady Bertram—all eyes and ears; and there was no introducing the main point before her.*

Henry is overlooking—or perhaps is too much a gentleman to take advantage of—how easy it would be to have Susan out of the way with just one surreptitious shove off the pier. But never mind, he makes himself as agreeable as possible, only speaking about general subjects, which has the benefit of entertaining Susan "in a way quite new to her." He talks about how he's been getting to know the tenants on his estate, which "was aimed, and well aimed, at Fanny," who's pleased "to hear him speak so properly"—but then, of course, he ruins it with his Henry thing of going too far, and hinting broadly at how much easier such good works will be when he has *sommmme*one at this side to help, someone who *maaaay*be might be quite nearby and whose name begins with F and what are you looking at, oh clever you, you guessed!

Fanny then does *her* Fanny thing of folding up like a bat and hiding; but even so, a little of his efforts has begun to work on her, for she admits to herself that he might turn out better than she ever supposed. This helps limit the damage when he doubles his original mistake by not only dropping another big hint about his super-faboo future with her, but twinning it with a sly reference to Edmund's coming bed of roses with Mary. And then, on the walk home, he manages to get Fanny alone long enough to make it clear that his visit to Portsmouth is for one purpose only: to see her. And while she wishes he'd just lay off that kinda talk already, it doesn't actually feel *quite* as annoying as it usually does.

> *[S]he had never seen him so agreeable—so* near *being agreeable; his behaviour to her father could not offend, and there was something particularly kind and proper in the notice he took of Susan. He was decidedly improved. She wished the next day over, she wished he had come only for*

> *one day—but it was not so very bad as she would have expected; the pleasure of talking of Mansfield was so very great!*

There's one dicey moment, which comes as they part: her father asks Henry to stay to dinner, and Fanny experiences "a thrill of horror" at the idea of him sitting down to a meal with them. You'd think Mr. Price was going to bring down a zebra with a club, and the entire family then go tearing at it with their bare teeth. But not to worry, Henry claims a prior engagement—which he doesn't actually have, he's just trying to avoid mortifying Fanny. Wait, wait...*this* is our cad? This guy? This considerate little love-bug? This pussycat? This *mensch?*

The next morning Henry intersects the Price family en route to church, which gratifies Fanny because this is the one day each week when they manage to pull themselves together and give the impression of not at all being a band of marauding Huns. "Her poor mother now did not look so very unworthy of being Lady Bertram's sister as she was but too apt to look," though how anyone can look like Lady Bertram's sister without a couch squeezed beneath her is beyond me. Henry attends the service with them, and afterwards accepts their invitation to walk on the ramparts, where Mrs. Price always bolts immediately after church to hook up with her friends for an orgy of good Christian gossip.

> *Thither they now went; Mr. Crawford most happy to consider the Miss Prices as his peculiar charge; and before they had been there long—somehow or other—there was no saying how—Fanny could not have believed it—but he was walking between them with an arm of each under his, and she did not know how to prevent or put an end to it. It made her uncomfortable for a time—but yet there were enjoyments in the day and in the view which would be felt.*

In fact, the weather's so fine and the prospect so pretty that despite the absence of a hedge of any kind, Fanny's soon in raptures. They saunter on in this way for two hours, during which time Henry scores some pretty serious points.

> *They often stopt with the same sentiment and taste, leaning against the wall, some minutes, to look and admire; and considering he was not*

> *Edmund, Fanny could not but allow that he was sufficiently open to the charms of nature, and very well able to express his admiration.*

But one of the views on hand isn't quite so pleasing to Henry's eye: that of Fanny's face, which "was less blooming than it ought to be." Gosh, y'think? A single exposure to the assembled Price clan would wilt every bloom in Kew Gardens as effectively as Agent Orange. And Fanny's been here a whole month, not to mention that she's also been working extra special hard to disapprove of *everything*. It's taken its toll.

Henry asks when she's to return to Mansfield, and Fanny tells him she's not sure; another month, but possibly more if it's not convenient for Sir Thomas to send for her. This causes Henry something like consternation—the first we've seen of anything in that nature from him. It makes an impression. He says, "I know Mansfield, I knows its way, I know its faults toward *you*. I know the danger of your being so far forgotten, as to have your comforts give way to the imaginary convenience of any single being in the family. I am aware that you may be left here week after week." And he insists that at the end of the two months, if no one's available to come for her, she's to send him word and he and Mary will fetch her home themselves. "You know the ease, and the pleasure with which this would be done. You know all that would be felt on the occasion." Fanny, we're told, "thanked him, but tried to laugh it off." And Henry—who's spent the entire novel up to now laughing—won't have it. He's *serious,* dammit. Just look at the set of his jaw! And that little vein in the middle of his forehead! Never saw *that* before, didja?

Austen is being very near reckless here; she's building up Henry so high—Mary too—that when she ultimately tears him down, there won't be any way to contain the fall; the plummeting wreckage might just (and in fact will) take the entire novel with it. I've said it before, but it bears repeating: I admire Austen's ambition, her desire to challenge herself, to take on the task of creating both a cad and a rival of greater shade and complexity than the more broadly sketched dastardliness of her earlier archetypes. But ultimately she's gone too far, and lost herself along the way. Our sympathies aren't where she means them—*needs* them—to be; and I have a strong suspicion that on some level, hers aren't either.

Finally, they say goodbye; Henry is leaving Portsmouth, perhaps for Norfolk, where he's thinking of reining in an errant estate manager who's thwarting him on the matter of a new tenant; but he's uncertain whether he should intervene. What does Fanny advise?

> *"I advise?—you know very well what is right."*
> *"Yes. When you give me your opinion, I always know what is right. Your judgment is my rule of right."*
> *"Oh, no!—do not say so. We have all a better guide in ourselves, if we would attend to it, than any other person can be. Good bye; I wish you a pleasant journey tomorrow."*

She deflects every compliment as deftly as though she were wearing a personal force field. And the tone of that goodbye...she might be seeing off an insurance salesman, or someone who's just installed a new roof.

And then she goes on in to dinner, or rather, not to dinner, because "she was so little equal to Rebecca's puddings, and Rebecca's hashes, brought to table as they all were, with such accompaniments of half-cleaned plates, and not half-cleaned knives and forks, that she was very often constrained to defer her heartiest meal, till she could send her brothers in the evening for biscuits and buns." Clearly she has no idea what little boys might think to do with biscuits and buns between the kitchen and her room. Believe me, those half-cleaned plates would be safer.

> *After being nursed up at Mansfield, it was too late in the day to be hardened at Portsmouth; and though Sir Thomas, had he known all, might have thought his niece in the most promising way of being starved, both mind and body, into a much juster value for Mr. Crawford's good company and good fortune, he would probably have feared to push his experiment farther, lest she might die under the cure.*

Fanny, of course, is as unlikely to die as she is to faint: her sheer, dogged pride will see to that. And as for this "cure"...well, just look at her now, huddled in her dim-lit corner, cold and hungry and weary and bereft, and thinking—what about Henry Crawford?

> *[S]he was quite persuaded of his being astonishingly more gentle, and regardful of others, than formerly. And if in little things, must it not be so in great? So anxious for her health and comfort, so very feeling as he now expressed himself, and really seemed, might it not be fairly supposed, that he would not much longer persevere in a suit so distressing to her?*

Sorry, Sir Thomas. Can you say "epic fail"?

CHAPTERS 43-45

Fanny Price, the supposed heroine of *Mansfield Park,* has spent pretty much the entirety of the novel standing off on the margins while the other characters provide all the plot action. Occasionally she's got in their way or underfoot, and they've had to talk over or around her, or to each other *through* her, but now that she's been removed to Portsmouth her essential irrelevance becomes harder to disguise. For the next several chapters, her role is reduced to no more than reading letters from (and about) home. In essence, she's fallen out of the novel and become one of us; Jane Austen, that Regency postmodernist, has gone meta. We read *Mansfield Park,* in which Fanny Price reads about Mansfield Park. Her text is our text; we peer at it over her shoulder.

The first letter is from Mary Crawford, and it's not exactly brimming with interest; she even says outright, "I have no news for you." By which she means, of course, no news of being engaged to Edmund; but it's true overall, as well. She actually avoids even mentioning Edmund, rattling on about her London frolics, till she can't sustain the effort anymore:

> *If I avoided his name entirely, it would look suspicious. I will say, then, that we have seen him two or three times, and that my friends here are very much struck with his gentleman-like appearance. Mrs. Fraser (no bad judge), declares she knows but three men in town who have so good a person, height, and air; and I must confess, when he dined here the other day, there were none to compare with him, and we were a party of sixteen.*

> *Luckily there is no distinction of dress now-a-days to tell tales, but—but —but.*

She signs off, "Your's, affectionately," then dives immediately into a postscript nearly as long as the original letter, admonishing Fanny not to stay at Portsmouth "to lose your pretty looks. Those sea-breezes are the ruin of beauty and health," as attested by her "poor aunt," the Admiral's wife, who apparently ended her life looking like filet of salt cod. Mary renews her brother's offer to ride in like the cavalry and rescue Fanny from so briny an environment:

> *I am at your service and Henry's, at an hour's notice. I should like the scheme, and we would make a little circuit, and shew you Everingham in our way, and perhaps you would not mind passing through London, and seeing the inside of St. George's, Hanover-Square. Only keep your cousin Edmund from me at such a time, I should not like to be tempted. What a long letter!—one word more.*

The "one word more" is of course actually several dozen, to the effect that while Mary is indeed ready at an hour's notice to sweep Fanny away from the purgatory of Portsmouth, that hour must not occur until after the 14th, because she and Henry have a party that evening—"The value of a man like Henry on such an occasion, is what you can have no conception of; so you must take it upon my word, to be inestimable"—and oh by the way, the Rushworths will be there, "which I own I am not sorry for—having a little curiosity—and so I think has he, though he will not acknowledge it." If Mary Crawford were alive today, she'd be a dedicated *Real Housewives* fan. If not one of its cast members.

Fanny's principal takeaway from the letter is, no surprise, that Edmund hasn't yet proposed. But she doesn't know what that means; hasn't he had the opportunity? Or has he changed his mind about Mary? Or has her behavior in a new circle (Fanny thinks her "cooled and staggered by a return to London habits") been sufficient to give him doubts about *her* feelings for *him?* Fanny of course can't know that answer, but she's pretty sure if Edmund does ask her, Mary will say yes. "She would try to be more ambitious than her heart would allow. She would hesitate, she would teaze, she would condition, she would require a great deal, but she would finally accept." And this realization prompts Fanny's first descent into open disgust.

> *The prospect for her cousin grew worse and worse. The woman who could speak of him, and speak only of his appearance!—What an unworthy attachment! To be deriving support from the commendations of Mrs. Fraser! She who had known him intimately half a year! Fanny was ashamed of her.*

I suppose Fanny, having been to exactly one dinner party that we know of, and that at the über-humble parsonage, can be excused for not knowing how dinner-party conversation works, and that for Mary to try to impress upon Mrs. Fraser anything more profound than how pretty a side of beef Edmund is, would be a tad, shall we say, uncomfortable in such a setting of lightness and gaiety. But I get the impression that Fanny at a London dinner party would fit in about as happily as Cotton Mather at a Roman orgy. And besides, Fanny, who has herself known *Mary* intimately for half a year, might be expected to sympathize with her attempts to find any support, in any quarter, for the better part of her nature—i.e., the part that draws her to Edmund.

But there's more: "That Miss Crawford should endeavour to secure a meeting between [Henry] and Mrs. Rushworth, was all in her worst line of conduct, and grossly unkind and ill-judged"—well, fine, I agree she doesn't have to be so *pert* about it; but she's writing to an intimate friend (or so she thinks), so why not be honest? There *is* a bit of prurient curiosity engendered by the occasion; we feel it ourselves. And certainly no one can reasonably expect Henry and Maria to spend the rest of their days avoiding each other...except Fanny, for whom avoidance is a guiding principle of life.

Fanny waits impatiently for the next letter to arrive, and we do too, because until it does we aren't going to be getting much in the way of actual novel. Austen seems to have grown bored with the Price family (or maybe just exhausted at having handled them for so many chapters in succession; it must be like juggling cats) and lets them recede into the background, except for Susan, who sits with Fanny up in her attic amidst all those books and learns...well, not to love reading, but to enjoy not appearing ignorant. To Fanny's dismay, she thrives more on conversation than on study. "The early habit of reading was wanting," she sighs.

But she's impressed enough by Susan's character and keenness to begin feeling real regret at the idea of leaving her behind when she returns to Mansfield. In fact, she goes so far as to fantasize about having a home of her own to invite her to—and if only she could bring herself to accept Mr. Crawford, she'd have exactly that. "She thought he was really good-tempered, and could fancy his entering into a plan of that sort, most pleasantly." This is one of those rare moments when you get a little jolt of genuine affection for Fanny; she edges into the realm of the likable. Of course, it's fleeting.

Eventually another letter arrives—a very looong one; in fact our hearts sink a little when we flip ahead and see that it runs six pages, because this time it's from Edmund instead of Mary, which means it won't be six pages of "Lady so-and-so accidentally sat on her pet ferret, I won't say Henry put it on her chair, certainly not on purpose," and will instead be six pages of, "Perhaps I might again presume so far as to press a claim on your good nature for the favor of your kind attention while I endeavor to say the following without imposing too much on your patience."

It turns out Edmund has come home from London empty-handed, i.e. without a fiancée, but he realizes Fanny must already know this from having heard it from Mary—except Fanny has heard exactly zip (which means neither have we).

> *So very fond of you as Miss Crawford is, it is most natural that she should tell you enough of her own feelings, to furnish a tolerable guess at mine.—I will not be prevented, however, from making my own communication. Our confidences in you need not clash.—I ask no questions.—There is something soothing in the idea, that we have the same friend, and that whatever unhappy differences of opinion may exist between us, we are united in our love of you.—It will be a comfort to me to tell you how things now are, and what are my present plans, if plans I can be said to have.*

You see what I mean? Edmund is king of the preamble. By the time he gets to his point, you need a shave.

The upshot is, he found Mary so changed by London society that he scarcely recognized her. "She was in high spirits, and surrounded by those who were giving all the support of their own bad sense to her too lively mind." This conjures up images of Mary swinging gaily from a chandelier, a saucer of champagne sloshing merrily from her free hand; but we swiftly realize it takes far less acrobatic mischief to shock poor Edmund. An ill-timed cackle over dessert would do it. He especially loathes Mary's chief friend, Mrs. Fraser, about whom he just can't think up enough bad things to say: she's shallow, vain, envious, mercenary, and ambitious, and so is her sister Lady Stornaway, and with every stroke of his pen he's convincing me that these are two women I would absolutely invite to every single party I ever threw, from now till the crack of doom. His main consolation is that these harpies seem fonder of Mary than the other way around.

> *...I am sure she does not love them as she loves you. When I think of her great attachment to you, indeed, and the whole of her judicious, upright conduct as a sister, she appears a very different creature, capable of every thing noble, and I am ready to blame myself for a too harsh construction of a playful manner.*

Well, *exactly*. For all her sophistication, Mary is still young, still lacks maturity; that she conforms herself to fit in whatever society she finds herself, couldn't make this more obvious. And so he won't—can't—give her up. "I have no jealousy of any individual. It is the influence of the fashionable world altogether that I am jealous of."

He's not a firecracker, but he's sharp. He sees how essentially unmolded Mary is; how the polish of her affectations conceals a character that's still being formed—and that, given the lack of guidance or counsel she had while growing up (under an uncle seems to have been equal parts Don Giovanni and Sweeney Todd), she's had to do the job all on her own. No wonder she grasps at the opinions and attitudes of everyone she encounters; she's trying on different personae, to see which suits her best. It's not too late to save her; to redeem her. And there's another reason he can't give her up:

> *Connected, as we already are, and I hope, are to be, to give up Mary Crawford, would be to give up the society of some of those most dear to*

> *me, to banish myself from the very houses and friends whom, under any other distress, I should turn to for consolation. The loss of Mary I must consider as comprehending the loss of Crawford and of Fanny.*

You have to laugh. Fanny's powers have so badly waned, that despite her still saying *no, no, no, no* to everyone and everything, it now falls on deaf ears—no one hears her; instead, they look at her—Henry, Mary, Sir Thomas, Lady Bertram, even Edmund who essentially created her—and all they see is, *yes, yes, yes.*

So Edmund won't give Mary up; but he doesn't know how to proceed with her. Should he go back to London after Easter, and give it another try? Or wait till she returns to Mansfield in June? Or, that being so far distant, should he send her a letter instead? He decides on the latter, as "I shall be able to write much that I could not say, and shall be giving her time for reflection before she resolves on her answer," but of course that's presuming he could get around to the meat of the matter before Mary grew bored, or tired, or died of old age. Or that, when he *did* reach the heart of the matter, somewhere around the eleventh page, it wasn't so couched in wherefores and given-the-circumstances and with-all-due-forethought-and-considerations that Mary would read it and not even realize what the hell he was talking about. Fortunately, he quickly abandons the letter plan after considering that Mary might consult Mrs. Fraser about it; and Edmund is sufficiently self-aware to realize that Mrs. Fraser going over his earnest lines one by one, adding her acid comments on all his elaborate hemming and hawing, might not be the most helpful thing for his cause.

But while he may have suffered a disappointment in Mary, he's a bigger fan of Henry than ever, being "more and more satisfied with all that I see and hear of him. There is not a shadow of wavering. He thoroughly knows his own mind, and acts up to his resolutions—an inestimable quality." He had the chance to see Henry and Maria come face-to-face at last, and "I acknowledge that they did not meet as friends. There was a marked coolness on her side. They scarcely spoke." Maria for her part seems contented, though Edmund hasn't had much opportunity to judge, having "dined only twice in Wimpole Street, and might have been there oftener, but it is mortifying to be with Rushworth as a brother."

He moves on to announce that the Grants are going to Bath; then closes the letter by reassuring Fanny of how much his mother misses her, how much *he* misses her, and that Sir Thomas intends to come and fetch her home himself, possibly after Easter, but if not certainly sometime before 1970.

Fanny—the meek, the humble, the accepting—now settles into a positive fit of angry impatience; Edmund's dithering has managed to provoke her to the point where she's all *for God's sake ask her already*—though she has no doubts about how it will all eventually work out:

> *"He will marry her, and be poor and miserable. God grant that her influence do not make him cease to be respectable!"—She looked over the letter again. "'So very fond of me!' 'tis nonsense all. She loves nobody but herself and her brother. 'Her friends leading her astray for years!' She is quite as likely to have led them astray... 'The loss of Mary, I must consider as comprehending the loss of Crawford and Fanny.' Edmund, you do not know* me. *The families would never be connected, if you did not connect them."*

There's something a bit thrilling in hearing Fanny *finally* get down to some trash-talking; but you can't really enjoy it, because at its core there's such a strain of cringeworthy hypocrisy. Fanny is spewing venom about people to whom she pretends friendship—and of whose friendship she's plainly availed herself of the benefits more than once. This isn't healthy, heads-together-over-the-fence social gossip; this is crazy-old-lady-on-the-street bilious muttering.

She eventually softens, at least towards Edmund, with whom she is still, we're told, in love (haven't yet been able to bring myself to believe it). "His warm regard, his kind expressions, his confidential treatment touched her strongly...It was a letter, in short, which she would not but have had for the world, and which could never be valued enough. This was the end of it."

We then, thank the sweet lord Jesus and all the saints and angels, get back to some much-needed comedy. Lady Bertram is very put out when she learns that Edmund has told Fanny about the Grants going to Bath, because she'd been hoping to tell her of it herself. And she'd been meaning to make quite a meal of it, so that it was "very mortifying to her to see it fall to the share of her thankless son, and treated as concisely as possible at the end of a long letter, instead of having it to spread over the largest part of a page of her own."

> *For though Lady Bertram rather shone in the epistolary line, having early in her marriage, from the want of employment, and in the circumstance of Sir Thomas's being in Parliament, got into the way of making and keeping correspondents, and formed for herself a very creditable, common-place, amplifying style, so that a very little matter was enough for her; she could not do entirely without any; she must have something to write about, even to her niece, and being so soon to lose all the benefit of Dr. Grant's gouty symptoms and Mrs. Grant's morning calls, it was very hard upon her to be deprived of one of the last epistolary uses she could put them to."*

Welcome back, J.A.! Missed your bad self. Now, how about those Prices...?

But this tone of genial mockery can't last; and in the next paragraph, Lady Bertram gets something to write about in spades, as her son Tom falls gravely ill. Not that I dislike Tom—quite the opposite, he's one of my favorites in the novel, right up there with the Crawfords—but I have to say, for this Austen reader at least, it's a nice change of pace to see a strapping young buck hover feverishly on the brink of death, instead of another dewy ingénue. Typically, though, it takes all of London's cavalcade of dangers and debauches to knock Tom for six, rather than the usual gust of damp wind that seems to topple the young ladies as effectively as a breeze from Chernobyl.

Anyway, Tom manfully resists giving in to his deteriorating state for a while, but soon is so weakened that Edmund rushes off to town to do what he can for him. Everyone is aquiver with fear for his life, though they all convey it with that wonderful Austenian reserve, in phrases like *I am quite fearful of his prospects indeed.*

Fanny reads all this in letters, which we read with her, so we're still in metafictional mode; at this point, it would seem as reasonable for a message to arrive summoning *us* to Mansfield Park as it would summoning her; or conversely, for her to put down her letter for a moment, get up, and go raid our fridge. It's only occasionally that we recall she's actually a character *in* the novel too, as when she finds "selfishness enough to wonder whether Edmund *had* written to Miss Crawford" before all this went down, which reminds us that Fanny has a stake in that particular event (and reminds us in a way not entirely flattering to Fanny, let me add).

There's a wonderful passage—another brief sketch, this time of Lady Bertram—that once again illustrates Austen's innate grasp of character and genius for human psychology:

> *Her aunt did not neglect her; she wrote again and again; they were receiving frequent accounts from Edmund, and these accounts were as regularly transmitted to Fanny, in the same diffuse style, and the same medley of trusts, hopes and fears, all following and producing each other at haphazard. It was a sort of playing at being frightened. The sufferings which Lady Bertram did not see, had little power over her fancy; and she wrote very comfortably about agitation and anxiety, and poor invalids, till Tom was actually conveyed to Mansfield, and her own eyes had beheld his altered appearance.*

Then, it seems, she turned pretty quickly into a Puccini heroine at the approximate climax of Act Three. Except she probably couldn't swoon as dramatically, being already spread out on the couch.

Tom's removal to Mansfield turns out to have been the classic bad idea; but apparently, like all suddenly stricken boy-men, he insisted on having his mommy near (and probably his dog, though Austen doesn't say so). At any rate, he's very much the worse for wear. The journey hasn't quite killed him, but he's close enough to the pearly gates not to have to hail a cab, if you get my drift. In fact a fever now claims him, and they are all "very seriously frightened." And Fanny...?

> *Without any particular affection for her eldest cousin, her tenderness of heart made her feel that she could not spare him; and the purity of her principles added yet a keener solicitude, when she considered how little useful, how little self-denying his life had (apparently) been.*

Wow. Sorry to say it. Bitch is *cold.*

We finally get another glimpse at the Price family, and find that they're all as unmoved by their cousin's suffering as can be expected.

> *Susan was always ready to hear and to sympathize. Nobody else could be interested in so remote an evil as illness, in a family above an hundred*

> *miles off—not even Mrs. Price, beyond a brief question or two if she saw her daughter with a letter in her hand, and now and then the quiet observation of "My poor sister Bertram must be in a great deal of trouble."*

Call me crazy, but I more honestly respect that momentary flicker of compassion, than the "purity" of Fanny's "principles" that can only approximate human feeling in the abstract...and even then, not without passing judgment.

But it seems Tom might be spared the horror of dying under the burden of Fanny's disapproval; the fever abates, his immediate danger is over, and he has a second chance to become a humorless, joyless automaton and earn his cousin's high esteem.

Or...does he? Fanny receives a new letter from Edmund, written "to acquaint her with the apprehensions which he and his father had imbibed from the physician...They judged it best that Lady Bertram should not be harassed by alarms...but there was no reason why Fanny should not know the truth. They were apprehensive for his lungs."

Further correspondence paints a picture of Edmund continually at his brother's bedside, the invalid's only real comfort given Lady Bertram's nervous twitterings and Sir Thomas's inability to "bring down his conversation or his voice to the level of irritation and feebleness." Aunt Norris isn't mentioned, which seems odd at first, because you expect her to be right in there, ordering clean linen every ninety-four seconds and personally shoving Tom's bed across the room to keep him in sunlight. But though Austen doesn't give us a reason for her absence, it takes us no time at all to supply one ourselves: *she's afraid of infection.* Not only will she not come near the house while Tom's in danger, she's probably busy packing up a trunk with the idea of visiting her sister Price after all, or maybe seeing the Great Wall of China.

So Edmund's really the beginning and end of Tom's support system, and Fanny's "estimation of him was higher than ever when he appeared as the attendant, supporter, cheerer of a suffering brother."

> *There was not only the debility of recent illness to assist; there was also, as she now learnt, nerves much affected, spirits much depressed to calm and raise; and her own imagination added that there must be a mind to be properly guided.*

Jesus, can't she just lay the hell off for *once?*

Fanny "was more inclined to hope than fear for her cousin—except when she thought of Miss Crawford—but Miss Crawford gave her the idea of being the child of good luck, and to her selfishness and vanity it would be good luck to have Edmund the only son."

Nope. She really can't lay off, can she? She's like a little wind-up monkey, endlessly beating her drum of judgment.

While Tom languishes, Easter comes and goes, and there's no word of anyone coming to fetch Fanny from Portsmouth. It's almost three months instead of two that she's been gone, and she's crawling the walls to get back. (She's probably not the only thing crawling the walls in that house, either.) She moons over Mansfield for several pages, realizing that there, not here, lies her true home; and it astonishes her that Julia and Maria, who have the means of going back any time they choose, are still lingering in town as if there were no family crisis of any kind. "It appeared from one of [Lady Bertram's] letters, that Julia had offered to return if wanted—but this was all.—It was evident that she would rather remain where she was." I don't know why this astonishes Fanny; she grew up with those girls, she knows full well how contemptuous they are of anyone beyond themselves. Imagine a jury filled with Marias and Julias; you could find yourself hanged for a parking ticket.

Fanny decides, in the manner of rednecks and yokels since time immemorial, that city life is to blame.

> *Fanny was disposed to think the influence of London very much at war with all respectable attachments. She saw the proof of it in Miss Crawford, as well as in her cousins;* her *attachment to Edmund had been respectable, the most respectable part of her character, her friendship for herself, had at least been blameless. Where was either sentiment now?*

The submarine is in range and the torpedo triggered. The long-foreshadowed sinking of Mary Crawford is at hand.

It comes by way of—what else?—another letter. (By this time the postman should have made an appearance or two in the story. He's at least as much an agent of the narrative as Fanny.) The letter is from Mary, and it's long, and the tone of it is so agitated with confused emotion that I imagine when Fanny sets it aside, the pages flutter against the tabletop like bird wings.

Mary begins by asking forgiveness for her long silence, then demands that Fanny fill her in on the news from Mansfield, meaning in this case, the current estimation of Tom Bertram pulling through. "I thought little of his illness at first," she confesses. "I looked upon him as the sort of person to be made a fuss with, and to make a fuss of himself in any trifling disorder, and was chiefly concerned for those who had to nurse him;" not the most promising start, and we can imagine Fanny's snort of derision, despite her own admission of no real affection for Tom, and her continued harping on the unflattering intersection of his illness with his character. Mary is more truly aggrieved, and "cannot help trembling. To have such a fine young man cut off in the flower of his days, is most melancholy." But then she doubles back:

> *Fanny, Fanny, I see you smile, and look cunning, but upon my honour I never bribed a physician in my life. Poor young man!—If he is to die, there will be* two *poor young men less in the world; and with a fearless face and bold voice would I say to any one, that wealth and consequence could fall into no hands more deserving of them...I put it to your conscience, whether 'Sir Edmund' would not do more good with all the Bertram property, than any other possible 'Sir.'*

Her assessment is unarguable; her expression of it, though, is in terrible taste. Mary's habit, which is to joke about everything, can be defended; is anything sacred, or isn't it? And if she's decided it isn't, then mortal illness shouldn't be either—and in fact her acerbic, cynical view is more in line with our modern way of behaving, in which gallows humor plays so valuable a role in coping with crises.

My mother died two years ago, after a long and grueling illness that ended up consuming much of the time and energy of my five siblings and me; our principal way of dealing with the anguish and the stress, was through black humor. An outsider who overheard us would have been shocked; but the greater the adversary, the bolder the joke required to disarm it. And death is sort of the big Kahuna in that regard. Mary Crawford's mistake—strategic more than anything else—

is to take this line of attack in a circumstance in which death doesn't threaten her with loss, but tempts her with triumph.

But Fanny, who's cracked maybe a dozen smiles in her entire life and probably regrets upwards to eight of them, can't possibly see this; doesn't want to see it; ultimately *won't* see it. What she sees instead is the Mary she requires to salve her feelings. What she sees is an unfeeling monster...worse, a voracious one.

Mary goes on to explain that she's appealing to Fanny for the scoop on Tom because Maria and Julia are no use to her; Maria in particular isn't even in town, she's staying with friends at Twickenham, having sent Mr. Rushworth down to Bath to fetch his mother. In a postscript, she reports that Maria is in fact now *back* in town—Henry has just seen her, and can confirm that she knows of her brother's probable decline.

She then concludes by renewing the offer, at this most urgent moment, of coming with Henry to fetch her home to Mansfield. "He and I can go to the Parsonage, you know, and be no trouble to our friends at Mansfield Park...you must feel yourself to be so wanted there, that you cannot in conscience (conscientious as you are) keep away, when you have the means of returning." In this, Fanny sees only an attempt by Mary to use her to get near Edmund again. And it's entirely possible—even probable—that this is in Mary's mind. But we know enough of her to know it isn't her *only* motive; she's made the offer before, for one thing, and she's also spent the entire novel showing genuine affection and solicitude for the Bertrams. She's a complex woman, and a contradictory one, and as I noted earlier, in many ways not fully certain of herself; but complexity is not something Fanny Price will allow for, in her view of the world. There is black. There is white. And it's her job to assign all of humanity to one or the other.

Fanny then shows us her priorities by refusing to consider returning to Mansfield in the company of "persons in whose feelings and conduct, at the present moment, she saw so much to condemn; the sister's feelings—the brother's conduct—*her* cold-hearted ambition—*his* thoughtless vanity. To have him still the acquaintance, the flirt, perhaps, of Mrs. Rushworth!—She was mortified. She had thought better of him." Yes, she had; for all the good that did either of them.

Anyway, it's clear the life-and-death situation at Mansfield weighs less with her than the icky idea of indebtedness to the Crawfords. She excuses herself from the offer of transport by claiming she couldn't possibly take the decision to return upon herself; it would be an abrogation of Sir Thomas's authority. If she's needed, he'll send for her. Which sounds perfectly rational, until we remember how she's been perfectly willing to abrogate Sir Thomas's authority before.

So she stays where she is. She evades possibility, declines to decide, makes no move, lifts no finger to alter her destiny in any way, good or bad; takes no risk, assumes no responsibility, rebuffs all affection. We know she barely eats; we can guess she scarcely moves. The air about her might be still as a vacuum. And very soon, when the walls come tumbling down, and everyone who's gone about the business of life with zeal and appetite, if not quite wisdom or restraint, is caught beneath the rubble, bloodied and bowed, Fanny will still be standing; Fanny will have won.

Absolutely goddamn crazy-making.

CHAPTERS 46-48

We rejoin Fanny where we left her last time—where we appear to have left her for the last geologic age; the Price clan might have been hunting mastadons when she arrived—sitting at home, doing nothing except receiving letters. But wait...apparently she's *not* receiving letters. After she declined the Crawfords' offer to come and steal her away from Portsmouth, she expected to be battered with exhortations to change her mind. But nope...nothing. Until after the space of a week, something does come from Mary Crawford, so skimpy a missive that Fanny is "persuaded of its having the air of a letter of haste and business"—possibly announcing Mary's arrival, with Henry, in Portsmouth to carry her off in a shackles if need be.

But no; the letter is instead a strange, cryptic thing, urging Fanny to ignore a "most scandalous, ill-natured rumour" that's just come to Mary's ear, and assuring her that "Henry is blameless, and in spite of a moment's *etouderie* thinks of nobody but you."

> *I am sure it will all be hushed up, and nothing proved but Rushworth's folly. If they are gone, I would lay my life they are only gone to Mansfield Park, and Julia with them. But why would not you let us come for you? I wish you may not repent it.*

Fanny is mystified. No scandalous, ill-natured rumour has reached her; in her little Portsmouth cocoon, it's a miracle if oxygen reaches her. "She could only perceive that it must relate to Wimpole Street and

Mr. Crawford, and only conjecture that something very imprudent had just occurred in that quarter to draw the notice of the world," though why she should care whether the Rushworths then beat a hasty retreat, and where they went, and whether Julia was with them, is beyond her. "As to Mr. Crawford, she hoped it might give him a knowledge of his own disposition, convince him that he was not capable of being steadily attached to any one woman in the world, and shame him from persisting any longer in addressing herself."

Yes, that would be best. Leave Fanny to her little airless existence where the taint of inconvenient human feeling needn't disturb her inertia. Think I'm being too harsh?...Here's Fanny's own POV on her situation.

> *She felt that she had, indeed, been three months [in Portsmouth]; and the sun's rays falling into the parlour, instead of cheering, made her still more melancholy; for sun-shine appeared to her a totally different thing in a town and in the country. Here, its power was only a glare, a stifling, sickly glare, serving to bring forward stains and dirt that might otherwise have slept. There was neither health nor gaiety in sunshine in a town. She sat in a blaze of oppressive heat, in a cloud of moving dust; and her eyes could only wander from the walls marked by her father's head, to the table cut and knotched by her brothers, where stood the tea-board never thoroughly cleaned, the cups and saucers wiped in streaks, the milk a mixture of motes floating in thin blue, and the bread and butter growing every minute more greasy than even Rebecca's hands had first produced it.*

Killer bit of writing there, btw.

It's in this scene of domestic oblivion that the scandalous, ill-natured rumour finally reaches Fanny's ear, from the unlikeliest source imaginable: her boozy old man and his borrowed broadsheet. He looks up from its pages and says, "What's the name of your great cousins in town, Fan?" and when she answers Rushworth, and confirms they live on Wimpole Street, he's tickled pink.

> *"Then, there's the devil to pay among them, that's all. There, (holding out the paper to her)—much good may such fine relations do you. I don't know what Sir Thomas may think of such matters; he may be too much of the courtier and fine gentleman to like his daughter the less. But by*

> *G— if she belonged to me, I'd give her the rope's end as long as I could stand over her."*

Which might not be too long, given that standing unassisted isn't exactly one of Mr. Price's superpowers. Still, the point is made: one of Sir Thomas's daughters has been extra-special naughty. Fanny takes up the paper and reads a report of "a matrimonial fracas in the family of Mr. R. of Wimpole Street," whose beautiful young bride (whose name "had not long been enrolled in the lists of hymen"—love that turn of phrase) has "quitted her husband's roof in the company of the well known and captivating Mr. C. ...and it was not known, even to the editor of the newspaper, whither they were gone." Why the editor of the newspaper should be expected to know above anyone else, I'm not quite sure. Possibly he's a Regency Bob Woodward or something.

Fanny insists that this is all a terrible mistake, even though she innately knows it's not. (Scarcely the first instance of Fanny deliberately obscuring the truth.) She speaks "from the instinctive wish of delaying shame," but she might have spared herself the trouble, because her father doesn't really give a good goddamn; now that he's scored a cheap point off her, he's fine just letting the whole thing drop. As for Fanny's mother, her reaction is hilariously typical.

> *"Indeed, I hope it is not true," said Mrs. Price plaintively; "it would be so very shocking!—If I have spoke once to Rebecca about that carpet, I am sure I have spoke at least a dozen times; have I not, Betsey?—And it would not be ten minutes work."*

Fanny meanwhile retreats to do what Fanny does best, which is languish and brood. She torments herself by going over everything again and again and again, like someone stuck in a time loop, and coming to the same inevitable (and, I'm betting, secretly satisfying) conclusions, especially with regard to Mary Crawford.

> *Her eager defense of her brother, her hope of its being hushed up, her evident agitation, were all of a piece with something very bad; and if there was a woman of character in existence, who could treat as a trifle this sin of the first magnitude, who could try to gloss it over, and desire to have it unpunished, she could believe Miss Crawford to be the woman!*

There's a lot of anguished reflection on how horrible, horrible, horrible it all is, to the point at which you begin to feel uncomfortable, like you're witnessing a sadomasochist wallowing in the sheer pleasure of self-inflicted agony. She spends an almost pornographic amount of time speculating on who will be most injured by the scandal, and decides Sir Thomas wins that particular prize, with Edmund the silver medalist, and in minutely considering their emotional devastation she works herself into a kind of melodramatic fit.

> *Sir Thomas's parental solicitude, and high sense of honour and decorum, Edmund's upright principles, unsuspicious temper, and genuine strength of feeling, made her think it scarcely possible for them to support life and reason under such a disgrace; and it appeared to her, that as far as this world alone was concerned, the greatest blessing to every one of kindred with Mrs. Rushworth would be instant annihilation.*

Jesus Harriet Christ on a moped.

We've come to expect morbidity from Fanny, but this really dials it up to eleven. The kind of mind that can't accommodate a family scandal without wishing for "instant annihilation" is of the febrile, unhealthy kind that is about the last thing I'd associate with an Austen heroine. And of course the risky thing about leaping immediately to the extremity of hyperbole when things go bad, is that it leaves you nothing to reach for when things get worse. Which they now do.

Another letter arrives. (Don't worry, it's the last. I wish we could have a celebratory bonfire of all the missives Fanny has received over the past few chapters, but if the blaze got out of hand it would wipe out half of Portsmouth.) It's from Edmund, confirming that Maria and Henry have indeed run off to nobody-yet-knows-where, and adding: "You may not have heard of the last blow—Julia's elopement; she is gone to Scotland with Yates. She left London a few hours before we entered it. At any other time, this would have been felt dreadfully. Now it seems nothing, yet it is an heavy aggravation." Poor Julia, always second best, even as a black sheep.

And then the silver lining to this double-dose of awful: Fanny is summoned home. Even better, Edmund is coming personally to fetch her. And—even more extra-super-duper—Susan is invited to come back with her. (I guess the Bertrams figure, they're two females down, better re-stock.) Fanny is now genuinely torn, between the nihilist attractions of wishing her nearest and dearest all wiped from the face of the Earth, and the giddy excitement of knowing she is at long last escaping the grease pit she grew up in. She has to keep reminding herself that life as she knew it is now over and all who love her forever doomed, even as she packs up her luggage with squeals of delight. Susan feels this conflict as well, though less strongly because she doesn't personally know the disgraced principals; "if she could help rejoicing from beginning to end, it was as much as ought to be expected from human virtue at fourteen."

Then the happy day arrives, and Edmund with it; and if you thought Fanny was melodramatic, get a load of this guy. He appears at the house with suffering etched into his face, and presses Fanny to his breast with the words, "My Fanny—my only sister—my only comfort now." All right, fine, it's a tad purple but arguably excusable under the circumstances; what's *not* excusable is that he appears to pay no compliments of any kind to the Prices. It's as though the Enormity Of His Suffering places him on a higher plane where he isn't required to engage in such bothersome niceties as Hello you must be my Aunt Price, what a pleasure to know you, and could this little rutabaga be my cousin Betsey? No, no, slumming with the Prices is good enough for a slick charmer like Henry Crawford, but not for the lofty Edmund Bertram. When he finds to his annoyance that Fanny and Susan haven't breakfasted yet, he goes off by himself till they're ready, "glad to get away even from Fanny," and spends an hour walking the ramparts, looking soulfully tormented and romantically windblown in case anyone is secretly filming him.

He returns in time to "spend a few minutes with the family, and be a witness—but that he saw nothing—of the tranquil manner in which the daughters were parted with." Edmund's eyes are fixed on one thing only, and that's Edmund. Then they pile into the carriage and set off. The journey is, as you can imagine, a silent one.

> *Edmund's deep sighs often reached Fanny. Had he been alone with her, his heart might have opened in spite of every resolution; but Susan's presence drove him quite into himself, and his attempts to talk on indifferent subjects could never be long supported.*

Eventually Edmund takes actual notice of Fanny—probably when he's grown bored of staring at the scenery, or his navel—and notices how haggard she is. Having been completely in a fog during his seventy-three seconds in the Price household, he has no idea that the stress of living in such a pressure-cooker has contributed to her withered looks, and he presumes, with all the egocentric arrogance of those who account theirs the only significant pain in all of human history, that she's just feeling a reflection of his own titanic torment:

> *[He] took her hand, and said in a low, but very expressive tone, "No wonder—you must feel it—you must suffer. How a man who had once loved, could desert you! But your's—your regard was new compared with —Fanny, think of* me*!"*

I have a standard response for people who resort to this "How do you think I feel?" line. I say, "I don't have to think. You always tell me." (I wish I could report that this actually shuts them up. But anyone that self-involved is usually immune to subtlety.)

When they reach the environs of Mansfield, Fanny can't help her spirits rising; here again are all those hedges she so much likes to heap with hosannas. And in fact she goes on for a paragraph delightedly noting all the changes in color and volume and clapping her hands and whistling and barking out the window. Unfortunately her two companions can't share in her enjoyment; Susan is suddenly fretting about how she'll manage to keep from betraying her vulgarity, and "was meditating much on silver forks, napkins, and finger glasses," while Edmund is still sunk into profound contemplation on the tragedy of being Edmund, "with eyes closed as if the view of cheerfulness oppressed him"; oh yeah, Edmund the contented clergyman is bit of a dullard, but Edmund the self-pitying martyr could bore the paint right off the walls.

So everyone is utterly morose, and we know that once they get home neither Sir Thomas, Lady Bertram, or Tom will be any livelier, so our only hope of relief is in Aunt Norris. But when we arrive at the house and the cast is reassembled, we can see that in many ways she's the worst off of the bunch. Maria was her particular favorite, and the match with Mr. Rushworth was one she personally arranged for her, so Maria's disgrace is her own, and she's feeling it big time. Her "active powers had been all benumbed" and she finds herself "unable to direct or dictate, or even fancy herself useful." The only spark of the old Aunt Norris is the searing hatred she feels at "the sight of the person whom, in the blindness of her anger, she could have charged as the demon of the piece. Had Fanny accepted Mr. Crawford, this could not have happened." She also works up "a few repulsive looks" for Susan, and we have hopes for more, but alas, nothing comes of it.

As for the other aunt in the house, "To talk over the dreadful business with Fanny, talk and lament, was all Lady Bertram's consolation." And while she is "no very methodical narrator," it's through her that Fanny begins to piece together what exactly the hell has happened.

It seems Mr. Rushworth had gone to Twickehnham for the Eastter holidays, leaving Maria with a family of "lively, agreeable manners, and probably of morals and discretion to suit"—you know, *urbanities*—and "to *their* house Mr. Crawford had constant access at all times." Julia wasn't around to provide even the featherweight of balance she might have offered, because she'd gone off to be somebody else's houseguest. Frolics and romps apparently ensued, because eventually a friend of Sir Thomas's wrote to urge him to come to town and use "influence with his daughter, to put an end to an intimacy which was already exposing her to unpleasant remarks," without specifying exactly what the unpleasant remarks were, which seems unfair to those of us who would really, really like to know.

Before Sir Thomas could load his valise onto the carriage, however, another letter arrived from the same friend—express, so you know it's some bad nastiness—with the news that Maria had absconded with Mr. Crawford. Sir Thomas lit out for London and hunkered down, no doubt ducking his head beneath the volleys of pernicious gossip flying across town (principally lobbed by Maria's mother-in-law's servant, who really seems to deserve a spin-off of her own), and persisted "in the hope of discovering, and snatching her from farther vice, though all was lost on the side of character." Hey, we're talking about Maria, here. All was lost on the side of character before she had permanent teeth.

And then, and *only* then, does he learn Julia has eloped with Mr. Yates.

Fanny can't but pity poor Sir Thomas, with three children now burdening him with worry (since Tom has had a setback on hearing all the woeful news). He also has to endure pity for his youngest son (who would insist on being pitied, if there were any doubt) in having been so brutally disappointed by the woman of his dreams, who it now seems will never be the wee little wifey of his country parsonage.

Because it turns out the final meeting between Edmund and Mary Crawford was about as final as it could possibly be, barring one of them actually shooting the other dead. He divulges to Fanny that he had gone to see her at Lady Stornaway's house, eager to commiserate with her and "investing her with all the feelings of shame and wretchedness which Crawford's sister ought to have known," only to have her bring up the subject in a breezy, mock-exasperated manner: "Let us talk over this sad business," she says. "What can equal the folly of our two relations?" When Edmund's face registers unmistakable shock—possibly his jaw drops sixteen inches and his eyeballs sproing out of his head like in a Tex Avery cartoon—she backpedals, noting gravely, 'I do not mean to defend Henry at your sister's expence."

> *"So she began—but how she went on, Fanny, is not fit—is hardly to be repeated to you. I cannot recall all her words. I would not dwell upon them if I could. Their substance was great anger at the* folly *of each... Guess what I must have felt. To hear the woman whom—no harsher name than folly given!—So voluntarily, so freely, so coolly to canvass it! —No reluctance, no horror, no feminine—shall I say it? no modest loathings!—This is what the world does."*

By which he means, "This is what the city does."

I'm not sure what Edmund wants here. Mary is putting the best face possible on things; she's stiffening her spine and striving to keep a cool head, and to patch up the mess as tidily as possible (she wants Edmund's aid in forcing Henry and Maria to marry). Her manner is practical, rational, resigned, unsentimental...*English.* Whereas Henry seems to want her to fall shrieking to the carpet, upon which the two of them can then wail and flail and tear their hair out at the roots like hysterical continentals.

Mary goes on to shock Edmund further, by laying some of the blame at Fanny's door.

> *'Why, would not she have him? It is all her fault. Simple girl!—I shall never forgive her. Had she accepted him as she ought, they might now have*

> *been on the point of marriage, and Henry would have been too happy and too busy to want any other object. He would have taken no pains to be on terms with Mrs. Rushworth again. It would have all ended in a regular standing flirtation, in yearly meetings at Sotherton and Everingham."*

This kind of sophistication just about gives Edmund renal failure. Never mind that she's absolutely right. Maybe that even makes it worse. But to us, the lightness with which Mary attempts to deal with the scandal is entirely natural; she's just a century or so ahead of her time. (I've said it before, but it bears repeating: she's a Noël Coward heroine in a Jane Austen novel.) To our eyes, the great affronted show Edmund makes of being shocked, *shocked* by everything she says, comes across as stuffy and excessive. "I do not consider her as meaning to wound my feelings," he says. "The evil lies yet deeper; in her total ignorance, unsuspiciousness of there being such feelings, in a perversion of mind which made it natural to her to treat the subject as she did." To treat it, he means, as a problem to be solved rather than the fall of western civilization. "Her's are faults of principle, Fanny, of blunted delicacy and a corrupted, vitiated mind...Gladly would I submit to all the increased pain of losing her, rather than have to think of her as I do. I told her so." Yeah, I just bet you did.

Mary's idea is that, once married to Henry, "and properly supported by her own family, people of respectability as they are, [Maria] may recover her footing in society to a certain degree."

> *"In some circles, we know, she would never be admitted, but with good dinners, and large parties, there will always be those who will be glad of her acquaintance; and there is, undoubtedly, more liberality and candour on those points than formerly. What I advise is, that your father be quiet. Do not let him injure his own cause by interference...Let Sir Thomas trust to his honour and compassion, and it may all end well; but if he get his daughter away, if will be destroying the chief hold."*

Honor and compassion...forgiveness and a chance at redemption... we're meant to find this despicable? Edmund says, emphatically, yes. In his opinion, Mary proposes nothing less than "a compromise, an acquiescence, in the continuance of the sin, on the chance of a marriage which, thinking as I now thought of her brother, should rather be prevented than sought"—and at about this point you might want to stop and say, Fine, buddy, what's *your* suggested plan for the lovers, then? Because it seems to be something along the lines of stoning them to death, driving stakes through their hearts, and stuffing their mouths with garlic.

Edmund delivers a thundering denunciation that leaves Mary "exceedingly astonished—more than astonished" and reduces her to sarcasm; which we of course recognize as the last angry recourse of wounded pride.

> *"It was a sort of laugh, as she answered, 'A pretty good lecture, upon my word. Was it part of your last sermon? At this rate, you will soon reform every body at Mansfield and Thornton Lacey; and when I hear of you it may be as a celebrated preacher in some great society of Methodists, or as a missionary into foreign parts.' She tried to speak carelessly; but she was not so careless as she wanted to appear."*

As Edmund heads out the door, she calls out to him; he turns around and she smiles—a "saucy playful smile"—and he keeps on going.

All right, let's not dwell on it. This is the nadir; the place Austen really jumps the rails and sends the whole train careening into the jagged canyon below. But it's the only time in her entire body of work she does so—and that includes her juvenilia and unfinished novels—so we can forgive her this momentary dementia.

Mention of the juvenilia prompts an interesting thought, which is that *Mansfield Park* represents a more or less thorough betrayal of the young writer who produced all those wacky, anarchic, calamity-choked mini-masterpieces; her spirit of wild invention, cheeky wit, and subversive hooliganism is the kind that's actively punished in the present novel, where every merrily expressed irreverence is an indelible mark of corruption. Maybe Austen exorcised her Puritan demons in the process; if so, we can only be thankful. Anyway, onward.

Now that Edmund has confessed his newfound horror of the woman he once loved, Fanny feels "at liberty to speak" and "more than justified in adding to his knowledge of her real character, by some hint of what share his brother's state of health might be supposed to have in her wish for a complete reconciliation." In other words, it's pile-on-Mary time. And it ain't pretty, believe me.

Then Austen clears the slate, proclaiming "Let other pens dwell on guilt and misery. I quit such odious subjects as soon as I can, impatient to restore every body, not greatly in fault themselves, to tolerable comfort, and to have done with all the rest." By this time we're ready to rassle her some over her definition of "greatly in fault," but it's the last bloody chapter, so we let it go in the interest of just finishing the thing.

"My Fanny," she goes on (and yes, thanks, you can have her), "I have the satisfaction of knowing, must have been happy in spite of every thing," and here she enumerates every reason in favor of that happiness, though if anyone could sniff out a square inch of misery in an acre of paradise, it's Fanny Price. And given that Austen repeatedly uses the conditional tense (she "must have been" happy), I'm guessing even she isn't a hundred percent convinced of it.

But if Fanny is happy, those around her certainly aren't; Edmund has taken his consumptive-Lord-Byron act to heights undreamed of in Portsmouth, and Sir Thomas is mired in regret and self-reproach for having raised up a pair of man-eating succubi. But news eventually arrives that somewhat redeems Julia; it seems her elopement with Mr. Yates was prompted less by selfish lust than by a strong streak of self-preservation. After Maria ran off with Henry, Julia realized her family's reputation was about to seriously crater, so she'd better grab whatever suitor was closest at hand and marry him *now,* or she'd end up on the shelf for the rest of her life. Mr. Yates just happened to be the one within reach. Sir Thomas eventually reconciles with his daughter, who is "humble and wishing to be forgiven," and reconciles himself *to* his new son-in-law, who while "not very solid" (in the manner that, say, Jello isn't very solid) is at least earnest and willing to be guided.

And then Tom's health improves, which further lessens the weight of Sir Thomas's worries, and indeed Tom is so chastened by his cha-cha-cha with death, and by his culpability in *l'affaire* Crawford ("he felt himself accessory by all the dangerous intimacy of his unjustifiable theatre") that he becomes "what he ought to be, useful to his father, steady and quiet, and not living merely for himself." Well, fine. Everyone has to grow up. Just tell me he could still crack his tongue like a whip, and that his dinner guests were always left gasping for breath by the cheese course.

Maria, however, remains intractable; Sir Thomas won't ever find a lessening of torment on her account.

> *She was not to be prevailed on to leave Mr. Crawford. She hoped to marry him, and they continued together till she was obliged to be convinced that such hope was vain, and till the disappointment and wretchedness arising from the conviction, rendered her temper so bad, and her feelings for him so like hatred, as to make them for a while each other's punishment, and then induce a voluntary separation.*
>
> *She had lived with him to be reproached as the ruin of all his happiness in Fanny, and carried away no better consolation in leaving him, than that she* had *divided them. What can exceed the misery of such a mind in such a situation?*

I'm pretty sure Maria's misery is exceeded when she learns Fanny has snared her brother on the rebound. But alas, Austen doesn't confirm this.

Mr. Rushworth has no trouble getting a quickie divorce, and Austen cautions us not to pity him: his wife "had despised him, and loved another—and he had been very much aware that it was so. The indignities of stupidity, and the disappointments of selfish passion, can excite little pity." This is harsh. Austen really is in Savonarola mode in this novel. Unfortunately, she was insufficiently able to restrict her own gifts, as to prevent herself from giving us that one moment in which Rushworth showed us his humanity—displaying a flicker of self-awareness and of suffering at Maria's open favoring of Crawford—so that we haven't been able to laugh at him as easily since, or to dismiss him so callously now. With a flick of her wrist she dressed him in flesh and blood, and I'm not entirely sure she even knew she did it.

The problem is, then, what to do with Maria. Aunt Norris, "whose attachment seemed to augment with the demerits of her niece," wants her to be received back home and resume her place as queen bitch of Mansfield, but Sir Thomas is basically over-my-dead-body. Which makes Aunt Norris glare daggers at Fanny, flitting around the very house Maria is now denied, and you can tell she wants to suggest, What about *her* dead body, but doesn't dare to.

Actually, Sir Thomas has a pretty clear idea of what to do with Maria, which is basically, lock her up somewhere far away, protected by him and "secured in every comfort," but basically under house arrest. If the technology existed, he'd put her in an ankle monitor. And for a companion, she'll have Mrs. Norris, which is a bit of an eyebrow-raiser, because so far from being a chaperon, Aunt Norris has proven herself many times over to be Maria's biggest cheerleader in every self-destructive thing she's ever done. But "shut up together, with little society, on one side no affection, on the other, no judgment, it may be reasonably supposed that their tempers became their mutual punishment." And Sir Thomas is more than ready to boot Aunt Norris's bony white ass out the door anyway.

> *His opinion of her had been sinking from the day of his return from Antigua; in every transaction together from that period, in their daily intercourse, in business, or in chat, she had been regularly losing ground in his esteem...To be relieved from her, therefore, was so great a felicity, that had she not left bitter remembrances behind her, there might have been danger of his learning almost to approve the evil which produced such a good.*

And what of Henry Crawford?...He has to live with his very real regrets of Fanny. Had he only been able to win her, "there would have been every probability of success and felicity for him. His affection had already done something. Her influence over him had already given him some influence over her." In a number of places Austen confirms, or at least hints, that both Henry and Mary would have been reformed by unions with Fanny and Edmund. That we've had to witness these two charming favorites shunted so brusquely aside, redemption denied them, is a pretty rum business. What is Henry Crawford's real sin, anyway?...Being human; being complex; being young.

> *...[B]y animated perseverance he had soon re-established the sort of familiar intercourse—of gallantry—of flirtation [with Maria] which bounded his views, but in triumphing over the discretion, which, though beginning in anger, might have saved them both, he had put himself in the power of feelings on her side, more strong than he had supposed.—She loved him; there was no withdrawing attentions, avowedly dear to her. He was entangled by his own vanity, with as little excuse of love as possible, and without the smallest inconstancy of mind towards her cousin.*

This is not a cad. Austen seems to be using him as the protagonist in a cautionary tale, dooming him to "vexation that must rise sometimes to self-reproach, and regret to wretchedness—in having so requited hospitality, so injured family peace, so forfeited his best, most estimable, and endeared acquaintance, and so lost the woman whom he had rationally, as well as passionately, loved." No starched-collared Victorian could have sentenced him with more scowling prejudice.

Mary too must go on blithely fluttering through life, regretting of, and pining for, Edmund; and the Grants—remember them?—are quickly hustled offstage (to a new living for the rector) because their continued presence at Mansfield is now too awkward to be convenient to the story. There's a whole lot of suffering going on here, and if these are the peeps Austen considers "greatly in fault" then you have to wonder what the hell happened to her. I mean, this is the woman who basically let Lydia Bennet and George Wickham get away with metaphorical murder. And Lucy Steele and Robert Ferrars, too. Part of Austen's appeal to me has always been her serene indifference to the success of her grinning predators. As long as her heroine (and hero) have ended up happy, she seemed content to leave everyone else alone—on the principle, I suppose, that the worst imaginable punishment is simply allowing them to continue being themselves. (Certainly true of Lydia and Wickham.) Here, she's chosen instead to channel some Old Testament prophet, and smite the sinners with an iron fist.

I don't want cautionary tales from Austen; if she reforms the human race at all, it will be through relentless mockery of its pretensions, hypocrisies, and delusions, not through moral fables about virtuous ingénues. She's strayed from her true path here, and we're left following her, stepping entirely too trustingly into stinging nettles and poison oak.

In one respect, however, she happily hasn't changed; she remains as indifferent as ever to what we moderns understand as "romance." The passage in which Edmund turns his mind from Mary to Fanny is almost plangently matter-of-fact, with him wondering whether, it being "impossible that he should ever meet with another such woman...a very different type of woman might do just as well—or a great deal better." He might be contemplating a change from planting radishes to beets. And then there's this:

> *I purposely abstain from dates on this occasion, that every one may be at liberty to fix their own, aware that the cure of unconquerable passions, and the transfer of unchanging attachments, must vary much as to time in different people.—I only intreat every body to believe that exactly at the time when it was quite natural that it should be so, and not a week earlier, Edmund did cease to care about Miss Crawford, and became as anxious to marry Fanny, as Fanny herself could desire.*

You feel the earth move?...Me neither.

The novel ends in several pages of self-congratulation, but it tastes a bit stale on the tongue. Especially since our author has admitted that both Henry and Mary Crawford would have benefited from their respective matches with Fanny and Edmund; their appetites curbed, their excesses restrained, their characters inclined more to responsibility. And Fanny and Edmund would have had to learn to accommodate, forgive, and even appreciate human fallibility; to love someone else for his or her faults, not in spite of them. All that is sundered on a single youthful folly; and Mary's practical approach to limiting the damage is viewed as evidence of a damaged character—while Edmund's refusal to do anything but wallow in the wretchedness of it all, like an especially highly strung Italian peasant, is set up as the height of moral perfection. I just don't get this. I don't get why we're meant to celebrate four people missing out on the unions that would have redefined and improved them; why we're meant instead to go all gooey over Edmund finding perfect peace and contentment with Fanny, who's been his lap dog since they were juveniles—a marriage that promises no friction, no compromises, no self-sacrifice, no soul-searching...it's static; a placid pool with nothing to disturb its smooth surface except, inevitably, the swift spread of algae. Mary and Henry are left unmoored and heartbroken...Edmund and Fanny retreat into the womb of their childhood...what? I'm supposed to rejoice?

Another point I must at least touch on: I've noted repeatedly how immune I remain to the Fanny-Edmund pairing. There's never, for me, even the slightest evidence of the kind of chemistry we saw between Lizzy and Darcy, or even Elinor and Edward Ferrars. I'm at least willing to admit that part of the reason—albeit a small part—is a cultural resistance to the idea of first cousins as lovers. I know things were different back in Austen's day; in a smaller population with clearly defined class boundaries, the dating pool was naturally more limited than it is for us. But the aversion to such a pairing in our own era isn't something we can easily set aside, and I find myself reading of Fanny and Edmund's coming together with a grimace of sexual distaste that I can't seem to wipe away. Couple that with the whole undercurrent of the Antiguan slave trade, and you've got a novel with some serious cultural handicaps all the way through. Clone a dozen Aunt Norrises and set them stampeding through its pages like a herd of raptors, and you still couldn't fix it.

But the primary and ultimately decisive problem is still the empty dress at the center of it all. When she began her next novel, Austen wrote to her sister, "I am going to take a heroine whom no one but myself will much like." But she was wrong; Emma Woodhouse is almost universally adored. It's Fanny Price who has borne the brunt of readers' dislike and disdain over the centuries. Inert, joyless, and judgmental, she stands to one side for the entirety of *Mansfield Park* while its other characters strive, battle, and fall, and in the end her strategy of doing nothing wins her everything she's ever wanted. Fanny, who never takes a risk, never tells a joke, is never silly or unwise or exultant or—frankly—human, triumphs over her enemies and her rivals by virtue of her sheer indomitable passivity.

And what of those enemies and rivals? They aren't as quite numerous as in Austen's previous works, though quality nearly makes up for scarcity. There's the fatuous Mr. Rushworth; battering Aunt Norris; gabbling Mr. Yates; and the wonderfully Neanderthal Price clan. But then, alas, we come to the main focuses of our intended ire: Mary Crawford and her brother Henry. They're witty, charming, incautious, unthinking...emotional and headlong and sensual and indiscreet. To our modern sensibilities, they're romantic heroes, complete with tragic flaws. Edmund, our nominal hero, is a good man, true, but he's parched soil, gasping for want of laughter and energy and magic; for the blessing of uncertainty; for *life.* Instead he winds up with Fanny; their union is a guarantee of spiritual and emotional barrenness. In so frictionless a pairing, nothing can ever alter, nothing ever change, nothing ever grow.

I've conjectured long and hard about why Austen wrote *Mansfield Park;* but whatever the reason, the good news is, she learned from the endeavor...and she shows as much in her next novel, which is basically

Mansfield Park turned on its head. Its heroine, Emma Woodhouse, is a revisionist Mary Crawford—a sly, feline charmer who's quick to judgment and carelessly glib, and who is made to pay for it; but this time, crucially, she's forgiven. Her rival, Jane Fairfax, is a new incarnation of Fanny Price—chilly, impenetrable, aloof; and like Fanny, her imperturbable stillness wins her her man in the end. But in this case it's exactly the right man for her: Frank Churchill, a second Henry Crawford, whose wily roguishness will force her to enlarge her own capacity for understanding; as her quiet determination will galvanize his. Because of this ingenious inversion, *Emma* scintillates where *Mansfield Park* stalls out; *Emma* delights where *Mansfield Park* frustrates; and *Emma* is beloved, where *Mansfield Park,* despite its many brilliant facets and enduring moments, seems fated to remain only tolerated.

I'll have much, much more to say about *Emma* in the second volume of *Bitch In a Bonnet,* as well as about *Northanger Abbey* and *Persuasion,* the novels of Jane Austen's full maturity as a social (and, in *Northanger Abbey,* cultural) satirist. Until then, I thank you for indulging me in my irreverent tear through her canon. It's not sacred ground; Austen would be as resistant to that idea as would any writer of merit. But it's *shared* ground, and shared by many, a fair number of whom I have roughly elbowed in the jaw in my progress over it. I'd apologize; but I'm actually rather hoping you liked it. If you come back for more, I'll know for sure.

ABOUT THE AUTHOR

Robert Rodi is the author of nine novels and two memoirs; he's also an accomplished monologist and musician. He lives in Chicago with his partner Jeffrey Smith and a constantly shifting number of dogs. For additional information visit his website, www.robertrodi.com

22624313R00265

Made in the USA
Middletown, DE
05 August 2015